State Capture

State Capture

How Conservative Activists, Big Businesses, and Wealthy Donors Reshaped the American States—and the Nation

ALEXANDER HERTEL-FERNANDEZ

Oxford University Press is a department of the University of Oxford. It furthers the University's objective of excellence in research, scholarship, and education by publishing worldwide. Oxford is a registered trade mark of Oxford University Press in the UK and certain other countries.

Published in the United States of America by Oxford University Press
198 Madison Avenue, New York, NY 10016, United States of America.

© Oxford University Press 2019

First issued as an Oxford University Press paperback, 2021

All rights reserved. No part of this publication may be reproduced, stored in a retrieval system, or transmitted, in any form or by any means, without the prior permission in writing of Oxford University Press, or as expressly permitted by law, by license, or under terms agreed with the appropriate reproduction rights organization. Inquiries concerning reproduction outside the scope of the above should be sent to the Rights Department, Oxford University Press, at the address above.

You must not circulate this work in any other form
and you must impose this same condition on any acquirer.

Library of Congress Cataloging- in- Publication Data
Names: Hertel-Fernandez, Alex, 1986-author.
Title: State capture : how conservative activists, big businesses, and wealthy donors reshaped the American states and the nation / by Alex Hertel-Fernandez.
Description: New York, NY : Oxford University Press, 2019.
Identifiers: LCCN 2018027144 (print) | LCCN 2018038838 (ebook) | ISBN 9780190870805 (updf) | ISBN 9780190870812 (epub) | ISBN 9780190870799 (hardback) | ISBN 9780197564264 (paperback)
Subjects: LCSH: Conservatism—United States—States. | U.S. States—Politics and government—21st century. | State governments—United States. | Business and politics—United States—States. | Americans for Prosperity (Organization) | American Legislative Exchange Council. | State Policy Network (Organization) | BISAC: POLITICAL SCIENCE / Political Process / Elections. | POLITICAL SCIENCE / Public Policy / General. | POLITICAL SCIENCE / General.
Classification: LCC JC573.2.U6 (ebook) | LCC JC573.2.U6 H398 2019 (print) | DDC 320.520973—dc23
LC record available at https://lccn.loc.gov/2018027144

For Nate, who reshaped my life

CONTENTS

Preface ix
Acknowledgments xv
Abbreviations xix

Introduction 1

PART I THE EVOLUTION OF ALEC: A CORPORATE-CONSERVATIVE ANCHOR ACROSS US STATES

1. "The Most Dangerously Effective Organization": A Smart ALEC Is Born 23

2. Policy Plagiarism: A Window into ALEC's Reach across US States 64

3. An Easy "A" with ALEC: ALEC's Appeal for State Lawmakers 78

4. "A Great Investment": ALEC's Appeal for Big Business 112

PART II THE RIGHT-WING TROIKA AND ITS FOES

5. A Little Help from Their Friends: Introducing the Right-Wing Troika 143

6. Transforming the Nation One State at a Time: The Right-Wing Troika and State Policy 174

7. "Feisty Chihuahuas versus a Big Gorilla": Why Left-Wing Efforts to Counter the Troika Have Floundered 211

Conclusion: State Capture and American Democracy   243

Appendices
   Chapter 3 Appendix   269
   Chapter 4 Appendix   274
   Chapter 6 Appendix   278
   Chapter 7 Appendix   291
Notes   295
Works Cited   319
Index   343

PREFACE

Gene Whisnant is a genial retiree from central Oregon who loves to talk baseball. After 27 years of service in the Air Force, Whisnant decided to get involved in politics. He has served in Oregon's lower chamber since 2003.[1] Shortly after arriving in the legislature, Whisnant was approached by a former state senator who encouraged him to join a national association of legislators called the American Legislative Exchange Council (or ALEC, for short). Describing his longstanding involvement in that group, Whisnant smiles. While all legislators are automatically members of the non-partisan, non-profit National Conference of State Legislatures, Whisnant eagerly notes, he made the decision to join ALEC on his own. Whisnant readily paid the $50 dues each year to stay involved in the group and now is the state's ALEC leader.

What makes Whisnant so proud of his participation in ALEC? The first thing to understand, he says, is how many state legislators in Oregon actually serve only part-time, "working their tails off" to get anything done. He is retired, giving him more time to spend on the job as opposed to his younger colleagues. Yet Whisnant does not have much help from expert staffers who could do research for him. His staff consists of his wife, who works half-time, and an aide who works three days per week when the legislature is not in session.[2] Whisnant's situation is far from uncommon. In recent years, Oregon legislators were paid about $23,500 per year—hardly enough for a family to live on without a second job or another source of income. Oregon, in fact, pays its legislators only a bit less than the national average in states that offer salaries to their members.[3] The state ranks at approximately the national average for the number of staffers working for each state representative and senator as well.[4] Across the United States, many state legislatures are run without either professional lawmakers or staffs.

Without formal help, how does a state legislator like Whisnant get the ideas, research, legislative language, talking points, polling, and expert witnesses that are needed to make policy? That's where ALEC comes in. For his $50-per-year membership dues, Whisnant gains access to nearly 1,000 prewritten bills on a variety of social, economic, and political issues, ranging from environmental standards to health insurance regulation to tort reform and voting requirements. These bills provide a clear and easy-to-use policy agenda for conservative, pro-business legislators to follow.

But it is not just policy proposals that ALEC offers. As an ALEC member, Whisnant also gains access to a deep bench of policy researchers and experts who would be happy to help him build the case for a particular model bill from the group's archives. He has had the opportunity to meet those policy experts in person many times at ALEC's annual conferences. Those convenings, typically held at appealing resorts and hotels across the country, are either free or heavily subsidized for legislators and their families. "We have such limited staff that [ALEC] helps us look at things and consider them," Whisnant explains approvingly about the group.

Whisnant's report in a 2011 newsletter nicely explains how the ALEC process works.[5] After attending several annual meetings and reading through the group's materials, Whisnant decided to take ALEC-inspired action on budget reform. He first hosted a local briefing in the statehouse, which was led by visiting ALEC staffers from Washington, D.C., and also included fifty Oregon legislators, aides, and local business leaders allied with ALEC. Following that convening, Whisnant took model legislation already developed by ALEC and introduced those bills under his own name. Among other things, they would have slashed staff positions and introduced more possibilities for privatizing state services. Whisnant, then, is able to supplement his lack of legislative staff with the private resources provided by ALEC to develop, promote, and ultimately change state policy.

Whisnant isn't alone in his enthusiasm for the group. ALEC's membership in recent years numbered at a little under 2,000 public officials, or just under a third of all state legislators.[6] This, of course, should come as no surprise given that legislators in so many states lack adequate resources to develop policy on their own. As a result, through processes similar to the one Whisnant used in Oregon, ALEC can claim credit for hundreds of bill introductions each year. Nearly one in five of those introduced bills, on average, turns into law.[7]

ALEC's model bills center, with laser beam–like focus, on corporate-friendly and conservative priorities. As we will soon see, the most common proposals disadvantage liberal constituencies; lift environmental, health, safety, and economic regulations on business; cut taxes on wealthy individuals and companies; and privatize state programs and agencies.

But where do those policy ideas come from? And where does ALEC obtain the funds necessary to provide such valuable services to legislators like

Whisnant? For answers to those questions, we must turn to the other half of the group's membership: corporations and conservative activists.

Enron's Pitch in the Big Easy

Before its leaders were found guilty of massive accounting fraud, Enron was a leader in the resale of electricity. Enron aimed, in essence, to develop a market for buying and selling contracts based on changes in the prices of electrical power. Its growth in this market, however, depended on its ability to buy and sell electricity across state lines and to dismantle local utility monopolies.[8] Those were decisions that largely rested in the hands of state legislators like Gene Whisnant.

Faced with fifty different state legislatures, each with different cultures, lawmakers, and constellations of interest groups, what was a single company like Enron to do? Although Enron invested in building a stable of its own lobbyists across the states, forging relationships with friendly consumer groups and coalitions, and relying on barnstorming by Chairman Kenneth Lay and other close allies, a key element of Enron's statehouse circuit strategy involved the same group that Whisnant praised so highly.[9]

Enron became active in ALEC in the mid-1990s, participating in the group's energy and environmental policy task force alongside Koch Industries, another company seeking electrical deregulation. Under Enron's leadership, that ALEC task force drafted and approved model legislation that would deregulate state energy markets.[10] It also produced several guides and research papers offering policy arguments and evidence in favor of deregulation that legislators could use to persuade their colleagues and constituents. Those bills and materials were then disseminated to all several thousand of the group's elected members in legislatures across all fifty states.

As a final pitch to ALEC's membership, Enron underwrote a substantial portion of ALEC's annual conference the following year in New Orleans. At the 1997 meeting in the city's Hyatt Regency hotel, Kenneth Lay delivered a keynote welcoming address to the assembled state legislators.[11] In that speech, Lay made the case for deregulation of state electrical utilities and the interstate sale of power. On the next day of the conference, there was also a special session for legislators interested in "Creating a Free Market and Consumer Choice in Electricity" on precisely those themes.[12]

Enron's aggressive campaign waged through ALEC paid off. Eventually, twenty-four states adopted some form of deregulation between 1997 and 2000 at the behest of ALEC and other groups pushing for loosening electrical rules.[13] "Enron was the only company out there lobbying and they were everywhere," remarked one environmental policy observer about the state deregulation battles.[14] Still, Enron didn't win everything it wanted from all states. In Whisnant's home state of Oregon, for example, Enron only managed to pass partial deregulation of the state utility marketplace. According to the Sierra Club's chapter in that state, Enron "came in like a house of [*sic*] fire and we cooled their jets. Once they realized they wouldn't be allowed to do what they wanted, they lost interest. They came in with a blatant attempt to roll the legislature and impress everyone with how important they were compared to podunk Oregon. We didn't like it."[15]

But the Sierra Club's partial victory in Oregon was not necessarily a big loss for Enron. The company was playing the whole field of states and had already won in many other legislatures. They could afford a few losses so long as there were bigger victories in other statehouses. In fact, ALEC has been emphasizing this point to businesses for some time. "In the states, if you're trying to get [something] passed and you've lost in Kansas, Nebraska and Texas, it's not a total failure. You may well win in Arizona, California and New York that year. You've got 50 shots," stressed one of ALEC's early executive directors in making a sales pitch to potential members.[16]

Enron's strategy in the case of electricity deregulation represents a broader lesson that other large national companies have learned since the 1980s. State governments not only set policies that affect corporate bottom lines. Statehouses also represent multiple battlegrounds where businesses have important advantages. For one thing, state legislators are often highly attuned to corporate demands, especially when businesses raise the prospect of layoffs or relocating to another state.[17] For another, most Americans do not pay much attention to what happens within the halls of state legislatures. Some 40 percent of Americans reported in 2016 that they could not recall the party in control of either their state's upper or lower legislative chambers.[18] That lack of scrutiny gives businesses more opportunities to shape policy without any opposition.[19] And state legislators, like Whisnant, often are strapped for ideas and research assistance, leaving them open to accepting substantial legislative help from private groups. ALEC lets businesses take advantage of all three of these characteristics of the states.[20]

In this regard, Enron was not unique in its turn to ALEC. The group has boasted a membership of around 200 of the largest and most prominent companies throughout the country. Although membership in the group is not public, in the past, its corporate backers have included businesses such as Amazon, FedEx, Google, UPS, Facebook, Kraft Foods, McDonald's, Visa, Walmart, and State Farm Insurance. ALEC's corporate members provide the main financial support for the group's annual budget of some $6 million to $10 million.[21]

Companies are not the only ALEC backers, however. Although a quick review of the model bills the group has produced reveals many proposals that clearly benefit ALEC's corporate members, there are still a number of bills not associated with business interests. It is difficult to identify a business constituency, for instance, for ALEC's legislative ideas related to curbing abortion access, restricting gay rights, and welfare reform. Instead, we must look to the third set of actors involved in ALEC's creation and expansion over time: conservative activists and donors.

Conservatives Go Local to Fight Government Spending

For years, conservative activists bemoaned the fiscal profligacy of state and federal governments. Bob Williams is one such budget hawk who has spent the better part of his career looking for ways to restrain the growth of public spending at all levels of government. After receiving his undergraduate degree in business administration from Penn State, Williams spent time as an auditor for the US Government Accountability Office before eventually running for the Washington state legislature, where he served five terms.[22] While in the legislature, Williams was responsible for proposing a number of measures related to state spending. "Without a limited and accountable government, individuals cannot enjoy the freedom and responsibility they need in order to mold a satisfactory life for themselves," Williams has argued.[23] Williams eventually realized he could have an even greater impact on fiscal policy working outside of the legislature. After he stepped down from office, Williams helped found the Evergreen Freedom Foundation, a state-level free market–oriented think tank operating first out of Washington and more recently in Oregon and California (it has also dropped the Evergreen from its name).

Although the Freedom Foundation focuses primarily on state-level policy, its reach now extends well beyond the Pacific Northwest. Thanks to a close association with ALEC, Williams has had the opportunity to promote proposals to reduce the size of the public sector across the United States as the private-sector chair of ALEC's tax and fiscal policy task force.[24] In that position, Williams has distributed a number of model bills to ALEC's legislative membership—including the same proposals that Gene Whisnant used in Oregon. Beyond disseminating specific model bills, Williams has also participated in workshops and trainings for state legislators as part of ALEC's annual meetings, outlining his perspective on state and federal budgets, as well as how ALEC's legislative members can more effectively collaborate with state-level free market institutes like the Freedom Foundation "to win more policy battles and lay a foundation for continuing success" in reducing the size of government.[25]

More recently, Williams has assisted one of ALEC's most ambitious initiatives to date: pushing state legislatures to pass resolutions calling for the convening of an Article V Constitutional Convention, in which state delegates could pursue amendments to the US Constitution directly, rather than by working through Congress.²⁶ ALEC's tax and fiscal policy task force envisions that state delegates to an Article V Convention could promote a "balanced budget amendment" to the Constitution, which would force the federal government, like nearly all states, to pass a balanced budget each year. Many mainstream economic experts believe that such a measure would devastate the federal government's ability to boost the economy during recessions and spell economic disaster.²⁷ Thus far, ALEC has obtained the required legislation in 28 states, including 10 passed between 2013 and 2016—only a few states shy of the threshold needed to invoke the Convention.²⁸ One of ALEC's early heads emphasized the value of this strategy, arguing that if conservatives wanted to move constitutional amendments—like a balanced budget effort—"they'll have to get 38 states to pass those things. You have to have an active support network in the states when ratification time comes." ALEC, in her view, offered exactly that kind of support to right-wing activists.²⁹

Just like Enron, then, conservatives have found that cross-state advocacy through ALEC has been an ideal way to advance their policy priorities. Despite years of effort and organizing, fiscal hawks, for instance, experienced little success moving balanced budget legislation in Congress.³⁰ But in the states, they found many more opportunities: failure in one state was not a huge loss, since activists like Williams could simply move on to another one. Casting the states as terrain on which political losers in one battle could simply transition to another was thus a key selling point of ALEC for both corporate and conservative America.

This move, first advanced by ALEC, and later, two other cross-state networks of conservatives, private-sector companies, and wealthy donors, amounted to a watershed change in US politics. Together, this advocacy has produced a stark rightward shift across the states, ultimately contributing to a dramatic redistribution of political power. Gene Whisnant has described that shift as ensuring an opportunity for the private sector to check the power of government, a "give and take with the private sector."³¹ Borrowing a term from my fellow political scientists studying developing democracies, I dub it "state capture"—or when small groups of well-resourced individuals and companies shape the political rules of the game to their advantage.³² The following pages spell out exactly how that capture has unfolded across the United States, one state capitol at a time, and what it all means for American politics.

ACKNOWLEDGMENTS

Achieving durable political change across the US states requires broad coalitions of diverse and committed supporters. The same, I have learned over the past six years, is true for dissertations and books. My graduate school advisers at Harvard—Theda Skocpol, Peter Hall, Cathie Jo Martin, and Kathy Thelen—have each provided their own invaluable mix of encouragement and advice. Kathy helped spark an interest in political economy and inequality during my undergraduate years at Northwestern, and has been a terrific mentor and collaborator ever since. Indeed, it was thanks to her that I saw Peter and Theda in action at a workshop on historical institutionalism in college—and decided to pursue a career in politics and public policy. After I arrived at Harvard, Peter's generous feedback helped me enormously as I developed the ideas for the dissertation on which this book is based. And Cathie has been a terrific sounding board and cheerleader throughout the whole process.

None of this project, however, would have been possible without my chair, Theda, who has taught me so much about the careful study of political organizations over time. It has been an incredible privilege to learn from—and ultimately collaborate with—her on our research related to the shifting US political terrain. Her model of rigorous and civically engaged scholarship is a standard to which I will continually strive, and as will be apparent to readers, Chapters 5 and 6 draw from our joint work together.

Beyond my committee, I have received the very helpful advice of other scholars in writing this manuscript. Nick Carnes, Lee Drutman, Jake Grumbach, Jacob Hacker, Steve Teles, Rob Mickey, Paul Pierson, and Vanessa Williamson were especially generous with their time and comments. Numerous presentations, including at the State Politics and Policy Conference, Midwest Political Science Association meetings, American Political Science Association meetings, the University of Maine, Stanford University's Junior Scholar Forum, the University of California, Berkeley American Politics Workshop, the Northwestern

University Comparative and Historical Workshop, the University of California, Santa Barbara American Politics Workshop, the Harvard University Seminar on the State and Capitalism Since 1800, the University of Iowa, the University of Oxford, the Tobin Project, and Yale University's American Politics workshop all honed the arguments and evidence presented in the following pages.

I have also been lucky in the colleagues I met in graduate school; they have provided me with emotional and intellectual sustenance—and made the whole dissertation and then book-writing experience fun. Noam Gidron, Kostya Kashin, Volha Charnysh, James Conran, Leslie Finger, Jeff Javed, Leah Stokes, and Matto Mildenberger deserve special thanks for their generosity of feedback and friendship. Joint work with Kostya informs the text analysis of ALEC model bills throughout the book, and joint work with Leah and Matto, in our 2017 survey of state legislators and staff, informs Chapters 6, 7, and the Conclusion.

I was fortunate to benefit from two book workshops that provided a helpful mix of feedback on the manuscript. In Washington, D.C., Steve Teles generously organized a "murder board" that included Lee Drutman, Mark Schmitt, Shayna Strom, and Vanessa Williamson. At Columbia, the School of International and Public Affairs faculty grants program supported a workshop at which Sarah Anzia, Devin Caughey, Martin Gilens, Matt Grossmann, Nate Kelly, Katherine Krimmel, Justin Phillips, Paul Pierson, Bob Shapiro, Suresh Naidu, and Margaret Weir all offered fantastic advice and reactions.

As this book makes clear, well-timed and generous philanthropic support can make a big difference. The research on which this book is based benefited from timely support from the National Science Foundation's Graduate Research Fellowship Program, the Harvard Multidisciplinary Program in Inequality and Social Policy, the Tobin Project, the Russell Sage Foundation, and the Institute for Social and Economic Research and Policy at Columbia University. Bob Bowditch also supported this book through the research project on the shifting US political terrain.

Many individuals and organizations donated their time for interviews that informed this book, including (but not limited to) staff at the American Legislative Exchange Council, the Center for Policy Alternatives, the Center for Media and Democracy, the Democracy Alliance, the Economic Policy Institute (and the Economic Analysis and Research Network), the Center on Budget and Policy Priorities (and the State Priorities Partnership network), Progressive Majority, the Progressive States Network, the State Innovation Exchange, and the State Policy Network. I appreciate their expertise.

At Oxford University Press, I am very grateful for the enthusiasm and patience of Dave McBride, as well as the anonymous reviewers for the manuscript. Their thorough comments and feedback were incredibly helpful in strengthening the book.

Above all, I am thankful for my family, who provided in equal parts support and inspiration. Throughout their careers in political organizing and higher education, my parents, Adriela and Tom, have modeled a commitment to mentorship, teaching, and service to which I aspire. My sister Sarah continues to teach me about the role that civic institutions, especially libraries, play in supporting inclusive communities. And my Minnesotan family—Melissa, John, and Anna—has shown me what a commitment to public service looks like firsthand.

Finally, I dedicate this book to my husband, Nate. He has been my best friend, cheerleader, and guide for over a decade—and has made my life whole.

Alexander Hertel-Fernandez
July 2018
New York, New York

ABBREVIATIONS

AALL	American Association for Labor Legislation
ACA	Affordable Care Act
ACCE	American City County Exchange
ACORN	Association of Community Organizations for Reform Now
AFL-CIO	American Federation of Labor and Congress of Industrial Organizations
AFP	Americans for Prosperity
AFSCME	American Federation of State, County and Municipal Employees
ALA	American Legislators' Association
ALEC	American Legislative Exchange Council
ALICE	American Legislative and Issue Campaign Exchange
CASLP	Conference on Alternative State and Local Policies
CBPP	Center on Budget and Policy Priorities
CEO	Chief Executive Officer
CPA	Center for Policy Alternatives
CSE	Citizens for a Sound Economy
CSG	Council of State Governments
CSI	Center for State Innovation
EARN	Economic Analysis and Research Network
EPA	Environmental Protection Agency
EPI	Economic Policy Institute
FGA	Foundation for Government Accountability
IRS	Internal Revenue Service
LGBT	Lesbian, Gay, Bisexual, and Transgender
NAACP	National Association for the Advancement of Colored People
NCSL	National Conference of State Legislatures

NEA	National Education Association
NFL	National Football League
NRA	National Rifle Association
PAC	Political Action Committee
PLAN	Progressive Legislative Action Network
PSN	Progressive States Network
RPS	Renewable Energy Portfolio Standard
SEIU	Service Employees International Union
SFAI/SPP	State Fiscal Analysis Initiative/State Priorities Partnership
SIX	State Innovation Exchange
SPN	State Policy Network

State Capture

Introduction

Appearing for a press conference the day after his party had suffered unexpectedly large losses in the 2010 midterm elections, a chastened President Barack Obama conceded that Democrats had taken a "shellacking" in Congress.[1] Most of the attention following those elections centered on the extent to which Obama's White House would be able to "sit down with members of both parties and figure out how we can move forward together," as the president had pledged to do.[2] "Deep rifts divide Obama and Republicans," led *The New York Times*, while *The Washington Post* went with "After midterm wins, GOP vows to block Obama's agenda."[3]

To be sure, the 2010 midterm elections did transform the possibilities for Obama's presidency, effectively ending any hope of additional legislative victories for the rest of his time in office. Yet in hindsight, the 2010 midterms ushered in an even more important consequence for Obama's legacy. It was a consequence that unfolded miles away from Washington, D.C., running through state capitols from Montgomery to Madison. Before the elections, Democrats were in full control of 16 states and Republicans only 9.[4] After election day, Republicans jumped to 21 and Democrats fell to 11. The GOP's legislative gains are among the largest that any party has achieved since the New Deal, while the losses endured by Democrats number among the deepest.[5]

As state governments began convening in 2011 with new Republican leaders in charge, a wave of remarkably similar proposals flooded legislative hoppers. Once-blue states like Wisconsin and Maine were now considering measures to cut back the ability of unions to engage in politics and collectively bargain; dramatically scale back access to abortions; retrench social programs like unemployment insurance, Food Stamps, and Medicaid; expand the ability of individuals to buy, carry, and use guns; and lower taxes on the wealthy and on businesses.[6] Perhaps most important for President Obama's immediate policy agenda, these newly Republican-controlled states now had the possibility of stymieing the implementation of his signature legislative accomplishment: the passage of comprehensive health reform through the 2010 Affordable Care Act.

In an era of sharply polarized parties that disagree on nearly every issue, it may not come as much of a surprise that Republicans would pursue a different legislative agenda from Democrats. But what made the 2010 state legislative transition so striking was the speed with which states began introducing and enacting a near-identical set of very conservative policy priorities.

Consider three examples: so-called stand-your-ground, right-to-work, and voter ID laws. Stand-your-ground, or "Castle Doctrine," laws expand the rights of individuals to use otherwise unlawful—and even lethal—force to protect themselves from perceived bodily harm. These provisions attracted significant attention in the wake of the 2012 death of Trayvon Martin. Martin was a Florida teenager fatally shot by an individual (George Zimmerman) whose ultimately successful defense rested, in part, on the law.[7] State right-to-work laws target labor unions, and remove the obligation of workers at unionized firms to pay union dues, even as unions are still legally required to represent the non-dues-paying workers just as they would dues-paying members. Right-to-work laws thus put pressure on unions' financial resources and organizing clout.[8] Voter ID laws, in turn, are measures that require Americans to present some form of identification when they head to the election polls. Although cast as neutral measures intended to prevent voter fraud, these provisions have the potential to make it substantially harder for minority, younger, and poorer individuals—who tend to support Democrats—to vote, since they are most likely to lack the required identification.[9] In private settings, some conservative sponsors of these bills admit that their purpose is to indeed reduce turnout of their political opponents.[10]

In short, all three of these bills represent conservative—and often controversial—priorities that have the potential to fundamentally change the landscape of policy across the states. As Figure 0.1 shows, before 2010 not many states had adopted all three measures. But following the GOP takeover of so many states in the 2010 elections, a number of states began adopting all three provisions, nearly simultaneously. The number of states with identical stand-your-ground, right-to-work, and required voter ID provisions jumped from just two in 2006 to eight by 2013. In all, by 2013, seven states enacted strict photo ID laws for voting, six states enacted right-to-work provisions, and four states enacted stand-your-ground laws. Where did this flood of new conservative legislation come from? In particular, how did so many states arrive at these same three proposals at nearly exactly the same time?

The answer lies with a concerted push from a trio of conservative groups operating within and outside of state legislatures. Take the explosion of voter ID laws following the 2010 elections. Of the 62 ID laws states considered during the 2011 and 2012 legislative sessions, more than half were proposed by lawmakers who shared a common affiliation: they were all participants in the American

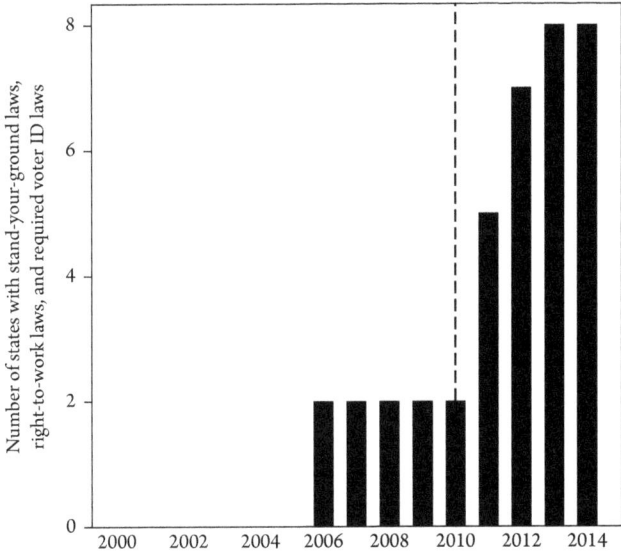

Figure 0.1. STATES ENACTING STAND-YOUR-GROUND, RIGHT-TO-WORK, AND VOTER ID REQUIREMENTS, 2000–2014. Author's review of state legislation.

Legislative Exchange Council, or ALEC.[11] In exchange for their payments of $50 per year in membership dues, those legislators had access to a draft proposal for strict voter ID requirements that ALEC's task force on "public safety and elections" had approved two years earlier, in 2009, during a meeting in Atlanta, Georgia.[12]

Minnesota was one of the first states to introduce legislation related to voter ID requirements after the 2010 elections. The bill was sponsored by ALEC's chairwoman in the state, Representative Mary Kiffmeyer. In interviews with the press, Kiffmeyer strenuously denied relying on ALEC for that bill, arguing that "for people who say this is just ALEC's bill is demeaning to me as a woman and a legislator—suggesting that we couldn't write our own bill for Minnesota." [13] "I might have a novel brain in my head and have a unique thought," Kiffmeyer stated defensively.[14] But a careful review by the Associated Press concluded that there were a number of similarities between the bill Kiffmeyer authored and the ALEC model bill.[15] ALEC, for its part, similarly denied in public that it had directly inspired any of the voter ID legislation introduced since 2009. An analyst for the group argued that ALEC has "never campaigned to promote these policies [including voter ID] in the states."[16] An internal publication from the group told a different story. In that piece, ALEC crowed that voter ID laws were "a strong step toward the prevention of fraud at the polls" and that the group was "uniquely positioned to raise awareness and provide effective solutions to ensure a legal, fair and open election system" through its proposals, including voter ID laws.[17]

The dramatic rightward swing in state policy goes well beyond access to the voting booth. As we will see, the advocacy of ALEC and other conservative cross-state networks, buoyed by outsized GOP control of the states, has threatened other accomplishments of the Obama administration, including President Obama's landmark health reform program, the Affordable Care Act (ACA). ALEC, for instance, has produced extensive materials for lawmakers interested in repealing or stymieing the implementation of the health reform program. These state-by-state efforts to undermine the ACA may wind up being far more consequential than the aborted efforts by the Trump administration to repeal the ACA wholesale in Congress in 2017.

At the same time, however, ALEC was not going up against the Affordable Care Act on its own. While ALEC marshaled opposition to health reform within state legislatures by introducing model bills that prohibited states from accepting new federal funds or enacting policies to implement the ACA, the State Policy Network (SPN), an association of over sixty state-level think tanks focusing on free market and conservative policy, published a steady stream of research and media commentary outlining the reasons why state lawmakers should avoid participating in the Affordable Care Act at all costs. As we will see, despite SPN's protestations to the contrary, the research and advocacy from its affiliates were anything but home-grown, often featuring the same experts writing similar reports for different states. One of SPN's Texas affiliates, the National Center for Policy Analysis, released a report arguing that the state should "chart its own course" when it came to Medicaid expansion—ironic phrasing given that the content of that report was not exactly original, recycling many of the same arguments against expansion that other affiliates had produced.[18] SPN was, in fact, nudging many of its affiliates to oppose Medicaid expansion by giving them grants to work on this issue, along with technical support.[19]

SPN and ALEC worked on convincing state legislatures using research, data, and expert commentary. A third cross-state conservative network—Americans for Prosperity (AFP)—adopted a more bare-knuckled approach. Activating over 2 million conservative grassroots volunteers across all fifty states, AFP regional and state staff organized protests and flooded state legislatures and governors' offices with mailers, phone calls, and emails threatening electoral retribution if politicians dared to touch the new health reform program. One newspaper article describes the blitz that AFP created when Tennessee was contemplating expansion of its Medicaid program as part of the ACA:

> AFP has spent about $300,000 on ads opposing Medicaid expansion, hosted around eight town hall meetings around the state and convinced

about 200 local activists to protest at the state capitol wearing red shirts. All six of its full-time staff have been working on the issue this year in some way, according to [AFP] Tennessee Director Andrew Ogles.... "When the governor began talking about it over the holidays, we really had to go into rapid-response mode," Ogles said.[20]

Beyond grassroots engagement, AFP also deployed its $150 million campaign warchest to run ads against GOP state lawmakers, threatening primary challenges should they cross the party line and participate in the ACA. Together, the three conservative cross-state networks—or the right-wing troika, as I dub them—played an important role in explaining why so many states, especially GOP-controlled states, passed up lucrative federal funds to expand their Medicaid programs and, as a result, left millions of poor adults without access to health insurance.[21]

Table 0.1 introduces the size, scope, and function of each of the three members of the conservative troika that I will explore in this book. Numbering at around 2,000 state legislators and several hundred large companies, philanthropies, and conservative advocacy groups, ALEC pushes policy ideas, written by politicians, conservative activists, donors, and businesses, on state legislatures. Those ideas are supported, in turn, by the research, communications, and media advocacy of the State Policy Network think tanks, as well as the grassroots activists, electoral contributions, and media campaigns provided by Americans for Prosperity, through its federated presence in over 36 states and volunteer rolls numbering over 2 million.

Where did the conservative troika, anchored by ALEC and supported in more recent years by SPN and AFP, come from? How is it that these cross-state conservative networks have developed such effective strategies of pursuing sweeping changes across all fifty states? What does their success mean for the substance of American public policy and the distribution of political power in an era of growing disparities of income and wealth? And why does the left lack its own cross-state network that could check the power of the troika?

This book answers those questions. It explains how, over decades, conservative activists, supported by corporate interests and individual wealthy donors, constructed the trio of political organizations that culminated in the post-2010 shift in state policy we are living through today. As I will document, these organizations were established well before the shellacking that President Obama and his fellow Democrats endured in the 2010 midterm elections and long before Donald J. Trump's election to the White House in 2016—dating back to 1973 in the case of ALEC. These groups also enjoyed significant political success throughout the 1990s and early 2000s even before the 2010 rout. Yet unlike other recent assessments of the right, this book argues that

Table 0.1. **Introducing The Right-Wing Troika.**

The American Legislative Exchange Council (ALEC; $8-10M per year)	The State Policy Network (SPN; $78M+ per year)	Americans for Prosperity (AFP; $150M+ per year)
• Thousands of state legislators, hundreds of large companies, and conservative activists/philanthropists • Develops and disseminates legislative language through policy task forces • Disseminates examples of introduced/enacted bills to lawmakers (100–200 bills based on ALEC models enacted each year) • Uses regular convenings and the provision of expert advice to encourage lawmakers (who often lack staff) to support the ALEC legislative agenda • Created in 1973	• Coordinates and supports more than 60 affiliated think tanks in all 50 states • Testifies for model bills produced by ALEC • Produces media coverage (op-eds, interviews, letters) in support of bills • Commissions polls with tailored wording to show public support for bills and regulatory measures • Many of its affiliates participate on ALEC task forces • Created in 1986	• Nearly 3 million activists and 500+ paid staffers; paid directors in 36+ states • Active during and between elections • Organizes rallies, petitions, and district contacts with lawmakers • Runs ads supporting and opposing legislators, model bills produced by ALEC • Develops coalitions with other right-wing organizations • Commissions polls with tailored wording to show public support for bills and regulatory steps • Created in 2004

the troika's policy victories were not inevitable. There was no "master plan," "blueprint," or "skeleton key" that ALEC, SPN, and AFP could draw upon, to quote from other recent accounts, and it would be a big mistake to read history backward and assume that the troika's present-day success was preordained from the start.[22]

Instead, conservative leaders had to learn as they went along, drawing from both their successes and missteps. That tricky and time-consuming process of building and maintaining coalitions of activists, donors, businesses, and politicians sheds important light on a broader debate on the relationship between interest groups, elected officials, and political parties. The troika, as we will see, illustrates how organized interest groups can reshape the policy priorities individual politicians—and even an entire party—end up pursuing.

Businesses, Donors, Ideological Activists, and Party Coalition-Building

A long tradition in political science considers political parties to be creatures formed by, and made up of, teams of office-seeking politicians trying to win elections.[23] In particular, this line of thinking views parties as solving certain dilemmas faced by ambitious politicians, including how to select and support the best-qualified candidates for office, how to mobilize potentially apathetic voters by creating a strong party "brand" and raising the resources to communicate that brand to the electorate, and how to decide which legislation to develop and vote on once in office.[24] In this view of the political world, political parties are driven by electoral pressures to formulate policies that cater to the median (middle) voter. Party platforms, then, should hew closely to what middle-of-the-road voters prefer to maximize votes and win elections.

Typically excluded, or at best neglected, in this picture, however, are the array of other activists, interest groups, and wealthy donors that also come to mind when we think about contemporary politics, like the highly politically engaged members and staff of deep-pocketed groups like Planned Parenthood on the left and the National Rifle Association on the right, or outsized campaign givers like billionaires Tom Steyer (who gave over $91 million in disclosed federal contributions to liberal candidates in 2016) or Sheldon Adelson (who gave over $82 million to conservative candidates in the same cycle).[25] Where do they fit in? Faced with this question, a group of political scientists has recently argued that we should think of "intense policy demanders"—well-resourced political activists and organizations seeking to change public policy—as forming the real base of political parties. Parties are best seen not as teams of politicians hoping to win and hold office (as in the older view), but rather as coalitions of activists and groups trying to change public policy.[26] Party policy platforms, in turn, flow not from what voters necessarily want, but rather from the positions staked out by the various interests represented in the partisan coalition.[27]

The organized interest-centered perspective offers a much more realistic assessment of party politics in the United States. For one thing, it corresponds to a broad body of research showing that most individual voters only have a murky view of government policy and tend to follow the cues given to them by politicians.[28] For another, it acknowledges the central role that interest groups and activists play in elections and, above all, in trying to change the substance of what government does and does not do.[29] Still, as political party scholars Katherine Krimmel, Nolan McCarty, and Lawrence Rothenberg have all pointed out, constructing alliances between groups and parties is no easy task—and it is one that the organized interests-as-parties perspective tends to underplay.[30]

To be sure, interest groups, activists, and politicians all benefit from a close alliance with one another: organized interests and activists get to define party agendas to match their priorities, and politicians get electorally valuable resources, like grassroots volunteers, campaign cash, and policy expertise.[31] But organized interests and activists sometimes have good reason to go at it alone and remain outside the orbit of any one given party, too. First, groups and activists may want to maintain ties to both parties to maximize their access when control of government switches. Second, organized interest groups banding together to support a party have to find ways of reconciling their diverse—and possibly divergent—preferences into a consistent platform. And lastly, organized interests might be wary of alienating their supporters or the general public by affiliating especially closely with one party over the other. All these concerns are especially acute for large businesses and trade associations. Not only do private-sector interests face a big downside risk of backlash from disgruntled customers or shareholders when they align themselves too closely with one party, but they also have good reason to play both sides so that they can retain access to policymakers regardless of the party in control of government.[32]

In a similar vein to organized interest groups and companies, politicians also have good reasons to play the whole field of activists and groups and avoid a permanent coalition with any one set of outside interests. Individual politicians might want to work with activists, businesses, and groups that their party coalition does not support (such as when a Democratic politician wants help from a pro-life group, or when a Republican politician gets assistance from a labor union). Politicians might also want to shift the set of interest groups with which they work because of changes in the political agenda or other electoral pressures. Perhaps most important, when entering into a long-term coalition with organized groups and activists, politicians have to give up control over their legislative platform to policy-demanding interests in return for the resources such groups offer.

Faced with these competing pressures, how can organized interests and activists—and especially private-sector businesses—form enduring coalitions with one another and with politicians? A close study of the troika, and especially ALEC, reveals fresh answers to this question. Tracing ALEC's changing organizational form over the years, we will see that it is indeed difficult for activists, donors, and businesses to enter into an enduring coalition with one another. Activists, donors, and businesses often want different things from government, and the pursuit of some goals by one camp may alienate others. ALEC, for instance, would need to come up with specific mechanisms to reconcile differences between ideological donors and activists, on the one hand, and more mainstream and risk-averse businesses on the other.

Examining ALEC leaders' rollout of these organizational strategies to get activists, donors, and businesses all on the same page adds important qualifications to the party-as-organized interests theory. In particular, it shows the specific steps that political entrepreneurs need to take to get coalition members to overcome different (and possibly opposing) preferences. These strategies include creating structures that let coalition members most invested in particular policy areas set agendas in those areas, establishing clear decision rules for who prevails in conflicts between coalition members over different policy priorities, and keeping coalition activities and membership secret.[33] The latter is especially important for publicity-shy corporate managers who might want the policy benefits of participating in a close alliance with activists and politicians—but not the potential reputational costs of angering customers, suppliers, or investors who might find companies' partisan ties unseemly.[34] As we will see, when this secrecy is breached, some companies face a big risk of backlash and pressure to cut their ties with conservative activists and donors.

A second lesson that emerges from the troika's development involves strategies for shaping legislators' stands on issues. The party-as-organized interests theory puts significant weight on party nominations as the main way policy-demanding groups and activists will try to shape the positions of a party. To get a party to support the issues that a coalition of activists and interest groups prefers, the theory goes, it is most effective to identify office-seekers who already agree with those positions and support their candidacy. Activists and interest groups can, of course, lobby already elected officials or try to sway candidates with promises (or threats) of campaign contributions and voter mobilization. Still, the authors of the parties-as-organized interests theory expect these tactics to be less effective than nominating allies right from the start. As the authors argue, "Lobbying works reliably only for policy demands that officials already favor," and efforts to sway candidates often falter because activist and interest groups "can never be sure they are getting what they bargain for."[35]

To be fair, the troika, mainly in the form of AFP, has sometimes made party primaries a priority.[36] But ALEC in particular shows a powerful alternative approach for interest group coalitions to redefine a party's legislative priorities. While the parties-as-organized interests theory proponents are right that it is hard to get members of Congress or presidents to change their minds on policy positions once in office, the picture looks entirely different at the state level.

While state legislative candidates may run as liberals or conservatives, in many cases they have not yet identified which specific policies they favor and oppose. Many state legislators, and especially incoming legislators, simply do not have the experience in government that might otherwise be necessary to formulate concrete positions on a range of issues. For instance, about 44 percent of state legislators surveyed in 2002 said that they had never held elective office before, and 41 percent said that they had never served in an appointed position either (about 35 percent had served in neither kind of position).³⁷

The lack of clear policy positions is readily apparent when perusing the campaign platforms of state legislative candidates. Take the example of the 2016 elections for the Iowa state senate, in which Republicans finally gained a majority in that chamber, granting them full control over Iowa government. As we will see later in the book, that transition had enormous implications for the direction of Iowa state policy—yet discussion of policy issues was virtually absent from the campaign discourse of the six GOP senate candidates who ultimately flipped control of the chamber. Reviewing the platforms on their campaign websites, the six candidates scarcely provided any policy content, instead listing generic conservative principles like "our families have to live within our budgets. We need to ensure that our state and federal government does the same," or emphasizing the need to "peel back needless regulations that hurt small businesses, kill jobs, and stop economic growth," and renewing a commitment to "making our communities better, healthier places to live and raise families."³⁸ Even once elected, moreover, many state legislators simply lack the time or staff help to formulate political platforms or agendas on their own. On the same 2002 legislative survey, only 23 percent of legislators reported that they spent the equivalent of a full-time job on legislative work.

The troika—and above all, ALEC—have learned to take advantage of this lack of concrete legislative preferences and capacities.³⁹ As we will see in more detail in the coming chapters, ALEC made an effort to provide precisely the legislative ideas, research, and political resources that many state legislators would have otherwise lacked. This has had the immediate consequence of reducing the cost to state legislators of pursuing ALEC model bills. But it has also meant that the businesses, activists, and wealthy donors participating in ALEC could, over years, define what it meant to be a conservative, pro-business state legislator. Put differently, when conservative state legislative candidates found themselves elected to the legislature, ALEC increasingly became their first resource to supply the ideas that those legislators should be promoting. This is a different, though equally important, avenue for interest group and activist coalitions to define the policy platform of a party compared to the nominations process emphasized in the parties-as-organized interests theory. In so doing, my narrative documents how interest groups like the troika may have contributed to mounting state partisan polarization and the nationalization of state politics.⁴⁰ And lastly, my account shows how efforts like ALEC's to provide model bills, research help, and political advice can not only subsidize the efforts of legislators who are already supportive of the same policy positions as lawmakers, but can also redefine the priorities and preferences those legislators hold in the first place.⁴¹

Understanding the Right Turn in US Politics Across States

Aside from shedding light on the relationships between activists, donors, interest groups, and parties, the picture I provide of ALEC, and later, SPN and AFP, contributes to our understanding of the "rightward turn" in American politics since the 1970s. A number of other scholars have tackled the question of how and why conservative activists, sometimes supported by allies in the business community and wealthy benefactors, began to mobilize into politics over this period.[42] But this book offers a distinctive, cross-state perspective on those developments. Panning out from the happenings in Washington, D.C., is important not only because it offers a wider set of cases of conservative and corporate alliance-building to examine. It is also important because right-wing activists and business leaders recognized that they could have even greater influence on American politics by pushing proposals simultaneously across the states, rather than only adopting the all-or-nothing tactic of new congressional legislation or executive action.

States, conservative organizational architects discovered, were potentially much more receptive to their proposals because of particular features of the state policy process—such as the fact that overworked and underpaid state lawmakers are often strapped for ideas for legislation and the assistance necessary to turn those bills into laws.[43]

Focusing on the states also meant that conservative activists and business leaders could get a second shot at promoting policy ideas that failed to stick at the federal level, or that were complete nonstarters to begin with. The US states thus offered fifty different alternative arenas for the troika to pursue their objectives. As the State Policy Network put it in a recent guide for their affiliate think tanks to retrench the power of labor unions, "The only way to curb union influence is through systematic reform efforts targeting *multiple* states" (my emphasis).[44] What is more, in recent times, these right-wing policy activists and corporate representatives could use legislative control of state government to stymie the progressive policies passed by liberal cities in those red states—for instance, blocking efforts by urban areas to raise minimum wages or enact paid family and sick leave programs.

By documenting the various ways that conservative activists, wealthy donors, and big business have become increasingly focused on cross-state political strategies, this book reaffirms the importance of the states as sites of policymaking. Observers of US politics and policy have all too often written off the states as trivial players on the American political scene—describing them as legislative "backwaters" or the mere "junior partners" to the federal government.⁴⁵ Indeed, some scholars have argued that the party in control of a state matters only a little for public policy outcomes.⁴⁶ Progressive activists, for their part, have all too often followed those conclusions to their logical ends, deciding to focus most of their energy on Congress and the White House, rather than the states.⁴⁷

The following chapters tell a different story. Far from being the second-class partners of Congress and the president, I find that the states have become heated battlegrounds over important policies with real stakes for ordinary Americans. In areas as diverse as employment rights, access to health insurance, the quality of schools for children, and climate change, it is the US states—and not the federal government—that are taking action. This book also shows that partisan conflicts—spurred on by cross-state advocacy groups like ALEC, AFP, and SPN—mean that who controls the states has large and enduring consequences for American politics. As we will see, some of the troika's most significant legislative victories—like cutting back union rights—have had knock-on effects that permanently disadvantage the liberal opponents of ALEC, AFP, and SPN for years to come. Corporate and conservative cross-state advocacy has also standardized the legislation pursued by Republican-controlled governments. The work of the troika means that the legislation passed by GOP legislatures and signed into law by Republican governors looks increasingly similar, often based on identical model bill language.

Beyond illuminating the important and growing role of the states in American governance, the analysis in this book puts earlier work on the development of the conservative movement in context. There are now a number of excellent biographical narratives of right-wing individual donors, especially the billionaire industrialists Charles and David Koch.⁴⁸ My approach in this book is to foreground the organizations that these donors, and especially the Kochs, have created and funded, explaining how these groups have evolved and why they have been so successful in changing policy in some states and not others. To understand the lasting political influence (or lack thereof) of wealthy donors like the Kochs, we have to focus on their organizations. It is ultimately these organizations, and not the donors themselves, that are recruiting political candidates, supporting political campaigns, and lobbying legislatures.

Understanding What Businesses Want— and Get—from Politics

This book has something to contribute to debates over the role of business in politics, too. Ask campaign finance reformers or activists if there is too much corporate money in politics and they are likely to shake their heads vigorously in affirmation, explaining to you all the ways that businesses use their financial clout to buy legislation that helps their bottom lines. But ask a political scientist the same question and you will probably get an entirely different response. In fact, one group of political scientists published a paper provocatively asking the reverse of my hypothetical question: "Why Is There So *Little* Money in U.S. Politics?" (my emphasis).[49]

In that piece and others, political scientists have struggled to show a clear link between corporate political spending and policy outcomes. Some scholars, focused on individual policy battles, have shown cases where it is clear that business' political activities have lowered taxes, slashed regulations, and maintained important subsidies.[50] But other quantitative work has failed to establish a systematic relationship between business' political spending, on the one hand, and Members of Congress' votes on the other, or between the stands of major trade associations, like the US Chamber of Commerce, and the fate of federal policy.[51] And it is challenging to detect a clear-cut relationship between the organizational heft of interest groups and their ultimate policy successes and losses.[52]

One important reason why it is so difficult for scholars to pin down exactly how business shapes policy is that corporate interventions often occur early on in the legislative process, shaping the agenda of alternatives that are considered by lawmakers and specific language that is drafted within a bill.[53] That means studies focusing on the later stages of policymaking, and especially roll call votes, will have difficulty detecting traces of business power.

In the following pages, I am able to take advantage of the operation of the anchor group within the troika—ALEC—to move beyond roll call votes and pin down precisely how troika policy proposals, including many corporate-drafted priorities, end up in state law. Because ALEC relies on model bills to lobby state legislatures, I can compare those proposals with actual legislation to see when and where state lawmakers borrowed text from ALEC proposals. This process offers a much richer picture of where businesses, operating through the troika, got their way in state policy. It shows that businesses are, in fact, getting quite a bit for their political investments.[54] It also underscores the importance of looking beyond traditional—and often crude—measures of business clout, such as counting up disclosed campaign contributions from businesses, to focus on long-term, enduring relationships between individual lawmakers and intermediary organizations, like ALEC, that grant corporate managers access to the policymaking process.[55]

A closely related payoff of this study of the troika, and especially ALEC, is that it shows how US businesses often keep their most controversial and ideological political participation off the public's radar. That, of course, is a deliberate strategy on the part of businesses to shield themselves from consumer or investor backlash. But it means that researchers inferring the political positions of businesses who look at companies' most public involvements, like political action committee contributions or disclosed federal lobbying expenditures, will necessarily miss out on corporate participation in groups like ALEC and SPN that represent more hardline stances and strategies.[56] Echoing the work of political scientists Jake Grumbach and Paul Pierson, this book thus underscores how some political observers may have too quickly assumed that big businesses are generally politically moderate.[57] As we will see, many of the largest and most prominent Fortune 500 companies with relatively anodyne electoral giving were also heavily supporting ideologically supercharged ALEC and SPN state affiliates over the 1990s and 2000s.

Lastly, this book shows how companies deal with the fragmented American political system, in which major policies can be pursued at multiple levels of government. Businesses are often torn between an impulse to push policymaking down to the lowest possible level of government and a preference for uniform, national action. To the extent that decentralization of public policy, especially tax and regulatory policy, forces states to compete with one another to attract capital and reduces public scrutiny of corporate lobbying, businesses may prefer leaving those obligations to the states.[58] But, on the other hand, large companies that do business across state lines—say, a major retailer or health insurer—may actually prefer national legislation over a hodgepodge of disparate state rules. Enter a troika member like ALEC, which lets businesses have the best of both worlds when it comes to federalism: individual companies can pursue policy at a level of government where lawmakers are especially attuned to the threat of footloose capital, all while pursuing a relatively more uniform set of rules across the markets in which managers do business.

Previewing the Rest of the Book

The oldest of the three troika members, ALEC, continues to be the most important of the three cross-state networks in generating policy proposals and reaching lawmakers. Yet despite its prominence, the organization remains poorly understood. Against conventional wisdom, as Chapter 1 lays out, ALEC is best understood as a coalition of politicians, businesses, conservative activists, and wealthy donors—one that combines the sometimes conflicting preferences of all four sets of actors. Drawing on archival evidence and interviews with organizational architects and state lawmakers, I trace the historical development of ALEC from its origins in 1973 to the present day. I highlight the key players involved in its creation, and track the various strategies—both successful and unsuccessful—it has deployed over the years to attract and retain its diverse constituencies.

Detecting the influence of a particular organization, or set of groups, on public policy is no easy task. Thanks to ALEC's strategy of pressing prewritten policy proposals on state legislatures, however, we can get a sense of the legislative reach of the right-wing troika by searching for instances of "policy plagiarism." Those are cases where state lawmakers, like college students facing down a last-minute deadline, have copied and pasted some or all their bills from ALEC models. In Chapter 2, I describe how I have compiled an original dataset that includes nearly all state legislation introduced or enacted since the mid-1990s, along with digitized versions of about 1,000 model legislative proposals drafted by ALEC. Using new methods of text analysis, I map out where individual lawmakers and states introduced and voted on bills that plagiarized from ALEC model legislation.

Having laid out the landscape of the troika's model bills over the past two decades through the lens of ALEC, I next turn to explain when and why legislators rely on ALEC for policy ideas, and even specific legislative language, in Chapter 3. I argue that ALEC recognized early on that many part-time and inexperienced state legislators lack the resources to develop legislation on their own. The organization could thus have great success by providing precisely the proposals, research assistance, and political support that many state elected officials would otherwise lack. I show that states were more likely to introduce and enact ALEC model bills when legislators were paid less, had fewer staffers, and were more pressed for time. I find similar results looking at the level of individual legislators, too: more inexperienced lawmakers were more likely to directly copy from ALEC model bills. Partisanship, ideology, and business pressures—though not campaign contributions—play a central role as well. Chapter 3 thus helps to explain ALEC's patterns of success across some states and not others, and lends broader insights into lobbying and policymaking in the United States by emphasizing the importance of policy capacity for where and when policy advocates can translate their ideas into law.

Whereas Chapter 3 examined the appeal of ALEC to lawmakers, Chapter 4 switches to another constituency of this anchor in the right-wing troika: individual companies. Chapter 4 asks why companies would want to invest the resources necessary to participate in ALEC. I draw out both the costs and benefits of participation for a given business, and then explore a range of potential explanations for why some companies decide to use ALEC to shape public policy across the states while others do not. An especially important explanation for corporate participation, I show, includes policy threats that cross state lines. Businesses were especially likely to join when they were faced with the risk of government regulation or taxation across many states at once—precisely the sort of access to cross-state lobbying that ALEC was selling to corporate executives. Case studies of the healthcare and IT industries further illuminate the importance of these cross-state policy threats to business participation in ALEC. The final section of the chapter assesses the factors that led companies to either retain their membership in the group or cut ties following public backlash in recent years. Altogether, Chapter 4 helps us to better understand how companies decide to participate in politics beyond the tactics that tend to receive the most attention in news coverage, like campaign contributions and hired guns from K Street, and how these tactics intersect with corporate characteristics and the broader political climate.

The first four chapters dedicate special attention to ALEC because of its centrality in the troika. But in more recent times, ALEC has not been acting on its own. Chapter 5 describes the evolution of, and interplay between, the two other members of the right-leaning troika of political organizations focused on the states: SPN, the network of state-level think tanks buttressing ALEC's proposals, and AFP, the new grassroots federation established by the Koch political network. Leveraging newly compiled organizational data and records for both groups, I describe how AFP and SPN have formed alongside ALEC and pursue complementary policy objectives.

What effect has the conservative troika had on public policy—and ultimately, real-world political outcomes? Chapter 6 draws on in-depth case studies of two policies—Medicaid and government employee labor relations—to trace how ALEC, SPN, and AFP have worked hand-in-glove with one another to reshape state policies. Each case study begins with a cross-state analysis, showing the relationship between measures of the strength, organization, and coordination of the troika groups and changes in public policy. I then explore legislative battles for each policy within key states in more detail. These examples illuminate the precise roles that each organization played in promoting a common agenda of policies—including opposition to the expansion of Medicaid as part of the Affordable Care Act and support of measures to curb the bargaining rights of public employees. These case studies also show the ways in which the troika has deliberately used public policy not just as a means of achieving narrow technical objectives, but also to reshape the political landscape in ways that bolstered their own position and weakened their opponents.[59] And lastly, the case of the Medicaid expansion battles illustrates how the troika sometimes finds itself going up against more mainstream business interests supportive of certain government programs. In these instances where the business community is internally divided, the troika often finds it harder to appeal to GOP politicians.

Switching from the right to the left, Chapter 7 poses the following question: Why were left-wing policy advocates caught so flat-footed after conservatives established and expanded the right-wing troika and began reshaping state policy? One inescapable refrain is that there is simply not enough money for liberals to fund their own cross-state networks. As I show, drawing on archival evidence, interviews, and surveys of state organizations, this easy lament from the left is only half right. Looking across major foundations and donors, I show that at least until recently, the aggregate resources available to progressive causes were roughly comparable to those on the right—so it was simply a matter of those resources being concentrated on national politics and local service delivery, rather than on cross-state organization-building. Funding from foundations and elite donors to progressive troika counterweights was spotty and inconsistent, and often encouraged the formation of competing groups that merely duplicated one another's functions. Public employee unions—perhaps the most natural left-wing counterweight to the troika—were indeed powerful cross-state lobbies in some regions, but their geographic reach was never as deep as the troika's. In addition, many government employee unions are now in decline across onetime strongholds thanks to advocacy by ALEC, SPN, and AFP and recent judicial decisions.

More generally, I also show that liberals were slow to even start considering the construction of their own cross-state networks because they had taken for granted the participation of conservatives in older bipartisan, national networks of government officials and focused their energy mainly on Congress, the White House, and, increasingly, the cities—but not the states. By contrast, right-wing political entrepreneurs realized that they could be more effective advancing their legislative agenda by building their own set of alternative state policy networks. Chapter 7 is therefore a story of incomplete and delayed political learning—one that shows how political entrepreneurs draw from their opponents to construct new strategies and organizations, but also the obstacles that those entrepreneurs can face in putting lessons from the other side into practice.

In the concluding chapter, I review the evidence presented in the preceding chapters. I next lay out the implications of my analysis for citizens and advocates who are concerned about the role of money in politics, as well as rising economic and political inequalities. In particular, I focus on the implications of troika-backed legislation for the quality of American democracy, and the ways that troika priorities—and even the troika's strategies for *pursuing* those priorities—might run up against goals of political equality. The troika dampens the representation of ordinary Americans in politics and also makes it harder for citizens to hold those politicians accountable.

On the other hand, I also discuss how the troika's activities are well within the constitutional rights enjoyed by citizens, businesses, and advocacy groups. As a result, efforts to legally ban either the money or participation of the troika are likely to be unsuccessful. Instead, I emphasize structural changes in the policymaking process that would open up the process to a broader set of actors who would bring different (and opposing) perspectives to state governance. I end the book with a call for opponents of ALEC, SPN, and AFP to construct their own organizational counterweights to the troika—rather than merely seeking procedural reforms to shut the troika out of politics.

What This Book Leaves for Future Work

Understanding the emergence, evolution, and impact of the troika is a tall order. As a result, I leave several important issues for future work. I do not, for instance, assess the economic and social effect of troika bills, instead focusing on their *political* causes and consequences. No doubt ALEC, AFP, and SPN's advocacy has shaped important areas of life for Americans in different states, but it is beyond the scope of this book to consider how they have changed outcomes like poverty, economic growth, unemployment, and inequality.[60]

Closely related, I leave open the role of racial and ethnic politics as they intersect with the troika. Many of ALEC, AFP, and SPN's policies surely have outsized effects on minorities—like ALEC's past advocacy of voter ID requirements, punitive sentencing laws, tighter enforcement of undocumented immigration, and cuts to major social welfare programs. But for the purposes of this book, I leave an assessment of their disproportionate impact on African Americans and Hispanic Americans—and the role of racial resentment in potentially promoting their spread—mostly to the side.[61]

And finally, although I zoom in on a number of legislative battles in the states throughout the book to show how ALEC, AFP, and SPN operate, this book is not primarily about individual states. I do not tell the story of any one particular state. (Though there are excellent books that do – like Dan Kaufman's *The Fall of Wisconsin*, *Janesville* by Amy Goldstein, and *Collective Bargaining and the Battle of Ohio* by John T. McNay.) Instead, I focus on how nation-spanning organizations on both the left and the right have used state politics to change American policy over time.

A Note on Methods

The methodological approach I pursue in the following pages is problem-driven; rather than tackling questions from any one particular methodology, I select the procedures and evidence best suited to the puzzles at hand. Accordingly, I employ diverse data and methods in each chapter, ranging from an analysis of archival materials, to new methods of text analysis imported from computer science, to more familiar methods of linear regression, and interviews with state legislators and political leaders. To ensure that the book is as readable as possible to all audiences, I refrain from presenting lengthy discussions of methods or raw quantitative output in the main text, placing such material in appendices to each chapter.

Another methodological point is in order regarding my ability to make claims about causality. Social scientists are becoming increasingly mindful of the difficulties in arguing that one factor causes another. The gold standard for identifying such a relationship is the randomized control trial often deployed in medicine. While political scientists have successfully imported this model to study the effects of different interventions on important political outcomes (like how different campaign tactics might affect voter turnout), the model of randomized control trials is more poorly equipped to answer questions about political development, especially those focused on political organizations.

In the case of this book, I cannot go back in time to establish whether a different strategy that the troika pursued would have resulted in a different path of organizational development or political clout. Instead, I rely on a combination of strategies to pin down causal relationships. In some cases, I employ a close reading of the historical narrative, deploying counterfactuals based on the content of firsthand materials, like organizational memos and interviews. Those primary sources help to illuminate the strategic choices that key actors faced, and permit me to make qualified assessments of what might have happened to the troika if one choice had been taken over another.

In other cases, I examine causal relationships while attempting to control for factors that might otherwise account for the relationship. And lastly, in still other cases, I attempt to test causal mechanisms at different levels of analysis—for instance, demonstrating that a relationship holds across the fifty states at a single point in time, within individual states over time, and across legislators within states over time. The fact that I find the same relationships at each level of analysis helps me to be more confident that the correlations do indeed reflect causal relationships, and not necessarily spurious associations. The claims I make in this book thus necessarily rely on a range of evidence, and so I encourage readers to make assessments about the plausibility of these causal claims looking at the totality of these analyses, rather than on the results of any one analysis or piece of evidence on its own. Just as the story of state capture encompasses a diverse array of actors—politicians, donors, activists, and businesses—so too does it require a diverse array of evidence.

PART I

THE EVOLUTION OF ALEC

A Corporate-Conservative Anchor across US States

1

"The Most Dangerously Effective Organization"

A Smart ALEC Is Born

"Pssst . . . Wanna Buy a Law?" teased the normally staid trade publication *Bloomberg Businessweek* in a 2011 article.[1] That piece explained how a relatively unknown group, the American Legislative Exchange Council (ALEC), could turn one bill idea from a business into "many, many, many laws" in exchange for hefty membership dues. "Corporations drop bills off at one end," concluded the journalists, "and they come out the other, stamped with the imprimatur of a non-profit, 'non-partisan' group of state legislators." In the journalists' assessment, that process made ALEC a corporate "bill laundry" for the states.

Investigative journalists from *The Nation* reached a similar conclusion, writing that ALEC's project was best summarized as "the complete business domination of American public life."[2] The good-government reform outfit Common Cause agreed, summing up their take on ALEC as a group in which "dozens of corporations are investing millions of dollars a year to write business-friendly legislation that is being made into law in statehouses coast to coast, with no regard for the public interest."[3] And in a book on corporate lobbying across the states, labor scholar Gordon Lafer has concluded that "above all, the corporate agenda [to shape state policy] is coordinated through the American Legislative Exchange Council."[4]

These assessments of ALEC paint a clear picture of a business front. That certainly squares well with some examples of the group's activities, like Enron's efforts at deregulation of state electrical markets throughout the 1990s. But the denunciations of ALEC as a "corporate bill mill" fit more uneasily with ALEC's other lobbying priorities. For instance, Common Cause has pointed out that in addition to lobbying for corporate tax breaks and cuts to regulation, ALEC has been at the forefront of efforts to introduce strict voter ID laws across the states. "If it's voter ID, it's ALEC," declared one of Common Cause's directors.[5]

And earlier ALEC pushes prevented states from expanding legal rights to LGBT Americans and women. Where is the narrow corporate interest in these social issues?

Another source of confusion comes from accounts of ALEC that emphasize its connections to Charles and David Koch, the two mega-wealthy libertarian industrialists who are often known colloquially as the "Koch brothers." The Center for Media and Democracy, a left-wing group of muckrakers closely tracking ALEC, the State Policy Network (SPN), and Americans for Prosperity (AFP), has been quick to point out that ALEC has long received support from the Koch brothers' main company, Koch Industries: "No one knows how much the Kochs have given ALEC in total, but the amount likely exceeds $1 million," estimated Lisa Graves, the Center's head.[6] That infusion of cash, Graves argues, has resulted in "hundreds of ALEC's model bills and resolutions" bearing "traces of Koch DNA: raw ideas that were once at the fringes but that have been carved into 'mainstream' policy through the wealth and will of Charles and David Koch."[7]

It is certainly true, as we will see, that ALEC has been supported by the Kochs' main corporate arm. But to call ALEC part of the vast "Kochtopus" of organizations created and managed by the two brothers mischaracterizes both ALEC and the Koch network. ALEC is not now, nor has it ever been, part of the Kochs' main network of political organizations.[8] As best as we can tell, funding for ALEC flows not from the Koch brothers' "seminars" of wealthy donors that finance their more ideological spending, but rather through their business. And unlike the other organizations that the Kochs direct, ALEC is not helmed by close Koch Industries operatives. So if ALEC is not part of the Kochs' main set of political organizations, what exactly is the relationship between the group and the Koch brothers?

The misunderstanding of ALEC's relationship with businesses, movement conservatives, and wealthy donors is understandable, as we will see in this chapter, because over decades the group has grown to include all these actors. It is neither simply a front for corporate lobbying, nor another piece of the Koch network. Instead, it is best seen as a coalition that has attempted to reconcile the varied preferences of big businesses, firebrand conservative activists, and wealthy donors. That task has not always been easy. ALEC has at various points leaned too far toward favoring one set of constituents over the others—sometimes resulting in backlash.

Importantly, ALEC's leaders would need new institutional designs to manage conflicts both within and between their constituent parts. Looking closely at these innovations sheds light on questions of coalition-building in the fragmented American political system. In particular, it helps us to understand when businesses are capable of sustained collective political organization in the United States—a surprising outcome for many observers of American politics.

Why ALEC's Development Is Surprising

In hindsight, it may seem obvious that an organization that brought together political conservatives with private-sector companies to lobby state governments would be a useful creation for corporate executives and right-wing activists seeking policy change across the country. Certainly, the parties-as-organized interests theory I outlined in the last chapter would anticipate that businesses seeking policy change would do well to develop close alliances with activists and politicians. Yet on the other hand, a long line of scholars has argued that groups representing businesses in politics in the United States will be too hamstrung by internal conflicts to adopt anything other than flat-out opposition to government.[9] According to these accounts, businesses are either too fragmented across sectors and regions to lobby together, or else are hampered by our two-party system in which business owners lack a dedicated party, as in some Western European countries. And similarly, unlike in Western Europe, there are no "peak" business associations that all companies are required to join that might organize corporate political activities. Why would American companies spend good money and time on joining a national business group—like ALEC—when they can simply free-ride off of the investments made by their competitors?

Other research suggests another reason that coordinated business action in politics should have become more challenging in recent decades: a fragmentation of corporate interests.[10] This line of work argues that American executives faced shared threats in the 1970s from an aggressive labor movement, a growing regulatory state, and a public increasingly skeptical of big business. Those threats, in turn, prompted collective action and mobilization through reinvigorated older groups—like the US Chamber of Commerce—and new ones, like the Business Roundtable. But since that period, business succeeded in eliminating their original threats—perhaps most notably the specters of aggressive national regulation and labor activism—so that the original motivation for organization no longer existed. As sociologist Mark Mizruchi has put it succinctly: "Having won the war, there was nothing left over which to fight. As a result, the corporate community began to fragment."[11]

But here too the historical development of ALEC runs against received wisdom: the group was least successful in the 1970s and early 1980s and most successful in the decades that followed, precisely during the supposed waning of other national business associations. Figure 1.1 plots the trajectory of ALEC over this period, showing that after growing steadily in the 1970s, legislative

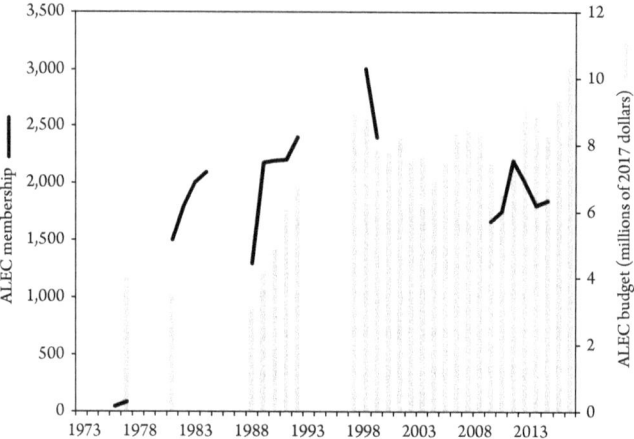

Figure 1.1. ALEC MEMBERSHIP AND BUDGET, 1973–2016. ALEC membership and budget, using data from various ALEC annual reports and tax filings.

and corporate membership dipped in the early 1980s as the organization went through a period of crisis, and then grew again in the late 1980s and early 1990s. Likewise, ALEC's budget remained relatively flat throughout the 1970s and 1980s, and did not steadily grow until the late 1980s and early 1990s—precisely when other prominent business groups, like the US Chamber and the Business Roundtable, were floundering. (Note that the data on ALEC's budget and membership are spotty and I have only included the years for which I have data either from ALEC's annual reports or from IRS filings.)

Why has ALEC succeeded where other business coalitions have failed? And what can ALEC's success tell us about the politics of business-conservative alliances in the United States? The answer to both questions lies with the structure of the group itself and, in particular, the strategies that its leaders deployed to overcome the obstacles to coordinated business action and coalition-building with conservative activists and donors. To attract businesses from a diverse set of sectors, ALEC needed to find perks the group could offer to managers that those companies would not be able to find elsewhere—and that would be sufficiently attractive so as to justify ALEC's steep membership dues and investment of corporate time and effort.[12] On top of that, ALEC also had to come up with an organizational structure that could adjudicate between the divergent (and potentially conflicting) preferences of companies from different sectors, and between corporate representatives and hardline conservative activists and donors. And ALEC had to find ways of protecting companies from potential backlash from investors and consumers, who might find corporate support for an ideologically conservative group off-putting. Secrecy would become an important way of providing that security to businesses from the prying eyes of journalists and the general public.

In the following sections, I describe the creation of ALEC and how initial missteps from 1973 to the 1980s pushed its leaders to settle on the specific organizational structures that permitted it to grow in size and legislative clout from the 1990s to the mid-2000s. As we will see, it took trial and error before ALEC managed to establish the structure that it has today—and even then, it was still vulnerable to public backlash, like the sort that the group endured in the mid-2000s. In particular, when the group failed to keep up the secrecy that protected its companies from public scrutiny, ALEC would find itself under significant financial and political pressure.

This staggered process of learning underscores the fact that ALEC was never the all-powerful lobbying force behind "vile machinations" that many of its progressive foes envisioned.[13] Rather, there were many moments when ALEC could well have fallen apart. Looking closely at why the group did not helps us to appreciate both the distinctive features of ALEC—and also the bigger picture of business, activist, and party relations in the United States.

A Conservative Coalition Forms and Initially Flounders: 1973–1983

When most people think about the modern conservative movement, the first name that comes to mind is probably GOP president Ronald Reagan or presidential candidate Barry Goldwater. But when asked to reflect on conservatives' history, former House Speaker Newt Gingrich added another name to that list, arguing that "no single person other than Ronald Reagan has done more to create the modern conservative movement than Paul Weyrich."[14] James Dobson, founder of the social conservative lobbying group Focus on the Family, similarly gushed that "had there been no Paul Weyrich, there would be no conservative movement as we know it."[15] Who was Weyrich—and what did he do to earn those right-wing laurels?

Born into a deeply religious working-class family in Racine, Wisconsin, Weyrich set out on a peripatetic career that would take him across the country in an effort to unite the GOP around a hard-right agenda.[16] Weyrich's start in politics came early, during his time as an undergraduate student at the University of Wisconsin. An invitation to a 1960 training conference with the Young Republicans gave him the opportunity to meet then–Vice President Richard Nixon and Senator Barry Goldwater and equipped him with valuable campaign and organizing tactics. While the other students were having a good time and enjoying the cocktail parties, Weyrich "took the conference very seriously" and soaked up all that the seminars offered.[17]

Social issues, especially reclaiming the role of religion in society, animated Weyrich's political interest. It was easy for social conservatives like Weyrich to feel alienated in those years between changing social mores and a long string of disappointing legal decisions. In 1962, for instance, the Supreme Court ruled that required prayer in school was unconstitutional and just three years later the Court made contraceptives widely available to all women.[18]

After a brief stint as a journalist in Wisconsin and then in Denver, Weyrich went on to work on Capitol Hill as a press aide for Colorado Senator Gordon Allott, alongside another future star of the conservative movement, George Will. While working for Allott, Weyrich discovered that his conservative comrades were badly outmatched in Congress. Few in number, fractious, and lacking any centralized direction, conservatives found themselves outgunned by the liberal coalition pursuing Great Society reforms and the civil rights movement agenda.[19] Conservatives simply "did not understand or believe in organization," Weyrich contended.[20]

Yet Weyrich did not simply despair over the state of conservatism. Putting his organizing training to work, he saw an opportunity to build a new infrastructure for supporting the recruitment and election of right-wing candidates, as well as the production and distribution of conservative policy ideas. So when Joseph Coors, heir to the Colorado beer fortune, reached out to Weyrich's boss asking about how he might invest in the conservative movement, Weyrich realized that his moment had come. Writing to Coors, Weyrich pitched an idea he had hatched with fellow legislative aide Edwin J. Feulner, Jr. for a new right-wing think tank, the Analysis and Research Association. With additional funding from Richard Scaife, another longtime conservative bankroller, Weyrich and Feulner's new think tank began its work in late 1971.[21] Early disputes over the role that the think tank should play—whether it should be a more staid research organization or adopt more aggressive advocacy tactics—would lead Weyrich and Feulner to split off two years later and form the Heritage Foundation.[22] Heritage, the duo believed, would not just respond to the agenda of Congress but take an active role in setting it in the first place.

Weyrich briefly served as the president of Heritage for its first year. But his real passion was building organizations, not necessarily helming them, and so between 1973 and 1974 Weyrich directed his energy toward creating four new groups to organize the political right. The Republican Study Committee would provide a home for conservatives in the House of Representatives, while the Senate Steering Committee would do the same for the upper chamber. The dramatically named Committee for the Survival of a Free Congress would find, train, and support conservative challengers to Congress. And the American

Legislative Exchange Council would support right-leaning state lawmakers in the production of conservative legislation across statehouses.[23]

Weyrich took up the reins of a group of midwestern politicians in Chicago who had already expressed interest in forming a formal organization of right-leaning state legislators. Under the auspices of the American Conservative Union, a group of Illinois state legislators, including State Senator Don Totten and State Representative Henry Hyde, met to plan the details for the new group.[24] Mark Rhoads, an Illinois state legislative staffer, first dubbed the group the Conservative Caucus of State Legislators, which was later changed to ALEC after members worried about seeming too outwardly ideological.[25] Weyrich, along with his Heritage cofounder Feulner, served as early board members at the insistence of the Scaife Foundation, which began funding the group.[26]

An initial public meeting in the winter of 1973 in Chicago provided a forum for potential new members. That convening, held at the O'Hare International Tower, spanned three days and was "open to all conservative legislators."[27] The event's speakers included free-market evangelist economist Milton Friedman; Robert Carleson, US commissioner of welfare and former welfare director for Governor Ronald Reagan; US Representative Phil Crane (a Republican from Illinois); and conservative New Hampshire GOP Governor Meldrim Thomson.[28] Two years later, ALEC formally spun off of the American Conservative Union, and two years after that, it had secured its official non-profit status with the federal government.[29]

In addition to Totten and Hyde, early ALEC members included Robert Kasten, a state senator from Wisconsin; Tommy Thompson, a state representative from Wisconsin and assistant minority leader for his chamber; John Engler, a state representative from Michigan; Terry Branstad, a state representative from Iowa; and John Kasich, a Hill staffer and later Ohio state senator. Many of these figures would go on to national prominence in the Republican Party, including Tommy Thompson as Wisconsin governor and 2008 GOP presidential candidate, John Engler as governor of Michigan and a top business lobbyist, Terry Branstad as governor of Iowa, and John Kasich as governor of Ohio and 2016 GOP presidential contender. These first members and leaders were also generally very conservative politicians, especially on social issues. As a later US senator, ALEC co-convener Henry Hyde was, for instance, one of the most persistent abortion opponents in Congress and spearheaded a measure that prevents Medicaid from paying for abortions for its beneficiaries to this day (the so-called Hyde Amendment).[30]

Why was Weyrich so energized about state legislators when the bulk of his work had been in Congress? The answer is that he was concerned about an increasingly liberal bent to other national associations of state lawmakers, like the National Society of State Legislators, as well as the rise of new interest groups, especially public-sector labor unions, that had a formidable presence in state government but were also part of a national federation, and thus could quickly disseminate policy proposals across the states.[31] In Weyrich's vision, ALEC could counter these opponents as a national group "led by legislators and staffed by conservatives with a shared belief in limited government, free markets, federalism, and individual liberty."[32]

A later executive director of ALEC further explained the yawning gap between left and right organizing in state and local politics at the time:

> The substantial policy initiatives taking place in the increasingly important state capitals have been and are generally liberal. It is ironic that one of our movement's great successes—the resurgence of federalism—presents us with one of our greatest, and yet unmet, challenges. Conservatism is weakest at the local level . . . [G]overnment at the state and local level is still overwhelming controlled by liberals, in large part because conservatives have concentrated too much of their attention and energy on Washington.[33]

That ALEC leader argued that in contrast to the conservative movement, "liberals understood the importance of the states some time ago," and that liberal state legislators "are supported by a vast array of special interest groups that have been active in the states for a long time," perhaps most notably public-sector unions and especially the "radically liberal National Education Association."[34] As another conservative leader and cofounder of ALEC explained, groups like the teachers unions "came up with model legislation, which [they] would push in several states at the same time" and then they "would use the argument, 'Well, if so-and-so passed it, it must be okay.' And so the bill would go forward, sometimes in 30 states and more. Usually, the liberal bill moved from committee to floor vote before you [the conservative activists] got prepared and marshaled your arguments, if then. The local [conservative activists] were on their own in each state—and they were overwhelmed."[35] The historical record backs up this perception of a lack of conservative or business groups focused on the states: according to a survey commissioned by the US Chamber of Commerce in 1965, only 7 percent of business groups reported having an exclusive focus on state government, compared to 35 percent focused on the federal government.[36]

In a later interview, another ALEC head agreed that the "most effective lobby in the state legislatures" at the time of ALEC's creation was the "National Education Association."[37] She continued: "Many people are deceived by believing that the National Education Association lobbies only for education-related legislation, but they don't. They oppose right to work laws, they oppose balanced budget resolutions, they support comparable work bills, they get involved in just about every piece of major legislation in the state legislature. They are very well organized, extremely well funded."[38] Weyrich also concurred with that assessment of the importance of public-sector labor unions for liberals, admitting several years after the creation of ALEC that he was trying to construct "a carbon copy of what the left has already done" by duplicating the success of the NEA, among other liberal groups.[39]

It is not difficult to see why the right perceived itself to be outgunned by the new public-sector labor unions. From 1960 to 1972, the share of states with collective bargaining for public school teachers, for instance, rose from 10 percent to nearly 80 percent (see Figure 1.2), and from 10 percent to 50 percent for state government workers. The growth of collective bargaining fueled the expansion of teachers unions into politics, and the number of states where a National Education Association affiliate had established a PAC increased from just 1 in 1965 to 22 four years later.[40] The rising threat of public-sector labor unions was only compounded by Democrats' seemingly unshakable grasp on state governments: Democrats controlled a majority of state legislatures in each of the years from 1960 to 1973 save for two. As we will see, ALEC—and later, SPN and AFP—would take aim directly at the public-sector labor unions in an effort to build and maintain conservative political power across the states.

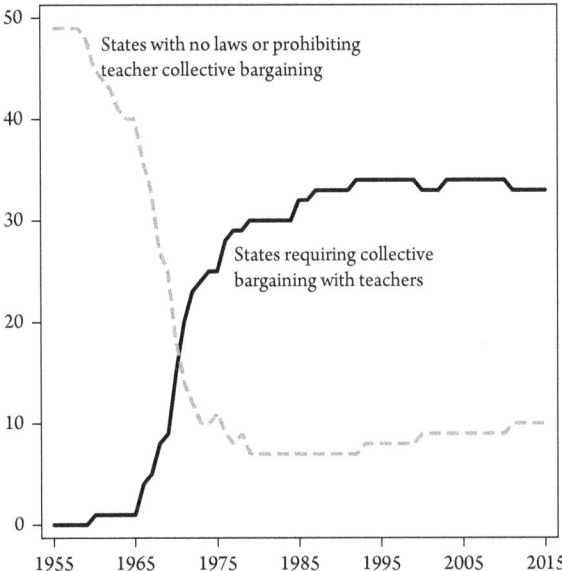

Figure 1.2. RISE OF PUBLIC-SECTOR UNIONS IN THE STATES. Adoption of state laws requiring collective bargaining with teachers. Author's analysis of Valletta and Freeman 1988 data, with updates from Kim Rueben and Leslie Finger. States requiring collective bargaining with teachers includes states with implicit or explicit duty-to-bargain provisions.

But what, exactly, did those early ALEC leaders hope to do with their new organization? In their view, ALEC was well positioned to remedy the organizational imbalance between the newly formed public unions and the conservative movement by providing an infrastructure of support to respond to liberal legislation. ALEC could also generate new conservative and pro-business legislation to spread across the states. These two goals are reflected in ALEC's bylaws, which describe the organization's mission as to "assist legislators in the states by sharing research information and staff support facilities; establish a clearinghouse for bills at the state level, and provide for a bill exchange program; disseminate model legislation and promote the introduction of companion bills in Congress and state legislatures; [and] formulate legislative action programs."[41] ALEC's central activity then—as now—involved recruiting individual state lawmakers as dues-paying members who would attend conferences, receive newsletters, and craft and disseminate model bills.

But while the general goals of ALEC had been established by the mid-1970s, it had not yet used these objectives to spell out how it was different from other conservative groups or business associations. Rather than focusing on ALEC's ability to promote business-backed and conservative policy ideas across statehouses—something that other groups were poorly equipped to do—in its initial years ALEC generally aimed at responding to the liberal policy ideas of the day at the national level. And, reflecting the importance of social issues for its founders, as well as the strong ties of ALEC's initial leaders to the social conservative movement, ALEC prioritized the defeat of high-profile liberal social policies, such as the passage of the Equal Rights Amendment, abortion rights, gun control, D.C. voting rights in Congress, and gay rights.[42]

In one policy paper circulated to its members provocatively titled "Homosexuals: Just Another Minority Group?," ALEC argued that the "highly organized and well funded movement in this country toward legal and institutional acceptance of homosexuality has had an impact too great and far reaching for Americans to ignore."[43] Why was ALEC so concerned about the militancy with which the homosexual community was arguing for equal treatment before the law? Drawing on questionable research from the social conservative advocacy group Focus on the Family, ALEC informed state lawmakers that homosexual relations and practices are "probably some of the most destructive and degrading institutions in America today," contributing to psychological damage, pedophilia, and a fetish for recruiting the young to homosexuality "as a learned behavior," and ultimately out-of-control promiscuity and health risks through venereal disease.

The recommendation from ALEC to lawmakers was thus to "consider the ramifications" of "homosexual rights" before deciding whether the "State [has] the right to dictate to parents the type of educational environment their children must have.... Can the State tell a private employer... that he cannot use his own discretion in employment selection [of homosexual employees]? And should tax and adoption laws be changed to give homosexual couples the same tax advantages and adoption privileges as traditionally married couples?" After the litany of dangers ALEC had given to readers of the policy brief, the answer was clear: lawmakers should stand up to attempts to "homosexualize society" and simply say no.

The heavily socially conservative tone of ALEC's initial work is also conveyed in the account of a group of Minnesota state legislators who attended one of ALEC's first meetings on welfare. Those lawmakers had hoped to learn about new solutions for controlling state welfare costs, but instead were dismayed to discover that the group served as "nothing more than a campaign school for far right political candidates."[44] I heard a similar story from a conservative southern state lawmaker I interviewed, who attended one ALEC meeting in the group's early years only to find that the group was too conservative even for him.[45]

What few economic issues ALEC did cover in these early years focused on either very general changes in state economic policy—such as requiring legislative review of state applications for federal grants or producing estimates of the fiscal and regulatory impact of potential legislation—or symbolic gestures, like calling for "free enterprise" education in schools.[46] As a result of ALEC's intense prioritization of social issues, the group had little to offer most individual businesses in these years, which were uninterested in wading into controversial debates over social issues. Writing about ALEC, one commentator observed at the time that "the potential allies with which [ALEC and other new conservative groups have] been most frustrated with is the moderate business community."[47]

Finding no interest among potential corporate members, most of ALEC's funding in its early years came from conservative foundation grants, especially from the Coors and Scaifes, who were funding Paul Weyrich's other projects, like Heritage, as well. Fully 95 percent of ALEC's funding in 1982 came from either grants or contributions, as opposed to corporate memberships or conference sponsorships.[48] These foundation grants were fairly modest, and tended to be earmarked for specific projects related to social issues, like education or welfare reform.[49] Reflecting that lack of appeal to businesses and reliance on relatively stingy foundation grants, ALEC was quite small in these early years—starting with only two volunteer employees, thirteen legislative members, and an annual budget of $2,700 (nearly $15,000 in 2017 dollars; all subsequent dollar figures in 2017 dollars).[50]

Without many resources, the legislative success of the group was very limited as well. As one investigative report cataloging the "new right" conducted by a teachers' union summed up, "During [ALEC's early] years of operation . . . except for laws requiring student proficiency testing," a major priority of ALEC's foundation backers, "the group's track record in getting its legislation enacted is not all that impressive."[51] One silver lining, however, to the group's shallow corporate support was that it did not need to find ways of navigating conflicts between its members. ALEC's archival records do not indicate many conflicts between the few participating companies or political advocacy groups.

ALEC's mediocre track record would begin to change in the mid-1980s, as leaders launched efforts to forge deeper ties with the business community.[52] It was aided in this endeavor by its tax-exempt status, meaning that donations to the group could be written off of a donor's tax bill.[53] One early episode in particular demonstrated to ALEC leaders how they could attract corporate backers. That effort involved participating in a coalition promoting state insurance reform.[54] The experience ALEC leaders had in this coalition would provide an important template for ALEC's strategies in later decades, specifically the advantages of marketing the group as offering a distinct set of benefits to companies that managers could not obtain from other business organizations and the possibilities for using policy to reshape the state political terrain.

Premiums for general liability insurance skyrocketed during the early 1980s, increasing the amount that entities as diverse as state and municipal governments, manufacturers, medical providers, and daycare centers needed to pay for their insurance coverage.[55] Insurers and their corporate clients blamed the tort system, pointing to frivolous lawsuits and calling for tighter caps on tort claims. Trial lawyers and consumer advocacy groups, on the other hand, responded by blaming the insurers and proposed tighter regulations to protect ordinary Americans.[56]

ALEC entered the debate by working closely with private insurers and other businesses calling for restrictions on tort claims, operating against consumer advocates and labor unions. ALEC's National Project on Risk and Liability "seeks to provide the basis for long-term fundamental reform for the state civil justice systems," explained a publication announcing the launch of the initiative.[57] It found its niche in the newly formed American Tort Reform Association, acting as the main pathway for national groups like the American Society of Association Executives, the National Federation of Independent Business, and the Mechanical Contractors Association to lobby state legislatures.[58] The head of the tort reform association, James Coyne, correctly identified the potential payoffs that ALEC could provide for his effort. Coyne would have had an easy time working with ALEC: both groups shared an office with the Heritage Foundation at the time, and several of the initial philanthropic backers of ALEC were also funding the tort reform initiative.[59]

As ALEC's executive director explained about the collaboration, "The states are the prime focus.... There are more than 1,000 bills out there addressing the [tort reform] issue."[60] "ALEC's National Project will have as its final product a compendium of model state legislation designed to effect fundamental state civil justice reform . . . culminating in the publication of ALEC's . . . *Source Book of American State Legislation*, which will contain model state legislation for tort reform."[61] That eventual package of model bills included proposals to "limit or cap damages [that claimants could receive], to modify the types of harms for which penalties and/or damages are allowed, to change doctrines of proof or causation, to extend (or shorten) statutes of limitations, to expand (or reduce) the class of those eligible for compensation (or subject to damages claims), [and] to publicly regulate attorney fees and modify allowable defenses."[62]

ALEC's lobbying blitz for each of these model bills ultimately paid off: after the campaign, 23 states would introduce caps for tort suit damages; 34 states would limit, or even ban, tort suit punitive damages; and 38 states would introduce a maximum amount for which a defendant could be held liable—all changes that would make it more challenging for consumers to bring suits against business.[63] The tort reform coalition ultimately brought a number of new corporate members within the ALEC fold as well; the group's civil justice initiative grew to include Amoco, the Alliance of American Insurers, the National Federation of Independent Business, the Chemical Manufacturers Association, and the National Association of Independent Insurers.[64]

Like ALEC's later offensive against public-sector labor unions, the civil justice project around tort and liability reform provided immediate benefits to the private-sector businesses seeking relief from legal claims against their goods and services, as well as the private insurance companies dealing with wildly variable legal payouts. But it also had the important additional consequence of taking aim at a longtime supporter of progressive Democratic causes and candidates across the states: the trial lawyer bench. "It's a double kiss," explained one conservative strategist in the tort reform movement, "Republicans get to force one of the biggest backers of Democrats to spend money just to survive and, at the same time, please everybody from the Chamber [of Commerce] to the drug companies, to the Realtors, doctors, you name it."[65] "[I]t's very clear what the program is—it is to defund the Democratic Party," explained one Democratic political operative, stating that for the Republican Party, "it's a double header: more income for your side, and you take income from the other."[66]

This strategy—of using public policy to reshape political opportunities—was one that ALEC founder Weyrich understood very well. During a speech at a religious right meeting in Dallas, Texas, Weyrich emphasized that his philosophy about political change was "different from previous generations of conservatives. . . . We are no longer working to preserve the status quo. We are radicals, working to overturn the present power structure of this country."[67] In the same speech, Weyrich explained that conservatives should use policy to limit access to the ballot box to weaken their opposition, declaring, "I don't want everybody to vote. Elections are not won by a majority of the people. They never have been from the beginning of our country and they are not now. As a matter of fact, our leverage in the elections quite candidly goes up as the voting populace goes down."[68] Weyrich—and the groups he founded—similarly sought to use policy to change the power structure available to their allies and opponents.

In part as a result of victories like these, one conservative magazine bragged that ALEC had now been dubbed the "most dangerously effective organization" in state politics by the National Education Association—a far cry from teacher unions' political assessment of ALEC just a few years prior.[69] Building in part on the lessons of its tort reform effort, ALEC also established close ties to the tobacco industry. Those companies were seeking to curb state regulation of tobacco sales, marketing, and use.[70] ALEC was more than happy to oblige. The group hosted, for instance, a 1986 seminar for state legislators on the issue, which argued that there was "no persuasive scientific evidence that substantiates a causal or exacerbating relationship between environmental tobacco smoke exposure and chronic health disturbances . . . [W]e seriously delude ourselves if we believe that the health implications of poor indoor air will be magically eliminated, even significantly ameliorated, by banning smoking."[71] (By 1986, the US Surgeon General's office had already published nearly twenty reports on the consequences of tobacco use, establishing a public health record showing its addictive and cancer-causing characteristics.[72]) Instead, ALEC recommended that states needed to adopt stiffer indoor ventilation standards that required technology produced by another firm affiliated with the group.[73] The tobacco industry would continue to provide an important source of funding for ALEC for many decades to come.

While the anti-smoking ban campaigns only succeeded in delaying the adoption of smoking regulations, the overall effort of reaching out to individual companies paid off handsomely for ALEC over this period. Thanks to new corporate members such as Edison Electric, Procter & Gamble, Mary Kay Cosmetics, Eli Lilly, Adolph Coors, and Atlantic Richfield, ALEC had amassed a budget of nearly $3 million and a staff of 20 by the mid- to late 1980s.[74] Boasted ALEC's executive director: "I have more big corporations who want to see me, get involved and become members than we can practically cope with."[75] These companies participated in ALEC as leaders on a newly created private-sector advisory board, as individual members, as donors for the group's annual meetings, and as sponsors of other events for state lawmakers.

ALEC had arrived at a valuable service for attracting corporate support: granting companies the ability to standardize policy across disparate state governments while keeping policymaking at a level that offered greater advantages to business interests. For both tobacco manufacturers and the businesses affected by tort suits in the 1980s, corporate executives had a strong interest in creating more uniform standards across the states—in both cases, curbing the spread of consumer-friendly regulations. As one top corporate executive would later explain in describing his business's decision to support ALEC, a growing concern during this era for him was "the proliferation of non-uniform state-by-state legislation that could be starting to undermine one of the key competitive advantages of US industry; namely, our large, unfragmented domestic market."[76] Those were companies that ALEC could now court for membership through its new "business policy board."

ALEC's pride in its increasingly successful corporate relations, however, masked continued tensions between its policy advocacy around controversial social issues and the preferences of its new corporate members. While acknowledging his company's strong support of ALEC's state activities, Rick Rothschild, director of government affairs for Sears, Roebuck & Company, explained, "I'm aware of no corporation that has a position on social issues."[77] Another corporate governmental affairs officer was even blunter: "We like ALEC's conservatism and probusiness attitude. But abortion, school prayer and the like are just not issues for us. We nod and accept the rest of it but we aren't supportive of it. You have to grin and bear it."[78] Ultimately, these more moderate business preferences on social policy prevailed. ALEC thus began to shift away from such controversial issues. Explained one lobbyist for a cross-state association at the time: "[ALEC's leaders] were very right wing, but they have tried to temper some of that to be more acceptable [to business]."[79]

ALEC was most successful at attracting business support when it could promote policies that financially benefited individual companies and sectors, rather than ideologically charged social issue legislation of little interest to corporate managers. Figure 1.3 plots the focus of ALEC's model bills proposed each year, and shows that a declining share of all model bills could be categorized as focusing on controversial social issues like abortion or drugs. The social issues category counts model bills related to English-language laws, abortion and religious freedom, gun rights, and measures condemning busing efforts for school integration. Nearly a fifth of model bills fell into this category in the 1977 to 1979 ALEC sourcebooks, compared to just 2 percent from 1993 to 1995. By contrast, model bills related to narrow business regulation issues rose from just 4 percent in 1977 to 1979 to nearly half of all bills by 1993 to 1995 (here, I count bills coming out of the task forces related to labor market issues, energy, the environment and natural resources, transportation, telecommunications, healthcare, real estate, banking, or financial services, and civil litigation). Criminal justice–related model bills, and especially those that supported the privatization of prison services, also rose sharply over this period.[80]

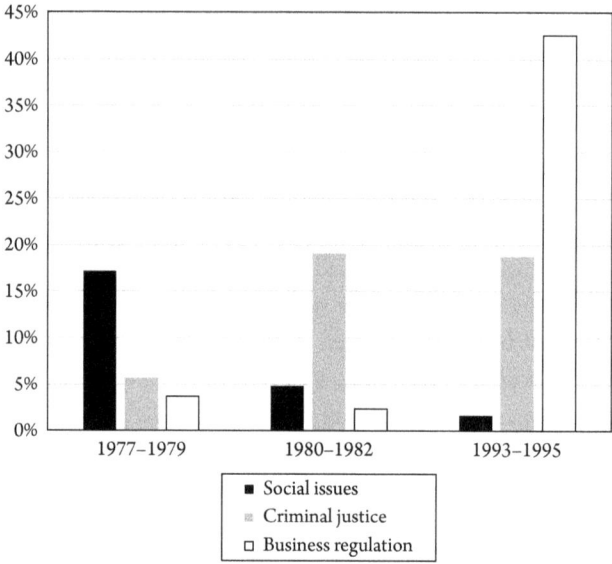

Figure 1.3. ALEC's DECLINING FOCUS ON SOCIAL ISSUES AND RISING FOCUS ON BUSINESS REGULATION. ALEC model bills proposed in annual sourcebooks that focus primarily on social issues, criminal justice, or business regulation; see the text for coding details (data from ALEC 1976, 1977, 1979b, 1980b, 1995b).

A Football Star Tackles ALEC's Finances: The 1980s Overhaul

ALEC also experimented with new organizational forms in the 1980s that would prove critical in the coming years. Inspired in part by the structure of President Ronald Reagan's Task Force on Federalism (in which many ALEC leaders participated), Sam Brunelli, ALEC's newly installed head, institutionalized internal "task forces" to facilitate discussion around specific policy issues between legislators, private businesses, activists, and ALEC staff.[81] This was an idea that had only been occasionally used before the late 1980s. According to Brunelli, task forces were only "loosely organized" and tended to come in and out of existence depending on the priorities ALEC was pushing in any given year.[82] The initial task forces he set up focused on civil justice (especially the tort reform agenda), healthcare (especially the promotion of medical savings accounts), and telecommunications policy (involving privatization and deregulation). As we shall see, these task forces would become an important route for businesses and activists to directly define ALEC's legislative priorities in the coming decades, helping to market ALEC's benefits to companies that might not otherwise join the group, as well as managing conflicts between members that threatened to undermine the group's success.

At first glance, Brunelli might seem like an unlikely figure to head ALEC during this critical reorganization, since he took a more winding path into politics than did his predecessor, Paul Weyrich. Born in rural Fort Morgan, Colorado, Brunelli attended Colorado State College.[83] There the 6-2 Brunelli became a star football player, and after graduation he went on to play professionally for six seasons as an offensive lineman for the Denver Broncos.[84] Following his retirement from the NFL, Brunelli launched and ran his own agricultural business in Colorado, Brunelli Farms, for several years.

Like so many other conservatives, it was Ronald Reagan who pulled Brunelli into politics. He was a "big Reagan man" in the 1976 GOP primary, and after campaigning hard for Reagan in the 1980 general election, Brunelli wound up working for Education Secretary Bill Bennett in that department's Office of Intergovernmental Affairs.[85] At the Department of Education, Brunelli was tasked with working on state educational reform, and despite all the energy that the Reagan administration had put into the effort, "It seemed like we were losing the battle . . . to all the different educational associations, especially the NEA."[86] Disillusioned with the lack of progress, he asked himself, "Why don't [I] go where the action is, in the states."[87] Looking across the sparse field of conservative efforts to date, he came up with ALEC, and although it was still a "small, fledgling operation," they were "of the like-minded."

Still, when Brunelli arrived at ALEC, he realized that there was a lot of work to be done. "They had a very limited scope of power and the ability of what could be done," he summed up to me; "They didn't have the vision and the agenda."[88] As if that wasn't enough, Brunelli discovered ALEC was "deeply in debt and mortgaged to the hilt . . . probably [with] a 2 million dollar unfunded liability." One of Brunelli's first challenges, then, was to figure out how to properly finance the organization, and that would involve the creation of the task forces. As he explained it, these new units would build greater appeal for corporate members and thus generate more revenue for the group.[89] Before Brunelli arrived, ALEC "would raise money around a certain project and nothing else would be funded and that's how they got all of those unfunded liabilities and went broke." Under Brunelli, no longer would ALEC exclusively appeal to individual philanthropies for specific projects. Instead, with the task forces in place, corporate executives could become "much more involved" in the group with the opportunity to "come where the [policy] action" was most relevant for their particular business.[90] Philanthropies could also participate on the new task forces, but they would need to pay dues like private-sector companies rather than offering project-specific funding.

Beyond inspiring the task force structure, the Reagan presidency proved to be a boon to ALEC's organizing efforts in other ways. With many conservative leaders affiliated with ALEC now serving in the administration, ALEC developed close ties to the White House. In addition to organizing an annual "ALEC White House Briefing" on domestic and foreign policy issues—a prime perk for dues-paying legislative and corporate members—the Reagan White House took a strong interest in ALEC. That meant integrating ALEC's work into the administration's priorities and regularly slotting in administration representatives at ALEC events. For instance, Reagan's EPA administrator, secretary of the interior, and education secretary all looked for opportunities to align ALEC's work with that of the administration.[91] "For state legislators who appreciate the critical value of free enterprise, ALEC offers the strong support of legislative research and networking. . . . ALEC and I are soldiers in a common cause," proclaimed Reagan on behalf of the group.[92] Far from abandoning the states after gaining control of the White House, conservatives in the Reagan administration used the formal authority—and also the trappings of their office—to encourage cross-state organizing through ALEC.

Another organizational innovation during this period would prove to be less successful. Motivated by their legislative victories across the states, ALEC decided to enter electoral politics by creating a political action committee. ALEC leaders hoped that the PAC would invest nearly $100,000 in 1984 and half a million dollars by 1986 into gubernatorial and state legislative races.[93] Not only would the new ALEC-PAC victories help to secure further legislative wins for the group, but ALEC leaders believed that new conservative majorities in statehouses would help Republicans to redraw legislative districts in their favor after the 1990 census.[94] Apart from offering direct contributions itself, ALEC-PAC hoped to train conservative state legislators, as well as to spur more contributions by other, larger PACs to candidates for state office—an arena of politics that ALEC felt was long neglected by potential donors.

Despite these ambitious aims, the electoral arm of ALEC fit poorly with its original focus on public policy, and ALEC eventually retreated from electoral politics after 1986 and returned to their primary mission of shaping state legislation among already elected state officials. ALEC remains a group that generally operates outside of electoral spectacle, instead focusing mostly on crafting state policy between elections.[95] That is, however, not to say that its legislative proposals are designed without elections in mind. An appeal of ALEC for legislators, as we will see in Chapter 3, involves its "signaling" quality to demonstrate to voters and donors that a state legislator is generally pro-business or conservative.

Growing Pains and the Development of New Strategies: 1990–2001

If the 1970s marked the formation of ALEC, and the 1980s saw ALEC's transformation from a collection of mostly socially conservative activists into a coalition of conservatives and corporate interests, then the 1990s were a period of rapid expansion and consolidation of ALEC's operations. ALEC entered the decade with a membership base of around 2,400 legislators (out of 7,600 nationwide), over 250 private-sector members, and annual revenues of about $7 million, roughly double the revenue the organization received in the late 1980s.[96] The vast majority of this revenue was generated by donations from corporate members through dues and conference sponsorships, although ALEC continued to receive support from conservative foundations, especially those associated with the Coors, Olin, Scaife, Milken, and Bradley families.[97] Still, as we shall see, the group carried considerable debt from its earlier era, when it was not as focused on attracting corporate support as it would later be.[98] This debt would generate an important source of pressure on the organization to further change its structure to attract and retain corporate backers.

Notwithstanding ALEC's considerable legacy costs, the group's growing legislative influence in the states during the early 1990s was readily apparent. In the 1990–1991 legislative session, a total of 240 ALEC model bills were introduced (with at least one in each state); of those, 92 bills were enacted in 46 states, for a passage rate of 38 percent, 20 percent higher than the average for all state legislation.[99] The success of ALEC led one progressive leader to lament to a journalist at the time that "big business is extraordinarily well-organized at the state level. The more progressive community has got to get organized at the state level, because frankly we're being taken to the cleaners."[100]

Brunelli's new task forces were quickly becoming a central component of the group, too, changing from being mere clearinghouses for discussions between ALEC members to formal bodies that each had their own official memberships, rules, boards of state legislators and private firms, and annual meetings.[101] These task forces, covering healthcare, tax and fiscal policy, civil justice, education, commerce and economic development, criminal justice and public safety, energy and the environment, telecommunications and IT, and trade and transportation, would now be individually responsible for producing and disseminating model bills directly to state legislatures.

The formalization of task forces fits with a broader effort on the part of ALEC leadership to explicitly adopt a "business philosophy" in order to rebuild the group's finances and pay off its sizable legacy debts. One board member estimated in the 1990s that ALEC might need a short-run infusion of around

$750,000, followed by a longer-term capital campaign to raise at least $2 million, even worrying that ALEC "will go under if there is not a significant influx of money in a short period of time."[102] (Koch Industries would eventually provide an important bridge loan to cover the group's short-run deficit, along with a grant from R.J. Reynolds Tobacco.[103])

At the same time that it acknowledged ALEC was a non-profit entity, a business report prepared for ALEC's leadership argued that "nevertheless, like a business, ALEC must generate sufficient revenue to cover operating costs, maintain a reserve fund, and have the resources to expand services and make capital investments. Therefore, ALEC must begin to function more like a business, and recognize that it has a product that it provides to a defined customer base for a 'profit.' In other words: *there can be no mission without margin*" (original emphasis).[104]

As the report put it bluntly, the "product" that ALEC was selling was state policy, and it was selling the opportunity to write state policy to private-sector businesses and advocacy groups.[105] ALEC, this report argued, needed to highlight and aggressively market the exclusive benefits it could offer that were unavailable in other business or lobbying groups.

Task forces would now be responsible for covering their own costs, so to that end, ALEC's board of directors encouraged task force staff to "identify 'hot topics' to generate enough interest to cover costs" using ALEC's unique ability to help companies and activists promote particular policy ideas across many different states at once.[106] Task forces that could not attract corporate support were told to turn to conservative foundations (as with welfare and education policy), or else they would be dropped from the group altogether.[107] The task forces that were abandoned were generally those without clear deep-pocketed sponsors (like those addressing substance abuse and child and family services), while those with clear corporate interest (like telecommunications or environmental regulation) endured over the whole period.

Although conservative foundations, like those associated with the Coors and Scaife families, had provided the seed money for ALEC, the group's leaders were increasingly skeptical of turning to philanthropies for support, preferring corporate grants. The reason was that conservative foundations had begun to attach many strings to shrinking grants. That, in turn, greatly limited the ability of ALEC to use the funds to cross-subsidize other activities—a perennial problem for non-profits.[108] In addition, foundations were slower than private-sector businesses at making funding decisions. While a company could simply cut a check to ALEC after a fundraising meeting, foundations "took time," since they had elaborate mechanisms for grant applications that had to pass multiple votes. "They had all of this infrastructure" that got in the way, summed up one ALEC leader at the time.[109]

ALEC thus borrowed the model of a private-sector business for its operations, and its task forces became a mechanism for selling specific—and distinctive—products to individual managers, offering "an invaluable resource to businesses seeking to prosper in today's challenging public policy environment."[110] In contrast to other national business associations or conservative policy groups, ALEC could credibly claim to interested executives that it was "uniquely positioned as a legislative network that crosses geographic, political, and economic lines. . . . No other organization in America has as many valuable assets . . . in as many key [state] decision-making positions as does ALEC."[111] In a crowded field of conservative think tanks and advocacy groups, trade associations, and national business groups, this organization was able to stand out thanks to the niche it had carved out in connecting businesses and activists with state legislatures.

Even as ALEC's increasingly entrepreneurial task forces addressed the challenge of attracting financial support in the mid-1990s, the group began facing another obstacle: conflicting policy preferences between its members. Here again, the task forces developed a solution. First, there would be an explicit division of labor between ALEC's task forces by substantive policy areas, so, for instance, only the agricultural task force could produce and disseminate policy proposals related to agriculture. ALEC's leaders developed highly specific and elaborate language for assigning potential model bills and policy activities (such as workshops and conferences) to each task force, and to deal with issues that might cross task force jurisdictions.[112] There were also "long-instituted gentlemen's agreement[s]" between ALEC's task force participants to "refrain from publicly attacking each other or otherwise throwing each others' ALEC model legislation into disrepute."[113]

This division of labor reduced potential conflicts about which issues and policies the group should be promoting. While other national political associations might find their membership deadlocked over deciding which legislative issues to prioritize each year, ALEC delegated its agenda to the companies and activists most invested in those corresponding policy domains. Thus, there were few cases where the group would need to choose whether to pursue, say, policy proposals related to agriculture instead of proposals related to healthcare. It also had the effect of giving the most voice within ALEC to the businesses that had the most to win or lose from a policy—like extractive resource companies fighting measures to address climate change, tobacco companies pushing bills to avoid public health regulation, and telecommunications companies trying to gain access to new markets.

The effectiveness of this strategy is evident in the diversity of policy proposals the group has advanced over time, and also by the fact that model bills produced by one policy task force have, in some instances, run against the intent of model bills produced by another task force. For instance, while its tax and fiscal policy task force members were promoting bills to reduce state spending, the criminal justice task force advanced bills that would have greatly increased state spending on prisons through more punitive sentencing laws.[114]

This delegation also explains why tech giants like Facebook and Google that would later join the group could be members in ALEC while also promoting initiatives to address climate change outside of ALEC. These businesses were participating in the telecommunications policy task force—and could credibly claim that they had nothing to do with ALEC's environmental policy positions or activities. As Facebook executive Bill Weihl explained when asked why the social media giant was a member of a group that opposed its other environmental policy priorities: "We're not an advocacy or a single-issue organization. We're a company. We are members of many different organizations, that one included."[115] The structure of the task forces also meant that even if there was majority support for a position among ALEC's corporate members, like addressing climate change, ALEC's energy policy would still be set by the minority of mining, oil, and gas companies that had the most to lose from shifting away from carbon-intensive energy production.

Of course, even as businesses were contributing to individual task forces, the money they directed toward ALEC still subsidized other activities as well, including the infrastructure for the whole organization. As Sam Brunelli reminded me, although companies came to ALEC to work on a "certain model bill," their "X dollars came in and it funded everything—the company's issue and everything else."[116] This ensured that the entire organization could be supported and, according to Brunelli, was a very explicit reaction to the earlier ALEC era in which ALEC sought project-specific funding from foundations to the detriment of the rest of the organization, which was how the group ended up with so many unfunded liabilities.[117]

While the strict delegation of policy to the task forces managed conflicts *between* policy issue areas, ALEC still needed to address the problem of opposing preferences *within* each task force. To do that, the group's leaders established clear criteria for which members would prevail in conflicts within task forces: businesses or activists that contributed more to the organization and enjoyed a higher level of membership would have the last word. The basic level of membership, for instance, qualified members to participate in task forces, but did not grant voting rights over task force decisions. For that, members would need to contribute at least three times more.[118] For an even higher level of membership, members could be guaranteed that their issues would be addressed by a task force: "In addition to the benefits of *Lincoln Club* membership, *Madison Club* members may have a Legislative Director work on their behalf on a specific project."[119] And for still higher levels of membership, corporate managers or activists could be assured that they would have specific input into the design of topics and speakers for the group's annual meetings.[120]

Thus, if a company found itself at odds with another corporate ALEC member over a particular model bill, both businesses would have a clear expectation of how that conflict would be resolved: the matter would come down to the amount that managers at each company were willing to pay to have that idea spread across ALEC's membership. This decision rule prevented ALEC from suffering many of the same intra-association conflicts described by other authors in groups like the US Chamber of Commerce or the Business Roundtable.[121] It also created bidding wars between corporate members of ALEC that helped bring in more revenue.

Some examples of these intra-task force disputes include telecommunications policy, which pitted the interests of national giant AT&T against more local Bell companies, and tobacco regulation, where Lorillard Tobacco (manufacturer of Newports and Mavericks) wanted legislation regulating the shelf space convenience stores would give to its competitors, including Philip Morris.[122] And the Solar Energy Industries Association, a trade group representing solar energy projects, joined ALEC at one point to push for greater renewable energy incentives—only to leave shortly thereafter when it became clear that they couldn't muster enough support on the extractive industry-heavy environmental policy task force.[123] But perhaps the best example of this strategy for managing interbusiness conflicts comes from state battles over electricity deregulation, which we saw earlier in the book. Both sides of this issue were active in ALEC during this period, with one camp represented by the Edison Electric Institute (the trade association for investor-owned utilities) and the other represented by Enron (which sought to sell electricity across the states) and Koch Industries (a major power consumer). The task force responsible for energy-related policy was deeply divided between these two sets of interests.[124]

Ultimately, however, Enron and Koch Industries decided to invest in greater access, and their position was reflected in a series of model bills, resolutions, and research produced by the group, as we have already seen.[125] Indeed, recall that Enron was such a large contributor to ALEC that the company's CEO was offered a keynote slot at the subsequent annual ALEC meeting in New Orleans. At that meeting, Lay made the argument for deregulated electrical markets before the assembled body of state legislators from all across the country. Had the investor-owned utilities been willing to offer greater contributions to ALEC, it would have been their representatives at the meeting instead of Enron.

In this way, ALEC was able to maintain its neutrality and let the opposing executives decide for themselves how much they valued ALEC's services. Summed up the Edison Electric Institute's manager of state government affairs: "It's a situation where you buy a seat at the table and then you have the opportunity to vote and drive policy. We don't have enough votes. If they are going to do something we like, they don't need our votes, and if they are going to do something we do not like, we can't stop them."[126] ALEC's executive director in the early 2000s disputed this characterization of the group, arguing that Enron did not always get its way. As evidence, he cited the fact that ALEC refused to endorse the Kyoto treaty requiring the United States to reduce its energy emissions—an Enron-favored position.[127] Yet ALEC's energy task force was dominated by extractive industry representatives during this time, including Shell Oil, Phillips Petroleum, Mobil Oil, and Marathon Petroleum, and so it should come as no surprise that Enron's unpopular position lost out. ALEC's structure was in some ways radically transparent, at least for its members. It is difficult to think of another political organization that so clearly articulates the decision rule dictating the issues it pursues: more money, more access.

Table 1.1 summarizes the leadership structure of the organization in the 1990s. ALEC was headed by a national board of directors, which, in turn, was split between the group's main constituencies: state legislators (on a public-sector board) and businesses and conservative activists and donor philanthropies (on a

Table 1.1. **Leadership Structure of ALEC, 1990s.**[a]

	Board of Directors, led by National Chairman (Legislator)	
Private Enterprise Board (Corporate Members and Conservative Activists)		Public Board (Legislative Members)
Private Enterprise State Chairs (At Least One per State)		Public State Chairs (At Least One per State)
	ALEC Task Force Chairs (Legislative and Private-Sector Chairs)	
	ALEC National Staff Administration, Development, Public Affairs, Meetings and Conventions, and Legislation and Policy	

[a] Author's review of ALEC materials.

private-sector board). Those two boards were led by a national chairman (a state legislator). Corporate members and state legislators were further represented through state chairmanships, with at least one private-sector leader and legislator representing each state (and with some states having up to three chairs). A major responsibility of these state chairs is the recruitment of new private-sector and legislative members. State legislative chairs, for instance, reach out to newly elected lawmakers to encourage them to attend ALEC's orientation summit for new legislators and to become members themselves (more on their strategies in Chapter 3). State private-sector chairs, for their part, would do the same for their corporate or advocacy colleagues whose organizations might benefit from participation in ALEC.

Incorporating locally recognized leaders in a federated structure helped ALEC to build membership in all states, including states where ALEC might not have initially seemed viable.[128] Indeed, football star–turned–ALEC head Sam Brunelli attributed the organization's success in part to the state chair structure. Before he took over the reins of ALEC in 1988, staff had "talked about" having state leaders embedded in the group's leadership structure, but they "hadn't worked out the requirements," so it was a "loosey-goosey affair."[129] To build up the state chair system, Brunelli traveled to some 40 states each year, seeking out respected Republicans and moderate or conservative Democrats who might be interested in joining the group.[130] He looked hard for members from both parties so that the group wouldn't only be identified with "strident Republicans"—a key selling point to corporate donors and to other prospective members. Having members from both sides of the aisle also protected the nascent group from being coopted by state GOP party operations.[131] Figure 1.4 shows a button that ALEC distributed to its members displaying a smiling Republican elephant and Democratic donkey together, emphasizing the bipartisan nature of the organization during this period.

Once he had identified interested state chairs, Brunelli set up a system of competition—inspired by his love of football—to encourage each of the chairs to recruit as many of their legislative colleagues as possible. Using the perks of fancier hotel rooms or subsidies for room and board at ALEC conferences as an incentive, ALEC's leadership rewarded the state chairs who recruited the most active new members from their states. In addition to sheer numbers of recruits, ALEC rewarded chairs who invited lawmakers from a more diverse array of legislative committees so that the organization as a whole involved legislators with a variety of policy responsibilities who could be of interest to businesses from different sectors.[132]

Thanks to these organizational innovations, by the early 2000s, the group had developed into a formidable player on the political scene, commanding a budget of between $7 and $8 million, with another $6 million in assets. It could count

Figure 1.4. ALEC ATTEMPTED TO ATTRACT CONSERVATIVE LAWMAKERS FROM BOTH PARTIES IN ITS EARLY YEARS. ALEC button provided by Bernie Grofman.

a legislative membership that exceeded 2,400 lawmakers (or nearly a third of all state legislators) and 29 staff members, according to the group's 2002 annual report.[133] With that reach of membership, it claimed the introduction of over 3,100 pieces of legislation in the 1999 to 2000 legislative cycle—and of those, over 450 were ultimately turned into law.[134]

The Activist–Business Balance in ALEC Shifts Back to Conservatives: 2005–2011

The 1990s and early 2000s saw a period in which ALEC was generally dominated by the business side of its membership, with movement conservatives retaining an important, but generally secondary role in drafting model bills and promoting policy. That balance of power within the coalition began shifting in the mid-2000s, however, with a return to the sort of hardline conservative stances that characterized ALEC's priorities in its early years, especially on three controversial issues: access to the voting booth, immigration, and gun rights.

Yet unlike the earlier period, big businesses were participating in the group. Rather, two other factors account for this shifting balance of priorities within ALEC. First, deep-pocketed advocacy groups behind these causes—especially restricting access to the ballot box and loosening limits on gun ownership and use—saw the success that ALEC was having for individual businesses, and sought to more aggressively leverage those same benefits for their own ends. In the case of gun laws, the National Rifle Association (NRA) had long been an ALEC member, sponsoring skeet-shooting events for legislators attending ALEC's meetings as far back as 1989. Yet throughout the late 1990s and early 2000s, you would be hard-pressed to find much significant activity in the criminal justice task force around firearms-related legislation.

We can see the shifting activities of ALEC's criminal justice panel from 2001 to 2009 in Table 1.2. In the early 2000s, the major accomplishments heralded by that task force generally focused more on a combination of tough state sentencing guidelines and various measures aimed at protecting particular industries from crime. Especially notable is the panel's emphasis on reducing the threat of retail theft by increasing penalties for those crimes. Those proposals were championed under the corporate leadership of Walmart (the

Table 1.2. **Evolution of ALEC's Criminal Justice Task Force, 2001–2009.** [a]

Year	Model Bills Considered	Private-Sector Chair(s)
2001	• Anti-Automated Enforcement Act (automated traffic violation limits) • Child Abuse Investigation Reform Act • Personal Information Security Act (personal information security protection) • Third Theft Felony Act (discouraging retail theft)	• American Bail Coalition • Guardian Interlock Systems
2002	• Animal and Ecological Terrorism Act • Affidavit of Mailing Act (permitting retailers to use regular postal service when reconciling checks) • Theft Using Emergency Exit (additional penalties for using an emergency exit, especially in retail stores)	• American Bail Coalition • Guardian Interlock Systems
2003	• Various prison privatization acts • Repeated Felony Theft from a Store Act • Amendments to Animal and Ecological Terrorism Act • Environmental Corrupt Organizations–Preventative Legislation and Neutralization Act (ECO-PLAN, limiting environmental or ecoterrorism)	• Vacant

(continued)

Table 1.2. **Continued**

Year	Model Bills Considered	Private-Sector Chair(s)
2004	• Anti-Skimming Act (for credit card theft) • Support of the PATRIOT Act • Targeted Contracting for Certain Correctional Facilities and Services Act (privatizing prisons) • Bail Forfeiture Payments Act; Bail Forfeiture Relief and Remission Act • Establishing Jurisdiction for Online Sale of Stolen Property and Online Theft by Deception Act • *Concealed Carry Outright Recognition Act; Concealed Carry True Reciprocity Act*	• Walmart stores
2005	• Sexual Offenses Against Children Act • Zero Tolerance for Underage Drinking Act • Organized Retail Theft Act • Bail Bond Expiration Act • Prisoner reentry programs • *Castle Doctrine Act*	• Walmart stores
2006	• Sexual Offenses Against Children Act • Stop Child Predators • Zero Tolerance for Underage Access Act	• Walmart stores
2007	No publications available.	• National Rifle Association
2008	• Child predator–related proposals • Human trafficking–related proposals • *Illegal immigration–related proposals* • Mortgage fraud–related proposals • *Voter ID proposals*	• National Rifle Association
2009	Name changed to "Public Safety and Elections Task Force" to reflect voter ID and election focus	• National Rifle Association

[a] Author's analysis of various ALEC publications. Italicized entries indicate the period of NRA leadership on the task force, as well as ideologically charged measures related to gun ownership and use, immigration, and voter ID laws.

task force's corporate chair from 2004 to 2006) and Home Depot, one of the panel's corporate participants.

The focus on the criminal justice task force began to change in 2004, when the NRA pushed two measures that would broaden recognition of concealed carry gun permits across state lines. A subcommittee of the criminal justice group evaluated those proposals, and model bills based on the NRA measures easily passed the criminal justice task force in December 2004 and were then distributed to the whole ALEC membership the following month.

Following its success with concealed carry permits, the NRA returned to ALEC for a criminal justice meeting in the fall of 2005. The NRA was hoping to promote a bill it had already passed in one state, Florida, earlier that year. Nicknamed the "Castle Doctrine," the proposal legalized lethal force for self-defense in one's home or property. The NRA's top lobbyist and former president—Marion Hammer—made a pitch to the criminal justice group for the measure at a meeting in Grapevine, Texas, accompanied by a Heritage Foundation policy analyst who had written a brief making the case for the Castle Doctrine for ALEC. The NRA later reported that Hammer's presentation was "well-received" and the "task force subsequently adopted the measure unanimously."[135]

Less than a year later, the NRA returned to ALEC's annual criminal justice meeting in the spring of 2006 to report "on the continuing success of the Castle Doctrine Act throughout the states."[136] Thanks to the NRA's advocacy, the bill had, in fact, become such a popular provision among ALEC members that the group highlighted it on a legislative scorecard issued in 2007, boasting that Maine, North Dakota, and Tennessee had all recently passed Castle Doctrine proposals.[137] The NRA would subsequently become the private-sector chair of the criminal justice panel from 2007 to 2011, leading that group's activities and helping to establish its priorities. The increasing involvement of the NRA in the criminal justice task force over this period thus helps to explain the panel's shift away from more explicitly corporate-friendly crime legislation to more conservative, gun rights–related issues.

It was during the NRA's tenure as head of the criminal justice task force that ALEC also approved its first model bill requiring the presentation of a photo ID to vote in elections and to crack down on illegal immigrants. Approved during the group's spring meetings in Hot Springs, Arkansas, the "Taxpayer and Citizen Protection Act" requires that "evidence of United States citizenship be presented by every person to register to vote [and] at the polling place prior to voting." Indicative of the increasingly socially conservative turn of the group, especially the criminal justice task force, the model bill also required that "state and local governments verify the identity of all applicants for certain public benefits" and "report United States immigration law violations by applicants for public benefits."[138] The model bill language made clear the reasons that states should be concerned about the identity of voters and social benefit applicants, stating plainly that "[State Name Here] Government has evidence demonstrating illegal immigration is causing economic hardship to states and that illegal immigration is encouraged by public agencies within states that provide public benefits without verifying immigration status."[139]

Where did the language for ALEC's model bill on voter ID and citizenship checks come from? Identifying the source of the text sheds light on the second reason why the balance of power within ALEC had begun shifting in the mid-2000s. It turns out that the author was a very conservative Arizona politician, Russell Pearce, who had been elected two years earlier to his state's senate and was by now serving on the executive committee of ALEC's criminal justice task force. Before running for the statehouse, Pearce had worked as a sheriff's deputy in Maricopa County. Pearce's boss in Maricopa, Sheriff Joe Arpaio, would later attract national scrutiny and face federal charges for defying a court order to cease deliberately targeting Latinos in police stops.[140] Under Arpaio's leadership, a US Department of Justice investigation concluded that the Maricopa County sheriff's office, including Pearce, "oversaw the worst pattern of racial profiling by a law enforcement agency in U.S. history, creating "a 'culture' of abusing the rights of Latinos" (President Trump would later pardon Arpaio during his first year in office).[141]

The experience working for Arpaio, Pearce would later argue, led him to worry about "the impact of . . . illegal immigration on families, taxpayers and citizens," and Pearce cited that fear as the reason he would lobby aggressively for a 2004 ballot proposition called the "Arizona Taxpayer and Citizen Protection Act."[142] That act, Pearce claimed, would prevent undocumented immigrants "from continuing to illegally defraud the taxpayers."[143] "Tough, nasty illegals and their advocates grow in such numbers that law and order will not subdue them. They run us out of our cities and states. They conquer our language and our schools," Pearce has bemoaned about the out-of-control "invasion" of illegal immigrants to his state.[144]

By now the content of the Arizona Taxpayer and Citizen Protection Act should be clear: the bill would have required a photo ID for citizens wishing to cast ballots, as well as extensive identity checks for applicants to state social programs. Proposition 200 passed, with 56 percent of Arizona voters in favor of the measure, and Pearce then took the exact legislative language to ALEC to introduce as a model bill proposal to the criminal justice task force.[145] Alabama, Georgia, and Kansas quickly passed near-identical versions of the ALEC model bill Pearce had introduced, and many other states introduced variants of it.[146]

The hardline stands of Russell Pearce found good company among ALEC's legislative members during this period. That is because ALEC's legislative membership was growing steadily more conservative over the 1990s, and especially in the early 2000s, following the overall rightward lurch of the Republican Party across the United States. Figure 1.5 plots the ideological positioning of the typical Republican state legislator nationwide along with the average ideological

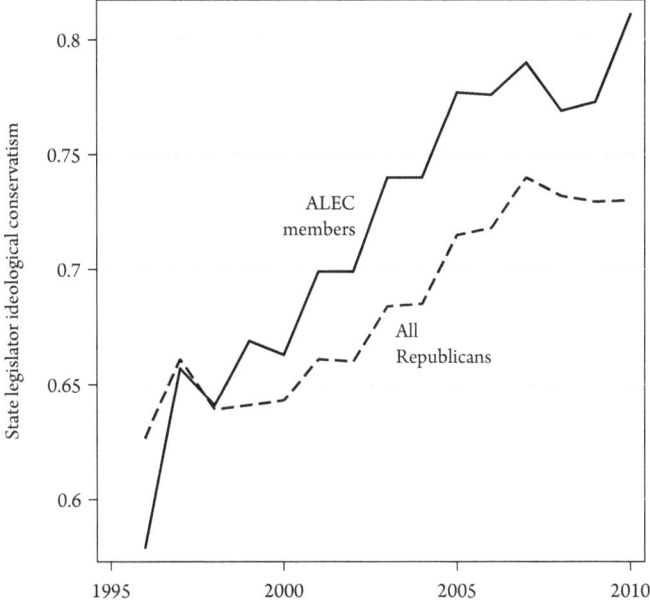

Figure 1.5. RIGHTWARD IDEOLOGICAL MOVEMENT OF ALEC MEMBERS OUTPACED THE POLARIZATION OF THE REPUBLICAN PARTY, 1996–2010. The median legislative position of all GOP state legislators and of identified ALEC members (based on leaked records). State legislative ideological placement from Shor and McCarty 2011.

positioning of the typical ALEC member from 1996 to 2010, drawing on leaked membership records of the organization paired with measures of state legislative ideology created by political scientists Boris Shor and Nolan McCarty.[147]

Two things stand out from the trends presented in Figure 1.5.[148] First, Republican state legislators as a whole were becoming much more conservative over this period—and that fits with the national GOP's pull to the right well documented by many political scientists.[149] Second, the ALEC membership was about as conservative as the typical Republican state legislator in the mid-1990s, but has since moved steadily to the right—and the speed and magnitude of the conservative shift of ALEC's membership have outpaced even the polarization of the GOP across the country as a whole. The typical state GOPer became about 17 percent more conservative over the fourteen years from 1996 to 2010, while the typical ALEC member became 40 percent more right-leaning.

The upshot of the transformation of the national Republican Party, as well as the GOPers participating in ALEC, meant that there was a much more receptive audience to the hard-right conservative stances of groups like the NRA and legislators like Russell Pearce. To be sure, ALEC has always attracted more conservative lawmakers from both parties. But especially since the early 2000s, the typical rank-and-file member was substantially more right-leaning than they were in the group's earlier years. It also meant that ALEC itself increasingly had the opportunity to define the policy positions of conservative GOPers who were seeking to build careers for themselves in state legislatures across the country as it became more closely affiliated with the conservative base of the Republican party. As David Dagan and Steven Teles have described about the group during this period, "For Republican state legislators who know they are conservative but do not know what positions to take on a range of unfamiliar issues, ALEC's model legislation provides an immediate signal of orthodoxy and a template for action."[150]

This transformation of the ALEC membership was especially striking within the criminal justice task force. Consider the eight legislative members of its executive committee who served alongside Russell Pearce from 2009 to 2010.[151] Over that period, the state lawmakers leading the criminal justice task force were more ideologically conservative than fully 88 percent of all other state lawmakers across the country. The panel's legislative leaders, in turn, were more conservative than 72 percent of all the other ALEC members in the group.

The ideological extremism of the criminal justice task force helps us to understand why there was such an appetite for Pearce's anti-immigrant and voter ID proposals within the panel. It also helps us to understand why, following the 2008 election of Democratic President Barack Obama, the criminal justice task force—now rebranded as the "Public Safety and Elections Task Force" to reflect its increased focus on voting and immigration—would double down on measures to restrict access of Democratic constituencies to the franchise in the name of combating voter fraud.

In the summer of 2009, ALEC ran an in-depth article in its internal publication that provided the group's own take on how voter fraud had contributed to President Obama's recent electoral victory—and what ALEC members could do going forward to be "proactive against serious threats designed to undermine the integrity of the most important element of our system of government."[152] "Our system of voting continues to be weakened by the threat of voter fraud. One form of fraud that has been frequently documented, especially in the months prior to the 2008 election, is voter-registration fraud," the piece argued. The authors pointed to conservatives' longtime bête noire—the liberal community organizing group ACORN—as being a prime reason for that fraud, submitting "incomplete, duplicates, or just plain fake" voter registration forms. The solution, the ALEC authors argued, was already clear, thanks to early legislative action in Indiana. "Voters in Indiana are required to produce a government-issued photo ID to vote," and ALEC's Indiana State co-chair had approvingly described the law as crucial to "maintaining the integrity of the elections" in his state. The authors of the piece concluded by happily reporting that ALEC's newly rechristened elections task force would be "actively working on these issues" through new model legislation and initiatives in the weeks and months to come.[153]

The Public Safety and Elections Task Force wasted no time working on its new mandate. First, it released a new model bill urging states to defund ACORN, arguing that the organization was "guilty of violating numerous laws and aiding and abetting criminal activity."[154] The ALEC panel also produced a dedicated mini-site on the ALEC website with additional materials aimed at "cracking ACORN," and linking to Heritage Foundation reports documenting the group's alleged abuses that helped to "illegally" elect Democrats across the country, including President Obama himself.[155] And by the summer of 2009, the panel had drafted new model legislation based on Indiana's voter ID measure—again spearheaded by Arizona's Russell Pearce. Thirty-seven states introduced sixty-two versions of voter ID legislation following ALEC's approval of the new voter ID model bill—and more than half were sponsored directly by ALEC members.[156] In many cases, as in Florida, state legislative sponsors invoked the specter of the now-defunct ACORN—using the same arguments that ALEC had provided to its members—as the reason for putting forward the new restrictions on registering to vote and casting ballots.[157]

In sum, by 2011, the center of gravity within ALEC—and especially within the Public Safety and Elections Task Force—had begun shifting away from the more narrowly focused, bottom-line interests of businesses like Visa, FedEx, Walmart, or Microsoft, and toward the more socially conservative—and highly controversial—issues related to immigration and voting favored by right-wing firebrands like Russell Pearce and the other members of his panel. To be sure, there were still some powerful corporate constituencies behind the Public Safety and Election Task Force's increasingly hard-right measures: gun and ammunition manufacturers in the case of the stand-your-ground law (with the NRA) and private prisons in the case of ALEC's model legislation increasing the scope for the investigation and detention of unauthorized immigrants (especially the Corrections Corporation of America).[158]

But the first-movers in introducing these bills were primarily the increasingly conservative members and activist groups participating on the task force. These new and hard-right social policies were not necessarily immediately problematic to ALEC's staider corporate members. Thanks to the deliberate obfuscation of corporate involvement in the group, few companies faced a publicity risk. And if pressed, those companies could claim that they only participated in ALEC on a narrow set of issues, and because of the task force structure of the group, that claim was, in fact, true. Such security, however, would soon change—underscoring the importance of secrecy and plausible deniability for ALEC's more controversial proposals.

Backlash to ALEC: 2011–2013

Until the mid-2000s, ALEC had successfully avoided attracting much media attention. Few outside the rarefied world of state politics recognized the group or appreciated its growing influence. Figure 1.6 shows media coverage of ALEC over time and in comparison to a similar organization—the National Conference of State Legislatures (NCSL)—that also represents state lawmakers and seeks to provide public policy resources to state governments. (It is worth noting, though, that the NCSL is distinct from ALEC in a number of important respects; we will review these differences in more detail in Chapter 7.[159])

To construct this figure, I searched LexisNexis for newspaper articles written with either NCSL or ALEC as a subject. On average, only about four newspaper articles were written each year about ALEC between the 1970s and 1990s, while about ten times as many were written about the NCSL, despite the fact that ALEC was growing rapidly during this period. Indeed, in no year between 1976 and 2011 did ALEC receive more than half of the newspaper coverage that the NCSL garnered—until 2012. The figure thus presents two key questions: First, how was ALEC able to maintain such a low degree of media coverage and public attention, even as it grew rapidly over time? And second, what happened in 2012 to increase public attention to the group?

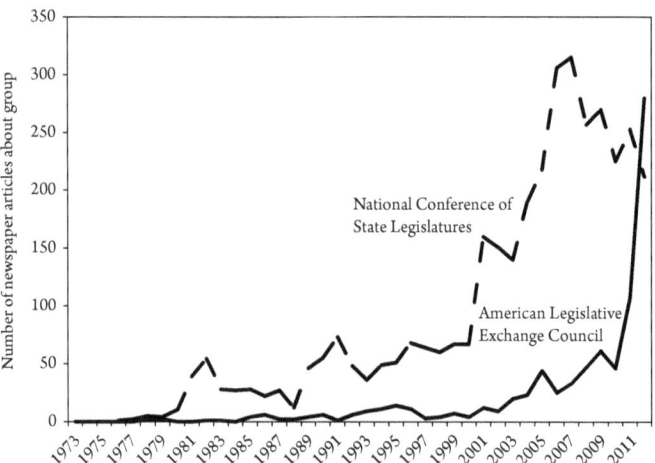

Figure 1.6. NEWSPAPER COVERAGE OF THE AMERICAN LEGISLATIVE EXCHANGE COUNCIL COMPARED TO THE NATIONAL CONFERENCE OF STATE LEGISLATURES. The relative media salience of two groups representing state lawmakers—the National Conference of State Legislatures and the American Legislative Exchange Council—as measured by the number of newspaper articles (extracted from LexisNexis) each year with each group as a subject. This figure shows that ALEC received substantially less media attention than NCSL until 2012.

Consistent with the expectation that companies sought to minimize the potential for backlash from consumer or investor controversies, ALEC deliberately lowered its visibility, making it harder for the public or media to identify its membership, and to obscure the role it played in spreading legislative ideas across the states. For example, ALEC members in some states, like South Carolina, Indiana, and Colorado, passed laws that explicitly exempted the organization from lobbying disclosure requirements by name.[160] So while other political groups had to report their interactions with state lawmakers, ALEC did not. As one shocked South Carolinian representative put it after discovering the ALEC exemption: "I can't get in a car with a lobbyist and drive up the street. But ALEC can give me a scholarship to fly across the country."[161]

In addition, access to model bills was limited to ALEC members only, and lists of the legislative and corporate members of ALEC were not made available to the public. And when ALEC's activities began to receive media attention at the national level in the mid-1990s, its board of directors became notably nervous; one leader in particular was "getting a little concerned that ALEC might be going off the deep end. [ALEC does] not need to get publicized. . . . ALEC is getting some publicity; don't know that it is really good."[162] The group was also especially sensitive to the perception that companies were "buying access" to policymakers. In response, ALEC's board of directors recommended changing their operations to "limit exposure in that area" by making it harder to publicly link specific companies to any particular ALEC event or deliverable.[163]

ALEC's leadership took similar steps again in recent years, when they changed the organization's rules to require that all model legislation originate with a legislative member. That makes it more difficult to identify the corporate backers of its policy ideas—even when lawmakers are simply serving as conduits for business ideas.[164] It's "total bullshit," summarized one investigative journalist when I asked him about the change in ALEC's policy. Thanks to open record laws, that journalist had obtained email correspondence revealing how businesses were simply feeding model bill proposals—and talking points—to ALEC legislative members to satisfy the new rule. One industry group, the Competitive Enterprise Institute, emailed Ohio State Representative Andy Thompson, asking him to propose a bill on self-driving cars at ALEC's December 2013 meeting. The industry group gave Thompson a slide show to present at the task force meeting, as well as the exact text of the model bill to introduce, explaining, "Here's the PowerPoint file. Nothing fancy. Just slides meant to go along with the line-by-line reading at the subcommittee and full task force." The bill was approved—and Thompson later thanked the Institute, even apologizing that "I could have been more help, I'm sure."

I experienced ALEC's publicity-averse nature firsthand when my requests to attend ALEC's annual meetings were repeatedly turned down at the start of this project. After other journalists and progressive activists sought to infiltrate these meetings—both as registered and unregistered guests—it is now standard practice for ALEC to have a heavy security presence at its convenings to screen out unwelcome attendees.[165]

If these strategies had worked well for so long—as Figure 1.6 suggests—then what went wrong in 2012? The answer is that in 2012, a coalition of progressive groups began a campaign to pressure corporate members to sever their ties to ALEC. The impetus for the new campaign was the death of Trayvon Martin, an unarmed African American teenager who was shot and killed by the neighborhood watch coordinator of the gated community where he was visiting his family.[166] The shooter initially justified his actions under Florida's so-called stand-your-ground, Castle Doctrine law. In investigating the origins of Florida's self-defense provisions, progressive groups discovered the link between ALEC, the NRA, and the Florida law that inspired the later ALEC model.[167]

The African American political advocacy group Color of Change, which had been trying to draw attention, relatively unsuccessfully, to ALEC model bills promoting restrictive voting requirements in the past, had finally found a compelling hook for its efforts.[168] Its members began bombarding ALEC corporate participants like Amazon, AT&T, State Farm, and Pepsi with phone calls and emails.[169] Color of Change was quickly joined by other progressive groups, like the Center for Community Change, Common Cause, and People for the American Way. Several large unions, including AFSCME, participated as well.[170] Soon, the anti-ALEC campaign's criticism expanded from focusing mainly on gun rights and self-defense laws to include a range of ALEC model bills that clearly were drafted to benefit specific corporate interests.

It is striking to note that liberal groups had tried—and failed—to raise attention to ALEC nearly a decade before, in 2003. In that year, People for the American Way and Defenders of Wildlife spearheaded the creation of a coalition of left-leaning groups to counter ALEC that included Public Citizen, the NAACP, the AFL-CIO, the NEA, and the Natural Resources Defense Council.[171] According to one of the coalition's leaders, a former labor operative, "When a spotlight is shone on the corporate, right-wing agenda [of ALEC], then ALEC's bills will no longer be able to slip quietly through state legislatures."[172] But unlike the later effort in 2012, this campaign was unable to get much traction without a broader connection to current events. This comparison to earlier efforts to bring attention to ALEC thus highlights the critical role of the Martin shooting for providing a focal moment for anti-ALEC campaigns in 2012.

Facing the new broad-based pressure in 2012, many of ALEC's more prominent corporate members left the group, including Coca-Cola, Pepsi, Kraft, Wendy's, and Walgreens. Said Walmart's government affairs representative at the time: "We feel that the divide between these activities and our purpose as a business has become too wide."¹⁷³ The Center for Media and Democracy reported that 49 corporations and 6 non-profits (including the Gates Foundation) left the group following the Martin controversy; leaked internal ALEC reports tell a bleaker story: more than 60 private-sector members dropped or let their membership expire.¹⁷⁴

That decline in membership also caused a corresponding drop in revenues, and ALEC faced a gap of $1.4 million in its June 2013 budget, or more than a third of its projected income.¹⁷⁵ Explained ALEC's director of public relations at the time: "Companies do not like controversy of any sort. It is also clear that—whether true or untrue—accusations made of ALEC cost members."¹⁷⁶ In response to the departure of these companies and the heightened public attention, ALEC reported that it would end its Public Safety and Elections Task Force, the panel responsible for disseminating self-defense and voter ID laws.¹⁷⁷

Since the initial backlash in 2012, public attention has not diminished, and if anything, has increased. Major media outlets, like *The New York Times*,¹⁷⁸ *The Nation*,¹⁷⁹ and *Bloomberg Businessweek*,¹⁸⁰ all have written (mostly critically) of the group, and progressive organizations, especially Common Cause and the Center for Media and Democracy, have closely tracked ALEC's activities—even showing up at ALEC's meetings to stage protests in conjunction with labor unions. What is more, the Center for Media and Democracy received an anonymous leak of ALEC model bills, and has posted those and corresponding analyses on a dedicated website ("alecexposed.com") in conjunction with *The Nation*. "A confluence of events created an opening for people to focus a little bit more on what this organization was about. Part of ALEC's modus operandi was to operate behind the scenes without a lot of visibility. It's getting that visibility now," explained Marge Baker of People for the American Way.¹⁸¹ Even national politicians began criticizing firms for their connections to ALEC, such as Senator Dick Durbin from Illinois, and Organizing for America, President Obama's grassroots campaign organization, used attacks against the businesses affiliated with ALEC in a 2014 fundraising bid.¹⁸²

Although it was the Martin shooting that initially drew national attention to the group, it was ultimately the focus of ALEC on corporate-drafted bills that sustained national interest and backlash to ALEC's activities. As one *New York Times* editorial put it pointedly: "Lawmakers who eagerly do ALEC's bidding have much to answer for. Voters have a right to know whether the representatives they elect are actually writing the laws, or whether the job has been outsourced to big corporate interests."¹⁸³ The existence of so many ALEC initiatives that so clearly benefited the financial interests of particular businesses and industries made such statements easy to make and public outrage from the left easy to sustain. The Martin shooting and its aftermath thus demonstrate how difficult it is to focus the public's attention on state politics, even when it involves high-profile policy debates. Yet it also shows how damaging such scrutiny could be for an organization like ALEC that depended on keeping the more ideological activities of large, risk-averse, for-profit companies secret.

ALEC leaders, for their part, were quick to attribute their recent losses to a well-organized sabotage campaign from the left. At their 2014 annual conference, ALEC officials hosted a session titled: "Playing the Shame Game: A Campaign That Threatens Corporate Free Speech," which explained to attendees that "union activists are out to get ALEC—that they're following Saul Alinsky's playbook on browbeating corporations into submission. Unions are often shareholders in public companies thanks to pension fund investments. That means they get to offer proposals, such as 'resign from ALEC,' in annual shareholder meetings."[184]

The recent controversy over ALEC demonstrates the limits of its efforts to mask corporate involvement in political coalitions with conservative activists. Clearly, high visibility and salience are liabilities for a group like ALEC that opens up companies to such public backlash. As Wisconsin State Representative Chris Taylor, who attended the 2013 ALEC annual meeting, opined, "ALEC cannot otherwise exist" without its corporate members being able to mask their relationship to ALEC from the public's attention.[185] *Bloomberg Businessweek* summed up ALEC's need for secrecy in a similar manner: "If ALEC operated with complete openness it would have difficulty operating at all. ALEC has attracted a wide and wealthy range of supporters in part because it's done its work behind closed doors. . . . Part of ALEC's mission is to present industry-backed legislation as grass-roots work. If this were to become clear . . . there'd be no reason for corporations to use it."[186]

Cities and Counties: The Next Frontier for ALEC?

Rather than folding in the face of the intense public pressure and scrutiny since 2012, ALEC has instead ramped up the activities that have made it such a powerful force in American politics. Expressing concern that progressives had begun to mobilize at the local and city levels in ways that directly threatened the political fate of conservatives and the bottom lines of businesses, ALEC has in recent years extended its activities to include not just state lawmakers, but also officials on city councils and county governments through a new arm: the American City-County Exchange (or ACCE).

Local deliberative bodies, ALEC recognized, not only represented an untapped resource for the conservative movement, but also could serve as a valuable profit center to help with ALEC's funding woes. As *The Guardian* pointed out in its coverage of ACCE, there "are almost 500,000 local elected officials, many with considerable powers over schools and local services that could be attractive to big business."[187] For dues ranging from $10,000 to $25,000 a year, private-sector companies can "participate in policy development and network with other entrepreneurs and municipal officials from around the country"—which includes the right to "present facts and opinions for discussion," and pitch ideas for new policy to ACCE's affiliated mayors, city council representatives, school board members, and county government officials.[188]

ACCE advertises benefits for local government officials that sound very similar to those offered to state lawmakers: "ACCE members receive academic research and analysis from policy experts who work with issues, processes and problem-solving strategies upon which municipal officials vote." "Provided with important policy education," ACCE advertising material continued, "lawmakers become more informed and better equipped to serve the needs of their communities."[189] Local officials are already responding positively to ACCE. "It's nice to have a group like this that can provide information to me as to how other people in other areas have done positive things in terms of reducing the size of government and the scope of government," reported one member of an Ohio city council approvingly.[190]

ACCE priorities include issues relevant to a range of business interests. The same conventional power producers that are increasingly susceptible to efforts to address climate change at the national and state levels, for instance, have trained their sights on local government, as cities have sought to encourage the use of renewable energy sources. Accordingly, ACCE is advancing proposals that would make it more challenging for local governments to provide incentives for the use of solar power and that would prevent municipalities from taking over power distribution systems.[191]

Another threatening local measure for natural gas producers and plastic products manufacturers involves the regulation of plastic shopping bags. A number of states and cities, including Washington, D.C., Austin, Cambridge, Chicago, Los Angeles, San Francisco, and Seattle, have passed measures to curb the use of plastic shopping bags to reduce their harmful impact on the environment.[192] Many other cities and counties are considering similar measures, given the success of the initial wave of bans and fees (all told, between 2015 and 2016, at least 77 measures involving bag use were proposed in 23 states).[193] Championed by progressive and environmental groups, plastic bag regulation poses a clear threat to companies responsible for producing the bags, which are made from natural gas. Spurred on by the natural gas industry, then, ACCE is encouraging cities and counties to stop the use of such bans or fees on plastic bags (ALEC separately encourages states to remove the ability of cities to pass bag taxes in the first place; such bills have passed in Missouri, Iowa, Wisconsin, Michigan, Indiana, Florida, Idaho, and Arizona).[194]

Sharing economy giants like Uber and Airbnb have also sent their lobbyists to ACCE meetings to push proposals that would prohibit cities from regulating their businesses.[195] And just as with ALEC, ACCE works with service-sector businesses, especially those in the fast-food and retail industries, to promote strategies to tamp down minimum wages and labor market regulations. At one recent ACCE meeting, a representative from the International Franchise Association argued for a "two-pronged strategy to beat back higher wages."[196] The strategy consisted of preemption efforts, which would make it harder (if not impossible) for localities to pass labor market measures, including minimum wage hikes, which exceed state law, and aggressive litigation against cities to stop legislated minimum wage boosts.

It is too soon to evaluate the legislative and organizational success of ALEC's move to the cities and counties. And there are some reasons to expect that the initiative may not carry as much clout as its parent organization given all the scrutiny it has been receiving in recent years. In fact, ALEC itself has downplayed ACCE's influence in interviews with the press, describing the group "like Boys and Girls State or Model UN" for city officials.[197] But there are also good reasons to think that ACCE has the potential to be quite successful. As we will see in the chapters that follow, ALEC has been most influential when lawmakers are strapped for ideas and resources. Local governments in the United States tend to be even more underresourced than state legislatures, potentially making ALEC all the more appealing to city and county officials.

Given these disparities, it should come as no surprise when ACCE's members report how pleased they are at how the group serves as "'an ideal lobbyist,' filling the void left by the lack of staff—and the ideas they might generate—at the local level."[198] Reported one new member of the group from a city council: "There's nobody feeding you . . . ideas for legislation [right now]."[199] The future for ALEC and ACCE, then, looks quite bright, as they prepare to feed their model bill ideas to the nearly 20,000 cities and towns in the United States, with more than 300 dues-paying members already enrolled.[200] Perhaps tellingly, several years into the ACCE initiative, ALEC's finances have already more than recovered from the earlier 2012 fiasco. ALEC's budget in 2016 was 44 percent *higher* than it was in 2010, before companies started pulling out of the group.

In this chapter, we have seen how a small but energetic group of conservative political leaders assembled an infrastructure for pressing their policy demands across state legislatures. Though they struggled in ALEC's initial years, these leaders eventually arrived at a set of strategies that would prove to be very successful in attracting new members, especially private-sector businesses, to their group. These companies brought with them deep coffers from which they could make generous donations to the group's burgeoning operations, as well as increased prestige and credibility within the conservative movement.

Companies, however, were not merely acting out of charity in their support of ALEC. Business leaders realized that the group could provide them with valuable benefits that they could not obtain elsewhere, helping corporate executives push their preferred policies across all fifty statehouses. In a testament to the value of those legislative benefits, some of the largest and most prominent American businesses—ranging from pharmaceutical giants to car manufacturers to online retailers—joined the group and sat on its board of directors. ALEC also appealed to conservative activists and donors who were tired of loss after loss in state legislative battles, and the group's founders included a number of conservative entrepreneurs who were helping to design an alternative set of governing institutions for the right throughout the 1970s and 1980s. Together, businesses and conservatives helped to create an agenda for idea-strapped right-leaning state legislators to carry out once elected to state legislatures.

Managing tensions between conservative activists and for-profit businesses was no easy task, however, and ALEC's leaders needed to come up with new organizational mechanisms for reconciling the preferences between dueling companies and across the divide separating the private sector from social conservative warriors. Even then, the balance of power within ALEC has shifted over time with the intense polarization of the GOP—and that itself has created exposure for the group in recent years as the organization began promoting heavily socially conservative proposals related to voting, immigration, and gun rights that attracted scrutiny from the media and progressive activists.

Having laid out the historical trajectory of ALEC and drawn out some of its implications for our broader understanding of coalitions between businesses, activists, donors, and politicians, we next turn our attention to the specific legislative proposals that ALEC has advanced over the years, where those proposals have and have not found their way into state law, and why ALEC has been more successful in some states and years over others.

2

Policy Plagiarism

A Window into ALEC's Reach across US States

From 2011 to 2017, Mike Parson served as a Republican state senator representing Missouri's 28th district, just southeast of Kansas City. A staunch conservative, Parson was a rising star in his state's party, going on to win a primary and then a general election in 2016 for Missouri's lieutenant governorship. Parson also has deep ties to the right-wing troika, especially in their efforts to defeat the implementation of the Affordable Care Act in Missouri. How do we know this? Because of a typo.

In 2014, then-senator Parson introduced a bill, SB 508, that aimed to make it more challenging for individuals to participate as "Healthcare Navigators" for the new health reform program.[1] Those navigators were intended to help Americans enroll in health insurance plans under the reform law. Parson's bill would have required that aspiring navigators complete a time-consuming and costly application process.

As it turns out, the idea of making it more challenging for Missouri to implement the health reform program was not Parson's alone. His bill was copied and pasted from an ALEC model bill dubbed the "Navigator Background Check Act."[2] In fact, Parson had so blatantly lifted the text of SB 508 from the original ALEC proposal that he forgot to change an error in the model bill referring to federal statute 92-554 instead of 92-544. The error in the ALEC bill was thus directly inserted into the Missouri legislation. In vetoing Parson's bill, Democratic Governor Jay Nixon cheekily chided Parson for his close reliance on the ALEC model: "Some state legislatures that have considered similar navigator-related legislation derived from ALEC model legislation have taken the opportunity to fix the incorrect reference from the ALEC model before enacting it. However . . . the Missouri General Assembly [has] simply parroted the incorrect reference from the ALEC model act without alteration."[3]

Mike Parson is in good company. Many other state legislators, in their haste to enact ALEC policy proposals, have also forgotten to tweak the group's suggested text when introducing model bills under their own names. Florida State Representative Rachel Burgin, for instance, introduced a 2012 resolution calling on the federal government to reduce corporate income tax rates—yet she forgot to remove the standard ALEC boilerplate that appears at the top of all model bills, stating that "it is the mission of the American Legislative Exchange Council to advance Jeffersonian principles of free markets, limited government, federalism, and individual liberty."[4] And Minnesota State Representative Steve Gottwalt was called out by one of his colleagues on the house floor for copying a bill proposal from ALEC.[5] When questioned about his proposal's origins, Gottwalt stated defensively that "this bill is my bill, it's not ALEC's bill." In response, Democratic representative Joe Atkins pointed out that Gottwalt had distributed a handout for his bill with a logo in the middle of the page—the same logo that appeared in the middle of the original ALEC model bill. "I hate to sound like Billy Baldwin's agent," quipped late-night news comedian John Oliver about the episode, "but you can't just copy everything that ALEC does."[6]

The fact that so many elected officials seem so eager and willing to copy text, verbatim, from ALEC proposals might make us doubt the work ethic of our state legislatures. But lawmakers' heavy reliance on the group is great news for me as a researcher. ALEC's use of model bills means that I can use "text reuse detection"—computer scientists' technical term for plagiarism detection—to see where lawmakers have copied text either in whole or in part from ALEC proposals. My assumption, which I believe is well founded, is that this sort of policy plagiarism indicates cases where lawmakers have actually turned to ALEC for help drafting legislation. After reviewing my new approach to detecting where and when lawmakers have turned to ALEC, I describe the spread of ALEC's model bills over the states in recent decades.

Copy and Paste Lawmaking

ALEC's model bills form the foundation of my approach to measuring the group's influence across the states. That is because the model bills offer a detailed picture of what individual businesses and conservative activists wanted from state policy, spelling out their specific demands in exact legal language. These bills thus provide a concrete method of gauging whether or not legislators relied on ALEC when drafting state legislation. If legislators used identical, or near-identical, language from the model bills when crafting state legislation, I assume that it was because they relied on ALEC and the business and conservative interests that the group represents. The model bills provide a sort of "smoking gun" test for ALEC influence (to borrow a term of art from detective work).[7] Although we might not have seen the suspect shoot the victim, observing the suspect holding a smoking gun while standing over the suspect's corpse gives us good reason to think the suspect might have been involved in the murder. Similarly, although we cannot go back and check whether each and every state lawmaker did, in fact, copy and paste their legislation from ALEC model bills, seeing plagiarized text should make us confident that the lawmaker did indeed rely on the group.[8] Ultimately, it is not the specific text that legislators copy that I care about; it is identifying the legislators who rely on ALEC model bills.

For readers who have not spent time wading through reams of ALEC model bills, it is helpful to get a closer look at how these proposals are structured. Their length ranges from just a single paragraph (for simpler policies) to several pages (for more complicated ones), and they generally start with a preamble summarizing their purpose, provide a title (and a short title), make a series of declarations of fact or argument, define key terms used throughout the legislation, and finally proceed on to the substance of the proposal. Here, I have copied excerpts from ALEC's Paycheck Protection Act, which would make it harder for public employee unions to gather funds from their members and use that revenue for political spending.

PAYCHECK PROTECTION ACT

This Act requires labor organizations to establish separate funds for political purposes, establishes registration for the fund, establishes certain criminal provisions governing a labor organization's political activities, and prohibits employees from authorizing automatic payroll deductions for contributions to a labor organization's political committee or fund except through an explicit, signed statement.

Model Legislation

Section 1. [Short Title.]

This Act shall be known as the Labor Organizations Deductions Act

Section 2. [Legislative Declarations.]

This legislature finds and declares that:

(A.) The integrity of the political process in the state of [insert state] can only be maintained through the voluntary and informed participation of its citizenry. Political contributions that are made without the knowing and informed consent of individuals, made freely without fear or retaliation, penalty or loss of rights, causes injury to the political process.

(B.) Workers have a right to control their own political contributions and a right to refuse to make political contributions without fear of retaliation, penalty or loss of statutory or other rights.

...

Section 3. [Definitions.]

(A.) "Political fund" means the separate segregated fund established by a labor organization for political activities according to the procedures and requirements of this part.

...

Section 4. [Limits on labor organization contributions.]

(A.) Except as provided in subsection (B.), union dues may not be expended for political activities.

(B.)

(1.) A labor organization may only expend money for lobbying, electoral, and political activities not bearing upon the negotiation, ratification or implementation of a collective bargaining agreement if the labor organization establishes a separate segregated fund to be used for such lobbying, electoral and political activities.

...

My general strategy, which I developed working together with an expert political methodologist, Konstantin Kashin, is to systematically compare every bill that state legislators have introduced and enacted with each ALEC model bill. For reasons of data availability that I will explain here, my focus is on state legislation introduced or enacted from the mid-1990s to 2013. The goal of these comparisons is to see whether legislators derived any part of an introduced or enacted bill or resolution from the text originally contained in an ALEC model proposal. What follows is a basic summary of the policy plagiarism detection, sketched in broad terms.[9] Readers less interested in the methodological guts of the procedure can skip to the next section, where I start discussing my findings.

The first step in my analysis was to collect all the ALEC model legislative proposals I could find. To do this, I relied on a variety of sources. I first compiled and digitized the model bills that had been published by the Center for Media and Democracy, the left-leaning watchdog group based in Madison, Wisconsin, that has been tracking ALEC for a number of years. In 2011, the Center published an anonymous leak of many model bills.[10] The Center for Media and Democracy leaked bills provided a very helpful start for my project, covering a number of ALEC model bills written in recent years. But I also wanted to go further back in time to get a more comprehensive picture.

I thus took an ALEC-inspired road trip across the country, visiting a number of state legislative libraries, as well as archives at the Library of Congress, the University of California, San Francisco, and the University of California, Berkeley, to compile and scan older ALEC model bills that were not included in the Center for Media and Democracy's original leaks.[11] The trick was that although ALEC model bills were not intended for broad public distribution, the group mailed copies of those proposals (along with other publications) to their legislative members. Many of those members, in turn, eventually donated the ALEC mailings to their state legislative libraries, forming a treasure trove of ALEC bills for my analysis.

Once I returned from my cross-country ALEC tour, Konstantin and I painstakingly converted each of the scanned documents from ALEC into digitized text. I then categorized each model bill by substantive policy areas (with 16 such areas in total). In all, we ended up collecting, digitizing, and compiling close to 1,000 unique ALEC proposals. To the best of our knowledge, this is the most comprehensive collection of ALEC's proposals outside of the organization itself. (All this would have been far easier, of course, had ALEC given me access to their own archived model bills—but the organization turned down my request to review their records.)

Table 2.1 shows the distribution of these proposals by substantive issue area. ALEC model bills were most likely to focus on criminal justice, healthcare, agriculture, energy, and the environment. There were the fewest model bills on guns, housing, and voting and election issues. Interestingly, model bills related to gun rights and voting laws have attracted the most controversy out of all the ALEC models, as we saw in the previous chapter, yet those are the areas in which the organization has been least active over the years, at least from the perspective of generating distinct model bills. This makes sense given that the return to increasingly socially conservative legislation happened relatively recently in ALEC's history.

The second dataset Konstantin and I compiled was even more comprehensive, spanning nearly all state bills and resolutions that were ever introduced and enacted from the mid-1990s (generally 1995) to 2013. In all, this dataset contains about 2.4 million bills and resolutions from individual state legislative websites. Unfortunately, due to limitations on electronic bill availability, the text

Table 2.1. **Unique ALEC Model Bills by Policy Domain.**[a]

Policy Area	Count	Share (%)
Guns	12	1
Housing	15	2
Voting and elections	16	2
Finance	33	3
Foreign policy	33	3
Labor unions	33	3
Social welfare and benefits	33	3
Transportation	35	4
Civil justice	74	8
Government reform	81	8
General regulation	87	9
Budget and taxes	90	9
Education	91	9
Agriculture, energy, and environment	113	12
Healthcare	116	12
Criminal justice	120	12

[a] Author's collection of ALEC model bills.

analysis misses out on enacted legislation from Indiana, New Jersey, New York, Pennsylvania, South Carolina, Texas, Virginia, Washington, and West Virginia (introduced bills from these states are still available, however).

Having gathered the ALEC models and state legislation, the next step was to "pre-process" all the text. This is a common preparatory step in working with text as data, and includes changes such as making all the text lowercase, shortening all words to their stems (thus "stemmer," "stemming," and "stemmed" all become "stem"), removing common "stop words" (such as "a," "about," or "after"), and removing punctuation marks, except for hyphens. Konstantin and I then converted all the pre-processed text from the legislative proposals and actual legislative text into n-grams, or sequences of n items from the text. (A bi-gram, for instance, would contain one pair of contiguous words or stems, like "student learn.") For the eventual text analysis, we used both bi- and tri-grams. We then calculated a variety of measures of similarity between each introduced or enacted state bill and each ALEC model bill, and estimated which bills contained identical—or near-identical—language to ALEC models.

Two years and many lines of computer code later, the end product of our work was a database of over 10,000 introduced or enacted pieces of state legislation that the matching program had deemed sufficiently close to ALEC model bills so as to suggest blatant policy plagiarism. (As we spell out in a supplemental technical paper, Konstantin and I manually checked a number of randomly selected ALEC matches and nonmatches to ensure that the computer algorithm was accurately classifying bills as ALEC-plagiarized; for instance, we found that our process regularly correctly identified 84 percent of randomly selected bills that we had previously coded as being ALEC-plagiarized.) For each match between an ALEC model and a state bill, we gathered the state in which the legislative text was either introduced or enacted, the bill's number, and the name of the original ALEC model to which the bill or resolution was matched.

In Table 2.2, I show examples of two state bills that were successfully matched to ALEC models, indicating passages that were taken verbatim, or near-verbatim, from ALEC-drafted language. These examples give a sense of the range of plagiarism in many of the bills that the matching algorithm identified. The first bill, introduced in Wisconsin in 2011, would permit students with special needs to receive school vouchers to attend the school of their parents' choice. It is based on an ALEC model by the same name, sponsored by the Goldwater Institute, intended to gradually introduce vouchers into state educational systems. The second bill, introduced in Arizona in 2013, is also based on a proposal from the Goldwater Institute intended to limit the ability of public employees to conduct union activities on the job. In both cases, one can easily see clear similarities between the original ALEC text and the state legislative language. While the Wisconsin bill contains more rewritten text than the Arizona bill, the intent—and, crucially, key legislative language—are still readily apparent. (For reference, the Wisconsin bill falls around the 22nd percentile of overall bill similarity, looking across all ALEC model bill matches, while the Arizona bill falls around the 93rd percentile.)

Mapping ALEC's Influence across States

What did the policy plagiarism detection reveal? One question is how ALEC bills have spread across the states over time. Figure 2.1 addresses this question, plotting out the share of all introduced bills (left plot) and all enacted bills (right plot) from the 1990s to 2013. I have overlaid the points with a smoothed trend line.

Table 2.2. **Examples of Matched ALEC Bill Use.**

Bill	ALEC Text	Bill Text
2011 Wisconsin AB 110 "Special Needs Scholarship Act" *More similar to ALEC model bills than 22% of all state legislation*	(A) A resident school district shall annually notify the parents of a student with special needs of the Special Needs Scholarship Program and offer that student's parent an opportunity to enroll the student in a participating school of their choice. Section 6. [Accountability Standards for Participating Schools] (A) Administrative Accountability Standards. To ensure that students are treated fairly and kept safe, all participating, private schools shall: (1) Comply with all health and safety laws or codes that apply to private schools; (2) Hold a valid occupancy permit if required by their municipality; (3) Certify that they comply with the nondiscrimination policies set forth in 42 USC 1981....	Annually, each school board shall notify the parents of each child with a disability enrolled in the school district of the program under this section. (4) Private school duties. Each private school participating in the program under this section shall do all of the following: (a) Comply with all health and safety laws or codes that apply to private schools. (b) Hold a valid occupancy permit, if required by the municipality in which the school is located. (c) Annually certify to the department that it complies with 42 USC 2000.
2013 Arizona SB 1348 "Prohibition on Paid Union Activity (Release Time) by Public Employees Act" *More similar to ALEC model bills than 93% of all state legislation*	Section 2-A A public employer shall not enter into any employment bargain with any public employee or union to compensate any public employee or third party for union activities. Any employment bargain that includes compensation to public employees or third parties for union activities is declared to be against the public policy of this state and is void.	Section 23-1422-A A public employer shall not enter into any employment bargain with any public employee or union to compensate any public employee or third party for union activities. Any employment bargain that includes compensation to public employees or third parties for union activities is declared to be against the public policy of this state and is void.

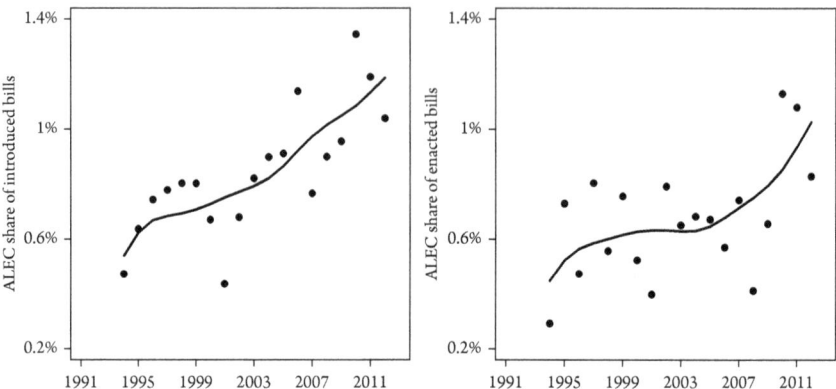

Figure 2.1. INTRODUCED AND ENACTED ALEC BILL SHARES OVER TIME. The proportion of introduced bills from ALEC model bills (left panel) and proportion of enacted bills from ALEC model bills (right panel). Lines indicate smoothed trend lines.

As Figure 2.1 indicates, state legislators have generally introduced and enacted more ALEC-copied legislation over the years. In 1995, legislators relied on ALEC models for about 0.5 percent of all introduced bills, and this reached a peak of 1.3 percent by 2010. Enacted ALEC-plagiarized bills were generally more stable throughout the 1990s, but exhibited a sharp increase in the mid-2000s, reaching a peak of 1.1 percent of bills in 2010. One percent of all bills might not seem all that impressive until you realize that US states consider and enact a huge number of laws every year. In 2012, for instance, the states considered over 100,000 bills and eventually enacted just shy of 17,000 bills.[12] At its peak, my estimates are that between 100 and 200 enacted bills came directly from ALEC proposals each year, which is consistent with ALEC's own internal scorecard records for the years in which they are available. In addition, some of these individual bills imply very dramatic changes to state policy—like passing right-to-work laws to hamper unions or enacting voter ID requirements—such that their substantive importance far exceeds their numerical frequency.

Another important question is how ALEC bill reliance varies across the states. My data suggest that there are a number of states that persistently relied on ALEC for their legislation from 1995 to 2013. Figure 2.2 plots this variation, separating bill introductions from enactments. As the maps indicate, West Virginia, Arizona, Missouri, and Pennsylvania introduced the greatest number of bills that were copied from ALEC proposals, while Connecticut, Ohio, Minnesota, and North Dakota introduced the fewest number of ALEC-plagiarized bills. Turning to bill enactments, we see that Utah, Arizona, Idaho, and Oklahoma enacted the most number of bills drawing from ALEC models,

(a)

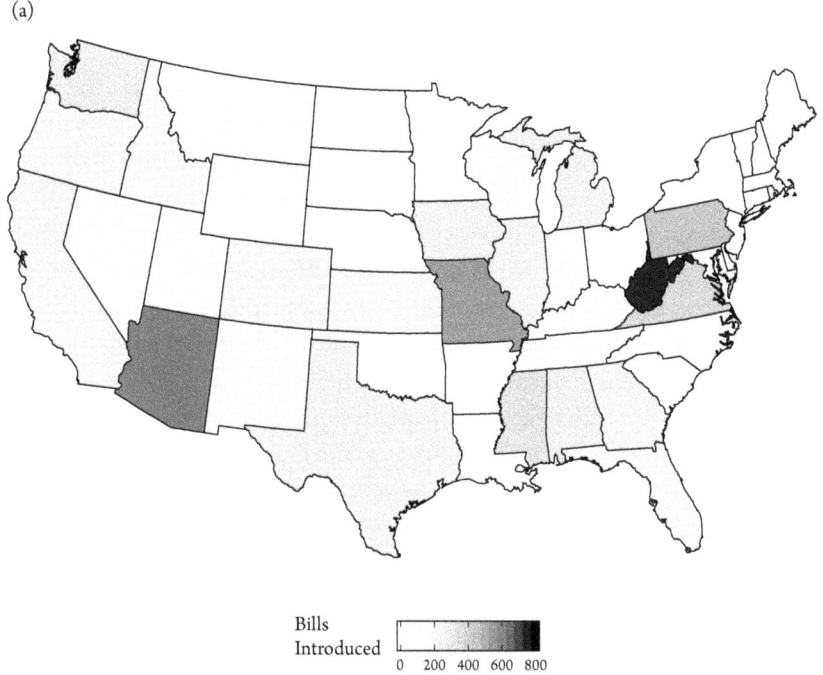

(b)

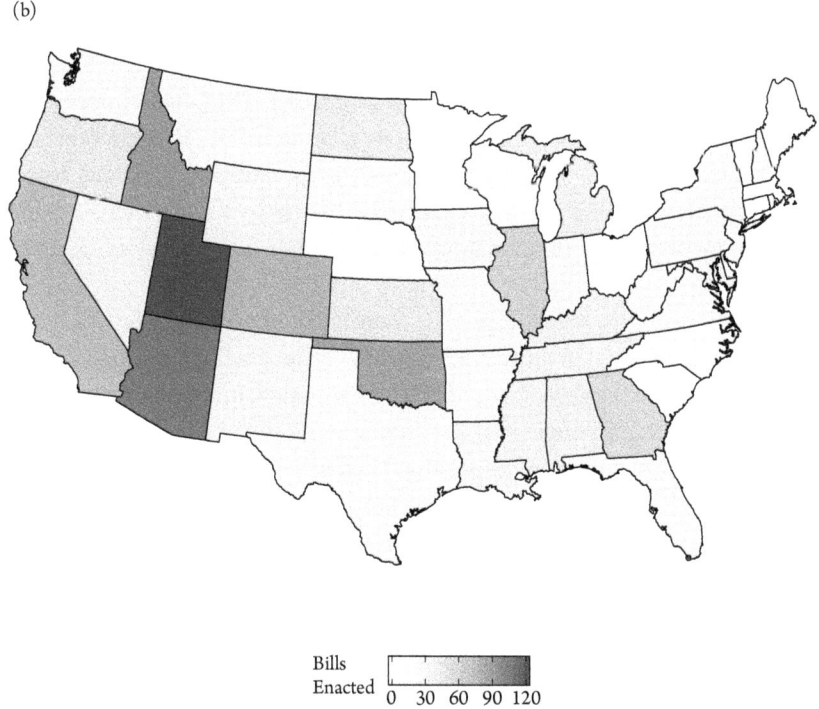

Figure 2.2. ALEC Bill Introductions and Enactments by State, 1995–2013. The total number of ALEC-plagiarized bill introductions (top panel) and enactments (bottom panel).

while states like Maine, Massachusetts, Nebraska, and Connecticut enacted the fewest number of ALEC-plagiarized bills.

Of course, part of these differences across states might be due to the fact that some states simply consider and enact more bills each year. Wyoming typically considers fewer than 500 bills per session and enacts well under half of that total. In contrast, Massachusetts lawmakers introduce an average of just under 9,000 bills per year and enact around 600 to 700 of those into law. To account for these underlying differences in legislative productivity, it is also useful to consider ALEC-copied bill introductions and enactments as a proportion of all bills introduced and enacted by states each year. Examining this measure, I estimate that Kansas, Arizona, Missouri, Wyoming, and West Virginia had the highest proportion of introduced bills that copied material from ALEC models, while Connecticut, Massachusetts, Louisiana, and Minnesota had the lowest introduction rates. Oklahoma, Kansas, Alaska, Wisconsin, and Arizona had the highest enactment rates, while Maine, Massachusetts, Connecticut, and Rhode Island had the lowest enactment rates.

Next, we can zoom in on specific ALEC proposals to get a sense of the most popular individual provisions from which lawmakers borrowed legislative language. Table 2.3 lists the top model bills enacted from 1995 to 2013. By far the most copied ALEC provision involved an education reform package originally passed in Indiana. In some ways, it makes sense that so many state bills drew from this package because the model bill is actually a compilation of seven individual ALEC proposals. Those proposals include measures encouraging the creation of charter schools, providing vouchers for students, changing teacher evaluation and licensing standards, cutting back the power of teachers unions, and encouraging the contracting-out of some educational services to private providers.

The second most popular proposal was another compendium of ALEC model bills related to medical liability reform, which generally limit the damages that individuals can claim when suing healthcare providers for harm or malpractice and make it more challenging for patients to bring such suits in the first place. The next two most common proposals related to long-term care and health insurance, while the fifth related to a foreign policy issue under the Obama administration. The remaining model bills were a hodgepodge of issues related to education, budgetary policy, health insurance, the environment, and federalism, and included symbolic resolutions as well as state constitutional amendments and bills.

While Table 2.3 focuses on individual ALEC model bills, we can gain another valuable perspective by zooming out to consider the popularity of ALEC proposals by policy area. These counts appear in Table 2.4. The vast majority

Table 2.3. **Top ALEC Bills Enacted, 1995–2013.**[a]

ALEC Bill	Enactments
ALEC Education Reform Package	314
Taking the Best: ALEC's Comprehensive Medical Liability Reform Proposal	178
Long-Term Care Insurance Act	56
High-Risk Health Insurance Pool Model Act	49
Resolution Urging the Obama Administration to Launch Negotiations for a Free Trade Agreement with Taiwan	42
College Savings Account Act	41
Resolution to Restate State Sovereignty	27
Resolution Calling for a Federal Balanced Budget Amendment	23
Rescission External Review Act	20
State Responses to Kyoto Climate Change Protocol	18
Vulnerable Adults Act	17
Resolution in Favor of a US Constitutional Amendment on Judicial Taxation	16
Expanded Consumer Choice in Financial Services Act	16
Resolution on Disease Management of Chronic Obstructive Pulmonary Disease	16
The A-Plus Literacy Act	16

[a] Author's analysis of state legislation and ALEC model bills.

of ALEC-derived bills (nearly half) were concentrated in just two policy domains: education and healthcare, followed by a distant third and fourth place for agriculture, energy, and the environment, and budget and tax policy. The heavy reliance on ALEC models from these domains likely reflects the fact that education and healthcare policies dominate state budgets. In fiscal year 2015, for example, states spent 25 percent of their budgets on K–12 education, 17 percent on Medicaid (state health insurance for the poor), and 13 percent on higher education.[13] Given that education and health programs tower over the landscape of existing state policy, ALEC—and its legislative members—are responding first and foremost to these issues.

In this chapter, we have seen what ALEC model bills look like and where and when these bills found their way into state laws. My approach of tracing how

Table 2.4. **ALEC Bill Introductions and Enactments by Policy Area, 1995–2013.**[a]

Policy Area	Introductions	Enactments
Healthcare	2,839	427
Education	2,065	414
Agriculture, energy, and the environment	734	167
Finance	229	72
Government reform	686	71
Budget and taxes	710	66
Criminal justice	557	64
Civil justice	679	58
Foreign policy	88	52
Transportation	252	42
Social welfare and benefits	245	39
Guns	322	30
General regulation	393	26
Housing	152	25
Labor unions	373	15
Voting and elections	46	5

[a] Author's analysis of state legislation and ALEC model bills.

ALEC's words and phrases were copied into state legislation and laws revealed that a considerable number of bills throughout the 1990s and 2000s—perhaps some 10,000 introduced bills and around 1,500 enacted bills—included text that came directly from ALEC model legislation. Those bills related to a range of issues, but most frequently health, education, and energy and the environment. They tended to prioritize privatization of previously public services, carving out favorable regulatory treatment for businesses, and ensuring low taxes on companies and their managers. The specific patterns of ALEC bill introductions and enactments have ebbed and flowed over time by issue, but the upshot was that a number of very consequential bills across a range of policy areas came directly from ideas and language developed by the companies, conservative activists, and wealthy donors participating in ALEC's task forces.

ALEC model bills, then, matter a great deal for the contours of social, economic, and political life across US states. But recognizing their importance raises a new question: If ALEC model bills have such consequential effects on state policy, why would state lawmakers so readily turn to the group in the first place? Why are legislators so quick to plagiarize ALEC's models—sometimes, as we have seen, so quickly that they forget to even tweak the legislative text to fit their own states?

3

An Easy "A" with ALEC

ALEC's Appeal for State Lawmakers

Imagine that you wake up tomorrow to find yourself elected to your state's legislature. As you start your day, you realize you are facing the responsibility of representing your constituents, overseeing the state's bureaucracy, researching policy, and writing and passing bills without previous experience doing any of those things. You would have a lot in common with Jim Fulghum, a neurosurgeon who was elected to the North Carolina legislature in 2012 without any prior work in state government. Reflecting on his first days in the Tar Heel state's lower chamber, Fulghum admitted that he had a lot to learn: "I'm not mechanically up to date on how to file a bill. . . . I'll know within a month how much I don't know, but I know I don't know a lot."[1]

One place you and Fulghum might turn as legislative novices is your staff. These individuals likely have been working during previous legislative sessions and could teach you both about the arcana of parliamentary procedure (such as how to file a bill) and also about the substantive policy details you would need to craft legislation. In a state like Pennsylvania, you would have access to year-round staffers who worked exclusively for you in both your capital and your district offices.[2] According to the most recent data from the National Conference of State Legislatures, there are well over 2,000 staffers for Pennsylvania lawmakers, or an average of about 9 staffers per member. Many of these staffers are highly trained and well compensated.[3] Those dedicated personnel, then, could be an invaluable resource for you, especially at the earlier stages of your legislative career.

But not all states spend as much as Pennsylvania does on staff for their legislatures, and you would be hard-pressed to get assistance in a state like Idaho, where you would only have access to shared staff members in your capital office, and no staff in your district.[4] And in Fulghum's state of North Carolina, staff work only part-time when the legislature is between sessions.[5] If your staff is not an option, where else might you go for help thinking through policy proposals and designing legislation? As Gene Whisnant, the Oregon representative we met in the Preface explained, one appealing option for resource-strapped legislators is ALEC, given that the group provides precisely the policy tools that many lawmakers—Whisnant included—lack.

In this chapter, I will document strong evidence for Whisnant's intuition. Legislatures where lawmakers have the fewest resources are precisely those that are most likely to rely on ALEC for legislative ideas. I first show that states that offer their lawmakers fewer staffers, have shorter sessions in office, and pay their lawmakers the least—thereby ensuring that lawmakers must maintain outside employment—are most likely to have introduced and enacted ALEC model bills. I then zoom in on individual lawmakers within state legislatures to show that it is most frequently junior and less experienced politicians who rely on ALEC bills—exactly what we would expect if ALEC is substituting for policy skills and expertise. Lastly, I show that although junior lawmakers are most reliant on ALEC for ideas, senior politicians and legislative leaders play an important role in the group as well.

Policy resources and model bills are not the whole story about ALEC, however, and this chapter also shows how partisanship and ideology fit into the picture. Conservative and Republican legislators are more likely to rely on ALEC even independently of their need for policy expertise. But the effects of partisanship are not constant over time. In the mid-1990s, ALEC bill reliance was a bipartisan affair shared by Democrats and Republicans alike. That began changing in the early 2000s, and by 2010, partisanship had become a much more powerful predictor of where ALEC proposals would crop up in state bills. Apart from partisanship, I also show that interest group pressure, especially at the individual lawmaker level, helps to explain which legislators decide to rely on ALEC more heavily. This chapter does not just document the factors that explain legislators' fondness for ALEC. It also shows that campaign contributions—perhaps surprisingly—do not help us to account for the spread of ALEC bills across the states.

An Easy "A" with ALEC

Let's return to the scenario just described, where you find yourself suddenly thrust into the position of serving in your state's legislature with no prior experience in elected office and without the sort of staff that lawmakers are lucky to get in states like Massachusetts, Pennsylvania, or New York. Now, a senior and well-respected lawmaker in your chamber approaches you on your first day in office to tell you about an organization that offers you prewritten bill ideas, down to the exact legal language you will need to introduce the bill wholesale, as well as all the research, evidence, and political talking points and polling you might need. You will need to arrange hearings on the bill, of course, but this organization can help you with that, too. And on top of it all, the senior lawmaker mentions that you will get to go with your family on a series of swanky junkets several times a year sponsored by this group—all expenses paid. My guess is that you—like me—would waste no time in signing up and planning your next free family vacation.

This is exactly how ALEC has built up its membership over time, according to Nebraska State Senator Jeremy Nordquist, who recounted to me how he found himself drawn to the group even as a left-leaning politician.[6] After Nordquist was elected in 2008, a senior member of the Nebraska State Senate whom he admired pitched the group to him. Nordquist contemplated the matter, and then eventually joined because he decided that he needed all the help he could get in a state where legislators are paid just $12,000 a year, meaning that lawmakers typically must hold another job outside of the state senate.[7] What is more, legislative sessions are relatively short (around two to three months of working days), meaning that legislators do not get much time to delve into legislation.[8] "When you're walking through the door of the legislature, you just got elected, you're just hiring staff, you don't know how to take your ideas and turn them into policy, so if there is a cookie-cutter, pre-written option, it would be very appealing," Nordquist explained to me about the allure of ALEC. In fact, at the time of our interview, Nordquist mentioned that a majority of his colleagues were ALEC members, including a majority of the senators who informally identify as Democrats (the state's unicameral chamber is officially nonpartisan).

Diving into each of ALEC's benefits and services helps us to understand ALEC's appeal, revealing why even Democrats like Nordquist would voluntarily join and take advantage of the group's resources. At a basic level, ALEC provides legislators with a portfolio of policy ideas that it has developed, with the exact legislative language necessary to implement those proposals. These bills are disseminated through ALEC's publications and events each year. All that is left for legislators is to introduce the model bills when they return to their home states. That in itself can be a huge benefit to legislators who are hungry for good ideas and are looking for policy proposals that already have been validated by outside experts, especially those—like ALEC—that can be claimed as business-friendly. A 2002 survey of state legislators, for instance, found that 66 percent of lawmakers believed they had to please a business constituency. ALEC could help lawmakers with doing precisely that.[9] As we saw in Chapter 1, ALEC had come to define itself as the source for legislation for pro-business, conservative legislators looking to fill out their broad ideology with specific policy ideas.

That signal that ALEC offered of business-branded ideas could sometimes even appeal to left-leaning legislators. Virginia Delegate Patrick Hope offered up weak policy resources in his state's legislature combined with the desire of legislators to signal that they were pro-business as an explanation for why his fellow progressives introduced and sponsored ALEC bills: "I'm co-chair of the Virginia Progressive Caucus," explained Hope in 2013, "I see some of our own members introducing some of these [ALEC] bills. . . . And you have to take a look back and say: What were they thinking? And because they've come in with this model, saying well this is just a pro-business bill, we haven't heard the other side of how this might impact the workers . . . we don't have the staff, we don't know what we don't know, and if we're only hearing one side . . . it's easy to get caught and not realize what you're doing. . . . I mean, probably before you even found out what this bill would do, the governor has already signed it, and it's already law."[10] Of course, ALEC's model bills are even more appealing to Republican state lawmakers. As former Republican Wisconsin state legislator, and later governor and US Secretary of Health and Human Services, Tommy Thompson recalled fondly about ALEC's model bills: "Myself, I always loved going to these [ALEC] meetings because I always found new ideas. Then I'd take them back to Wisconsin, disguise them a little bit, and declare that 'It's mine.'"[11]

In addition to the ideas for legislation, ALEC provides policy expertise and political strategy to state legislators in support of the model bills. Legislators who have questions about a particular proposal can turn to the task forces that ALEC organizes or to ALEC's bill tracking and research services. One publication crowed that ALEC responded to 100 to 200 research requests from state legislators each month, many times offering advice in a matter of hours.[12] ALEC, according to that publication, was becoming the "first" and "last" call for state legislators when researching policy. Aside from direct research assistance to lawmakers, ALEC offers its members and staff as expert witnesses who can testify on behalf of its model bills (or against opposing bills) in legislative hearings.[13] ALEC also organizes multiple events each year that provide opportunities for members to learn about specific policy issues in more detail. For example, at the 2012 ALEC policy summit, the tax and fiscal policy task force held briefings on public pension and fiscal policy reform, and offered discussions with economists and representatives from a variety of policy groups and think tanks.[14] Newly elected members are offered special orientations at these summits, too, describing the legislative issues and strategies most relevant for lawmakers to pick up early in their tenure.[15]

These research services have long been appealing to lawmakers who would otherwise have minimal resources to work with in their home legislatures. In a 1981 fundraising letter for ALEC, Virginia legislator Lawrence Pratt explained that "any legislator, and particularly those of us in a citizen's legislature like the Virginia General Assembly, gets overwhelmed by the volume of bills that is introduced and voted on. . . . I can tell you from experience that even if a legislator tries (and a lot of them don't) it is simply not possible for one person to read every word of over 1,600 complicated documents in 5 short weeks." Pratt then made the sales pitch for ALEC's services: "For just $4,000 [about $11,000 in 2017 dollars], ALEC can provide the staff needed to *read the bills*, and then give regular reports to key legislators about what they're being asked to vote for ... help us secure a conservative research assistant for our legislators."[16]

Indeed, ALEC made no secret of the fact that it was able to exploit weak legislative resources to build interest in its services. In a corporate grant proposal from the 1980s, ALEC argued the following about its services (focusing specifically on economic policy): "State legislator's [sic] today are confronted with a wide array of complex tax and fiscal policy issues. A typical legislator must be able to make many important decisions on issues ranging from economic development to increased demands for new and expanded state programs and services.... Yet, most state legislators lack the staff and resources to be truly informed on all these issues.... ALEC is uniquely qualified to provide the information services necessary for the success of effective and responsible state tax and fiscal policy."[17]

A 1985 interview with ALEC's executive director, Kathy Teague, also confirms this recognition. Teague highlighted the resources the group provided to legislators who would otherwise lack such capacities: "For the great majority of state legislators, being a lawmaker is their second career.... And so, the need for information is acute. Also in the majority of the states the state legislator has no or very little staff support. In most of the states there is a majority and a minority legislative research office, and that research office has to provide research background information for all of the state legislators in that state."[18] For these undersupported legislators, ALEC offered clear benefits that included the model bills—but went beyond those proposals. "We will help them develop it, tailor it for their state. We will put them in touch with legislators in other states who have been the sponsors of similar bills, who can discuss with them the legislative intricacies of the bill, the strategy, the witnesses who were brought in to testify in favor of it, et cetera," Teague summed up.[19]

In another revealing interview, ALEC's national legislative chairman explained that state legislators were more receptive to business lobbying groups, such as ALEC, compared to national lawmakers because of the lack of staff at the state level: "I think that state legislators are more accessible than Congressmen; they're very close to the lobbying bodies, trade associations, etc.... Congressmen interact with professional Washington lobbyists through their staffs, whereas State Legislators have a more direct line of communication with actual industry people. This is one advantage or opportunity that business should recognize in the lessening of federal interference through federalism."[20]

It is not just ALEC members and leadership who acknowledged the linkage between policy capacity and business influence. ALEC's critics have offered similar assessments, too. For example, the Natural Resources Defense Council and

Defenders of Wildlife—two groups that have been highly critical of ALEC's role in weakening state environmental standards—offered an analysis congruent with the evidence from ALEC itself in 2002: "ALEC exploits a weakness of state legislatures. Forty-one states have only part-time legislators, and 33 of those have no paid legislative staff. Many state lawmakers are overwhelmed by the hectic, often-frenzied pace of annual sessions. ALEC's 'model' bills and packets of background information on key issues frequently shape the supposed solutions to a wide range of state problems and issues."[21] And Charles Monaco, a spokesman for the Progressive States Network, a group established to represent progressive state legislators (more on them in Chapter 7), echoed this sentiment about ALEC's strengths, stating that "there's a real need in a lot of legislatures that are not full-time or fully staffed to share best practices."[22]

The other key to ALEC's success has been making its mix of policy ideas, research expertise, and political assistance especially appealing by offering it as part of a broader opportunity for state legislators to meet and network with other political leaders and representatives of major corporations in posh retreats. The 1997 annual ALEC meeting, for instance, was held in New Orleans.[23] Between the official workshops, panels, and briefing sessions, state legislative attendees were invited to join the "ALEC Mixed Golf Tournament" on the Oak Harbor Golf Course (with representatives from Reynolds Tobacco, the event's sponsor). Alternatively, if golf was not your sport, you could participate in the mixed tennis tournament side by side with friendly associates from pharmaceutical giant Pfizer (at the Hilton Racquet and Health Club). Or, you could go hunting at the Tallow Creek Shooting Club with leaders from the National Rifle Association. All lawmakers were further invited to the event's grand opening reception with Big Easy–inspired cocktails, music, and Cajun food at the French Market Hall. "At the blast of a jazz band's brass horns, you will be drawn into the ballroom foyer where you will find a recreation of a Southern mansion garden, complete with a three-tiered fountain, flowers, gazebos, and tivoli lights. . . . Twenty Louisiana restaurants will offer samples of their house specialties." "It will be a night not easily forgotten!," promised ALEC's organizers.[24]

The balance of participants at ALEC conferences is split roughly equally between state lawmakers and private-sector businesses—and state legislators' expenses for these meetings are frequently paid for by those corporate members of ALEC through scholarship funds.[25] As a further incentive for state legislators to attend ALEC events, elected officials are encouraged to bring their families and take advantage of heavily subsidized childcare. ALEC even offers political training sessions for legislative spouses.[26] "Many political spouses develop their own public identity as part of the family campaign plan. Should you develop issues of your own? How do you start? This session is based on successful examples," described one 1989 conference agenda item for the "Spouse Program: Your Role in Public Life."[27] Another session focused on the leadership image of spouses, giving "tips on how to make the best impression in public. You'll learn how to make a good first impression, how to always get a good introduction, and how to dress for the podium." Lest male spouses of female lawmakers feel out of place, the conference program stressed that "a specially prepared slide show includes tips for the male spouse."[28]

Figure 3.1 reproduces a flyer advertising ALEC's 1991 conference in Seattle, Washington, that places equal emphasis on the substantive policy discussions as on the numerous social outings available to members at the legislative confab, including golf and tennis tournaments and clinics, skeet and trap shoot, and bicycle and boat tours of the region.[29] Participation was free for legislators, but ALEC charged steeper fees for the corporate participants who might want to join the legislators on these various social outings. Of particular interest are the extensive opportunities for spouses and children of legislators, who could participate in ALEC-organized tours of Seattle landmarks like the Pike Place Market, Pioneer Square, and the Emerald City, as well as complimentary childcare for the younger children attending the annual meeting. ALEC even helped lawmakers plan a whole family vacation before or after the convening, encouraging legislators not to "miss the opportunity to take advantage of special cruise rates to Alaska and British Columbia. ALEC is making arrangements for package tours both before and after the Annual Meeting." For those legislative families not so keen on cruises, ALEC also offered a special bike tour of the Puget Sound Region, "departing just following the conclusion of the Annual Meeting." The emphasis on attracting lawmakers' families continues to the present day. According to a leaked list of registrants for ALEC's 2017 summer conference, fully 9 percent of registrants were the invited guests or spouses of other attendees, like the state legislators.

At first glance, the social programming—especially the family outings and vacations—might seem at best a distraction from ALEC's core activities, and at worst a waste of resources. Yet the social ties fostered at the events in between official policy discussions have wound up being one of the most valuable investments that ALEC and its corporate sponsors have made over the years. ALEC's social programing matters because it directly increases the value of attending the group's meetings and, through that attendance, increases the appeal of the group to individual lawmakers. As we have learned, many states do not make it easy to be an elected official between the low pay, frantic schedules, and minimal legislative resources. Add to that the scorn legislators increasingly receive from a public with little respect for politicians, and it is not hard to see that a little investment on the part of ALEC in showing state legislators a good time can go a long way in fostering goodwill.

Special Events Registration

Name _____

Legislature/Company _____

___ ALEC's MIXED GOLF TOURNAMENT AND CLINIC
Sponsored by R.J. Reynolds Tobacco Company

Monday, August 26—8:00 a.m.-4:00 p.m.

Please schedule me for:
___ Round 1—8:00 a.m.-12:00 noon
___ Round 2—1:30 p.m.-4:00 p.m.

Note: If both sections are not filled, Tournament will be played in the morning (Round 1).

___ Handicap (needed for pairings)
___ I will need to rent clubs.
___ Right Handed ___ Left Handed
___ $100 Registration Fee for Non-Legislators (State Legislators' entrance fees are complimentary)

Registration Fee Includes: Green and Cart Fees, Golf Skills Clinic, Transportation to Course, Refreshments and Club Rental (if needed).

___ ALEC's MIXED TENNIS TOURNAMENT AND CLINIC
Sponsored by Philip Morris USA

Monday, August 26, 1991—10:00 a.m.-2:00 p.m.

___ I will need to rent a tennis racquet
___ $75 Registration Fee for Non-Legislators (State legislators' entrance fees are complimentary)

Registration Fee Includes: Court Fees, Tennis Skills Clinic, Transportation to Tennis Courts, Refreshments and Tennis Racquet Rental (if needed).

___ ALEC's SKEET & TRAP SHOOT
Sponsored by the National Rifle Association

Monday, August 26, 1991—10:00 a.m.-2:00 p.m.

___ $25 Registration Fee for Non-Legislators (State Legislators' entrance fees are complimentary)

Registration Fee Includes: Shotguns, Shells, Clay Targets, Ear and Eye Protection, Safety Training Course, Transportation and Refreshments. Shooters are to be grouped by experience.

Don't miss the opportunity to take advantage of special cruise rates to Alaska and British Columbia. ALEC is making arrangements for package tours both before and after the Annual Meeting. For more information, call the ALEC office.

For a free Destination Washington Travel Planner: a full-color 172 page guide with everything you need to help plan your visit: call 1-800-544-1800.

Progressive Travels of Seattle is offering a special bicycle tour of the Puget Sound Region, departing just following the conclusion of the Annual Meeting. (August 30-September 2). This four-day bicycle tour features the wonderful sights just outside of Seattle, such as beautiful Whidbey and Bainbridge Islands, the Victorian city of Port Townsend, and the Norwegian enclave of Poulsbo. Don't miss out on a chance to experience the area Conde Nast Traveler magazine called "one of the 10 best vacation destinations in the world". For more information and a free brochure, contact the ALEC office, or call Progressive Travels at 1-800-245-2229. Call soon, space is limited.

Special Programs for Spouses and Guests

Visit Pike Place Market, Pioneer Square and the Emerald City. Enjoy a leisurely lunch at Kiana Lodge (film location for television's "Twin Peaks series). Enjoy a scenic ride through the foothills of the Cascade Mountains to breathtaking Snoqualmie Falls. Travel north to the home of Washington's premier winery, Chateau Ste. Michelle.

Tour tickets are available through Convention Services Northwest. For additional information, contact the ALEC office at 202-547-4646, ext. 224.

Youth Programs/Child Care

For children of registered Annual Meeting participants, complimentary child care will be provided at The Westin Hotel for children ages 0-12. Child care facilities will be open during all official Annual Meeting activities.

Children ages 6-17 may participate in a get acquainted breakfast cruise, visit the Seattle Center, the Seattle Aquarium and enjoy a special evening at The Westin Hotel while their parents are participating in ALEC's Annual Awards Banquet. For more information, contact the ALEC office at 202-547-4646, ext. 224.

Figure 3.1. ALEC PLACES A HIGH PREMIUM ON SOCIAL EVENTS AT ITS CONFERENCES. Conference advertisement for 1991 ALEC meeting; see ALEC 1991.

Of course, in most cases, ALEC was not even spending from its own coffers to run the various conference events—the private-sector corporate members of the group typically pick up most or all of the tab for the social gatherings for lawmakers and their families. "We do a nice job with special events. We just kind of take it on ourselves because I want things to be nice for these guys who make 24,000 dollars a year," explained one corporate sponsor of the annual ALEC conference.[30] The motivation for corporate sponsorship of conference events is not simply charitable, however. As ALEC has put it in advertising sponsorship opportunities to companies, "No other legislative gathering, especially at the local level, provides the private sector members the unequaled opportunity to work directly with legislators in forming policy and defining the direction state government will take in the immediate future"—and as we have seen, that boast was grounded in reality.[31]

For a company interested in pushing one of its model bill proposals across the states, the chance to spend hours chatting up state legislators on the links, at a cocktail reception, or between tennis matches is indeed an unparalleled opportunity to build relationships with lawmakers who will be much more inclined to sponsor and enact those proposals in the future. That explains why year in and year out large companies like Time Warner, Reynolds Tobacco, Seagram Liquors, and AT&T were so willing to spend their executives' time and shareholders' money on sponsoring ALEC events. Reflecting on his company's longtime sponsorship of ALEC programming, the executive in charge of government affairs for GTE (now AT&T) was quite frank about what his company's investments in ALEC's social events were buying. According to him, GTE's contributions bought an "exchange of ideas and information [between] corporate and business members of ALEC and legislators."[32]

It is difficult to pin down the exact contributions that companies have made to ALEC events, but we can piece together a partial picture from leaked records. At the 2015 annual meeting, for instance, corporate sponsors could give between $5,000 and $100,000 for recognition and a chance to interact more closely with state legislative attendees. Assuming that companies gave the minimum amount in each "tier" of recognition, we can estimate conservatively that ALEC raised at least a million dollars in named sponsorships for that one meeting alone (or about a sixth to a seventh of their annual budget). Table 3.1 lists selected named corporate sponsors of ALEC's 2015 meeting, and reveals that many large American companies—like Reynolds American Tobacco, AT&T, Chevron, UPS, and FedEx—continue to give relatively generous donations to support ALEC's programming even after the negative publicity and scrutiny the group had received since 2012. Especially for large and public-facing companies like UPS or AT&T that are particularly sensitive to the potential for consumer

Table 3.1. **Top Corporate Sponsors of 2015 ALEC Meeting.**[a]

President's Level: $100,000	Reynolds American Tobacco
Chair's Level: $50,000	American Electric Power (AEP)
	AT&T
	DentaQuest
	Luminant/Energy Future Holdings
Vice Chair's Level: $25,000	Altria/Phillip Morris
	Diageo
	Encore Capital Group
	ExxonMobil
	Guarantee Trust Life
	Takeda
	UPS

[a] Source is leaked documents obtained by the Center for Media and Democracy.

backlash, their willingness to continue to sponsor these convenings is testament to the value of the gatherings for corporate bottom lines.

Another way of estimating corporate contributions to ALEC events is through the scholarships that the group offers to legislators to cover the registration, travel, lodging, and food costs of those lawmakers (and their families) attending annual convenings. Drawing on data from open records law requests made by investigative journalists at the Center for Media and Democracy, I estimate that companies spent over $3 million from 2006 to 2011 on room, board, and travel expenses to bring lawmakers to ALEC annual meetings.[33]

Not all states were equally likely to receive support from corporate sponsorships, however, and over this period the unlucky lawmakers in New Jersey, New York, and Massachusetts received no scholarship donations to attend ALEC events. In contrast, each lawmaker from Ohio and Arizona received an average of nearly $2,200 in corporate scholarships to hobnob at the ALEC meetings. Figure 3.2 summarizes the scholarship money from ALEC's corporate backers flowing to lawmakers in each state for the rest of the country, dividing the states into six equally sized groups. The darker-shaded areas indicate that a greater proportion of funds were flowing to lawmakers traveling to ALEC conferences and meetings from those states. We can interpret Figure 3.2 as revealing the states in which a greater proportion of lawmakers attended ALEC meetings—and where companies had a strategic interest in building relationships with precisely those legislators.

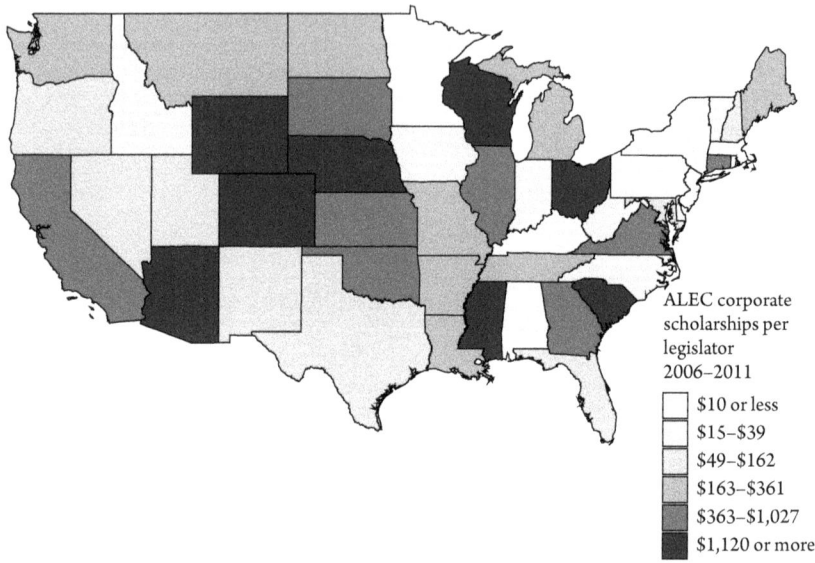

Figure 3.2. CORPORATE SPONSORSHIPS TO STATE LEGISLATORS FOR ANNUAL ALEC MEETINGS, 2006–2011. ALEC corporate scholarships for state legislators by state. Data on ALEC corporate scholarships from Graves 2012b.

If it is difficult to uncover how much companies contribute to ALEC sponsorships, it is even harder to reconstruct the relationships that are formed between lawmakers and ALEC staff or private-sector ALEC representatives or activists at these meetings. Still, there is good reason to think that these events regularly achieve their intended goals. As one state legislator and ALEC attendee reported to me in an interview, because of all of the benefits ALEC offers, "most ALEC members [may not start out as] true believers, but . . . go and participate in the group for the free food, free drinks, free trips, and connections"—and then wind up becoming more committed to the group over time with each passing meeting.[34]

Consider also the glowing letters that many legislators sent to the companies that sponsored their trips. John Adams is a state representative from Ohio and active ALEC member who wrote a kind note to AT&T's vice president of government relations after attending the 2010 ALEC convening with his fellow state lawmakers on AT&T's dime. "I can't say thank you enough for making our trip out to San Diego for the ALEC conference such a success. Thank you also to AT&T for their generous contribution and sponsorship of the Ohio Night event! Because of your help . . . the trip to ALEC was made possible for our [Ohio] legislators."[35] Adams then went on to emphasize that the meeting had helped to provide him with the "information [needed so] that the Ohio Legislature will pass and repeal laws to make Ohio a much more business friendly state" to companies like AT&T.

Testing Explanations for ALEC's Appeal across the Fifty States

We have seen compelling evidence from the historical record, from ALEC's leaders, and from legislators' own accounts that emphasize the valuable resources and services that ALEC provides to lawmakers. But do these explanations hold up when we look systematically across all fifty states? One way of answering this question is to return to the ALEC-plagiarized bills I identified in the previous chapter and see if states where lawmakers had fewer resources to write and pass bills were more likely to introduce and enact legislation copied from ALEC proposals. To get at the resources that lawmakers need to develop legislation on their own, I employ a summary measure that political scientists have created. This measure, dubbed "legislative professionalism," neatly captures several different aspects of state legislatures that matter for how easily lawmakers can draft, distribute, and enact bills. These aspects include legislative pay, the length of legislative sessions, and spending on legislative staff support and services. I expect each one to matter for lawmakers' reliance on ALEC model bills.

As we have already seen, state legislative pay varies dramatically across the country, with some states, like Montana, Utah, Wyoming, Texas, and Kansas, offering their lawmakers salaries less than $15,000 per year. New Hampshire stands alone in offering its legislators a mere $200 per year.[36] Even after taking into account its 424-person legislature (larger than many nations), the total amount that New Hampshire spends on salaries for its whole legislature is less than the average annual salary for a single legislator in California (around $100,000)— and about the same as a single Pennsylvania lawmaker (just over $85,000).[37] When lawmakers are paid less—especially below the levels needed to support an individual and their family—elected officials will need to turn to outside employment. That leaves less time for politicians to focus on legislation, researching different policy alternatives, putting together proposals, and building the political strategy necessary to enact bills. We should expect that states with lower legislative pay would be more reliant on ALEC's prewritten bills and research assistance and support.

Legislative pay is not the only characteristic of state legislatures that matters for ALEC reliance, however. The length of legislative sessions also varies enormously across the states, with some states, like New York or Michigan, meeting for nearly the whole year, every year.[38] Other states, like Arizona or Washington, might only meet for a few months every year.[39] And still other states, like Montana, Nevada, North Dakota, and Texas, only meet every other year.[40] Shorter sessions give lawmakers a smaller window to consider and deliberate over legislation, and therefore I expect that states with shorter sessions would be more pressed for time and more reliant on ALEC model bills that come ready to go out of the box.

The third and final element of legislatures that I consider is the staff support that lawmakers can count on. Just as with the length of sessions and pay, the presence and scope of legislative support staff range wildly across different states, from fewer than one paid staffer per lawmaker in New Hampshire, Vermont, and North Dakota to nearly 18 staffers per lawmaker in California.[41] The typical state gave its legislators just 4 staffers. And just as with legislative pay and the length of legislative sessions, the staff support offered to legislators ought to shape politicians' demand for ALEC ideas and assistance. Where lawmakers have fewer staffers, staffers who work part-time, and staffers who are shared across different legislators rather than assigned to a single lawmaker, politicians should have less help and expertise to draft and move bills through the legislature. That should make the private staffers offered by ALEC much more appealing—and increase those lawmakers' willingness to copy from ALEC model bills.

Figure 3.3 maps my summary measure that combines all three of these features of legislatures into a single index.[42] This measure registers highest for states like California, Pennsylvania, New York, and Illinois, and lowest for Wyoming, Utah, New Hampshire, and North Dakota (Louisiana falls roughly in the middle between these extremes).

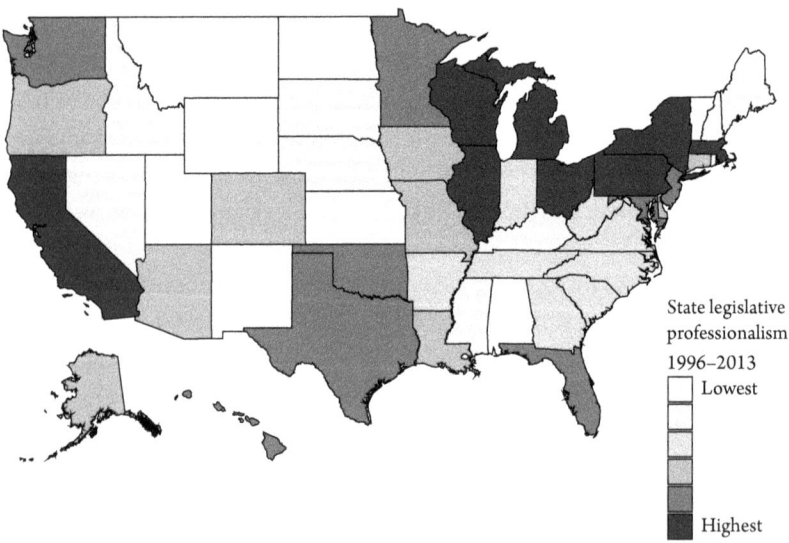

Figure 3.3. LEGISLATIVE PROFESSIONALISM ACROSS THE STATES, 1996–2013. Legislative professionalism for each state legislature. It is a summary index of legislative pay, length of legislative sessions, and spending on state legislative support (see text for more details). Index averaged from 1996 to 2013.

The measure corresponds well to more general characterizations of state legislatures: while we tend to talk about "professional politicians" in states like California and New York, New Hampshire, Vermont, and Montana all pride themselves on being states characterized as "citizen legislatures."

How does the picture from Figure 3.3 map onto the landscape of ALEC-plagiarized bills? Figure 3.4 answers this question by plotting the summary measure of state legislative professionalism from Figure 3.3 against the average proportion of a state's introduced bills (left-hand plot) or enacted bills (right-hand plot) that I identified as copying and pasting from ALEC model bills from 1996 to 2013. In both cases of introduced and enacted bills, we can see a strongly negative relationship between legislative resources and ALEC bill reliance. Over the 1990s and 2000s, states with higher legislative pay, longer sessions, and more staff assistance—like Massachusetts, Michigan, New York, Pennsylvania, and California—introduced and enacted far fewer ALEC model bills than did states like Wyoming, Idaho, Kentucky, or Kansas, which all offer fewer resources to their state legislatures. (Breaking out the summary legislative resources measure into its three parts, I find the strongest relationship between ALEC plagiarism and legislative salaries and staff spending, and a substantially weaker relationship between ALEC plagiarism and legislative session length.)

The trend lines implied by Figure 3.4 suggest that moving from California (the state with the highest level of legislative resources) to Wyoming (the state with the lowest level of legislative resources) would increase the proportion

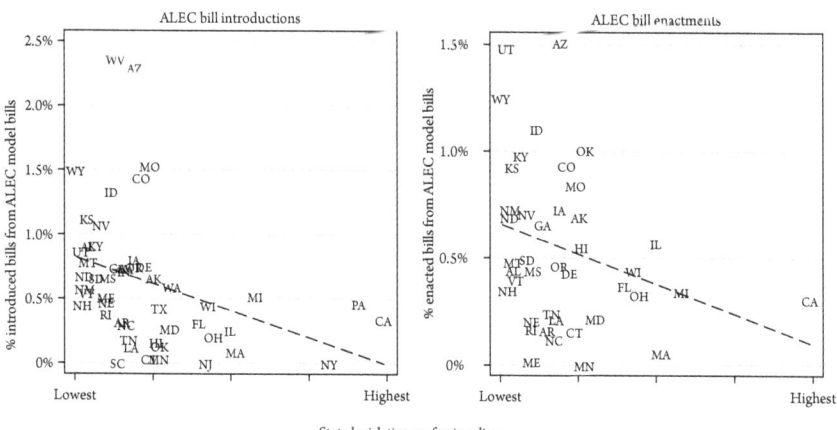

Figure 3.4. STATE LEGISLATIVE PROFESSIONALISM AND ALEC-PLAGIARIZED BILLS, 1996–2013. The relationship between state legislative professionalism and ALEC bill plagiarism for introduced bills (left panel) and enacted bills (right panel). Legislative professionalism is a summary index of legislative pay, length of legislative sessions, and spending on state legislative support. Index averaged from 1996 to 2013,

of a state's introduced bills plagiarized from ALEC by about 0.82 percentage points and enacted bills copied from those models by 0.55 percentage points. Those predictions are large given that the average state copied ALEC model bills for about 0.63 percent of its introduced bills and 0.54 percent of its enacted legislation.

This relationship also holds up accounting for a variety of other factors, including partisan control of government, union strength, mass public opinion on economic policy, and state unemployment, as well as examining variation in ALEC reliance within states over time (see the Chapter 3 Appendix for these analyses, which include state and biennium fixed effect regressions). The relationship between state legislative resources and ALEC bill introductions and enactments therefore cannot be dismissed as simply a story of partisan control or state political culture. Controlling for all these other factors, I estimate that a move from legislative resources in Wyoming to California is estimated to reduce ALEC bill introduction rates by about 1 percentage point and enactment rates by 1.23 percentage points.[43]

Figure 3.4 and the supplementary regressions thus provide strong evidence in support of the idea that lawmakers turn to ALEC when their states do not offer them public help and assistance drafting and moving legislation. But cautious readers might wonder if the plagiarized bills really are the best way of gauging reliance on ALEC. Might it be the case, for instance, that lawmakers rely on ALEC for all sorts of other services, while neglecting to copy and paste model bill text into their legislation? In that case, Figure 3.4 would be missing out on many other forms of ALEC reliance—and could possibly be understating reliance on the organization in certain states.

To address that concern, I added questions to a national survey of state legislative candidates fielded in 2014 that asked politicians whether they had ever relied on ALEC when considering or drafting economic policy (the question was "Thinking specifically about economic issues, have you ever relied on any of the following organizations when considering, drafting, or evaluating legislation? Check all of the organizations whose resources you have relied on.").[44] In all, 1,887 state legislative candidates responded to the survey for a final response rate of about one in five state politicians, similar to other studies that have been done of state lawmakers. Fortunately, the candidates who took the survey were not appreciably different from those that did not in terms of their region, party, or other characteristics.[45]

Because the survey was of political candidates—and not legislators—I focus on the more limited set of politicians who said that they had previously served in a state legislature. It would be these politicians—and not legislative newbies—who could have conceivably relied on ALEC in the past. Based on the responses among these politicians, Table 3.2 summarizes the states with the highest and

Table 3.2. **States with the Highest and Lowest Proportion of Lawmakers Reporting Reliance on ALEC, 2014.**[a]

State	Share of Candidates Relying on ALEC (%)	State	Share of Candidates Relying on ALEC (%)
HI	0	AL	42
FL	0	TN	40
OK	0	NM	33
MN	0	OH	33
NY	0	GA	32
IA	0	ND	31

[a] Data from the 2014 National Candidate Survey. Only candidates who held state legislative office are included in this table.

lowest proportions of candidates reporting reliance on ALEC. At the low end, no respondents in Hawaii, Florida, Oklahoma, Minnesota, New York, or Iowa reported relying on ALEC, while over three in ten candidates from Alabama, Tennessee, New Mexico, Ohio, Georgia, and North Dakota said that they had turned to the group when crafting policy.

Of course, we are not merely interested in whether lawmakers reported relying on ALEC—but whether lawmakers were *more likely* to report turning to the group in states that offered lawmakers fewer resources and assistance. Figure 3.5 graphs self-reported reliance on ALEC against the same summary measure of state legislative resources I used earlier. We see exactly the same picture in Figure 3.5 that we did when looking at ALEC model bill plagiarism. States that offered more extensive resources to their lawmakers—like California, Pennsylvania, and New York—were much less likely to have politicians reporting reliance on ALEC. In contrast, the greatest number of politicians reporting reliance on ALEC came from states like Alabama, Tennessee, New Mexico, and Georgia, which all offered their lawmakers far fewer resources to make policy—with shorter legislative sessions, lower legislative pay, and fewer staffers.

Though the patterns in Figure 3.5 are striking, skeptical readers may object to the conclusions I draw based on the fact that New York, Pennsylvania, and California are so far away from the rest of the states. Does the relationship between legislative resources and ALEC reliance continue to hold if we ignore those three outlier states? The dashed trend line answers that question, and indicates that we still see a sharply negative relationship between state legislative resources and ALEC reliance even when we focus on the remaining, lower-resourced states. The bottom line is that lawmakers, in their own words, report relying on ALEC more frequently where they have fewer publicly provided options.

Figure 3.5 helps us to see that the story about ALEC's appeal remains the same regardless of whether we ask lawmakers themselves or look at plagiarized legislative text instead. But another potential objection is that my measure of legislative resources—the summary index of state legislative professionalism—is at the state level. Might there be other characteristics in states with low legislative resources that are really responsible for the relationships I am identifying? The supplementary analyses I report in the Chapter 3 Appendix help to address this concern. They show that my findings hold up when I examine variation in ALEC activity and legislative capacity within states over time while controlling for other state features that vary from year to year. But an even more convincing test would look at individual lawmakers' demand for policy resources and their dependence on ALEC within particular states, rather than across whole states.

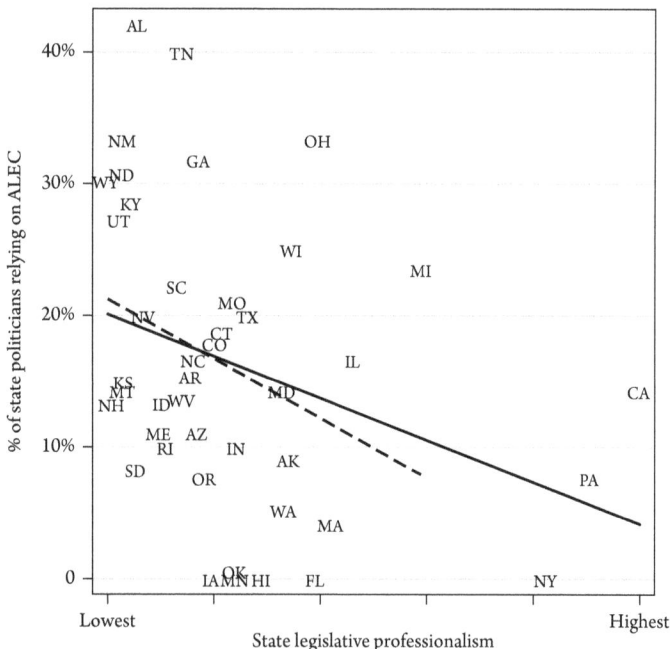

Figure 3.5. STATE LEGISLATIVE PROFESSIONALISM AND LEGISLATORS' SELF-REPORTED RELIANCE ON ALEC, 2014. The relationship between self-reported ALEC reliance among legislators and state legislative professionalism. ALEC reliance from 2014 National Candidate Survey; legislative professionalism is a summary index of legislative pay, length of legislative sessions, and spending on state legislative support. The solid black line is a regression line for all states. The dashed black line is a regression line excluding NY, PA, and CA. Only candidates who held state legislative office are included in this plot.

To do this, I return to the plagiarized set of bills, and look to see which state lawmakers were responsible for authoring the legislation that I identified as copying and pasting from ALEC models. This gives me the opportunity to look at reliance on ALEC on an individual lawmaker-by-lawmaker basis. Identifying the authorship of these ALEC-plagiarized bills is only half of the story, however, since I also need a measure of the legislative resources and expertise of individual lawmakers. Unfortunately, there are no readily available or agreed-upon measures of how much help and policy expertise individual legislators possess.

As a result, I rely on a cruder—but more readily available and comparable—measure: how long lawmakers have served in office. My assumption is that legislators who have had more years of experience will generally have more expertise and knowledge about the legislative process and specific policy areas, and will thus have less of a need for outside groups like ALEC. Obviously, there are likely to be exceptions to this pattern, like freshman legislators who come into office with considerable policy expertise because of their education or past careers. Similarly, there could be senior lawmakers who have little interest in digging into the weeds of policy analysis. Nevertheless, I believe it is reasonable to argue that more senior lawmakers should have more policy knowledge than their more junior colleagues.

A survey of state legislators from 2002 provides some justification for my use of legislative tenure as a measure of expertise.[46] One question on the survey asked lawmakers how important senior colleagues were to them when they were first elected to the legislature. Respondents could provide an answer on a 1 through 5 scale, where 1 indicated that senior colleagues were "not important at all" to them and 5 indicated that senior colleagues were "very important." In all, 43 percent of lawmakers said that senior colleagues were very important, and another 35 percent said that senior colleagues were somewhat important. The responses to this question suggest that more senior lawmakers indeed have more expertise than recently elected members.

Assuming that legislative experience is a good measure of expertise, do more senior lawmakers rely less on ALEC than more junior members? Using data on legislator experience from 2003 to 2013, I divide lawmakers into five equally sized groups based on their years of legislative experience. I then estimate the average number of bills legislators in each group sponsored that were blatantly plagiarized from ALEC models. To account for the fact that some legislators are much more productive than others in authoring many more pieces of legislation, I look at the proportion of a lawmaker's authored bills that come from ALEC, rather than the total number of ALEC model bills a lawmaker sponsored. (Looking at ALEC bill authorship as a percentage of all of a lawmaker's authored bills also accounts for the fact that some legislatures impose limits on the number of bills a legislator can introduce per session.)

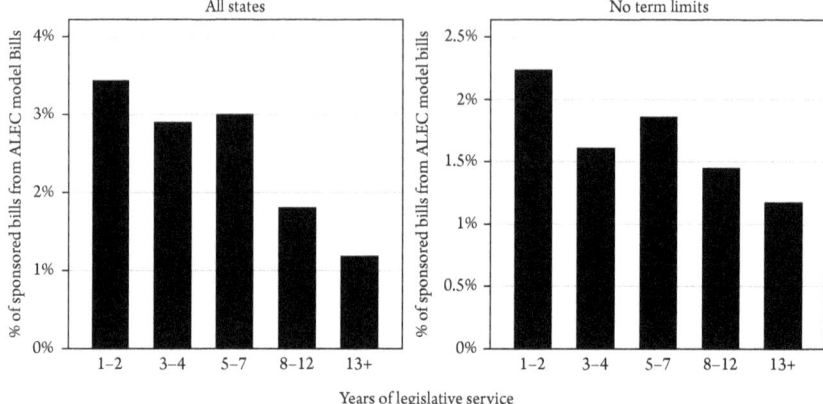

Figure 3.6. LEGISLATIVE EXPERIENCE AND ALEC BILL SPONSORSHIP, 2003–2013. The proportion of lawmakers' sponsored bills copied from ALEC model bills by the number of years a lawmaker had served consecutively in office. Legislators divided into five equally sized groups (quintiles). The left panel shows all states, the right panel states with no term limits. Years of legislative service from state legislative records.

The left panel of Figure 3.6 shows the results of this analysis, and indicates a negative relationship between years of legislative experience and lawmakers' reliance on ALEC for the bills they draft—or claim to draft. The most junior lawmakers (with 1 to 2 years of experience) relied on ALEC for over 3 percent of all the bills they sponsored. Legislators with about 3 to 7 years of experience showed a similar reliance on ALEC models, but that dropped off sharply for lawmakers with 8 to 12 years of experience (who relied on ALEC for only 2 percent of their authored bills), and especially for the most senior lawmakers with 13 years or more of experience, who relied on ALEC for only around 1 percent of their legislative activity. More senior lawmakers are much less dependent on ALEC-plagiarized bills for the legislation they introduce under their own name, consistent with the cross-state story I presented earlier.[47] This is true even when we look at the states without term limits, which artificially truncate the potential tenure of legislators; see the right-hand plot of Figure 3.6; the Chapter 3 Appendix results also show that the results hold up controlling for a variety of other factors.

Beyond Policy Resources: How Partisanship, Ideology, and Interest Group Constituencies Shape ALEC Reliance

So far I have focused on policy resources as an explanation for legislators' reliance on ALEC, and we have seen a range of evidence that states giving fewer resources to their lawmakers are indeed more likely to turn to ALEC, just as less experienced lawmakers are more likely to author ALEC model bills under their own names. This gives us valuable leverage to understand the puzzle of why some states and legislators turn to ALEC at any given point in time. But policy resources and expertise are less helpful in explaining why ALEC's legislative success has changed over time. States do vary year-to-year in the resources that they provide to their lawmakers, as in deciding how much to allocate to staff spending or how long their sessions will be. For the most part, however, the states that offered their lawmakers the most assistance in 1996—like New York, California, and Pennsylvania—are exactly the same states that offered lawmakers the most resources in 2000 and in 2013. Similarly, states like Wyoming and Montana that do not offer many resources to their lawmakers stayed roughly at the bottom of state rankings over the whole period that I studied.

To understand the changing over-time success of ALEC, then, we need to consider the characteristics of states and lawmakers that also change over time. The best place to start, in turn, is partisanship. As the two political parties become more distinct from each other in their ideologies and positions on a range of policies, partisan control of government by one party or the other increasingly means having a very distinct set of policies for a state's citizens.[48] Does your state have a GOP governor and legislature? You are likely to see school voucher and charter school expansion, tax cuts, limits on access to abortion and contraceptives, cuts to union rights, new restrictions on voting, and a reluctance to increase the minimum wage. But if you instead have a Democratic governor and legislature, your politicians are likely to enact increases in the minimum wage, measures to expand voting, tax hikes on businesses and wealthy individuals, and expansions of social programs like Medicaid or unemployment insurance. Against that background of partisan polarization, we might expect that the Republican Party would find ALEC's ideas and legislation more appealing than Democrats, especially in very recent years as both the GOP and ALEC have lurched to the right. The upshot of these changes is that we should expect that party control of state government ought to matter above and beyond policy resources in explaining the spread of ALEC's bills across the states. An increasingly conservative Republican Party means that we should expect ALEC will have greater success in translating its policy ideas into law in fully GOP-controlled states.

Figure 3.7 offers a first look at the importance of party control of state government for ALEC's legislative victories. Using my list of ALEC-plagiarized bills from 1996 to 2013, the figure divides states by the partisan control of their government over this period. To do this, I look at control of states' governors, upper legislative chambers, and lower legislative chambers, and then plot the proportion of a state's enacted bills that copied directly from ALEC models.

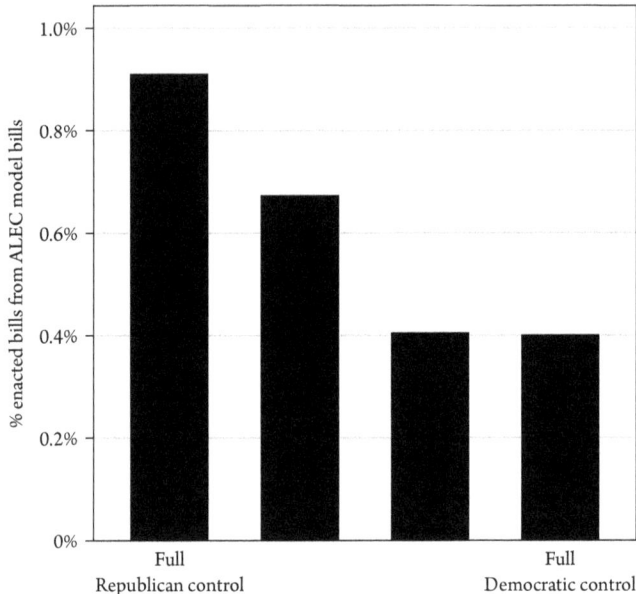

Figure 3.7. PARTISAN CONTROL OF GOVERNMENT AND ALEC-PLAGIARIZED BILLS, 1996–2013. The proportion of bills enacted from ALEC model bills by partisan control of state government, ranging from full Republican control to full Democratic control. Partisan control counts of a state's lower chamber, upper chamber, and governorship.

We can see a very strong relationship between partisan control and ALEC bill enactments: states under full GOP control were more than twice as likely to enact ALEC model bills compared to states under full Democratic control, and as states moved toward greater GOP control of one or two branches of government, the likelihood of ALEC bill enactment became higher.

Equally interesting from Figure 3.7 is that a surprising number of Democratic legislatures passed ALEC model bills that Democratic governors went on to sign into law. On average, fully 0.3 percent of the bills that Democratic state governments enacted from 1996 to 2013 came from plagiarized ALEC model bills. In all, I identified 254 pieces of state legislation that copied in whole or part from ALEC that were passed by Democratic legislatures and governors. What do these bills look like?

Just like the overall distribution of ALEC bills, Democratic states tended to rely on ALEC most heavily for education, energy, environmental, and healthcare reforms. Education in particular was an area where reform-minded Democrats were willing to implement ALEC ideas related to expanding charter schools, loosening state requirements for collective bargaining and the influence of teachers unions, and introducing more opportunities for students and parents to choose between different schools. Democratic governments in states as varied as traditional blue strongholds (like California and Hawaii) as well as more moderate and conservative enclaves (like Missouri or Oklahoma) were willing to enact these ALEC proposals. That makes sense given the extent to which the Democratic Party has been divided internally between a more reform-oriented, moderate wing willing to experiment with new models of teacher pay, accountability, and charter schools, and a more progressive wing closely tied to teachers unions historically skeptical of those reform measures.[49]

In healthcare, the most common Democratically passed ALEC proposals related to medical liability reform measures, which would make it more challenging for patients to bring legal suits against their doctors for malpractice—a longtime priority for medical care providers and facilities. Given the importance of medical providers for many local communities, it is easy to see why these proposals might be appealing even to Democratic politicians. Within the third area of activity—agriculture, energy, and the environment—many of the proposals represent concessions to extractive industries that dominate particular states' economies, and were popular in Democratically-controlled states that depended heavily on those sectors, like Kentucky.

We can also examine the importance of partisanship for individual lawmakers' reliance on ALEC bills, too, by returning to the data on ALEC bill sponsorships between 2003 and 2013. Figure 3.8 graphs those results, and shows that Republican state lawmakers relied on ALEC model bills for about 3 percent of all their authored legislation, nearly one full percentage point more

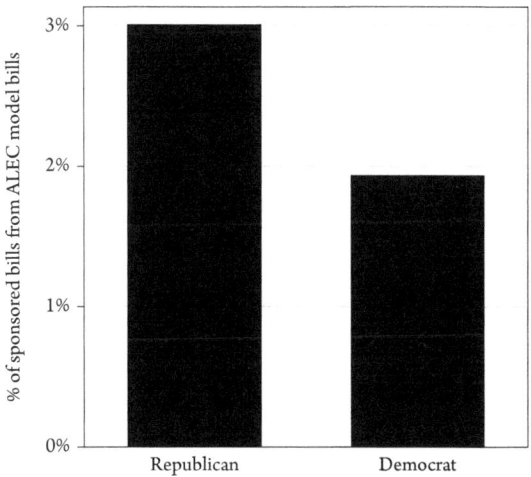

Figure 3.8. LEGISLATOR PARTY AND ALEC BILL SPONSORSHIP, 2003–2013. The proportion of lawmakers' sponsored bills copied from ALEC model bills for Republicans and Democrats separately.

than Democratic state legislators, who relied on ALEC model bills for a little under 2 percent of their bills. That is a relatively large difference—similar to the one we observed when looking at ALEC bill enactments across the states.

These findings across states and lawmakers suggest that partisanship, in addition to state legislative resources, goes a long way in accounting for the spread of ALEC bills over time in many states. But my description of partisan polarization did not only indicate that Republicans should be more likely than Democrats to rely on ALEC. It also suggested that Republican control of government should be an *increasingly* important explanation for ALEC bill reliance as the GOP and ALEC both moved further to the right and as ALEC increasingly came to define what it meant to be a conservative, GOP state lawmaker. An ever-more-conservative GOP ought to find ALEC's ideas more welcome. Democrats, on the other hand, would increasingly want to distance themselves from the right-leaning views of the group.

We can gauge the importance of partisan control of government for ALEC bill passage over time by calculating, for each legislative session, ALEC bill reliance for GOP- and Democratically-controlled state governments. Figure 3.9 plots this trend and shows that Republican-held state governments are relying on ALEC's proposals for an increasing proportion of their enacted legislation (especially in recent sessions), while Democrats are relying on ALEC for a diminishing proportion of their bills when in power. Figure 3.9 thus confirms that partisan control matters more now for ALEC's success than in the past.

Thinking about the increasing importance of partisan control leads us to the final factor that matters for ALEC's appeal: the interest groups to which

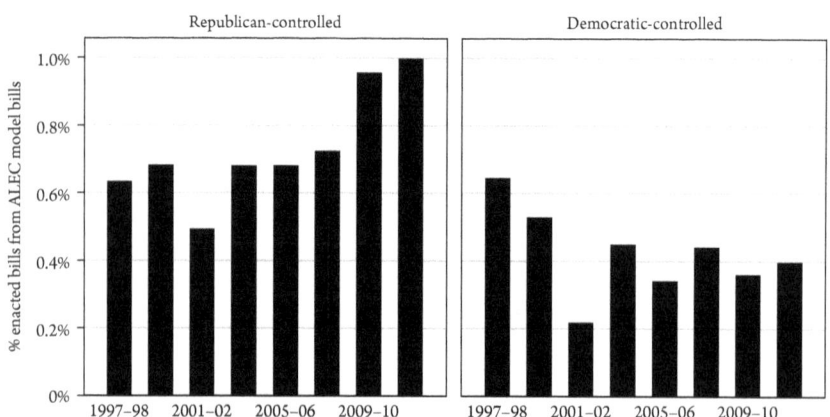

Figure 3.9. ENACTMENT OF ALEC-PLAGIARIZED BILLS OVER TIME IN REPUBLICAN AND DEMOCRATIC STATES. The proportion of bills enacted from ALEC model bills in fully GOP-controlled states (left panel) or Democratically-controlled states (right panel) over time.

politicians are accountable. While the changing ideological positions of the two parties help us to see why Democrats might find ALEC less appealing over time, it does not provide much leverage over why *within* the Democratic Party there are still lawmakers who might rely on ALEC—and why not all Republicans, even more junior GOP lawmakers, turn to ALEC's model bills. To understand why lawmakers might rely on ALEC independently of party or experience, we need to focus on lawmakers' bases of political support within their legislative districts.

Politicians may have a variety of reasons for seeking elected office—enacting certain policies, improving the lives of their constituents, or building a public profile—but all those objectives have the common requirement that politicians first need to win elections.[50] To do that, politicians need the support of organizations that can provide the resources necessary for successful elections. Those include things like activists who can turn out voters, money to buy campaign ads, and high-profile endorsements. In return for this support, political organizations will extract promises from politicians to change public policy.[51]

I anticipate that these policy-demanding groups will help shape lawmakers' demand for ALEC. If lawmakers are supported by groups with policy interests that go directly against ALEC, we should expect that those lawmakers would be less likely to think of ALEC as being a useful resource to them. Even if a legislator is strapped for resources and expertise, if his or her base of political support is staunchly opposed to ALEC's priorities, the legislator probably will not have much to gain from relying on ALEC's proposals, research, and contacts. Similarly, if the base of political support in a district is strongly aligned with ALEC's policy objectives, legislators would have good reason to work with the group, regardless of their need for expertise and capacity. To test the importance of legislators' bases of organized group support, I consider two different sets of interests: public-sector labor unions and emissions-intensive businesses. The former should be intensely opposed to ALEC, whereas the latter ought to be much more supportive of the group's priorities.

As we saw in Chapter 1, the public labor movement is ALEC's public enemy number one—and so we should expect that lawmakers who are more dependent on support from government employee unions would be less likely to turn to ALEC regardless of party or legislative expertise. Figure 3.10 evaluates this idea, using employment in state and local government in each legislator's district as a measure of politicians' reliance on public-sector unions. (More direct measures of public union membership and strength are lacking at the state legislative district level, but employment in public-sector jobs ought to be a good enough approximation of the strength of unions in those districts.) I look at Republicans and Democrats separately, and within each party divide lawmakers into five equally sized groups based on the level of public employment in their districts.

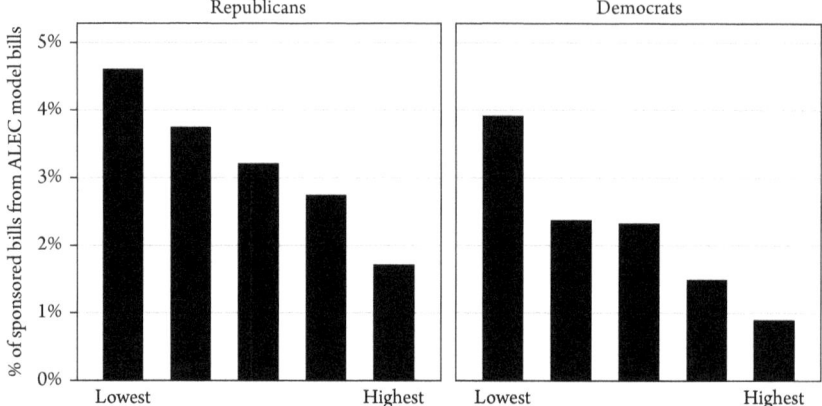

Figure 3.10. PUBLIC EMPLOYEE STRENGTH AND SPONSORSHIP OF ALEC-PLAGIARIZED BILLS, 2003–2013. The proportion of lawmakers' sponsored bills copied from ALEC model bills by the share of employed workers in public administration (divided into quintiles) for Republicans (left panel) and Democrats (right panel). Public administration employment data from the American Community Survey.

Across both parties, we can see a clear relationship between public employee strength and ALEC bill authorship. Politicians who represented more public employees were far less likely to sponsor ALEC-plagiarized bills.[52] Figure 3.10 thus helps us to better understand why some Democrats might feel comfortable turning to ALEC—if they are representing districts without many government employees, there is little threat of blowback for their reliance on ALEC legislation. On the other hand, Figure 3.10 also helps us to understand why some Republicans might be more reluctant to turn to ALEC if they represent a large government employee constituency. In fact, both Democrats and Republicans representing districts with very low levels of public-sector employment were about equally likely to introduce ALEC-copied bills.

This logic explains why North Dakota legislators like Representative Corey Mock and Senator Mac Schneider—two Democratically affiliated members—have introduced multiple ALEC model bills under their names while their Democratic colleagues like Senator Richard Marcellais and Representative Marvin Nelson have not. The explanation cannot be state legislative resources—all four lawmakers have access to roughly the same resources. It cannot be party, either, since they are all Democrats. Instead, it should come as no surprise that government workers account for nine times more of Marcellais' and Nelson's districts than Mock and Schneider's constituents. The costs of attending ALEC meetings and relying on the group's services are thus much lower for Mock and Schneider than for Marcellais and Nelson—and that is exactly what we see in their record of bill authorship.

We can also see the importance of public employee constituencies for legislative demand for ALEC's ideas and services in the 2014 survey data. Looking across the respondents to the 2014 survey of state legislative candidates, I found legislators who indicated that they relied on support from teachers—one of the most politically active public employee constituencies—were substantially less likely to report turning to ALEC for bill ideas and help. (The question text was "Thinking about your run for office this year, were there any groups that were especially important early supporters?" and one of the choices was "Teachers.") Only 6 percent of legislators who said that they relied on teachers for political support had also relied on ALEC, compared to 28 percent of legislators who did not rely on teachers.

Public-sector employees are a well-organized constituency that stands to lose big under ALEC legislation. But what about groups that would benefit from ALEC models? One such set of businesses are those that are involved in emissions-intensive production and extraction—that is, environmentally "dirty" industries. These companies, concentrated especially in mineral and oil discovery, extraction, and refining, as well as manufacturing, are contributing to the process of global warming and climate change by throwing up carbon emissions into the atmosphere.[53] Measures to deal with climate change thus pose potentially significant losses to these companies.[54] Policies to tax carbon emissions, for instance, would fall disproportionately on these dirty industries. Oil and coal production businesses would also suffer if the federal and state governments were to shift to cleaner renewable energy sources, like wind or solar power. Responding to these corporate concerns, ALEC has developed model bills intended to squelch efforts to increase environmental regulation and address climate change—even calling the science behind global warming into doubt.[55]

Given all that extractive resources and manufacturing companies would benefit from ALEC's policies, then, we should expect that lawmakers who count on greater political support from these industries would be more likely to rely on ALEC—even independently of their partisan affiliation or need for legislative capacity. I again measure the political relevance of the extractive resource and manufacturing industries through employment in a legislator's district, under the assumption that when these businesses represent a greater share of a lawmaker's constituency, those businesses will be a more important source of political support.

Figure 3.11 divides Republican and Democratic lawmakers into five equally sized categories of manufacturing and extractive resource

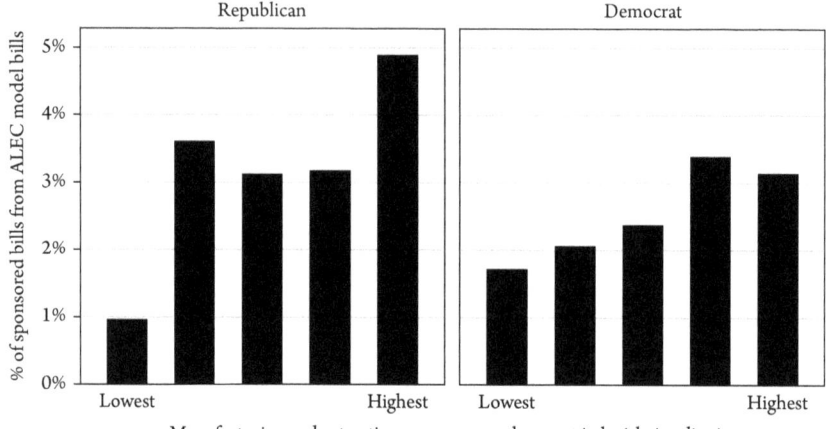

Figure 3.11. MANUFACTURING AND EXTRACTIVE RESOURCES STRENGTH AND SPONSORSHIP OF ALEC-PLAGIARIZED BILLS, 2003–2013. The proportion of lawmakers' sponsored bills copied from ALEC model bills by the share of employed workers in manufacturing and the extractive industries (divided into quintiles) for Republicans (left panel) and Democrats (right panel). Manufacturing and extractive resources employment data from the American Community Survey.

employment, and presents the reverse image of what we saw with government unions. The more a lawmaker depends on these environmentally dirty industries in their constituency, the more likely they are to have drawn on ALEC model bills for their legislation—even independently of their partisan affiliation.[56]

Political support from manufacturers and extractive industries—and the threat of losing that support—can thus explain why Democratic lawmakers like Kathleen Willis, an Illinois state representative who represents a district where one out of every four workers comes from the extractive resources and manufacturing sector, has decided to rely on ALEC model bills, while her Democratic colleague Mark Walker, who represents a district where such employment is much less important, declined to work with the group.

The 2014 survey of state legislative candidates reveals a similar relationship between legislators who perceived a need to appeal to a general business constituency and reliance on ALEC. Thirty percent of legislators who indicated that they relied on early campaign support from businesses turned to ALEC for ideas and research assistance, compared to only 3 percent of legislators who said that business was not one of their early supporters.[57] Legislative experience and resources help to account for ALEC's reach across the states—but so too do partisanship and the organized interests, like business and public employee unions, supporting lawmakers.

What Campaign Contributions Don't Contribute to Our Picture of ALEC

In a report written by Common Cause, a left-leaning watchdog group dedicated to reducing the influence of money in politics, the authors summed up their perspective on how ALEC has been so effective: "Through [campaign contributions], ALEC's corporate leaders help secure a receptive constituency for their legislation.... Common Cause's review suggests that much of the political spending of ALEC's largest corporate backers can be linked to their business interests."[58]

For the authors of that report, the source of ALEC's power in state legislatures was clear: businesses gave generously to state legislative campaigns—nearly $400 million over the past decade—and the money has "reinforced ALEC's issue agenda, spelled out in the group's model bills."[59] John Nichols, a political reporter for *The Nation* who has been tracking ALEC for a number of years, expressed a similar sentiment when talking about why companies participate in ALEC—and why legislators do their bidding—on Bill Moyers' television show *Moyers & Company*: "If you really want to influence the politics of this country you don't just give money to presidential campaigns, you don't just give money to congressional campaign committees. Smart players put their money in states."[60] Beyond Common Cause and Nichols, this conclusion is underscored by countless other political observers and reformers who link corporate campaign contributions to the success of business-friendly legislation at both the state and the federal levels.[61]

If we follow the logic from the Common Cause report and these other observers of state politics, then we ought to expect that ALEC would be more successful in states where businesses gave more money to political candidates. Still, there are reasons to be skeptical about this avenue for influence. We have seen that ALEC's appeal tends to rest on the resources it provides to understaffed and underresourced lawmakers, as well as lawmakers who depend more heavily on business support within their constituencies (and conversely, less support from labor unions, especially in the public sector). None of these pathways directly—or even necessarily—involve campaign contributions.

Turning to the data, Figure 3.12 plots the share of a state's introduced and enacted bills plagiarized from ALEC models along the vertical axis, looking at the entire period from 1996 to 2013. The states are arrayed along the horizontal axis by the extent to which business campaign donations dominate labor contributions, averaging election spending from 1996 to 2013 (the specific measure is total business contributions divided by total labor contributions). I use this ratio to standardize the varying costs of elections by state. Simply

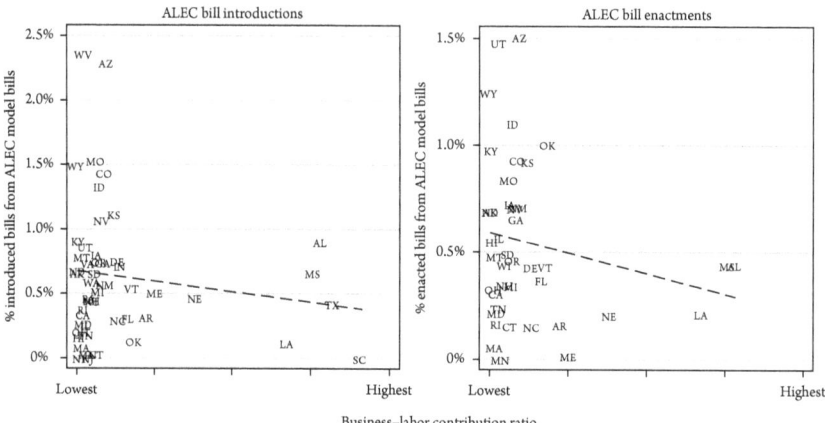

Figure 3.12. CAMPAIGN CONTRIBUTIONS AND ALEC-PLAGIARIZED BILLS, 1996–2013. The relationship between the ratio of business to labor campaign contributions in state elections against the share of introduced (left panel) and enacted (right panel) ALEC model bills. Data averaged across the period from 1996 to 2013. Campaign contribution data from the National Institute on Money in State Politics.

plotting the total amount of campaign spending from businesses would be misleading as it would ignore that state legislative campaigns in New York are substantially more expensive than campaigns in New Hampshire—and so we would expect more contributions from business (as well as all other interest groups) in New York compared to New Hampshire. This measure has the added benefit of getting at the power of business relative to its frequent political opponent—labor—and it also implicitly takes into account varying campaign finance rules across the states.

If ALEC bills were more common in states that were dominated by campaign spending from private-sector businesses, then we ought to expect that there would be a strongly positive relationship between the business–labor contribution ratio and introduced and enacted ALEC bills. Yet this is not what we see in Figure 3.12. If anything, the relationship between the business–labor contribution measure and ALEC bills slopes downward, especially for enacted ALEC bills, indicating that states where business dominates electoral giving rely *less* on ALEC. That might be because businesses facing greater political threats need to spend more on elections and other outward political battles, rather than working behind the scenes through ALEC.[62] It could also reflect the fact that business invests more in electoral spending in states with higher levels of legislative capacity.[63] Either way, there is no evidence that campaign contributions help to explain which states end up introducing or passing more ALEC bills—running directly against the popular perceptions of the organization in the media and among political reformers.

The Limits of Inexperience: Present (and Future) Legislative Leaders in ALEC

We have seen that more inexperienced lawmakers tend to rely on ALEC model bills for a greater proportion of their legislative activity. But it would be a mistake to conclude that ALEC's only mechanism for influence in state legislatures runs through junior backbenchers. More senior leaders in state parties and legislative chambers also play a big role in explaining ALEC's success across the states in several different ways.

To begin with, senior legislative members, especially caucus or chamber leaders, are an important way that ALEC recruits *new* members into the organization. As we saw at the start of the chapter, a common pathway into the group is for senior, well-respected leaders in the legislature to reach out to newly elected members and personally encourage them to try out ALEC membership—perhaps by inviting them to one of ALEC's annual meetings or new member orientations. Indeed, one of Sam Brunelli's key innovations was to recruit state chairs who held leadership positions and thus would be better positioned to build up a broad membership of lawmakers across all states.

Brunelli's recipe for success has continued to the present day. In 2014, for instance, many of ALEC's state chairs held leadership positions as whips, caucus leaders, minority or majority leaders, or floor leaders. And looking at the state legislative candidate survey from the same year, we can see that states where ALEC had installed more well-respected leaders as state chairs were more likely to see higher levels of ALEC reliance. In states where ALEC had no state chairs, only 5 percent of survey respondents reported relying on ALEC; that figure was 14 percent in states where ALEC had one state chair, and 19 percent of legislators in states with two or more chairs. (That relationship holds up even when I control for legislators' ideological orientation, partisanship, and self-reported reliance on business, as I indicate in the regression results provided in the Chapter 3 Appendix.)

Aside from recruitment, ALEC membership among senior legislative leaders matters in setting the agenda for especially ambitious initiatives, like advancing a high-profile ALEC proposal or blocking major legislation ALEC opposes. ALEC's efforts to curb union rights, especially public-sector union rights, offer an instructive example. The two highest-profile instances of ALEC's offensive against public employee unions include Wisconsin (in 2011) and Iowa (in 2017), where legislators pushed bills that stripped many public workers of their rights to collectively bargain with the government while simultaneously making it costlier for those unions to collect revenue and sustain their memberships (we will examine these two battles in much more detail in Chapter 6). In both cases, ALEC could count on strong support from not only legislative backbenchers, but also senior chamber leaders and governors who had longstanding ties to the group.

Before running for governor in 2010, Wisconsin's Scott Walker was an active participant in ALEC and had even sponsored several model bills related to criminal justice, public service privatization, and efforts to curb union rights.[64] In the case of the sentencing reform bill he had championed, Walker was quite open about his reliance on ALEC: "Many of us, myself included, were part of ALEC. . . . Clearly ALEC had proposed model legislation. . . . And probably more important than just the model legislation, [ALEC] had actually put together reports and such that showed the benefits of truth-in-sentencing and showed the successes in other states. And those sorts of statistics were very helpful to us when we pushed it through."[65] In Wisconsin's state senate, the GOP majority leader—Scott Fitzgerald—had previously admitted to being a "proud member of ALEC" since he joined the legislature in 1994 and had also served as a state chair.[66] Like Walker, Fitzgerald has spoken highly of ALEC's ability to disseminate bills across the states, arguing that "[ALEC's] committees crank out what I would consider boilerplate legislation, stuff that's sweeping the nation," allowing lawmakers to "pirate bills from one state that they think is a good idea."[67] Both political ambition and ALEC reliance run in the Fitzgerald family. Fitzgerald's younger brother Jeff served as the speaker of Wisconsin's lower legislative body during the 2011 public employee reform debate and had himself been participating in ALEC since 2001.[68]

A similar story played out in Iowa after the 2016 elections. The state's GOP governor, Terry Branstad, was, in fact, one of the earliest participants in ALEC (as we saw in Chapter 1) and a longtime fan of the group. Again, both the majority leader in the Iowa state senate—Bill Dix—and the speaker of the state's lower chamber—Linda Upmeyer—were longtime members of ALEC, with Upmeyer even serving on ALEC's national board of directors.[69] The constellation of strong gubernatorial and legislative leader support for these ALEC initiatives was crucial in getting them over the finish line, especially given the fierce opposition these measures received from liberal groups—above all, the embattled public employee unions. Had these bills attacking public employee unions only been supported by legislative newbies, it seems unlikely that they would have survived the controversy and backlash they generated. These bills needed support from the full Republican establishment to succeed. As the Milwaukee *Journal Sentinel* summed up, as heads of Walker's legislative push, the Fitzgerald brothers "faced down the crowds that stormed the Capitol during the height of the controversy over Gov. Scott Walker's bid to curb collective bargaining for most public employees" and were ultimately responsible for shepherding "through the Legislature ... bills that may reshape the state for a generation."[70]

Senior and more experienced legislators play a third role beyond new member recruitment and bill passage for ALEC. ALEC is a valuable resource for ambitious state legislators seeking to build a name and statewide profile for themselves for future elections—be it for a state's upper chamber, a governorship, another statewide elected position, or even Congress. ALEC's model bills and legislative resources allow these upwardly minded politicians to position themselves as productive lawmakers with a proven track record of writing (and potentially passing) business-friendly legislation. ALEC's social events and broader network also help politicians build ties with activists and donors within their own state and across the whole country.

It is, of course, in ALEC's interest to nurture the future careers of their most junior lawmakers as well, as it makes the advertising pitch to potential activist, donor, or corporate members all the more appealing. In 1995, for instance, ALEC boasted to potential corporate and activist members that the group counted as members 32 speakers in lower chambers, 25 upper chamber presidents, 34 majority leaders, and 28 minority leaders.[71] Similarly, in a 2000 publication for potential donors, ALEC heavily emphasized that "well over 100 ALEC members hold senior leadership positions in their state legislatures, while hundreds more hold important committee leadership positions," as well as the fact that their alumni network now included 7 sitting governors and more than 80 members of Congress, including chamber leaders like Speaker Dennis Hastert, Majority Whip Tom DeLay, and Assistant Senate Majority Leader Don Nickles.[72] And in 2017, ALEC counted as alumni 7 sitting governors, 72 members of the House of Representatives, and 13 US senators, including senior members like Joe Manchin (West Virginia), Lindsey Graham (South Carolina), Michael Enzi (Wyoming), and Richard Shelby (Alabama).[73]

A defining characteristic of American state legislatures is the great diversity in their capacity to design and implement legislation. Some states, like New York, California, and Pennsylvania, have in recent decades offered their lawmakers large teams of staffers to help with legislative work. Combined with year-round sessions and generous salaries, these conditions allow professional lawmakers to immerse themselves in the substance of policymaking. Other states, like Oregon, Wyoming, Idaho, and Alabama, fall on the opposite end of that spectrum, treating legislative seats as part-time positions with corresponding part-time work schedules, pay, and staff help.

In this chapter, we have seen that these differences across states matter enormously in explaining why some legislatures—and some lawmakers within those states—find ALEC so appealing. It is a relatively simple question of supply and demand: legislators have a demand for ideas, research assistance, and political advice. If the government is not supplying those things directly or giving politicians the time to develop expertise on their own, then lawmakers will look elsewhere—and ALEC has explicitly marketed itself as the private-sector alternative to a lack of public-sector resources.

The irony is that by attempting to make state legislatures more accessible to ordinary citizens by turning those positions into part-time jobs, legislatures like those in Montana or Mississippi have simply outsourced their policy development to the deep-pocketed activists and companies participating in ALEC.[74] Idaho's legislature, for instance, argues that the success of its laws "can be attributed to the fact that Idaho's legislators are 'citizen' legislators, not career politicians. They are farmers and ranchers, business men and women, lawyers, doctors, sales people, loggers, teachers. . . . Idaho's citizen legislators are able to maintain close ties to their communities and a keen interest in the concerns of the electorate."[75]

Yet precisely because of the lack of resources and time that the citizen legislators in Idaho possess compared to their colleagues in more professionalized legislatures, Idahoan lawmakers are turning to interests well outside of their state—national (and multinational) corporations, political activists, and mega-donors—for the very text of their legislation and assistance in passing those model bills. Thus, an important lesson of this chapter is that states cannot expect meagerly funded and poorly staffed legislatures to make policy on their own without outside help.

Legislative resources did not provide the whole story about why lawmakers relied on ALEC, however. We also saw that independently of their staff or expertise, Republican lawmakers were more likely to introduce and enact ALEC bills, especially in more recent years. Lawmakers' interest group constituencies mattered, too. And while more junior legislators were more likely to turn to ALEC for a greater proportion of their authored bills than more experienced legislators, ALEC still relies heavily on senior lawmakers, especially legislative leaders and governors, in promoting its legislative agenda. These leaders help recruit new members, shepherd big initiatives through the legislature, and foster a broader alumni network of ALEC politicians across all levels of government, which the group can then tout to potential activist, donor, or corporate members looking to have an enduring effect on policy across the United States.

Just as relevant as these findings is the *lack* of any relationship between ALEC reliance and campaign contributions. Contrary to all the sound and fury that such electoral giving garners from academics, citizens, and journalists alike— and contrary to the speculation from observers of ALEC in the media—I found that campaign contributions were unrelated to legislators' reliance on ALEC.

As I will explain in more detail in the conclusion to the book, this finding should give money-in-politics reformers pause about prioritizing measures to curb contributions as a way of curtailing business influence in government. My results in this chapter suggest that ALEC—and the corporate interests affiliated with the group—would continue to be successful at inserting their ideas into law even if all fifty states had stricter limits on electoral giving. Trying to squeeze money out of politics as a means of silencing ALEC and its backers is unlikely to have much of an impact for the underresourced lawmakers in Idaho, Wyoming, or Kansas.

A final conclusion implied by this chapter is that investing in ALEC has potentially big payoffs for its affiliated activists, and especially for-profit businesses. But why is it that some companies have realized the potential for that return and joined the group, while other businesses have not?

4

"A Great Investment"

ALEC's Appeal for Big Business

Faced with federal inaction on climate change, a number of state governments have begun to move on their own, passing legislation that encourages the use of clean energy.[1] Two of the most common approaches that states have used are renewable energy portfolio standards (RPS) and net-metering. RPS laws create goals or even mandatory requirements for state utilities to obtain a certain share of their energy from renewable sources, like wind or solar. Net-metering policies take a different approach, and permit energy customers who generate their own power—perhaps through a solar panel on their roof—to feed that electricity back to the power grid. Customers are then only billed for their net energy usage. That means households could receive payments back from utilities if they generate more power than they consume. Together, these two policies have received strong support from both parties, and as of 2017, 29 states had passed RPS requirements and 38 states had put net-metering programs in place.[2]

The popularity of RPS policies goes well beyond state lawmakers. These programs have received strong support from the mass public, and in 2015 a careful survey found that nearly three-fourths of Americans agreed that state governments should "require a set portion of all electricity to come from renewable energy sources such as wind and solar power."[3] That included 82 percent of Democrats and, perhaps surprisingly, even 60 percent of Republicans.[4] Beyond individual citizens, there are a range of renewable energy producers, too, that stand to benefit handsomely from requirements that states buy power from cleaner sources. The American Wind Energy Association, for instance, estimates that through 2025, markets for renewable energy spurred on by RPS policies will drive the development of 153,000 gigawatt-hours of renewable electricity (1 gigawatt-hour represents the energy needed to power perhaps just under a million homes for 1 hour).[5] Of that, 135,300 gigawatt-hours (or about 88 percent) could come from wind—a windfall (if you will) for the members of the Wind Energy Association.[6]

Yet while state RPS and net-metering policies are popular among the public and renewable energy companies, they spell bad news for traditional, fossil-fuel-intensive energy companies. Power bought from renewable energy sources represents lost sales for traditional power generators. Some conventional energy firms, like Shell, have begun investing in clean energy as a hedge on future disruption from climate change reform.[7] But many other oil and coal businesses have not been so willing to depart from their carbon-intensive roots. At a recent shareholder meeting, then–Exxon CEO Rex Tillerson (and later secretary of state for the Trump administration) said that his company wouldn't "fake it" by investing in renewable energy to address climate change. "We choose not to lose money on purpose," Tillerson acerbically quipped to loud applause.[8]

What could traditional energy businesses like Exxon do in response to the mounting renewable energy threat from the states? If the threat to their industry came from Congress, the answer would be straightforward: launch an aggressive lobbying campaign to sway the votes of the handful of pivotal representatives and senators on key committees. (Many of those energy companies had done exactly that during talks over legislation to address climate change in 2009 and 2010.[9]) But given that the threat from renewable energy standards was coming from across the states, rather than Congress, these companies were faced with ninety-nine different legislative bodies, each with their own rules and cultures. Enter ALEC. Instead of establishing their own grassroots presence in each of the states to push for repeal of RPS and net-metering policies, companies could instead join ALEC to push measures to undermine clean energy bills across all fifty states at once. ALEC, as we have seen, could easily promote anti-RPS and net-metering provisions through its system of model bill production and distribution.

This is exactly what fossil fuel–based interests have done over the past few years. Originally sponsored by the Heartland Institute, a fossil fuel–funded State Policy Network (SPN) affiliate, ALEC's energy and environment task force officially turned the "Electricity Freedom Act" into model legislation in October 2012.[10] That bill would repeal any state law that requires utilities to procure energy from renewable sources.[11] According to the bill proposal, "Forcing business, industry, and ratepayers to use renewable energy through a government mandate will increase the cost of doing business and push companies to do business with other states or nations, thereby decreasing American competitiveness."[12] To support the Electricity Freedom Act, ALEC members turned to an analysis published by another SPN affiliate, the Beacon Hill Institute, which claimed to show how renewable energy standards would impose steep costs on state governments and their citizens.[13] In 2015 alone, 26 ALEC-inspired bills to roll back RPS policies were introduced in 18 states (2014 saw 14 such bill introductions; 2013 saw 26).[14] West Virginia became the first state to repeal its renewable energy standards in 2015, shortly after Ohio froze its mandate. Though ALEC's efforts at stopping renewable energy standards have largely been stymied in other states, their anti-RPS legislative blitz continues.[15]

This was not the first time that ALEC helped businesses concerned about environmental regulation to defeat or co-opt potentially onerous state bills. Nearly three decades prior to debates over renewable energy standards, ALEC was drawing attention to the "dangerous legislative trend" of state governments introducing "command and control" strategies for preventing pollution and managing toxic chemicals.[16] A 1989 series of publications written for ALEC's corporate members with a stake in environmental policy decried the "draconian" plan the California Air Resources Board approved to manage smog in southern California.[17] That plan, which ALEC claimed "easily qualifies as the most radical air pollution reduction initiative ever seriously proposed anywhere in the world," would have prohibited the sale and use of certain common consumer goods and called for the use of alternative fuels, better automobile fuel efficiency, and cuts to toxic emissions from industrial and utility plants.[18] ALEC similarly warned about measures in Pennsylvania, Florida, Rhode Island, and South Dakota that would ban certain packaging materials in consumer goods, as well as proposals to require businesses to draft hazardous waste–reduction plans for approval by the state.[19]

ALEC's solution to this onslaught of "dangerous, ill-considered reduction proposals" was to develop a measure of their own to address environmental regulation, drafted by the members of the environmental task force and led by aluminum production giant ALCOA.[20] The bill, dubbed the "Pollution Prevention Act," set up a business-friendly system for regulating the release of toxic chemicals and hazardous waste while minimizing "the regulatory burden imposed upon ... citizens."[21] That model bill was quickly adopted by Georgia, Mississippi, Tennessee, Washington, Louisiana, and Maryland in subsequent legislative sessions.[22] The success of that model bill at staving off more burdensome environmental rules in those states led ALEC to boast at an annual meeting that its members were "instrumental in stopping radical environmental initiatives dead in their tracks."[23]

ALEC's extractive industry-backed offensive against renewable energy standards, and earlier moves to curb regulation of toxic chemicals and emissions releases, offers a cautionary tale to environmental advocates and reformers hoping to turn to the states in an era when the federal government is controlled by politicians wary of regulation. These examples also highlight the deeper dynamics of corporate membership in ALEC that I will explore in this chapter, namely, why companies—especially large, multinational businesses—decide to join forces with conservative activists and wealthy right-wing donors to collaborate on model legislation.

Examining fresh data I have assembled on ALEC's corporate members over the 1990s and 2000s, I show that companies were more likely to join and participate more intensively in ALEC when they faced a greater onslaught of state legislation related to their core business practices. That cross-state regulatory pressure, as we have seen, is exactly the sort of policy threat that ALEC is well positioned to address. When companies either want to stymie potentially arduous regulations or promote bills that open markets and reduce tax burdens, ALEC provides the means of ensuring that corporate managers can shape policy simultaneously and easily across all fifty states. Case studies of two sectors—healthcare and IT—further illustrate these mechanisms in more detail.

In the final section of the chapter, I move from exploring the factors that lead companies to join ALEC to considering the more recent era where the group has had to deal with intense backlash from the media and left-leaning political groups. I flip my original question to ask which businesses were most likely to sever their ties to ALEC given the scrutiny and potential for backlash membership subsequently entailed. By the end of the chapter, then, we will have a much better understanding of what draws companies to the model bills, annual confabs, and task forces that ALEC organizes—and the limits of that appeal in the face of substantial consumer, investor, and public pressure.

"An Invaluable Resource to Businesses Seeking to Prosper in Today's Challenging Public Policy Environment"

Writing in a 1994 proposal to potential corporate members, ALEC pointed out that "many businesses focus their government affairs efforts on Washington, D.C., believing that the only important government action takes place at the national level. This is a flawed strategy."[24] Why should businesses be focused on the states? As ALEC explained it, "The budget woes and the growing institutional political gridlock at the federal level have reduced the influence that the Congress and the White House exert on policy. In contrast, state legislatures," ALEC warned, "have become increasingly activist on a wide range of issues, including environmental regulation, health care, civil and criminal justice, labor, insurance, and tax and fiscal policy." ALEC offered businesses, like those reading the prospectus, the opportunity to develop "model legislation and policies that will set the terms of debate in all 50 state capitals"—"an invaluable resource to businesses seeking to prosper in today's challenging public policy environment."

What kind of companies might find this pitch appealing? I expect that one of the most important factors driving business participation in ALEC will be corporate exposure to the sort of state legislative initiatives that ALEC was describing. That is, the more that companies have to worry about disparate state rules establishing onerous regulations or taxes, the more valuable companies will find ALEC's legislative network.

The specialty chemicals manufacturer FMC Corporation—which makes ingredients needed for agricultural, health, and nutritional products—nicely summed up this motivation for supporting ALEC in a presentation it made to a new crop of state lawmakers who considered joining the group in 1990. The company's chairman and CEO, Robert Malott, described the problems his company faced from state policy initiatives at the time as being twofold.[25]

The first issue was simply getting a handle on the volume of legislation produced by the states that could plausibly affect his business. Which bills were being introduced, which bills had a chance of being enacted, and what would they mean for his company? "FMC's geographical and product diversity, typical of many large companies, magnifies the challenge of tracking state legislation and ascertaining its growing impact on our company and our ability to compete nationally and internationally," Malott described.[26]

But the problem for FMC wasn't just keeping track of these bills—a clear benefit that ALEC could offer to its corporate members. It was also the broader threat of state governments producing a patchwork of regulations on his company that would raise compliance costs for doing business across state lines. As Malott explained, "Growing state activism—or more precisely, the specific form this activism has been taking—creates serious problems for U.S. industry. . . . The proliferation of non-uniform state-by-state legislation . . . could be starting to undermine one of the key competitive advantages of U.S. industry: namely our large, unfragmented domestic market."[27] "By forcing companies to package, label, or configure products differently in different states," Malott summed up, "these laws and regulations significantly reduce economies of scale, increase overhead, and ultimately raise costs to consumers."[28]

You might think that facing down the prospect of fifty different state regulatory regimes would mean that his company would prefer a single national standard from the federal government. Yet Malott was careful to say that he still preferred giving as much power as possible to state legislatures to dictate public policy over his business. That was because in his experience, "state legislators are generally more attuned to economic realities than the legislature in Washington. Both the costs and rewards of a particular course of action tend to be felt more immediately at the state level. State legislators also—like business managers—have the added goal of competition: Most [state legislators] recognize that truly onerous tax or regulatory policies will simply drive employers next door. Finally, legislators in most states must—by constitutional decree—produce a balanced budget."²⁹ States, in Malott's view, were thus more amenable to business in ways that Congress could never be.

The solution that ALEC provided to FMC was therefore the opportunity to ensure that all fifty states—or at least most of them—set the standards preferred by the company when it came to environmental and production regulation. To use the phrase I introduced in Chapter 1, ALEC helped FMC to get the "best of both worlds" from America's federal system. FMC could keep regulatory policy at the state level, where lawmakers were more attuned to the needs of business. Instead of facing a patchwork of different regulations, however, FMC could promote a single standard across the states through ALEC.

Extrapolating beyond FMC, we should expect that other companies facing the prospect of patchwork regulatory threats across the states would be the ones most likely to join ALEC. To test this intuition more systematically, I first assembled a new database of all ALEC-affiliated companies from 1996 to 2013, using the records I compiled of ALEC publications, internal memos, and companies' own disclosures. While this is the most comprehensive list of businesses participating in ALEC of which I am aware, it surely misses out on some corporate members of the group. I have no reason, however, to believe that these companies would be necessarily biased toward having particular characteristics. Still, to address the concern that in some cases I did not know for how long particular companies participated in the group, I looked at any corporate membership in ALEC from 1996 to 2013, rather than participation in any given year.

Identifying corporate ALEC members was not enough, however, as I also needed a group of non-ALEC members to understand the factors that predict ALEC participation. I therefore settled on the list of the 500 largest publicly traded companies over the 1996-to-2013 period.³⁰ I did this for both practical and substantive reasons. Practically, I needed to define the universe of my analysis, and the list—essentially the Fortune 500—makes for a reasonably sized group of companies that represents a population of particular interest—major publicly traded corporations in the United States—with sufficient information about each firm. (Information on privately held companies, unfortunately, is much more limited.)

Substantively, I found the participation of these Fortune 500 companies in ALEC quite interesting, since many of these businesses are so visible to the public, making their involvement all the more puzzling given the potential costs of negative media exposure. These larger companies might also have alternatives to ALEC for dealing with state legislation, like their own in-house lobbyists.

In all, I determined that 25 percent of the companies in my sample of the 500 largest public businesses in the United States from 1996 to 2013 had participated in ALEC in some way over that period. Table 4.1 gives a sense of the distribution of these ALEC participants across the American economy, showing the industries with the highest to the lowest ALEC membership rates (out of sixty-four possible industry classifications). Companies in the transportation, healthcare, food production, energy and resource extraction, and IT industries were especially likely to participate in ALEC, while businesses in the hospitality, construction, and business-services industries were the least likely to do so.

Table 4.1 suggests that the companies most invested in ALEC throughout the 1990s and 2000s were indeed those potentially subjected to more cross-state regulatory threats—like private mail providers, tobacco companies, railroad businesses, and Internet service providers. To gauge companies' exposure to legislation and regulation across the states more rigorously, I searched the database of introduced and enacted legislation from 1996 to 2013 described in Chapters 2 and 3 to look for bills that targeted each industry of the 500 businesses included in my analysis. For each industry, I reported the average number of new bills relating to regulation of companies in that line of work. So, for instance, to track the exposure of Internet service providers to state legislation, I checked each year for state bills with keywords relating to "Internet service provider" and "regulation." States averaged about 193 bills mentioning the regulation of Internet service providers. By comparison, the average company was exposed to only

Table 4.1. **Industries with the Highest and Lowest ALEC Membership Rates, 1996–2013.**[a]

Industry	Membership Rate (%)	Industry	Membership Rate (%)
Advertising/marketing	0	Trucking	50
Apparel	0	Waste management	50
Automotive retailing, services	0	Gas and electric	53
Computer peripherals	0	Health insurance	55
Construction	0	Pharmaceuticals	73
Outsourcing services	0	Prepared food	75
Engineering, construction	0	Internet services	80
Healthcare: Medical facilities	0	Mail	100
Home equipment, furnishings	0	Railroads	100
Hotels and resorts	0	Tobacco	100

[a] Table shows the industries with the highest and lowest membership rates in ALEC; see the text for more details. There are 64 possible industry classifications in total.

about 53 bills from 1996 to 2013. That means Internet service providers had a much greater threat of piecemeal state regulation than did the typical large American company throughout the 1990s and 2000s. (The Chapter 4 Appendix spells out my strategy for coding regulatory threat in more detail.)

Table 4.2 gives a sense of the industries with the highest and lowest state regulatory risks over this period. By far and away the companies most subjected to risk from state government include those involved in petroleum production and processing, and health insurance and managed care providers, which both had well over 1,000 state bills introduced and enacted each year from 1996 to 2013 that would have regulated their operations. On the other side of the table,

Table 4.2. **Industries with the Highest and Lowest State Regulatory Threats, 1996–2013.**[a]

Industry	Average Number of State Bills	Industry	Average Number of State Bills
Household products	0.3	Internet services	193.3
Financial data services	1.7	Telecommunications	231.4
IT services	1.8	Commercial banks	337.7
Publishing	2.1	Diversified financials	339.2
Scientific equipment	2.9	General merchandisers	431.3
Semiconductors	2.9	Energy	621.9
Home furnishings	3.8	Securities	646.8
Industrial machinery	3.9	Beverages	760.2
Wholesalers	4.6	Insurance: Life, mutual	771.7
Other	4.7	Insurance: Life, stock	771.7
Outsourcing services	8.5	Food and drug stores	855.4
Temporary help	8.5	Tobacco	890.3
Advertising/marketing	8.6	Hotels and resorts	929.6
Motor vehicles	9.4	Gas and electric	996.7
Computer equipment	10.7	Petroleum	>1,000
Forest and paper products	12.7	Health insurance and healthcare	>1,000

[a] Table shows the industries with the highest and lowest state regulatory threat, measured as the average number of state bills introduced and enacted from 1996 to 2013 relating to an industry; see the text for more details. There are 64 possible industry classifications in total.

businesses making household products, selling financial data, and involved in information technology consulting tended to be least exposed to state regulatory threats. Both these examples make practical sense: we should expect more potential state regulation related to healthcare and the extractive energy industries than other sectors.

Comparing Tables 4.1 and 4.2, it certainly appears as though companies more heavily exposed to state regulation were more likely to participate in ALEC. But we can assess this question more rigorously by plotting the relationship between the two variables. Figure 4.1 divides the companies in my sample into five equally sized groups based on their exposure to state regulatory risk, and plots the proportion of each group participating in ALEC. The figure shows that companies facing greater regulatory threats from the states were substantially more likely to participate in ALEC than those that did not face such risks. Only about 15 percent of the companies exposed to the lowest state regulatory threats participated in ALEC, compared to nearly 40 percent of the companies in the highest fifth of regulatory exposure. Figure 4.1 thus provides evidence to back up the account from FMC's CEO that companies find ALEC useful for dealing with a slew of piecemeal state regulation that could potentially threaten their ability to do business across state lines.

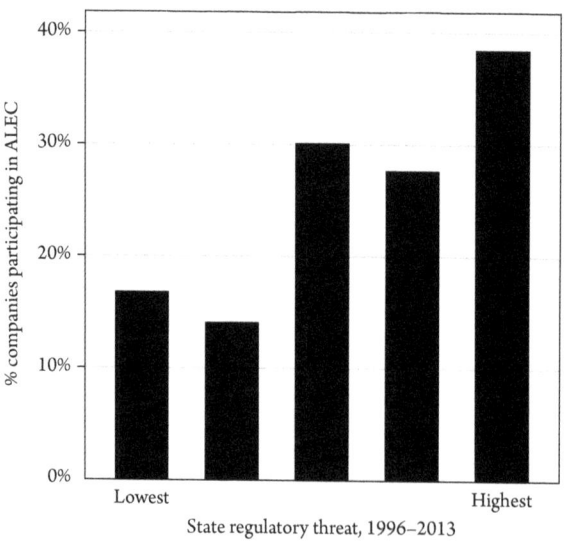

Figure 4.1. STATE REGULATORY THREATS AND CORPORATE PARTICIPATION IN ALEC, 1996–2013. The relationship between a company's exposure to cross-state regulation and participation in ALEC. Companies are divided into five equally sized groups based on state regulatory threat (quintiles). State regulatory threat is measured as the average number of state bills introduced and enacted from 1996 to 2013 relating to an industry (see the text for more details).

Exposure to state regulation is not the only threat that might move companies to join ALEC, however. Companies might also be interested in using ALEC's legislative reach to stymie their competitors. Businesses operating in cutthroat markets might join ALEC to impose onerous regulations on their competitors to drive them out of business. Similarly, incumbent companies in heavily consolidated markets might use ALEC to erect barriers to entry in their industries. Despite ALEC's professed enthusiasm for the free market, it has at times supported both kinds of policies (as in the case of the telecommunications sector).[31]

Given these examples, we might thus expect to see a U-shaped relationship between the degree of competition in a particular industry and corporate participation in ALEC: at very low levels of competition—where one or two businesses control an entire industry—we might expect that companies would try to use model legislation to keep out new entrants. At very high levels of competition, on the other hand, we would also expect to see these sorts of tactics deployed to rid the market of competitors. To measure the competitive pressure felt by businesses, I rely on a standard measure called the Herfindahl–Hirschman index. The index is scaled to range from 0 to 1, where greater numbers indicate a higher degree of market concentration.[32] Figure 4.2 plots the degree of market concentration faced by each company in my

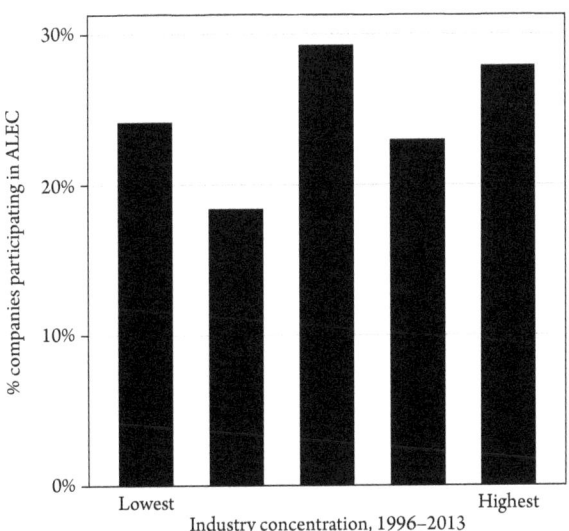

Figure 4.2. MARKET COMPETITION AND CORPORATE PARTICIPATION IN ALEC, 1996–2013. The relationship between a company's exposure to industrial concentration and participation in ALEC. Companies are divided into five equally sized groups based on industrial concentration (quintiles). Industrial concentration measured with the Herfindahl–Hirschman index, using data from Compustat.

sample, divided into five equally sized groups, along with the proportion of companies in each group participating in ALEC. In contrast to the results for state regulatory threats, Figure 4.2 does not show much of a relationship one way or another. There is no evidence of a clear positive or negative relationship between market concentration and ALEC participation, nor much evidence of a U-shaped relationship.

This means we are one for two when it comes to threats motivating corporate participation in ALEC: state regulatory threats seem to motivate participation, while threats of market competition do not. A third and final relevant threat for businesses to consider when contemplating an ALEC membership involves labor unions. While the labor movement's overall position in the national economy is quite weak, there are still some sectors where labor commands a formidable presence. In 2016, for instance, about 25 percent of utility workers were members of a union, as were 25 percent of transportation and warehousing workers (contrast those figures with the 6.4 percent membership rate across all private-sector workers).[33] Businesses in those industries, then, have to face the prospects of collective bargaining and pressure from labor leaders to raise employee wages, benefits, and working standards. The costs associated with such labor activity may thus lead companies to seek legislative provisions that would weaken labor unions.

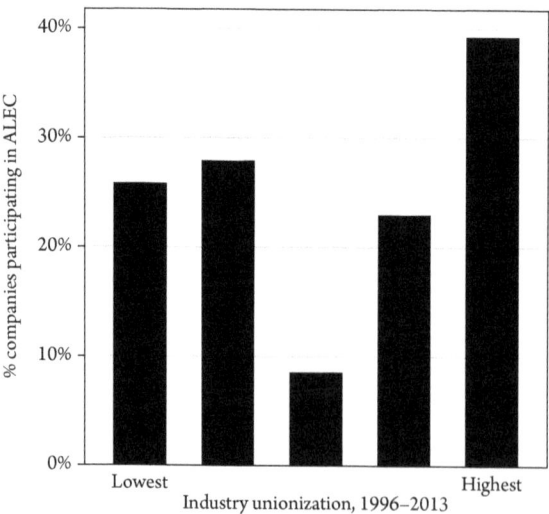

Figure 4.3. INDUSTRIAL UNION MEMBERSHIP AND CORPORATE PARTICIPATION IN ALEC, 1996–2013. The relationship between a company's exposure to unionization at the industry level and participation in ALEC. Companies are divided into five equally sized groups based on industrial union membership (quintiles). Union density from UnionStats.

Figure 4.3 examines the evidence for this prediction, plotting out the average level of union membership in a company's industry from 1996 to 2013 against corporate participation in ALEC, again dividing companies into five equally sized groups. Unlike with industrial market competition, we can see somewhat of a U-shaped pattern of ALEC membership—with companies in weakly unionized and strongly unionized industries much more likely than companies in the middle to participate in ALEC. This plot thus gives us some evidence suggesting that ALEC is appealing to companies hoping to either continue holding the line against unions (as in the retail sector) or to erode what few union strongholds remain (as in the transportation, utilities, warehousing, and communications sectors).

The explanations for ALEC membership I have explored so far have centered on businesses' motivations for joining the group. But corporate resources should matter, too. Participating in ALEC is costly and requires companies to make an investment of capital (in the form of membership dues and in-kind donations), as well as staff time and expertise. To take full advantage of ALEC, companies need to send representatives from their government affairs or communications teams to regular task force meetings, attend and sponsor the annual convenings, and draft model bills. All this should be easier for larger companies than smaller companies.

The idea that larger companies should be better-situated than smaller companies to engage in politics is not new. A long line of scholars of corporate political activity have argued persuasively that larger companies will have more money, time, expertise to contribute to political activities.[34] Consistent with this idea, bigger companies are more likely to hire lobbyists, to spend more on those lobbyists, and to have political action committees making generous contributions to candidates. Do we see a similar relationship for business participation in ALEC?

Figure 4.4 assesses this question by plotting ALEC participation against company size.[35] I have divided companies by their revenue (averaged from 1996 to 2013) into five equally sized groups. We see a striking positive relationship: larger companies were substantially more likely to participate in ALEC than were smaller companies—even among the subset of the 500 largest companies operating in the United States over the 1990s and 2000s. Corporate membership in ALEC remains below 20 percent for the first three quintiles of corporate revenue, jumping to 27 percent for the fourth-largest group of companies and 55 percent for the very largest companies. Larger companies, then, were plainly more likely to participate in ALEC as compared to smaller businesses, consistent with the idea that these bigger companies can afford to spend more to sponsor ALEC's swanky social gatherings, sit on ALEC's expensive task forces, and subsidize the participation of state legislators and their families in ALEC conferences.

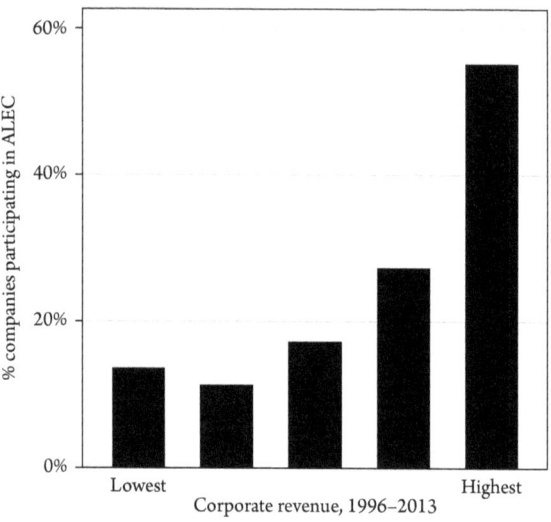

Figure 4.4. COMPANY REVENUE AND CORPORATE PARTICIPATION IN ALEC, 1996–2013. The relationship between a company's revenue and participation in ALEC. Companies are divided into five equally sized groups based on average revenue from 1996 to 2013 (quintiles), using data from Compustat.

The final explanation for corporate participation in ALEC that I examine relates to companies' existing involvement in politics. As past research on corporate political engagement has indicated, companies, like individuals, are more likely to engage in political activities if they have had prior experience in politics.[36] Businesses are more likely to establish a political action committee if they already have a government affairs office, and they are more likely to give contributions if they are already participating in business associations. Another reason why businesses engaging in other forms of national political participation might find groups like ALEC appealing is that ALEC deals with state politics, something that other national associations do not. Thus, managers could view engagement in ALEC as a valuable complement to their existing activities at the national level. Following this explanation, we would expect that businesses with greater exposure to national politics—for instance, greater involvement in other national political associations or experience with federal lobbying and electoral contributions—will be more likely to join ALEC. And there could be network learning effects, too. Through participation in another association—like the US Chamber of Commerce—corporate managers could learn about ALEC and its potential benefits for their businesses.

The left panel of Figure 4.5 assesses the relationship between corporate political giving—measured as the sum of a company's spending on federal lobbying and campaign contributions divided by a company's revenue—and

ALEC membership.[37] The right plot of Figure 4.5 looks at the relationship between a company's involvement in the US Chamber of Commerce, the National Association of Manufacturers, and the Business Roundtable from 1996 to 2013, seeing if a company that sits on the boards of directors of these three associations was more or less likely to participate in ALEC.[38] In both cases, we see that companies that were more involved in national politics—whether by donating more to congressional or presidential candidates or participating in other national business associations—were substantially more likely to participate in ALEC, too. There is no evidence, then, that ALEC is a substitute for these other forms of corporate political participation—and strong evidence that ALEC is a complement to such political activities.

Methodologically oriented readers should note that the relationships I have identified in Figures 4.1 through 4.5 are generally consistent when estimating regression models that control for the full set of potential corporate characteristics (see the Chapter 4 Appendix for these results).[39] Larger companies, companies facing greater cross-state regulatory threats (but not national regulatory threats), and more politically active businesses were all more likely to participate in ALEC. (Union strength, however, is not consistently related to ALEC membership.)

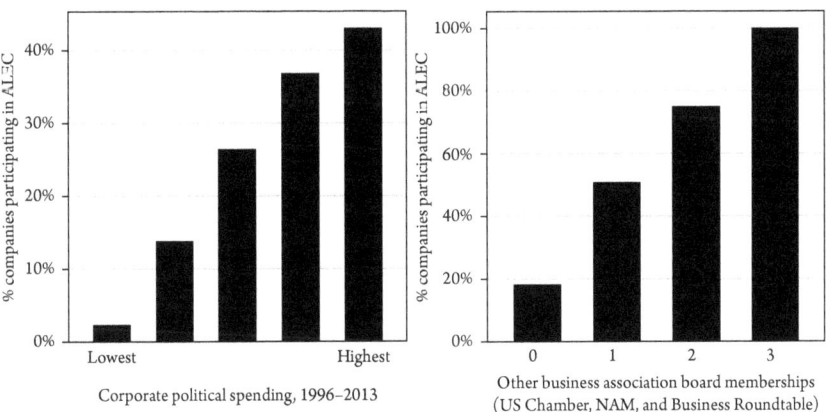

Figure 4.5. OTHER POLITICAL ACTIVITY AND CORPORATE PARTICIPATION IN ALEC, 1996–2013. The relationship between a company's political spending (federal campaign contributions and lobbying spending as a share of corporate revenue) and participation in ALEC (left panel) and a company's participation in other business associations and participation in ALEC (right panel). Companies are divided into five equally sized groups based on average political spending from 1996 to 2013 (quintiles) in the left panel and by the count of other business association participation in the right panel. Corporate political spending data from the Center for Responsive Politics; business association board membership from IRS tax filings.

Examining the Policy Threat Explanation in Two Industries

We have seen the broad relationship between threats from government, especially state government, and corporate decisions to participate in ALEC. But how has this relationship played out in practice? To illustrate these mechanisms in more detail, I turn to two examples from very different industries that show how common policy threats spurred businesses to join ALEC. In the first example, we will see how ALEC has helped companies fend off potentially costly regulations, using cross-state advocacy to pressure the federal government into dropping unwanted legislation, while the second example shows how ALEC can address a wave of new, onerous taxes with the potential to spread across the states.

Health Insurers, Pharmaceutical Manufacturers, and the Clinton Health Reform Plan

In some ways, the health insurance and pharmaceutical manufacturing sectors offer the clearest example of the policy threat argument. Much more than other sectors, health insurers face considerable regulatory pressure at the state level, as states have historically set rules on the benefits insurers must provide, the rates insurers can charge, and the populations insurers must cover. Similarly, pharmaceutical manufacturers must deal with a heavily regulated process for developing and selling their products to the public. As a result, these are two of the most politically active industries in both state and federal politics.

The fierce battle that ALEC waged on behalf of the insurance industry and pharmaceutical manufacturers against major federal health reform under the Clinton administration provides an excellent case study of the ways that these two sectors found a comparative advantage working with ALEC to advance their policy interests. The battle over health reform in the 1990s also nicely illustrates the different strategies that ALEC could offer to business. In this case, ALEC not only helped companies to promote business-friendly standardization of policy across the states, but also leveraged its cross-state network of lawmakers to help pressure Congress into dropping legislation threatening the health-services sector. In this way, the healthcare case study shows not only how ALEC can promote policy change across the states, but also how the group can use the states as battlegrounds to shape congressional policymaking from the bottom up.

Many insurers and pharmaceutical companies had added ALEC to their arsenal of lobbying tools during the group's early battles over state tort reform and corporate liability laws in the late 1980s, discussed in Chapter 1.[40] Just a few years later, it became clear that a major overhaul of the healthcare system was on the horizon—and ALEC helped to organize the corporate response. Healthcare was a big issue during the 1992 presidential primaries, and continued to be hotly debated throughout the ultimately successful campaign of Democratic candidate Bill Clinton.[41]

In response, ALEC's healthcare task force, which had now grown to include forty-one private-sector members, assembled a report intended to stake out the group's principles for health reform to rebut any forthcoming measures from the incoming Clinton administration.[42] Insurers and pharmaceutical companies had every reason to be concerned about the impact of legislative action, as their industries were the prime targets for Democrats deploring the rapidly growing ranks of uninsured and underinsured Americans who could not afford quality health coverage. These worries affected not only the poor, but increasingly the middle class as well, who were discovering that their expensive plans did not adequately protect them against the risks of large and unexpected health costs. Two public opinion analysts found at the time that some 60 percent of Americans worried that they would not be adequately insured in the future.[43]

Given their stake in the healthcare battle, insurers and pharmaceutical manufacturers were well represented in ALEC's group authoring the report on health reform.[44] Twenty out of the 41 private-sector representatives on the task force came from pharmaceutical firms, including large companies such as Hoffmann-LaRoche, Schering-Plough, Merck, Burroughs-Wellcome, and Glaxo, and pharmaceutical trade groups like the Nonprescription Drug Manufacturers Association and the powerhouse Pharmaceutical Research and Manufacturers of America (or PhRMA). Nine other members were insurers, including the industry's main trade group and major companies such as Humana and Golden Rule. Published 15 months later in January 1993, this panel's report provided business-friendly options for state legislatures that would create "accessibility and affordability for all Americans" by "instilling competitive incentives into the health care marketplace."[45]

Unsurprisingly, the model bills outlined in ALEC's 142-page report hewed strongly to the interests of the companies represented on the task force's private-sector panel. To improve the affordability of health insurance, the report recommended providing "stripped down, bare bones health insurance" to individuals and businesses that could not afford more comprehensive plans.[46] It also called for a review of benefits that states required insurers to provide by law, such as maternity coverage, as well as limits to the oversight that states had over insurance premium rate hikes.[47] States were further encouraged to provide tax credits for individuals to purchase plans directly from insurers, and to spur the creation of medical savings accounts. Such accounts were a big priority for

Golden Rule Insurance, an ALEC member that was championing their spread across the country.[48] Together, these measures represented a very stark divergence from even the more centrist managed-competition plans under discussion in the Clinton administration. Nevertheless, state lawmakers took up the report in earnest, and in 1993 over 100 of ALEC's health care proposals were introduced across the states and 17 were eventually enacted into law, providing a clear victory for the insurers and pharmaceutical firms that had helped author the report.[49]

The publication of this document also helped to establish ALEC as a player in the burgeoning health reform debate, and was even enough to help get the group invited to a briefing at the Clinton White House with the president, the first lady, the treasury secretary, and the administration's top healthcare staffer to discuss the health reform proposal the Clintons were drafting.[50] But while the report that ALEC developed had provided a path forward for business-friendly health reform in the states, it did not directly undermine the advancing Clinton proposal, which itself still posed a major risk for the insurance and pharmaceutical sectors.

As a result, ALEC's task force on health reform redoubled its efforts throughout 1993 to come up with a state resolution that would oppose a key funding provision of the forthcoming Clinton health reform plan, which ALEC viewed as being a crucial liability of the proposal.[51] ALEC had calculated that it could effectively draw attention to the increase in the tobacco excise taxes that the Clintons were proposing to pay for their reform. Focusing on this component of the legislation also had the added bonus of attracting support from the tobacco industry, which was understandably worried about the proposed tax hike.[52]

ALEC's plan was to encourage its state lawmakers to pass a resolution against the healthcare financing mechanism, using it as an opportunity for state legislatures to signal their disapproval of the broader Clinton proposal. That in turn, ALEC hoped, would put pressure on Congress to vote against an eventual health reform bill and could also be used to rally other important actors to ALEC's efforts.[53] The timing of state resolutions, ALEC leaders stressed, ought to be "contemporaneous with or just prior to release of the Hillary Clinton-led Health Care Task Force Reform report."[54]

Later that year, ALEC made the Clinton health plan a centerpiece of its annual meeting, holding a session for state lawmakers on the "Federal Health Care Debate and Its Effects on the States," which discussed the negative "direct effects a 'Clinton style' health care plan would have."[55] In a sign of how seriously ALEC was taking this debate, the panel included ALEC's own executive director at the time, Sam Brunelli, as well as the chair of the ALEC healthcare task force, conservative Arizona Representative Jon Kyl, and Dr. John Goodman, a health policy expert from one of Texas' SPN think tank affiliates.[56] Other sessions also touched on how state lawmakers could push back against the reform effort. They included a keynote panel from Representative Kyl, a workshop organized by the president of the pharmaceutical manufacturers association, and a panel of states that had enacted their own, more business-friendly versions of health reform with ALEC models.[57]

ALEC's model bill proposals and sessions at its annual meetings decrying the Clintons' health reform initiative were surely important in fostering opposition to the measure among their members. But another significant way that ALEC helped to stymie the health reform bill occurred once the legislation was under consideration by Congress in 1994. At that point, ALEC commissioned two university-based researchers to author a study that would document the costs of the legislation. The eventual report, *Concealed Costs*, used a series of questionable assumptions and methods to estimate that the Clintons' Health Security Act would result in massive declines in personal income, state and local revenue, and employment.[58]

Importantly, the report included state-by-state estimates of each of these losses, which permitted ALEC to partner with a number of other conservative advocacy groups to hold local town halls and briefings in state capitols across the country. At these events, ALEC would have its legislative members, often paired with a US representative or senator, discuss the findings of the *Concealed Costs* report for their own state, emphasizing the reasons why the Clinton plan needed to be defeated. One of the most frequent partners for these events was Citizens for a Sound Economy (CSE), a conservative grassroots advocacy group cofounded and funded by Charles and David Koch (and the precursor to Americans for Prosperity or AFP—more on these groups in the next chapter). CSE counted some 250,000 citizens as grassroots members, and recruited them in their blitz against the Health Security Act.[59]

A local Oklahoma newspaper provided a typical description of how CSE and ALEC worked together in one of these joint events.[60] ALEC sponsored a forum in Oklahoma City, timed to coincide with a visit from First Lady Hillary Clinton to discuss the administration's reform proposal. Two prominent Oklahoma politicians—US Senator Don Nickles (a former ALEC member) and State Representative Mary Fallin (a current ALEC member)—held a press conference in which they released a state version of ALEC's study on the Clinton plan.[61] An op-ed based on the report was timed to be released in a state newspaper that week.[62] Shortly after ALEC's legislative briefing ended, CSE then organized a protest on the steps of the Capitol with many of its 4,000 Oklahoma members present.[63]

Similar joint ALEC–CSE events were convened in many other states with key congressional votes for the Clintons' Health Security Act, including Illinois,

Louisiana, Texas, and Minnesota.[64] ALEC bragged that their forums had caught liberals so much by surprise that it was not until well into 1994 that pro-reform groups managed to start organizing counterprotests at ALEC events.[65] All that mobilization ultimately paid off, putting grassroots pressure on members of Congress from both parties and forcing politicians to acknowledge the appearance of swelling opposition to the health reform bill.[66]

It is hard to parse out just how much of an effect ALEC's individual efforts had on the demise of the Clinton health reform bill, itself an overdetermined outcome.[67] Still, there is some evidence to suggest that ALEC's role was significant. According to Senator Paul Coverdell, a Republican who led the charge against the Health Security Act in Congress: "Of the various private-sector groups I worked with in opposing the Clinton Health Care Reform plan, ALEC had the most impact."[68] And regardless of its contribution to the overall failure of the Clintons' health reform, ALEC certainly provided a crucial mechanism through which the health insurance and pharmaceutical industries could defend their interests against the threat of federal regulation. ALEC was, in the words of its leader at the time, indeed a great investment for health insurers and pharmaceutical manufacturers alike.[69]

Online Retailers and Internet Sales Taxes

Health insurance and pharmaceutical manufacturing are two industries that have historically leaned strongly to the right. The insurance industry has given nearly twice as much in direct federal campaign contributions to the GOP than to Democrats from 1990 to 2016, and the breakdown for pharmaceutical firms is about the same.[70] As a result, it might not come as a surprise that these firms have worked with ALEC in the past.

But what about more traditionally liberal-leaning industries? Have businesses in these sectors also worked with ALEC in response to policy threats? Here, the technology sector provides a useful example. Much more strongly identified with the left, especially on social issues, high-tech firms like eBay, Amazon, and Microsoft have tilted heavily toward the Democrats in their federal giving from 1990 to 2016 by over a two-to-one margin.[71] In addition, tech-sector leaders have tended to be much more supportive of efforts to address issues increasingly identified with the Democrats, such as climate change and immigration reform.[72] Yet despite the liberal tendencies of these companies' executives, when push comes to shove on key policies that threatened the high-tech sector's core interests, these firms have joined ALEC to protect their bottom lines.

The taxation of out-of-state Internet sales proved to be one such area that posed a major threat to the profits of online retail giants like Amazon, eBay, and Overstock.com. A 1992 Supreme Court ruling, *Quill v. North Dakota*, established that states and localities could only require businesses to collect sales taxes if that retailer had a "physical nexus"—a legal concept referring to a physical presence—within the taxing state.[73] Mailing products to customers from another state—like Amazon did—wasn't enough to qualify. The *Quill* decision thus effectively exempted sales made online from the reach of most state and local taxes. (Though customers are legally required to file taxes with their state on these out-of-state purchases, few actually do in practice.)

This arrangement suited online retailers just fine, since it gave customers a good reason to prefer online stores over their brick-and-mortar counterparts. Although the electronic commerce giant Amazon has repeatedly denied that it benefits from low or nonexistent state sales taxes on its products, other corporate documents suggest otherwise. When describing why he located Amazon in Washington state, as opposed to California or New York, founder Jeff Bezos had an easy answer: "It had to be in a small state. In the mail-order business, you have to charge sales tax to customers who live in any state where you have a business presence. It made no sense for us to be in California or New York."[74] Similarly, in Amazon's filings with the Securities and Exchange Commission, the company more directly acknowledged the degree to which it depends on states and localities not taxing its products, writing that "a successful assertion by one or more states . . . that we should collect sales or other taxes on the sale of merchandise or services could . . . decrease our ability to compete with traditional retailers and otherwise harm our business."[75]

What was good for Amazon and its fellow Internet retailers, however, was bad for state budgets. By failing to tax the sale of these goods and services, state and local governments were losing out on a large and growing base of potential revenue. One estimate, from the National Conference of State Legislatures, was that states lost around $23 billion annually from untaxed out-of-state Internet sales.[76] A separate estimate from a *Forbes* journalist was that just shy of nine out of ten Americans lived in a state that charged a sales tax Amazon did not collect.[77]

Facing mounting losses in sales tax revenue, some lawmakers from cash-strapped states got creative about satisfying *Quill*'s requirement to capture Internet sales. In 2008, New York's legislature passed AB 9807, which expanded the state's definition of taxable vendors to include out-of-state retailers that paid sales commissions for website ad referrals by New York residents.[78] In essence, New York was claiming the right to collect sales taxes from online retailers that used so-called associate programs to advertise for the retail store on the websites of third-party individuals. Amazon had one of the largest associate programs at the time, with over 2 million participating affiliates who linked back to Amazon on their personal websites in exchange for commissions when users clicked on Amazon's ads.[79] Given that some of those Amazon affiliates lived in New York, the new law would require Amazon to collect sales tax on all purchases made by the state's residents.

Amazon and Overstock.com immediately sued New York, claiming that it had violated the *Quill* decision.[80] With a deep bench of Internet retailers on its communications and technology task force, ALEC came out strongly against the New York law, filing a friend of the court brief on behalf of Amazon and Overstock.[81] ALEC also issued publications decrying the measure that it distributed to its members, arguing that "New York's new sales and use tax law is plagued by serious constitutional problems. Most significantly, AB 9807 improperly usurps the power of Congress to regulate interstate commerce," perhaps an ironic argument for a group that prefers state over federal authority.[82] Ultimately, the expanded New York tax law was upheld in the state's highest court. The US Supreme Court then declined to hear the appeal, effectively ending the legal challenge.[83]

Recognizing that their tax advantage was at risk as other states could follow New York's lead, the trio of Amazon, Overstock, and eBay turned to ALEC once again to squelch additional legislative proposals. The timing of the New York ruling was not good for Amazon and its allies. The decision came as many states were scrambling to fill budget holes created by the Great Recession, and any low-hanging revenue—including Internet sales taxes—seemed very appealing. By 2010, two other states had adopted their own versions of the New York Amazon law, and a dozen others were weighing proposals to do the same.[84]

With ALEC's backing, three states—Virginia, Texas, and Iowa—had taken action to protect their in-state businesses from out-of-state sales taxation based on an ALEC model bill developed by the communications and technology task force.[85] ALEC promoted that measure as a solution for state lawmakers to preempt any further taxation of online sales, and at its 2010 communication and technology task force meeting, online retailers like eBay strategized with state lawmakers and conservative activists to discuss "how to mobilize grass roots opposition to new state sales taxes being imposed on online ad referrals by in-state affiliates."[86] The following year, Amazon was a headline sponsor of ALEC's annual meeting, which included extensive discussion of the Internet sales tax issue as part of the communications and technology task force and a special working group on "21st Century Commerce and Taxation," including a legal workshop on "Leveling the Playing Field on Sales Tax Collection: State Efforts to Further Define Physical Nexus."[87] Sales tax issues continued to dominate the task force's activities throughout the following year, and ALEC has been successful in staving off further state action for several years.[88]

The example of the online retail industry further solidifies the logic that ALEC is the place for major businesses to go when faced with a potential policy threat across the states. As the CEO of Overstock.com explained to the Center for Media and Democracy when asked about their membership in the group, "Our association concerned a state sales tax issue, and we joined to allow better contact with state legislatures on our issue. . . . [I]t's necessary for us to communicate with policy makers involved in deliberations over future legislative actions on the subject."[89] In a similar vein, eBay responded to the same question by saying that they "only work with ALEC on one area and that is to support small businesses and help to protect them from threats including unfair tax legislation and state and local legislative issues."[90] Policy risks meant that these businesses had no other choice but to work with ALEC. But what happens when companies face cross-pressures between their desire to shape policy through ALEC and investor and consumer backlash for that very membership?

"Should I Stay or Should I Go?"

As we saw in Chapter 1, a confluence of events led to increased scrutiny and backlash to ALEC starting in 2012 and only accelerated over the next few years. The Trayvon Martin shooting drew attention to the group's promotion of expansive gun laws, and consumers, investors, politicians, and pundits began calling on companies to sever their ties to ALEC. What explains why some companies—like Walmart and Visa—decided to jump ship and leave ALEC, while others, like railroad company CSX and oil giant ExxonMobil, did not?

We can answer this question using the same set of companies I used for the earlier analysis. This time, however, the outcome is not whether one of the 500 largest companies in the United States *joined* ALEC, but whether an ALEC member *left* the group following the media firestorm. In all, about 28 percent of companies that had been participating in ALEC left the group, according to ALEC's own internal records. To compile the list of leavers, I rely on a leaked document from ALEC's 2013 board of directors meeting, in which the directors reviewed the companies that had left the group in the wake of the controversy.[91] I also add to the list companies that released public statements in 2012 and 2013 announcing that they had cut ties with the group. I consider all the same explanations for joining ALEC now for leaving the group, with two important additions: I add the exposure of businesses to consumer markets, as well as whether a company was at least partially owned by a public employee retirement fund.

Consider first whether businesses were exposed to consumer markets. The difference between Safeway and Johnson Controls makes for an instructive comparison. Both are large Fortune 500 companies yet have very different exposure to everyday, individual shoppers. Safeway, a national chain of supermarkets, depends on sales to ordinary Americans through its stores. In contrast, Johnson

Controls has much less exposure to individual consumers, since its goods and services are generally bought by other companies (among other activities, Johnson makes parts for automobiles to sell to car manufacturers). I expect that facing similar controversy in the media, consumer-oriented firms will be more likely to change their political behavior than non-consumer-oriented firms.[92] This is because the former will be more concerned about public protests and boycotts that could harm their bottom lines.

To gauge this factor, I coded each industry according to whether that industry was primarily engaged in direct sales to mass consumers, as opposed to sales to other companies.[93] I coded 42 percent of my sample of 500 companies as being primarily consumer-facing. Some examples of these consumer-facing industries included airlines (e.g., United Airlines), apparel manufacturers (e.g., Nike), and automobile manufacturers (e.g., Ford).

Were the consumer-facing companies more likely to leave ALEC as I expected? The evidence strongly bears out this expectation. Of the existing ALEC members, 41 percent that were in primarily consumer-facing industries ended up dropping their membership after the scandal broke, compared to only 13 percent of businesses that did not sell their products and services on a mass market. In other words, consumer-facing companies were more than three times more likely to leave ALEC than non-consumer-facing businesses.

The other new characteristic I consider is whether companies were owned by public employee pension funds. It may seem strange to focus on the retirement savings of government workers, like teachers and city sanitation engineers. Yet, over recent decades, the funds holding these pensions have become among the most important investors in the corporate marketplace. Out of the 200 largest pension plans in the United States, around two-thirds of total assets are held in plans for government employees.[94] What makes these public employee retirement funds especially important investors is that they are increasingly attempting to use their ownership of major companies to boost political disclosure of potentially controversial corporate political activities, including participation in ALEC.

For instance, AFSCME, a major public employee union, teamed up with an investment consultancy to pressure institutional investors—especially public retirement funds—to push companies to reveal and sever their ties to the US Chamber of Commerce and ALEC.[95] Describing their campaign, AFSCME wrote that it made good business sense for institutional investors to consider corporate political spending as a criterion for investment, explaining that "corporate reputation is an important component of shareholder value, and controversial lobbying activity can pose significant reputational risk."[96]

Did pressure from AFSCME and other institutional investors make a difference in forcing companies to cut their ties to ALEC? To gauge whether this investor-side pressure might have been responsible for pushing businesses out of the group, I examined whether any of the 500 companies in my sample were held by public employee retirement funds from 1996 to 2013.[97] The evidence strongly bears out the idea that public employee–held companies were much more likely to drop their ALEC ties compared to companies that were never held by government worker retirement funds. Twenty-seven percent of nonpublic employee fund–owned companies left ALEC, while 43 percent of the companies held by public employee funds ended up cutting off their membership.

What about the other factors that I explored earlier? Most of the characteristics that help to account for why companies joined ALEC in the first place fare poorly when assessing why companies left the group. Neither state nor national regulatory exposure seemed to matter much; companies facing many more pieces of potential state or federal legislation challenging their operations were just as likely to leave as companies that faced less regulation. Market threats were similarly unhelpful: companies were equally likely to leave ALEC regardless of whether they operated in highly concentrated or competitive markets. And unionization was only able to explain a little of the variation across companies in staying or leaving ALEC.

One factor, however, consistently stands out as being the other best explanation for ALEC departures aside from exposure to consumer and investor backlash: companies' other forms of political engagement. Companies that were already more involved in politics, either through leadership positions on the boards of major business associations or through campaign contributions and lobbying, were much less likely to leave ALEC compared to companies that were less politically experienced.

Figure 4.6 plots the proportion of corporate ALEC members leaving the group by company participation on the boards of directors of the National Association of Manufacturers, the Business Roundtable, and the US Chamber of Commerce (left-hand plot) and by spending on lobbying and electoral contributions over the 1990s and 2000s (right-hand plot). As the left-hand plot indicates, businesses that were not participating in other national business groups beyond ALEC were more than twice as likely as those companies serving in leadership roles to sever their ties to ALEC when faced with public backlash. The right-hand plot shows a similar story for political spending. Although not a perfectly one-to-one relationship, we can see that companies were generally less likely to leave ALEC if they were spending more on elections and lobbying in national politics.

Given that highly regulated companies were no more likely to leave ALEC compared to less regulated companies, it does not seem to be the case that these more politically involved companies maintained their membership in

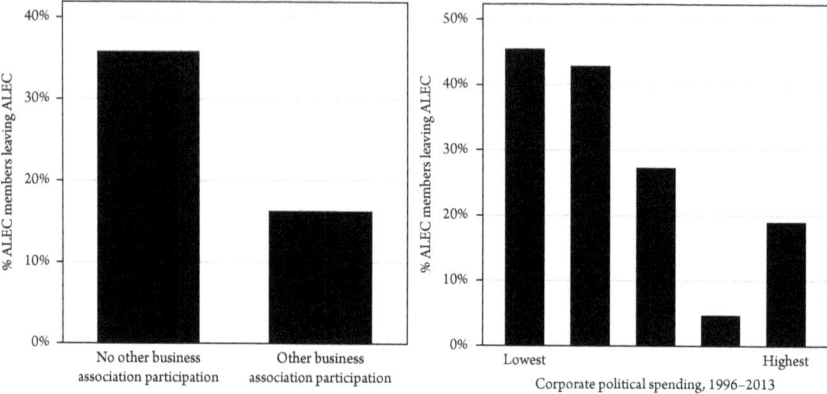

Figure 4.6. POLITICAL ACTIVITY AND CORPORATE DEPARTURES FROM ALEC, 2013. This figure only includes companies that were ALEC members going into 2011; it shows the relationship between any other business association participation and leaving ALEC (left panel) and corporate political spending and leaving ALEC (right panel). Companies are divided between those that had any other business association participation and those that did not (left panel), and then into five equally sized groups based on corporate political spending based on ALEC members (quintiles). Corporate political spending is the sum of federal campaign contributions and spending on lobbying as a proportion of corporate revenue, averaged over 1996 to 2013. Corporate political spending data from the Center for Responsive Politics; business association board membership from IRS tax filings.

ALEC because they were invested in particular policy battles in the states. Instead, a much more likely explanation rests with companies' levels of comfort and experience dealing with political controversies. As political scientist Lee Drutman has argued persuasively, corporate political engagement tends to be self-reinforcing and hard to change.[98] Once companies start to participate in politics, they rarely ramp down their involvement. The reason is relatively straightforward: after a company hires a team of government affairs and public policy experts, those employees have a strong incentive to keep finding opportunities for their business to stay involved in politics. Corporate executives, in turn, become more comfortable thinking about politics as a means through which their business can advance its interests. In the case of ALEC, then, we can understand the results in Figure 4.6 as showing that more politically engaged companies are more comfortable with participation in the group. These more politically experienced companies also might be better positioned to weather the storm of public backlash from their ALEC ties given their past experience with political battles.

We can get a sense of this mechanism by looking at the companies that voluntarily chose to headline ALEC's conferences in 2014, 2015, and 2016—immediately after the fallout from ALEC's publicity crisis. Who were these businesses that not only remained involved in ALEC but also decided to publicly endorse the group by serving as the top sponsors of ALEC's annual convenings? These companies include a number of energy and utility firms, such as American Electric Power, Chevron, ConocoPhillips, Duke Energy, and Exxon; pharmaceutical giants like Bayer, Lilly, and Pfizer; tobacco manufacturers like Reynolds America and Philip Morris; and telecommunications providers like Comcast, Time Warner, and AT&T.[99] What these companies have in common is that they are some of the most politically active businesses in the United States—and have indeed weathered a number of political crises in the past. By comparison to the tobacco industry's past troubles, for instance, the ALEC backlash must seem trivial to executives of Philip Morris or Reynolds America.

In the prior chapter, I documented the reasons why state lawmakers choose to join and participate in ALEC: the organization found a clear niche that it could fill in the state policy landscape, providing policy resources for conservative, understaffed, and overwhelmed part-time legislators. In this chapter, I have flipped the perspective to examine why companies would choose to pay the hefty dues—and potential reputational costs—to join and stay involved with ALEC. We saw that larger and more politically active businesses were much more likely to fund efforts to shape state policy through the right-wing, corporate network compared to their smaller and less active counterparts. Companies were also much more likely to participate if they were exposed to greater threats from state governments or labor unions, and these two objectives are reflected in the legislative priorities pursued by ALEC.

Once ALEC began to attract controversy, it tended to be the companies that had the most to lose from continued membership—those most exposed to consumer boycotts or investor pressure from activist retirement funds—that were most willing to sever their ties to ALEC. By contrast, those companies that were already highly experienced navigating the turbulent waters of politics were much more likely to remain in the group.

Together, the results in this chapter offer insights into why ALEC has managed to sustain such a deep and committed bench of corporate backers since it began reaching out to the private sector in earnest in the 1980s. As the results presented in this chapter show quite clearly, ALEC helped companies to deal with policy threats in a way that other associations—and even companies' own in-house lobbying teams—could not do themselves.

The results also suggest the key weaknesses of a group like ALEC, which is dependent on shielding its corporate members from potential public backlash. As we saw in Chapter 1, the group was able to do that for a number of years by keeping a low profile and carefully guarding lists of members—but the pressure from the Trayvon Martin shooting and the ensuing crisis proved to be too much for ALEC to suppress. That left it vulnerable to having consumer and investor-exposed companies picked off by media-savvy boycotts and activist investor–led campaigns.

Indeed, this is a weakness that ALEC's leaders have acknowledged themselves. During a 2013 board meeting, leaders were tasked with brainstorming recruitment strategies for new corporate members. One proposal involved the hospitality and tourism industry, focusing on the risk of state hotel taxes, wage and labor laws, and cruise line regulations—all policies that ALEC was well positioned to address. But a potential "con" voiced by some board members was that "individual companies that join will be very susceptible to dropping ALEC if there is public pressure."[100] A similar concern was raised about targeting the consumer-oriented financial-services sector, whose members "failed to renew at ALEC due to controversy."[101] Clearly, exposure to consumer pressure is now a big liability for ALEC.

Looking beyond our immediate picture of ALEC, the results in this chapter suggest that some business associations continue to be very important ways by which companies shape policy, even as lobbying through other national associations has declined over time.[102] While corporate lobbyists may now be able to go it alone when pushing legislation on Capitol Hill, they still can reap important benefits when pursuing state-by-state policy change through ALEC, given the organization's well-developed networks of access and influence across the country.

My findings also have implications for debates over the effectiveness of consumer protests to change corporate political behavior. This is an increasingly important subject in the post–*Citizens United* era, as many citizens and political advocates search for ways of curbing corporate influence beyond campaign finance or lobbying reform.[103] My analysis of businesses that severed their ties with ALEC provides some measure of optimism for those seeking to limit corporate political activities through consumer protests and investor pressure.

Nevertheless, this chapter also indicates that companies already engaged in many other political activities are unlikely to change their political behavior, regardless of consumer pressure. And to further put the ALEC episode in context, at the end of the day, only about a third of ALEC's corporate backers ultimately left the group in the immediate wake of the crisis. Consumer and investor action, then, cannot entirely (or even mostly) replace other strategies.

Understanding the limits of private-sector solutions to deal with the outsized political influence of businesses and wealthy donors will become only more essential as we turn our attention to the two other organizations formed in recent years that have buttressed and expanded the reach of ALEC across the states. These two other members of the "right-wing troika" are even less likely to be affected by public pressure than ALEC, making their potential influence all the more significant.

PART II

THE RIGHT-WING TROIKA AND ITS FOES

5

A Little Help from Their Friends

Introducing the Right-Wing Troika

Coming out of the 2012 elections, Michigan Democrats had good reason to be cautiously optimistic. President Barack Obama won reelection in their state by a wide nine-point margin. And statehouse Democrats, buoyed by the national elections, won new seats in the lower legislative chamber. Although Republicans still held both the legislature and the governorship, Democrats were now well within striking distance to retake control.[1] Any hopes state Democrats had that the election would dampen Republicans' conservative zeal, however, were dashed just a month later when the lame-duck GOP legislature announced that it was taking up a bill to make Michigan a "right-to-work" state. That measure would ban unions from requiring workers to pay dues—even if those workers were reaping the benefits of union-negotiated collective bargaining agreements and job protections. Right-to-work proponents argued the bill would protect Michiganders from supporting organizations with which workers disagreed. In practice, right-to-work measures tend to make it harder for unions to collect dues and attract members, leading labor supporters to decry the proposal as a means of weakening unions and the progressive movement more broadly.[2]

Right to work had previously seemed unthinkable to many political observers in and out of Michigan. The state was, after all, the birthplace of industrial unionism in the United States in the automobile manufacturing plants GM, Ford, and Chrysler ran. And even though the United Auto Workers (UAW) union had suffered big blows as manufacturers fled the state for cheaper, non-union workers in Mexico and the South, Michigan still remained one of the last strongholds of industrial union strength in the country. The state's private-sector union membership rate was until recently nearly twice the national average.[3]

Perhaps most importantly, the state's GOP governor, Rick Snyder, had pledged over the previous two years that he would not take up the right-to-work issue.[4] Though undoubtedly conservative, Snyder had a well-earned reputation for being a business-minded pragmatist rather than an ideologue, so

Michiganders had real reason to take him at his word. Snyder was, for instance, the only GOP governor *not* to sign a 2011 letter from the Republican Governors Association calling for Obamacare's repeal.[5]

But on December 4th, in an abrupt turnabout, Snyder announced that right to work was "on the agenda" in Michigan.[6] Hours later, the legislature produced language on the measure, and just two days later, both chambers approved bills that would apply right to work to private- and public-sector unions alike in the state. It is hard to imagine the bills passing any faster than they did; the legislature did not even bother to hold committee hearings on the bills, and votes in each chamber were taken in rapid succession of each other.[7] When the bills cleared final approval the following week, Snyder quickly signed them into law, proudly announcing that Michigan had become the 24th state to prohibit unions from collecting dues or fees from workers. "This is a major day in Michigan's history," Snyder boasted.[8]

The speed with which the legislature acted on right to work belies the months and years of preparation invested in the measure—a familiar pattern across the states. Start with the actual legislative proposal for right to work. The two bills the legislature drafted contained language that was nearly identical to ALEC's "Right to Work" model bill.[9] Three of the proposal's main legislative backers— Senator Arlan Meekhof, Representative Tom McMillin, and Representative Pete Lund—also had longstanding ties to ALEC.[10] Meekhof had been an ALEC member back when he was serving in the lower chamber. McMillin had previously introduced a bill that drew heavily from another ALEC model related to healthcare. And Lund was an active member in ALEC's commerce, insurance, and economic development and public safety and elections task forces. Lund and other Michigan legislative members of ALEC had, in fact, discussed their intention to introduce right to work months earlier at ALEC's annual Spring Summit in Charlotte, North Carolina.[11] The Michigan lawmakers no doubt found support for their plans at this meeting, since right to work has long been a central objective of ALEC, as we saw in Chapter 1.

ALEC, then, was at the heart of the Michigan measure. But ALEC was not operating by itself. Along the way, ALEC received big assists from two other organizations that were present on the ground in Michigan with ties to national networks that could redirect resources and technical assistance as the right-to-work battle raged in Lansing. The Mackinac Center for Public Policy, a conservative, free-market-oriented think tank operating in Michigan since 1987, played a key role in supporting the bill.[12] From its 44-person office in Midland, Mackinac publishes research reports, media commentary, and testimony supporting right-leaning policy in the state and across the country. Active on a range of issues, including education, taxes, regulation, property rights, and labor relations, Mackinac bills itself as among the country's largest conservative state-level policy institutes. Its budget of $4 to $5 million per year certainly puts it at the top of the pack. Affiliation with the State Policy Network (SPN), the national association of conservative, state-level think tanks across the country that share resources, tactics, and information, further bolsters Mackinac's reach.

Along with SPN, the Center has long pushed right-to-work bills in Michigan, promoting their purported benefits for the state's economic development, migration patterns, wage growth, and employment since at least 1990.[13] After the legislature's announcement that it would be considering right-to-work legislation, Mackinac staffers went on a media spree, appearing on CNN, Fox Business, and other news outlets to support the proposal.[14] And aside from those outside pressures, Mackinac had also been working closely behind the scenes with GOP lawmakers elected in 2010 to help orchestrate a right-to-work push.[15]

Apart from Mackinac, right to work was further buoyed by the state chapter of Americans for Prosperity (AFP), a national advocacy group that is a crucial part of the political network organized by right-wing industrial magnates Charles and David Koch.[16] Though AFP is centrally directed from its Arlington, Virginia, headquarters, it maintains a federated, state-by-state presence across the United States, with paid staff directors in over a third of states as of 2017. That structure permits AFP to have considerable leverage in shaping both national and state politics. Like Mackinac, AFP—and the broader network of Koch political groups—have made retrenching labor union rights a central priority. The six-year-old AFP chapter in Michigan was a big champion of the 2011 right-to-work campaign. "Michigan passage of right-to-work legislation will be the shot heard around the world for workplace freedom," AFP-Michigan proclaimed in an early December press release after Snyder announced his intentions.[17] The group further explained that a victory "in a union stronghold like Michigan would be an unprecedented win . . . that would pave the way for right to work in states across our nation."[18] Drawing from a common political playbook, AFP-Michigan recruited some 300 activists to rally near the capitol to support the bill, and organized a "Workplace Freedom Lobby Day," on which AFP grassroots activists visited their elected officials to urge them to support right to work.[19] As the temperature dropped, AFP-Michigan used the promise of free food and drink, gas gift cards, and a heated tent in front of the statehouse building to encourage protesters to march on Lansing before the vote.[20] After Snyder signed the bill, AFP-Michigan praised the measure and pledged their support during the governor's subsequent reelection bid. That is notable since AFP had opposed the governor for his more centrist deal-making earlier in his term.[21] "Right to work . . . used to be something economic conservatives could only dream about," explained AFP-Michigan's state director. "We can't forget to thank state policymakers, including Governor Snyder, who helped make those dreams a reality."[22] Further evidence of the close ties of AFP to the right-to-work push: just a few years later, in 2015, right-to-work legislative champion Pete Lund would go on to run Michigan's AFP state chapter.[23]

Together, AFP and SPN's local Michigan affiliate provided important support for the ALEC lawmakers' advocacy of right to work at every step of the way, building the intellectual case for the measure (in the case of Mackinac) and offering grassroots pressure (in the case of AFP-Michigan). The close collaboration between these three national networks in Michigan is not an isolated episode. As we will see in this chapter, it provides an important reason for ALEC's growing success.

The IKEA Model of Conservative Policy Advocacy: State Think Tanks in a Box

In September 2013, a group of nearly 800 conservative policy experts, activists, donors, and corporate executives from 48 states (dubbed "freedom pioneers") descended on the Renaissance Hotel in Oklahoma City, Oklahoma.[24] The assembled participants were invited to "stake a claim for freedom" as they attended break-out sessions on the major policy threats of the day, such as Common Core educational standards, state-level efforts to subsidize renewable energy, and the implementation of the Affordable Care Act. But the event was not only about discussing upcoming policy battles, or even sharing political strategies. It was also an opportunity for current and prospective leaders of conservative policy groups across the states to share advice for the day-to-day operation of their organizations. So wedged between fiery debates over pension and tax reform were sessions with the more mundane titles of "Turn Likes into Dollars: Use Social Media to Fundraise," "Moving Your Development Program from Candy Sales to Protein," and "The Challenge (and Benefits!) of Building a Highly Effective Board." This was the twenty-first annual meeting of the SPN, the association of state-level, right-wing think tanks in which Michigan's Mackinac Center participates.

At the 2013 convention, SPN President Tracie Sharp gave a useful summary of what SPN was all about.[25] Sharp described SPN as pursuing an "IKEA model" of conservative policy advocacy, named after the Swedish home goods conglomerate made famous for its inexpensive assemble-it-yourself furniture. But instead of selling cheap beds and end tables made of pressed wood, SPN conceived of itself as producing policy change across the states around a common set of policy goals: stymieing implementation of President Obama's landmark healthcare and environmental programs, reducing the power of labor unions, tightening voting requirements, cutting labor market and environmental regulations, and privatizing state services. To achieve these goals, SPN provided "raw materials" and "services" from a "catalogue" to its affiliated conservative policy groups operating within each state, materials that SPN members could use to design legislative campaigns that worked best given their own local political and economic climates. "Pick what you need," Sharp explained to SPN's gathered members, "and customize it for what works best for you."

Sharp went on to single out Mackinac for praise for its involvement in spearheading the right-to-work battle in Michigan, bestowing the group's highest distinction, the Thomas A. Roe Jr. Award, on Mackinac's president. Sharp held the Center up as a prime example for other SPN affiliates to follow, recognizing how Mackinac had taken advantage of propitious political and economic conditions in their state to push through a longstanding national priority for the network.[26] As Sharp has explained elsewhere, "Most observers thought such a victory would be IMPOSSIBLE in Michigan, the birthplace of Big Labor. But [Mackinac] ignored the critics and naysayers and united behind a winning effort."[27] The payoff was enormous, in Sharp's view: "Declining [union] membership rolls ... has resulted in $8 million annually being drained from ... union coffers" (original emphasis).[28]

SPN's annual convenings did not always have as large a crowd or as significant policy victories to celebrate. When the organization was founded in 1986 as the Madison Group, it was at best a loose-knit partnership of twelve state-level think tanks, named after the Madison Hotel in Washington, D.C., where the think tank representatives were meeting.[29] Administrative duties were housed in the Heartland Institute, a Chicago-based right-leaning policy group. Constance Heckman, a former executive director of ALEC, chaired the group.[30] By 1991, the Madison Group had grown to include 55 public policy institutes across 29 states, with an additional 24 national groups, such as ALEC, the Heritage Foundation, and the National Rifle Association, serving as common resources for the state affiliates.[31] Membership dues in the Madison Group entitled enrollees to a bimonthly newsletter, shared communications across members, and regular workshops and conferences organized by the Heritage Foundation and the Free Congress Foundation, the conservative lobbying group led by ALEC's cofounder, Paul Weyrich.[32] Most of the initial funding for Madison Group members came from the same sources as ALEC—conservative foundations and private-sector businesses.[33]

It was not a coincidence that SPN relied on nearly the same funding sources as ALEC during these early years, or that many of the Madison Group's initial staffers had previous ALEC ties. That was because in the 1980s ALEC's head Sam Brunelli saw that the Madison Group's initial attempts at fundraising "basically fell by the wayside" in an already crowded field of right-wing political advocacy groups.[34] Brunelli took the relatively unprecedented step of opening up ALEC's donor list to the Madison Group, and even inviting the Madison Group to use ALEC's contacts at various companies and foundations to raise much-needed capital for the burgeoning network of think tanks. As he noted, most of the time with conservative non-profits, "everyone is all proprietary," saying, "you can't come, you can't see our list" given that every new group represented a potential competitor for scarce donor resources. Brunelli also "got [the Madison Group] participating" on a regular basis in ALEC, and even waived ALEC's hefty task force and conference participation dues to encourage Madison Group attendance at ALEC's events.[35]

Of course, Brunelli was not simply acting out of the goodness of his heart. He readily explained that "the more I can do to get [other groups] involved, working with more state legislators, the better for me. I never did see it as a zero-sum game," he summed up; "Let's make a bigger pie."[36] That attitude would prove to be essential for both the rapid growth of SPN over time, and also the development of a close relationship between SPN and ALEC.

Major changes would come to the Madison Group in the early 1990s, when the association was formally incorporated as a non-profit organization dubbed the State Policy Network. The number of states with SPN members inched up by ten over the next five years, as indicated in Figure 5.1, which tracks SPN's presence across the states and the contributions that the national SPN office has received from philanthropies, companies, and individual donors. Still, SPN's overall resources remained minimal over this period; on average, SPN was only

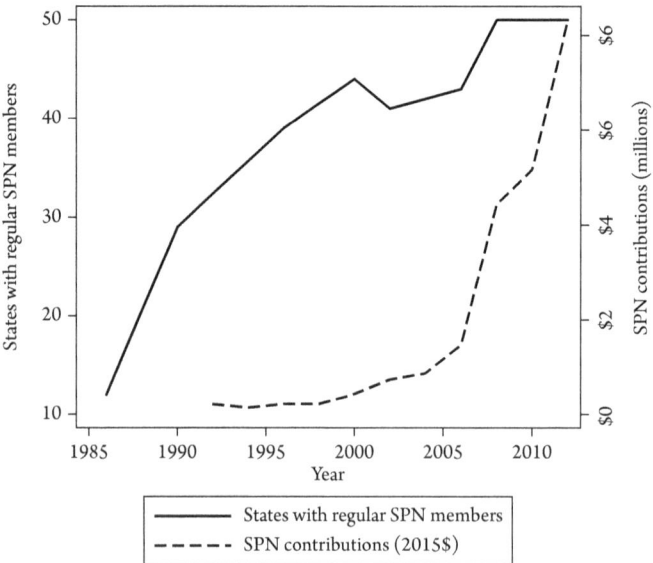

Figure 5.1. THE GROWTH OF THE STATE POLICY NETWORK, 1986–2012. SPN contribution data from IRS tax filings; SPN affiliate information from archived websites.

receiving $192,000 per year in contributions from its donor base and its national staff remained quite small (alternating between one and two staffers per year). Things began to look up after an additional round of reforms to the group in 1998 and 1999. SPN reorganized its board, focused more intensively on corporate fundraising, and began to provide a much more comprehensive set of services to its members. The results were soon felt at SPN's annual meetings, which grew to a record 138 attendees by 2000.[37]

SPN also enacted a number of new changes to further institutionalize its presence in the states, including an overhaul of its aging website. The redesigned site provided new internal resources for affiliates, like member lists, quarterly newsletters, and opportunities to interact with top industry executives who might also become donors to affiliates. Like ALEC, SPN also recognized the importance of building deep and enduring social ties between its members, and in the 2000 revamp of the group, its leaders focused on building out membership through targeted regional meetings, in addition to continuing to grow their annual national meeting. At one western regional meeting, cohosted by the Pacific Research Institute in California, over seventy attendees were able to share ideas about proposals that might be viable to push even in the otherwise very blue enclaves of California and Hawaii. Notably, ALEC's chairman at the time led that discussion.[38] Another regional meeting, held in Birmingham, Alabama, brought together some twenty southern state think tanks to brainstorm new policy proposals with the help of national groups, including ALEC, the Heritage Foundation, and the Reason Foundation, that would be welcomed in more moderate and conservative states.[39]

In an important organizational innovation for SPN, it began to field newly bolstered surveys of its members in an effort to gauge their effectiveness, strategies, the landscape of opposition and allies they faced in each state, and what the national network could provide to affiliates to better support the work that they did. As one of the first comprehensive surveys explained, SPN was hoping to solicit member responses "to assist existing organizations with comparative data on their counterparts in other states," "to assist individuals in the establishment of new think tanks, especially in states where no market-oriented organization exists," and "to provide accessible data to inform current and potential contributors of the needs and successes of state-based, market-oriented think tanks."[40] The questions ranged from the more general—explaining an affiliate's origins—to the very specific—listing salary ranges for all personnel and computer equipment used by those staffers. SPN also used the opportunity of the survey to encourage affiliates to reach out to other conservative think tanks and advocacy groups outside of the network, especially ALEC.[41] In a rather leading question attached to the new survey, SPN leaders asked affiliates, "Would someone from your staff participate on an American Legislative Exchange Council (ALEC) task force? If so, who and for what issue?"[42]

Beyond closer ties with ALEC, the results of the survey also pointed to new resources that the network began providing to its affiliates. Those new benefits included collaborations with more national organizations and state-based organizations that had national reach; more of a focus on privatization efforts, including training sessions and intensive conferences; and more leadership and management training for SPN affiliate heads, such as training modules and online how-to manuals for new think tank presidents. The latter efforts were a particular focus for SPN, and over the next three years, SPN's national staff would establish a permanent "think tank school" to "provide certification in relevant think tank skills, foster professional standards, and advance state think tank work as a vocation."[43]

SPN coupled these ambitious reforms along with a more aggressive push for fundraising from wealthy individual donors, not just the foundations and in-state donors that most affiliates had traditionally relied upon to date. In one newsletter to SPN affiliates in the spring of 2001, an article implored affiliates to work together to find new donors, rather than competing for their own resources individually. As the piece's author argued, "SPN affiliates should realize that they have a common interest in encouraging philanthropy and in cooperating in finding new donors, just as they now cooperate on public policy matters through the SPN. An expanding list of donors for the state-based free market movement will mean an expanding resource base in which all can share."[44]

Another SPN funding strategy during this period was to encourage affiliates to build relationships with private businesses, as ALEC had done. At one regional SPN convening in Philadelphia, local affiliates could hobnob with representatives from the pharmaceutical manufacturers trade group PhRMA, pitching proposals to them to "support state-level health . . . reform projects . . . with free-market health care policy."[45] The case of the Washington Policy Center (an SPN affiliate in Washington state) and Microsoft was another instructive example offered up to affiliates of how a corporate partnership could work in practice. Although it might have seemed "obvious . . . that corporations such as Microsoft . . . should easily recognize the value of think tanks' efforts to ensure a market-friendly policy environment," it wasn't in practice.[46] Microsoft had to be persuaded by the SPN affiliate in Washington state of the value of supporting think tank work. But the persuasion paid off: Microsoft began funding both the local state affiliate in Washington state and the SPN national association as a whole. "It's up to you to demonstrate that you're not just a worthy organization with good ideas, but an effective partner that delivers bottom-line value for long-term benefit," concluded Microsoft's business affairs and policy communications manager at SPN's annual 2001 meeting.[47] She would be the first to know.

She was previously the head of the Washington Policy Center who had made the initial ask of Microsoft to donate to the think tank and SPN.

Taken together, SPN's new focus on building ties to wealthy individual donors and big businesses reaped handsome returns, leading to a sharp jump in contributions to the national network. From 2005 to 2010, contributions to SPN grew by over 300 percent. By the late 2000s, things were looking very good for SPN. The group could count over 60 think tanks as members across all 50 states, and was active in a range of policy debates. And by 2013, SPN members collectively commanded budgets surpassing $78 million and averaged about 267 annual citations apiece in local, state, and national newspapers.[48] SPN was also offering a much more extensive set of benefits and services for its affiliates. Thanks to the generosity of its new corporate donors, SPN was able to provide grants to affiliates for general operating support, as well as specific projects. In 2014, SPN's national office made 32 grants averaging about $56,000—a significant amount given that the typical think tank's budget that year was just under $700,000.[49] And, of course, SPN was hosting larger meetings each year for its affiliates, donors, and other partners, like the one that honored Mackinac in 2013.

As with ALEC, SPN has also tried hard to keep its efforts out of the public eye. In 2013, I signed up to attend SPN's annual meeting in Oklahoma City, paying the general registration fee and booking a flight and hotel room. Just days before the conference, however, I was contacted by an SPN staffer, who informed me that I would not be able to attend. (The conference was theoretically open to all students interested in free-market policies; at the time, I was in graduate school at Harvard and very interested in free-market policies and politics.) When I explained that I might still fly to Oklahoma City to interview conference participants off-site at the hotel, the SPN staff offered to reimburse me for the costs of canceling my hotel and flight plans. Sensing that a trip to Oklahoma would be fruitless, I took them up on their offer.

What Do SPN Affiliates Do?

To get a sense of SPN's activities in the present day (aside from paying nosy graduate students not to attend their conferences), I have reviewed the updates provided by each state affiliate to the SPN national newsletter in 2016. These updates offer a brief but lively description of their major activities, goals, and accomplishments in recent months. Here's an example from the Georgia Public Policy Foundation in January 2016: "The Foundation paved the way [for education reform] with a December event . . . with the Reason Foundation and Allovue and [and] Thanks to [the Foundation's] copious research, market-based alternatives to Medicaid expansion are gaining support in the legislature."[50] Using these brief summaries, I coded the policy issues that each affiliate mentioned (like repealing the Affordable Care Act), their main strategies (like issuing reports or holding events), and the target of their efforts (the state legislature or the governor, for instance). While these summaries do not capture each and every activity pursued by the SPN affiliates, they do provide an indication of what affiliates wanted to highlight out of all their work each year. We can thus think of these codings as representing a sample of SPN's most prominent and public involvements.

Table 5.1 provides a look at how frequently affiliates listed various issues in their updates. By far, the most commonly reported issue was education reform, especially involving the creation or expansion of vouchers for students to attend private schools of their parents' choosing. The Nevada Policy Research Institute, for instance, reported that it had created a website to promote its "Education Savings Account" proposal and was holding "dozens of community events" to convey to the public why they should push the state's legislature to adopt the plan. Tax reform, generally involving cuts to income taxes, was a close second, followed by opposition to Medicaid expansion. SPN affiliates in Medicaid expansion holdout states—those not choosing to expand health insurance as part of the Affordable Care Act—were all focused on keeping their legislatures from bringing up the issue again in 2016.

Table 5.1. **Issues Pursued by SPN Affiliates in 2016.**[a]

Issue	Count	Issue	Count
Education	16	Environment	3
Tax reform	11	Right to work	3
Medicaid expansion	6	Regulation	3
Civil asset forfeiture	5	Occupational licensing	2
Infrastructure	5	Government reform	1
Pension reform	4	Elections	1
Public union reform	4	Federalism	1
Minimum wage	4	Constitutional reform	1
Property rights	4	Privatization	1
Budget	3	Criminal justice reform	1
Affordable Care Act repeal	3		

[a] Author's review of SPN affiliate updates.

Not all affiliates pursued the same strategies while working on these issues. By far, the most common strategies employed by SPN affiliates included holding public events (twenty-one affiliates mentioned this strategy explicitly in 2016). Those events were often paired with the release of publications or reports on a specific policy topic, a strategy that came in second (with seven affiliates reporting publications). Events and publications were followed closely by the release of legislative scorecards that coded the fealty of state or local politicians to affiliate agendas. As the Advance Arkansas Institute put it, its Freedom Scorecard "lists and rates the voting records of every member of the Arkansas General Assembly" and is "the most thorough of its kind ever produced in Arkansas." And three affiliates mentioned leadership training programs for young people or aspiring grassroots political leaders, including the James Madison Institute in Florida. The Madison Institute runs a program "designed to encourage and promote the growth, development, knowledge, and networks of under-40 professionals living and working in the Sunshine State."

Lastly, we can consider the targets of affiliates' efforts. The most commonly cited target was the general public (22 affiliates), followed by the legislature (14 affiliates), the media (13 affiliates), with governors coming in at a distant fourth (4 affiliates). Of course, these categories are not mutually exclusive. Efforts to shape public opinion and fire up grassroots volunteers in the short run may also be intended to move legislators' votes. But these codings do indicate that the typical SPN organization tends to focus their efforts on public-facing activities. You might suspect that SPN think tanks would be more likely to engage in public-outreach efforts in conservative states where they would find a friendly audience—but the opposite turns out to be true. SPN affiliates were substantially more likely to report the public as a target—and to report engaging in publicly oriented activities—in states where Democrats controlled most or all of the legislature and the governorship. When SPN think tanks face a friendly state government, they tend to report more inside contacts with government officials and resort to public pressure when having to deal with the opposing party in power.[51]

While our review of affiliate activities, along with Figure 5.1, gives a sense of SPN's national scope and its growth over time, it necessarily glosses over the specifics of what each SPN affiliate looks like—and how those affiliates shape policy. While I cannot tell the story of each and every one of the SPN affiliates, we can take a brief tour across the United States to review the origins and activities of two think tanks that typify two different models of SPN members. The *Goldwater Institute* in Arizona is one of the largest and oldest SPN affiliates, and, like several other SPN think tanks of its size, operates both within Arizona and nationally. In contrast, the *Maine Heritage Policy Center* is a good example of a mid-sized SPN affiliate operating mostly within its state's borders. Figure 5.2

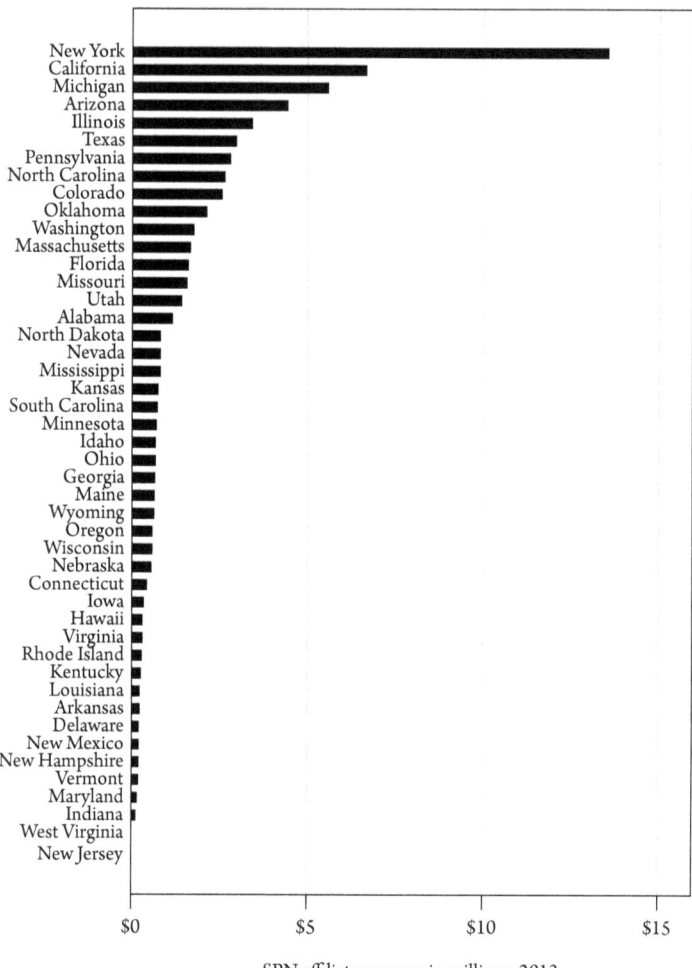

Figure 5.2. AVERAGE SPN AFFILIATE REVENUE BY STATE, 2013. Average SPN affiliate revenue for 2013 by state based on IRS tax filings. Where there are multiple SPN affiliates per state, the chart averages the total of all affiliate revenue within a state. WV and NJ data unavailable.

summarizes average SPN affiliate revenue by state as of 2013, indicating where each of the organizations we will visit falls in the overall distribution of SPN members.

The Goldwater Institute as a Model of Large SPN Affiliates

Founded in 1988, the Goldwater Institute has built up an annual budget of between $4 and $5 million per year. Only four other SPN affiliates—in Texas,

Michigan, California, and New York—have similar or larger budgets. Goldwater's staff of 60 focuses primarily on economic regulatory issues, education policy, and healthcare. Each year, the Institute holds around 30 to 50 public events and policy briefings, writes around 5 to 10 major policy reports, and generates about 40 to 50 new policy proposals.[52] Goldwater also focuses on garnering media attention for its policy experts and reports, claiming around 2,000 to 3,000 media "hits" or mentions of its work each year.[53]

In an unusual practice for SPN affiliates, Goldwater goes beyond standard policy analysis, writing, and communication to engage in lawsuits around their policy priorities through its Center for Constitutional Litigation. In 2015, Goldwater handled around a dozen such cases, three of which resulted in eventual victories (five in 2016).[54] One of those cases involved taking aim at a longstanding government employee union practice in Arizona, in which unions would negotiate provisions in their contracts that permitted certain employees to be paid for work they did for the union—dubbed "release time." After discovering the practice in 2011, Goldwater filed suit against the city of Phoenix to prevent police officers from being paid for work they did with their union.[55] Goldwater's size permits it to go beyond Arizona, and as in other litigation efforts, the institute has brought release time cases in other states, like Texas, where there is a good shot of eliminating the provision based on state constitutions.[56]

The fight against release time fits with a more general priority of Goldwater—like many SPN affiliates—to retrench labor rights, especially for public employees. Goldwater has pushed for "paycheck protection" measures, both in Arizona and elsewhere, that would make it more challenging for government employee unions to collect dues from their members' paychecks to spend on union and political activities.[57] Goldwater has also promoted state constitutional amendments that would prevent a labor-friendly federal government from expediting the process of forming a union by replacing a formal, secret-ballot election with a simple majority of workers who signed a union card.[58] Constitutional amendments based on the Goldwater model opposing labor election reform were ultimately added in four states, including Arizona.[59]

Beyond union policy, Goldwater is also active in promoting alternatives to public schools by drafting model legislative language and hosting delegations of state lawmakers from around the country. One of Goldwater's longstanding proposals is the creation of state-funded accounts that parents can use to pay for private-sector educational alternatives.[60] Arizona has already adopted that approach, and was soon followed by Florida, and more recently, Mississippi. As with labor issues, Goldwater has paired traditional policy advocacy with legal strategies, and was involved in litigation in Oklahoma around the creation of state scholarship funds that could be used to pay for independently chosen private schools.[61]

Goldwater's efforts in this area have benefited from their participation in ALEC. The think tank has been a longtime member, promoting model bills based on its priorities in education, healthcare, and labor policy.[62] Goldwater has authored ALEC model bills related to public funding for private schools, state opposition to national educational standards, opportunities for public school districts to request exemptions from state educational standards, opposition to the Affordable Care Act, and banning certain public employee practices, including release time and automatic government employee union dues collection.

As with other SPN affiliates, Goldwater receives a substantial amount of funding through Donors Capital Fund, a conservative donor-advised charity that channels philanthropic giving to right-leaning causes.[63] Goldwater has also received funding from Koch family philanthropic organizations. Yet most of Goldwater's funding does not flow from foundation giving. Only about $1.4 million of its annual budget in recent years came from philanthropic foundations, compared to over $4 million from individual wealthy donors.[64]

Given that Arizona has seen full GOP control of both legislative chambers and the governorship since 2009, Goldwater has generally maintained close and productive relationships with state leaders. Under the most recent governor, key staffers moved seamlessly between the Institute and prime posts in government. In 2016, GOP Governor Doug Ducey appointed the Institute's vice president of litigation to the state's Supreme Court. That was an important move not just for bolstering the organization's credibility, but also because it will undoubtedly provide another friendly audience for litigation that Goldwater brings against the state.[65] Another top Ducey staffer, serving as the deputy chief of staff for budget and policy, left the administration toward the end of 2016 to serve as Goldwater's president and chief operating officer. In all, Goldwater thus shows the ways in which large and well-institutionalized SPN think tanks not only guide policy across a range of areas in their own home states but also craft proposals for governments all over the country.

A Medium-Sized SPN Think Tank in Maine

As should already be clear from Figure 5.2, Goldwater's national scope and broad set of activities are the exception, not the norm, for SPN affiliates. For a picture of what a more typically sized SPN affiliate does, we can move from the dry mesas of Arizona to the rocky coastland of southern Maine, where the Heritage Policy Center is located. Founded in 2002, the Heritage Center has grown from an annual budget of only around $150,000 per year and one full-time staffer to a budget of around $600,000 per year with eight full-time staff members.[66] The Center was initially helmed by Bill Becker, a former GOP campaign operative, who sought to insert a more conservative perspective into the state's policy debates. "We really felt it was important that Maine—the media, legislators and the business community—was able to hear about policy solutions from a conservative point of view," Becker said of the group's creation. "I often say when I give speeches, I'm here to tell you 'conservative' is not a bad word," he has summed up.[67]

Like Goldwater, the Maine Heritage Center was a member of SPN nearly right from its start. The Heritage Center also focuses on a similar set of issues as Goldwater, albeit on a smaller scale. Those include labor relations, health policy, education, and tax and fiscal policy. The Center has long pushed for a so-called Taxpayer Bill of Rights, which would require voter approval on all tax and spending decisions.[68] On education, the group has promoted the benefits of privately provided online instruction, working as a participant in ALEC's educational policy task force. And on healthcare, the Center has opposed the state's efforts to expand health insurance coverage, initially under Democratic Governor John Baldacci, and later in response to the Obama administration's health reform program.

Despite its small size, the Center has benefited from a close relationship with Maine's current governor, the very conservative Republican Paul LePage. Elected in 2010, LePage attracted controversy for his explicit and often offensive comments.[69] Beyond his record for controversial commentary, LePage has also sought policies very much in line with the Heritage Center. LePage has, for instance, turned to the Center to develop his early budgets, which included large cuts in the state income tax.[70] LePage also picked up the Center's call to completely abolish the state's income tax (a proposal that has yet to be enacted).[71] The Center has worked closely with the state administration in its opposition to implementing the Affordable Care Act, including stopping the establishment of a state health insurance marketplace and expansion of Medicaid to poor adults.[72] (Progressive activists recently bypassed LePage and put Medicaid expansion up for a ballot measure in 2017, which won by large margins. At the time of this book's writing, LePage is still holding out on expansion.[73]) And the Center has supported the executive and the GOP legislature in their bids to pass right-to-work legislation in the state.[74]

Collaboration between a right-wing GOP governor and a conservative think tank might be expected in any state, but the Heritage Center has had a big leg up in its connections to LePage. The head of the Center chaired the governor's transition team, and an education policy specialist became commissioner of education. As one critic of the Center has described it, "Once in office, the [Heritage

Center] became the [LePage] administration's policy arm, wielding nearly unchecked influence on the governor and his team."[75]

Although most SPN affiliates tend to blend political communication with policy research and advocacy, the Heritage Center is unusual within the network for taking its political messaging even further by running its own online news and opinion service, called the "Maine Wire." "Dedicated to your right to know," the Maine Wire argues that "it has proved to be an invaluable resource in reporting on stories that would otherwise be ignored by the Maine media, providing a much-needed critical eye to the actions of Maine government, and providing a go-to location for conservative thought leadership."[76] The site offers up a mix of summaries of major national and state political stories, as well as commentary from a roster of contributors who range from college students to one of Maine's congressional representatives, Bruce Poliquin. The articles will commonly link to issues the governor and the Heritage Center are pursuing, such as one post that applauded a recent bill that would "solidify many of LePage's executive actions on welfare reform into state law"—executive actions that the Heritage Center had originally put forward.[77] The tone that the Wire adopts is often hard-edged, as are its tactics. As one political journalist for the *Bangor Daily News* explained, the Maine Wire's "modus operandi was to attack liberal politicians and Democratic sacred cows, such as welfare and Medicaid, and [the site] was unafraid to use controversial techniques, such as secret recordings [of liberal activists], to do so."[78] One thing that both the Center's critics and fans can agree on, however, is that the organization has enjoyed mounting influence, especially in recent years. With its new CEO installed in 2014, the organization plans on capitalizing on its close relationship to the administration, as well as GOP gains in the legislature, to continue "leading a charge for conservative policymaking in Augusta," as one journalist put it.[79]

Better Together: ALEC and SPN

Despite their different strategies, areas of policy focus, and resources, participation in ALEC is one common through-line for the affiliates we visited in Arizona and Maine. ALEC offered both organizations valuable resources that they could not find elsewhere. One benefit is the opportunity to take policy ideas on the road to other states by supporting and drafting model bills. These think tanks also got a chance to market themselves as resources for policy research, commentary, and ideas for lawmakers and companies looking for precisely that support. Even with its large budget and staff resources, Goldwater would not have been able to obtain the national reach that it did without its participation in ALEC. As an ALEC member, Goldwater could take some of its most important proposals relating to public union cutbacks and educational vouchers to the ALEC labor and education task forces, and work with the corporate and legislative members of those panels to disseminate model legislation based on its proposals that ultimately spread across the states. And in the case of Maine's smaller SPN affiliate, ALEC offered valuable support to the Heritage Policy Center's efforts to push back on progressive legislation. The Heritage Policy Center hosted ALEC staffer Christie Herrera at a 2010 event detailing ALEC's strategies for defeating the Affordable Care Act.[80]

In short, ALEC and SPN have been closely linked ever since Sam Brunelli opened up his funder list to the Madison Group and helped get the precursor to SPN off the ground. On an institutional level, SPN is a member of ALEC (and vice versa), and many SPN members serve as private-sector members on ALEC's task forces. At last count, some twenty-two affiliates had formal membership in ALEC working groups. SPN encourages such ties, seeking donor funding to pay for more of its affiliates to cover the hefty dues to join ALEC's task forces (think tanks, in principle, pay similar rates to private-sector companies). This was a special priority for current SPN head Tracie Sharp, who made a push for fundraising to pay for ALEC dues beginning in the mid-2000s. After that, SPN affiliates "have been at the table with state legislators and other private sector members to draft model legislation," glowed one SPN newsletter in 2009.[81] Sharp was recognized for her efforts to bring the two groups closer with the receipt of the 2009 ALEC Private Sector Member of the Year Award.[82] As one SPN think tank president noted: "This is a well-deserved award. Not only have SPN members assisted legislators in drafting [ALEC] model legislation, they've been key in killing some proposals... [along with ALEC]."[83]

A leaked 2013 fundraising document from SPN to the Searle Freedom Trust, a conservative philanthropy, further illustrates how funders were strategically funneling money through SPN's national headquarters in ways intended to encourage collaboration with ALEC. That fundraising document indicated that many of the awards the Trust was considering regranting to SPN affiliates were based on the past collaboration between think tanks and ALEC. For instance, in internal notes about a $40,000 grant intended for the Goldwater Institute in Arizona, SPN staff wrote in support of the proposal that "Goldwater was able to pass model legislation at the ALEC in 2012, and the legislative action received a great deal of media attention."[84]

Examining the sources of the deep ties between ALEC and SPN highlights a strength of SPN as an association. On the one hand, SPN affiliates are institutionally and legally separate from SPN national headquarters. This lets each affiliate make the case to lawmakers, journalists, and political observers that they are homegrown operations, run by staff who are deeply embedded in their local political scenes. For instance, the Josiah Bartlett Center for Public Policy, the SPN affiliate in New Hampshire, bills itself as an "independent think tank focused on state and local public policy issues that affect the quality of life for New Hampshire's citizens." The Center also draws heavily on its ties to New Hampshire politics in talking about its history and mission—especially the central role of its namesake, Josiah Bartlett, for the state's heritage.[85] SPN President Tracie Sharp has further expanded on this feature of the network, calling the affiliates participating in the group "fiercely independent."[86] "There is no governing organization dictating what [affiliated] think tanks research or how they educate the public about good public policy," Sharp added.[87]

Yet even as the SPN think tanks bill themselves as institutions that have been independently created and run within each state, the national network—through SPN headquarters—steers individual affiliates toward particular policy agendas and priorities through sizable grants earmarked for specific purposes—like defeating Medicaid expansion or participating on specific ALEC task forces. Through that strategically directed support, SPN can get the benefits of the appearance of affiliate independence while also ensuring that those affiliates are generally on the same page when it comes to resources and policy coordination.

Returning to the carefully choreographed battle waged by ALEC and SPN over enacting right-to-work legislation in Michigan that opened the chapter, we can say that the Wolverine state is by no means an outlier. Instead, there is good reason to think that ALEC's legislative advocacy is easier in states that have active SPN affiliates that can back up the work of ALEC's lawmakers through reports, media coverage, research, and political assistance. At the same time, SPN was not the only conservative network coordinating with ALEC to defeat the Michigan labor movement. We now turn to the third member of that right-wing troika bolstering ALEC and SPN's efforts: Americans for Prosperity (or AFP).

The Eight-Hundred-Pound Gorilla of the Koch Network: Americans for Prosperity

At an estimated wealth of nearly $50 billion each, Charles and David Koch were tied for sixth place in the Forbes 400 ranking of the richest Americans in 2017.[88] (Their combined wealth puts them above even Bill Gates.[89]) The brothers' wealth comes in large part from their industrial business conglomerate, Koch Industries, that has grown into the second-largest privately held business in the United States.[90] Employing around 100,000 workers, Koch Industries produces goods and services across a range of sectors as diverse as oil processing, finance, paper products, and ranching and sells recognizable products like Brawny Paper Towels, Dixie Cups, Stainmaster Carpets, Lycra Fabrics, and Thermolite Insulation.[91] Charles and David's political activities have increasingly become as ubiquitous as their products. Indeed, the mere invocation of the moniker "Koch brothers" now brings to mind for many an image of billions of dollars in "dark money" flowing throughout the American political system.[92]

Yet for all the scrutiny that the Kochs and their maneuverings have received in a steady stream of investigative journalism, biographies of the brothers, and tirades from progressive activists, their political network remains largely misunderstood. Much reporting on the Kochs tends to focus on the brothers as individuals, considering unusual details of their upbringing, the spats between the brothers over control of the family company, and, of course, the massive investments that Charles and David have personally made in politics, especially during recent elections. When reporters or pundits shift their focus away from the brothers themselves, they tend to think about Koch political advocacy as merely a front for the brothers' business interests. Liberal activists, for instance, are quick to note that the political positions taken by the Koch network often provide clear benefits for Koch Industries' bottom line. And separately, campaign finance experts tend to think about the Kochs as scattering money like a "secret bank" across broad swaths of the conservative movement. As we will see, each of these three common approaches to thinking about Charles and David Koch—and the political network that they have constructed—is at best misguided, and at worst makes it harder to get an accurate picture of the role that Koch organizations actually play in contemporary American politics.[93]

Let's start with the first misconception about the Koch network: that it is all about the brothers themselves. It is certainly true that Charles and David have invested large and unprecedented sums of their own money into politics, including recent elections.[94] In 2016, for instance, Charles and his wife donated a total of over $4 million to Republican candidates for federal office, according to disclosed Federal Election Commission records. Yet the most important part of the Koch political story is *not* the brothers, *nor* election-time giving. Rather, it is the overlapping set of organizations that they have created over many decades. Not only do those organizations raise funds that easily surpass the brothers' individual giving, but these groups wind up being more influential, hiring staffs of hundreds of political organizers and strategists who oversee efforts to intervene in politics year in and year out, in both elections and policy debates and across levels of government.[95] It is these core organizations that have either been created by the Kochs and their top associates, or that are mostly (if not entirely) supported by Koch funding streams, that merit our attention.

Given their centrality to the Koch network, Figure 5.3 zooms in on the core organizations directed by the brothers, dividing each group by their function and historical development. By arraying the Koch groups in this manner—both by function and age—we can see the step-by-step expansion of the Koch network, and in particular, how they have moved from a more limited set of political

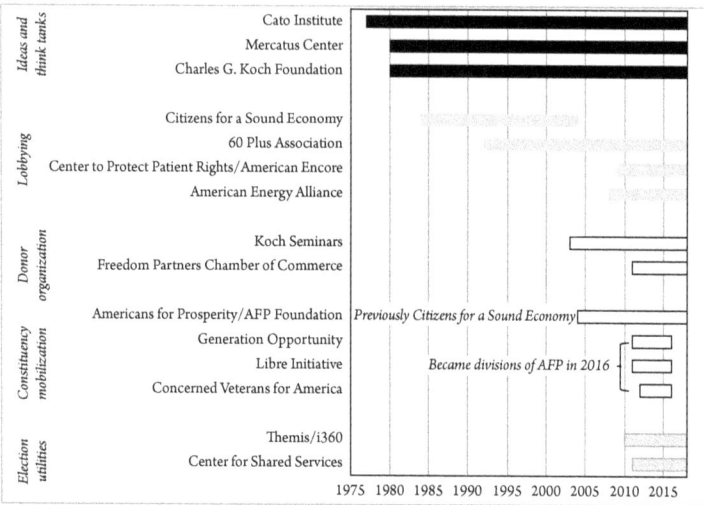

Figure 5.3. A TIGHTLY INTEGRATED—AND GROWING—KOCH POLITICAL NETWORK, 1975–2018. The development of core Koch political organizations by age and function. Adapted from Skocpol and Hertel-Fernandez 2016a, 2016b.

engagements in the 1970s to a fully integrated set of reinforcing and overlapping groups by 2015.

The first organizations the Koch network supported are now the oldest standing components of the brothers' political empire. That these earlier initiatives include three organizations dedicated to developing and disseminating libertarian political philosophies and policy ideas is no coincidence. Core to the Koch brothers' vision of political change is the notion that politicians reflect rather than create "the prevalent ideology" in a country, which is in turn set by "intellectuals . . . and all others who disseminate ideas."[96] A historian of the Koch brothers quoted a longtime network aide explaining this theory in more detail, perhaps channeling from John Maynard Keynes' famous formulation: "Politicians, ultimately, are just actors playing out a script. The idea is, one gets better and quicker results aiming not at the actors but at the scriptwriters, to help supply the themes and words for the scripts—to try to influence the areas where policy ideas percolate from: academia and think tanks."[97]

That perspective explains the Kochs' creation of and longtime support for the Cato Institute, the nation's premier think tank specializing in libertarian policy analysis. They have also provided longstanding support to the Mercatus Center at George Mason University, which churns out a steady stream of academic research intended to support widespread deregulation of federal and state governments. The Charles G. Koch Foundation's inauguration in 1980 provided an additional means of investing in individual academics, university centers and departments, and scholarly non-profits and think tanks "supporting the study of free societies"—precisely the sort of script-writing that could shape the actions of politician-actors in years to come.[98]

By the mid-1980s, the Kochs began expanding the scope of their activities beyond funding scholarly work and policy analysis to support a pair of new lobbying organizations: the 60 Plus Association and Citizens for a Sound Economy (CSE). These organizations resembled more traditional "astroturf" operations intended to build grassroots support for corporate-backed policy priorities in Congress and the states.[99] While the 60 Plus Association remained a sleepy affair until later battles over the estate tax and Social Security privatization in the 2000s, CSE was a much more ambitious operation right from its start.

At its launch, CSE billed itself as "a bold new development in the public policy process—an organization that combines ideas with people dedicated to improving the well-being of America by reducing government interference in the economy."[100] Beyond the priorities of the Koch brothers themselves, CSE created campaigns for other companies interested in pushing more specific policy changes to boost their bottom lines. As one investigative journalist reported in the early 2000s, "More than $1 million in contributions from the tobacco giant Philip Morris came when CSE was opposing new cigarette taxes. Donations totaling $1.25 million from US West coincided with CSE's lobbying for phone deregulation that would let US West offer long-distance service. Florida's three biggest sugar companies contributed nearly $700,000 when CSE fought a federal plan to protect the Everglades by restricting sugar cane growing on several thousand acres of land."[101] In essence, CSE served as a pass-through for companies looking to build the appearance of outside grassroots support for their preferred policies.

Foreshadowing a strategy later employed by CSE's successor, AFP, the group quickly enrolled hundreds of thousands of committed conservative grassroots volunteers—at least 250,000 if the group's reported totals are to be believed—to mobilize in attending rallies, contacting members of Congress, and turning out for elections.[102] These volunteers, however, had little actual input in CSE's policy agenda, which was set by the companies funding the organization.[103]

CSE would ultimately fall apart as tensions mounted between the Kochs and Dick Armey, the former House majority leader who joined the group as its chairman after stepping down from elective office.[104] In a common pattern across Koch-supported organizations, the brothers demanded near-total control of key decisions.[105] In this case, the brothers were pushing for the dismissal of several employees, which Armey and the board refused to carry out. Reaching an impasse, the Kochs pulled out of CSE by the end of 2003.[106] While Armey would still control the political arm of CSE (its 501c4 component, later rebranded as FreedomWorks), the Kochs took with them the non-profit, 501c3 foundation associated with CSE along with $5 million in funding. The Kochs would convert those remains of CSE, including some of its grassroots presence across the states, into a new organization called Americans for Prosperity (AFP). This rebranded organization had its own twinned political arm and charitable foundation, much like its precursor. Since its creation in 2004, AFP has become the central component of the overall Koch political network.

Aside from the creation of AFP, the other most significant move that the Kochs made in the early 2000s was to start convening twice-yearly donor meetings, or "seminars," as the brothers have called them. Participating in those invitation-only seminars are fellow conservative millionaires and billionaires, typically businessmen running or directing companies of their own, as well as their spouses.[107] Initially, they began as rather dry intellectual salons, with Charles, David, and invited speakers lecturing about the philosophical foundations of libertarian values.[108] (By some accounts, the first convening was so dry that many of the first round of attendees did not return for the second meeting the following year.[109])

Starting in 2007, and continuing after Barack Obama's victory in 2008, interest in the brothers' seminars steadily grew. More recent attendance numbers have ranged from 400 to 500 participants.[110] The seminars correspondingly took on more structure and practical purpose. While the more abstract lectures on political philosophy are still present, those panels are intermingled with more grounded sessions on political strategy, including presentations by key Koch network operatives reporting on recent victories and setbacks. Seminar donors also have opportunities to hear speeches from established and up-and-coming conservative politicians. Political candidates, for their part, covet such invitations, as they often result in a flood of new donations.[111]

Recent convenings have made ample room for mingling, turning the seminars into an important means through which wealthy right-wing donors living all across the country can foster social ties with one another, and with conservative political leaders. The primary goal of these seminars, however, is to raise money for the conservative movement—and above all, the core organizations directed by the Koch network. Throughout the convenings, top Koch operatives arrange for "one-on-one" sessions between potential donors and organizational leaders. Some seminars apparently end with an opportunity for donors to stand up and publicly pledge their giving in front of the rest of gathered attendees, making for a revival or auction-style scene.[112] In recent years, a new organization—the Freedom Partners Chamber of Commerce—has taken over the formal functions of running the seminars and managing these donations, further signaling the institutionalization of these events.

One top Koch staffer summed up the seminars in the following way to a journalist, who relayed the quote to me: "The seminar network is a group of hundreds of business leaders from across the country who get together a couple times a year ... to drive social change. And what they mean by social change is ... free people are capable of extraordinary things. The seminar network invests across what they would call the key institutions of society: education, business, policy, and politics."[113]

The Koch seminars have quickly become an incredibly influential source of fundraising for the right. While concrete numbers are hard to come by, the brothers have, at times, either publicly disclosed the total pledges they have received from their donors or that information has leaked to the press following seminar convenings.[114] In 2007 to 2008, the seminars raised just shy of $100 million; in 2009 to 2010, that number grew to over $150 million, and by 2011 to 2012, to $400 million. More recently, the Kochs pledged to raise between $700 and $900 million between 2015 and 2016, with another $300 to $400 for the 2018 cycle.[115] Those sums are vast on their own—and become even more impressive when we compare them to the money the GOP has raised in recent years. In 2015 to 2016, the Republican Party raised just over $850 million—or about the same amount of money the Kochs planned to raise privately for the same election cycle. The Koch network, it is fair to say, is playing on the same field as an entire political party.[116]

But where does all this Koch-raised money go? Investigative journalists have tended to focus on the "maze of money" that the Koch network has distributed through its "secret bank" of the Freedom Partners Chamber of Commerce to hundreds of disparate right-leaning groups. Working with *The Washington Post's* money in politics team, the Center for Responsive Politics assembled a tangle of organizations—ranging from the National Rifle Association to the US Chamber of Commerce—that had received Koch backing in 2012.[117] Important as that work is, trying to parse the "labyrinth of tax-exempt groups and limited-liability companies" obscures just how concentrated Koch giving really is in recent years. Though the Koch network has at times made an array of grants to many different conservative organizations, most of the money raised at the seminars flows to a handful of the main Koch-directed and controlled groups. From 2013 to 2014, nearly 80 percent of all Koch-raised funds in the Freedom Partners "bank" flowed to just nine of the main Koch groups identified in Figure 5.3—and of those core funded Koch organizations, the largest share went to AFP.[118] By 2015, over 90 percent of Freedom Partners grants were directed to the Kochs' main groups, and again mostly to AFP.[119]

Given its weight in the Koch network, Theda Skocpol and I have dubbed AFP the "800-pound gorilla" of the Koch network. And the more that we have examined AFP, the more unusual of a creature we have found. In some ways, AFP mirrors its predecessor, CSE. Like CSE, it combines central direction—policy agendas and broader strategy are set from AFP's national headquarters—with grassroots volunteers and activists who can be mobilized as needed for political campaigns. Yet AFP goes well beyond CSE's initial structure by establishing a clear federated operation that has institutionalized state and regional staff embedded in the local political landscape.[120] These directors organize grassroots supporters to stage rallies, write, call, and visit elected officials, and contact the media. Directors are generally responsible for raising money from in-state donors themselves to run their operations, but can also count on funds from the treasury controlled by AFP's headquarters to run television, print, and radio ads supporting issues and candidates as part of national campaigns. Most state directors have previously served in Republican politics, and many will return to work for GOP campaigns, legislative offices, and organizations after their tenure at AFP, giving these directors an important source of influence and pressure within their local Republican establishment.[121]

Further unlike CSE—and unlike many other organizations operating in US politics—AFP directs this political clout in both policy and electoral campaigns, seamlessly moving from electing very conservative state and federal lawmakers to aggressively lobbying those same politicians to enact their preferred legislation.[122] AFP's policy goals generally follow the Koch network's hardline libertarian priorities. That entails, as AFP puts it, "reining in public employee unions, expanding worker freedoms, blocking Medicaid expansion, advancing free-market energy policy, lowering taxes, reducing spending [and] expanding school choice."[123]

AFP has grown rapidly since its separation from CSE, as indicated in Figure 5.4. In 2005, AFP had a budget of around $4 million, 19 paid staffers, and an institutionalized presence in 5 states. Just two years later, those figures jumped to a budget of $9 million, a staff of 58, around 700,000 volunteers, and a presence in 15 states. Since then, AFP has continued to expand across the country under the expert supervision of Tim Phillips, a former Christian right political organizer, and by 2015 AFP could count on a budget of around $150 million, about 500 paid staffers, over 2.4 million activist-volunteers, and a presence in states that encompass around 80 percent of the US population.[124] Importantly, the states in which AFP works are not simply deep-red enclaves. AFP also has a presence across the Midwest, including battleground states like Michigan, Wisconsin, Ohio, and Pennsylvania, and in the purple Western Mountain region as well. AFP even counts a number of grassroots volunteers in states where it does not have a paid state staff presence.

Why join AFP as a volunteer? As AFP's website implores, citizens should "volunteer with AFP and make a difference for your community, state, and our nation!"[125] Working with AFP, the site further explains, "you can help educate your fellow citizens about the issues, hold politicians accountable, and advance policies that expand freedom and lower the tax burden. Whether it's on the

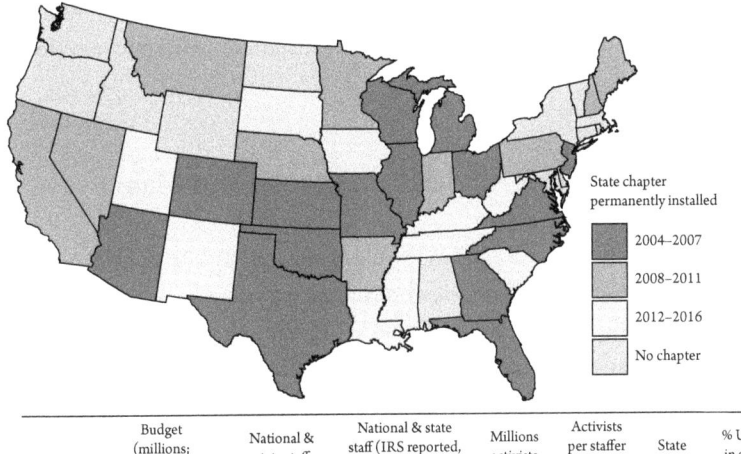

	Budget (millions; combined AFP/Foundation)	National & state staff (AFP reported)	National & state staff (IRS reported, combined AFP/Foundation)	Millions activists nationwide	Activists per staffer (AFP reported)	State directors	% US pop in staffed states
2005	$3.8	19	17	0.2 est		5	16%
2007	$9.2	58	50	0.7	12,069	15	47%
2009	$27.1	74	88	0.9	12,162	19	61%
2011	$50.8	106	177	1.58	14,868	25	70%
2013	$57.6	115	437	2.24	19,443	28	75%
2015	$150	500	902	2.43	4,858	34	80%
2017	At least $67.4	650		2.8	4,308	36	82%

Figure 5.4. THE RAPID GROWTH OF AMERICANS FOR PROSPERITY. The development of AFP from 2005 through 2017. Adapted from Skocpol and Hertel-Fernandez 2016a, 2016b.

phone, at a neighbor's front door, or on the steps of the state capitol, we need citizens like you who are willing to stand up and make their voices heard."[126]

AFP enrolls volunteers by hosting events and rallies, knocking on the doors of known GOP voters, making phone calls to potential conservative allies, and relying on sign-ups on its social media and Internet pages.[127] The reasons that grassroots volunteers sign up are varied.[128] Some join because they are committed to the specific agenda of AFP, like lower taxes or less environmental regulation. Others may be more interested in the social issues that AFP studiously avoids—like immigration, gay rights, or abortion—but are willing to support the same ultra-conservative politicians AFP backs.[129]

In many cases, AFP draws from existing conservative groups in the states, especially local Tea Parties.[130] And sometimes AFP simply pays individuals to sign up as volunteers. In 2012, for instance, Florida's AFP chapter paid local Tea Parties $2 per volunteer they signed up for AFP.[131] "It's an opportunity for tea parties to raise dollars for their organizations by helping AFP with an awareness and membership drive," explained AFP-Florida's director.[132] Regardless of how they are recruited, grassroots volunteers have little say on the agendas and activities of their state or local AFP chapters. By all accounts, AFP is directed just like other Koch operations: from the center, with tight control and little room for error. Poorly performing state directors, for instance, can expect a transfer or even dismissal.[133]

Touring AFP Affiliates in Arizona and Maine

How do the state affiliates of AFP shape elections and public policy? Similar to our tour of SPN affiliates in Arizona and Maine, we can take a quick trip across AFP chapters in those same states. These AFP state chapters were founded at different moments—Arizona in 2007 and Maine in 2010—and thus represent affiliates with varying degrees of institutionalization. That gives us as good a picture as any of the different models AFP has adopted across the states.

AFP-Arizona

The older of the two chapters, AFP-Arizona got a big head start in organizing because AFP staff could build on an existing right-wing grassroots organization in the state, the Federation of Taxpayers. The Federation was an anti-tax-oriented advocacy group that scored state political candidates on the basis of their support for reducing the size of government and slashing taxes.[134] A small organization with a volunteer-only staff, the merger between the Federation and AFP was beneficial for both sides. While the Federation received an infusion of funds and staff, as well as national support, AFP was able to gain an inside perspective on the Arizona political scene and a well-recognized brand to work from.

One of the first activities that the merged AFP-Federation group tackled in 2007 was producing a local version of the statewide scorecards on taxes the Federation had issued in the past. "Too many local government officials seem to be under the impression that no one is watching them," warned AFP Chapter Chairman Chad Kirkpatrick.[135] "With this scorecard, they now know the taxpayers are watching," he summed up.[136]

Those scorecards would become a defining characteristic of AFP's Arizona activities, providing a basis for guiding their grassroots volunteers toward particular candidates in elections. They also threatened potentially wayward lawmakers on how to vote on pending bills that AFP considered to be especially important. As AFP warned Arizona legislators on a pending vote on a budget plan: "Budget votes are a large part of AFP Arizona's scorecards, which measure bills based on their annual dollar impact to taxpayers, producers, and consumers."[137]

Beyond scorecards, the Arizona AFP chapter activates its grassroots volunteer base to contact their elected officials during key legislative debates. For instance, in deliberations over tax changes in 2009, AFP alerted its members that "our Legislators and our new Governor need to know that YOU are watching them, and that you are working with AFP Arizona to keep Big Government from growing."[138] AFP then provided its grassroots base with the necessary information to contact their elected officials. But AFP-Arizona's grassroots contacting does not only target the state legislature; the group also set its sights on the executive branch. In one 2011 debate over a measure that would permit greater privatization of state services, the group warned "all Arizona Taxpayers and Tea Partiers" that "Governor Brewer is under intense pressure to kill the reform from government-worker unions, many city council members, and some business lobbyists."[139] Accordingly, the AFP chapter urged its members to "please call and email Governor Brewer TODAY"—and AFP gave the contact information for the governor, as well as the personal email address of each of the three members of the governor's staff in charge of the issue.

The Arizona chapter has also organized its own state-level version of AFP's national conference—the "Defending the American Dream Summit." That summit brings together grassroots volunteers, state chapter leaders, allied state lawmakers, and national conservative figures to discuss ongoing policy debates within the state and across the country. At the 2008 Arizona version of the event, SPN's in-state affiliate, the Goldwater Institute, offered two of its analysts for policy presentations, as did representatives from two other SPN-affiliated groups from other states (the Reason Foundation from California and the Institute for Justice from Virginia).[140] Other prominent speakers included *The Wall Street Journal* economic columnist Stephen Moore, anti-tax warrior Grover Norquist, and conservative pundit Dinesh D'Souza.[141] A key selling point of the event was the chance to see—and ride—a hot air balloon that the national AFP headquarters was flying throughout the states to decry "hot air" political talk involving "lost jobs, higher taxes, and less freedom."[142]

AFP-Maine

Launched three years after Arizona's chapter, this one did not have the same advantage of an existing grassroots organization to merge with. Still, the group hit the ground running with lots of hope for policy reform. "Maine has the potential to be one of the most economically competitive states in the country," declared AFP-Maine's inaugural state director. "The Maine chapter of Americans for Prosperity is ready to work with its members to urge the next governor and legislature to rein in wasteful spending and get a hold of the state's runaway budget," he summed up optimistically.[143] One of the Maine chapter's first activities was to host a grassroots activist training session, a common practice for AFP chapters. More than seventy-five activists-to-be attended the gathering, which a state senator led. The training, as in other states, offered basic lessons about government spending, crafting and delivering an "effective and winning message," and deploying grassroots strategies to pursue the chapter's agenda through election campaigns and legislative debates.[144]

Given the appeal of that first meeting, AFP began making workshops a regular occurrence, ultimately partnering with the Maine Heritage Policy Center to train citizens on how to run a grassroots campaign, from writing letters to the editor to contacting elected officials more effectively.[145] "It's to help provide the next step so that people can move from rallies to getting more engaged in the political process," explained AFP-Maine's head.[146] Jointly with the Heritage Center, AFP-Maine committed to training at least 1,000 activists across every county by the end of the year.[147]

Aside from intensive grassroots training, AFP-Maine has also engaged in more traditional strategies for shaping state policy. The state chapter's director, for instance, delivered testimony in support of Governor LePage's 2012 budget, which promised deep cuts in taxes—precisely what AFP promotes across the states and in the federal government. In delivering that testimony, AFP-Maine Director Carol Weston bolstered the credibility of her argument by noting that she was speaking on behalf of the 4,000 members of her chapter.[148] Weston also publicly backed a constitutional amendment to eliminate the state income tax altogether—another priority of the Heritage Center, as we saw earlier.[149]

Weston, AFP-Maine's current head, provides a nice example of the career trajectories of AFP directors. Before joining AFP, she had served in Maine's lower legislative chamber (for five years) and upper chamber (for nine years).[150] While a lawmaker, she was highly involved in ALEC, serving on the telecommunications and information technology task force and eventually winning the group's "Legislator of the Year" award for her close work with ALEC in 2008.[151] That pattern is typical of many other states; AFP tends to choose directors who have strong connections to their state's Republican establishment and to other members of the troika.

Beyond its own state legislature, AFP-Maine has used its grassroots base to pressure the state's national representatives as well. One of the signature activities of AFP's national headquarters has been the "No Climate Tax Pledge." Modeled after Grover Norquist's very successful "Taxpayer Protection Pledge," barring lawmakers from supporting any and all tax increases, AFP's version targets any legislation "relating to climate change that includes a net increase in government revenue."[152] Signed by nearly the entire Republican caucus in Congress, the legislation effectively rules out the possibility of pricing carbon emissions, an essential policy step for dealing with climate change. The pledge is more than cheap talk: investigative journalists have discovered that AFP's advocacy around the pledge was important in scuttling negotiations over bipartisan climate legislation under President Obama.[153] In 2010, as the debate over that bill was still raging, AFP-Maine celebrated the fact that it had successfully gotten the state's gubernatorial candidate Paul LePage and two US House candidates to sign that pledge.[154] "The one thing elected officials should be able to agree on is that global warming shouldn't be used as an excuse to hike taxes on citizens and businesses," explained AFP-Maine's state director. "We encourage all of Maine's elected officials and candidates for office to sign the pledge."[155]

The Strengths and Limits of the Troika's Close Partnership

As both of these brief glimpses into the chapters in Arizona and Maine indicate, AFP offers conservative advocates access to a base of energized citizen-activists ready to contact lawmakers, participate in rallies, and turn out voters in elections. AFP's national headquarters also has the funds to deploy flurries of ads against state and federal politicians who support policies the organization opposes. (Of course, AFP's capacity to run those ads means that the mere threat of an ad blitz can often achieve the same outcome.) Those resources have made AFP a valuable partner for both SPN and ALEC in the pursuit of a common agenda since AFP's creation in 2004, and particularly since AFP's rapid growth from 2007 onward.

ALEC's 2017 summer conference neatly captures how the three components of the troika come together in pursuit of the same set of policies. Sixty-three staffers from 30 SPN affiliates across 21 states registered to participate in the conference. So too did 58 staffers from various Koch network groups, including 39 staffers from AFP. AFP's CEO and COO were registered attendees, as well as state directors or deputy directors from 23 states. Figure 5.5 maps out the states represented by SPN affiliates and AFP state chapters. It shows that all three members of the troika—ALEC, SPN, and AFP—were well represented in 2017 in a number of key states for upcoming political battles, including Colorado, Illinois, Kansas, Michigan, Minnesota, Ohio, Virginia, and Wisconsin.

Still, coordination between the troika members is not perfect, or universal. When it comes to promoting private alternatives to public schools, including the use of vouchers and school choice, limiting environmental regulations, curbing labor market rules, cutting taxes, especially on business and wealthy individuals, and weakening labor unions, AFP, SPN, and ALEC are entirely on the same page. That makes collaboration between the three groups relatively straightforward on those issues. But the situation becomes more complicated when business-friendly regulations or spending is on the agenda.

As we have seen, ALEC and SPN represent coalitions between corporate *and* conservative interests. As a result, many of the corporate bills that ALEC

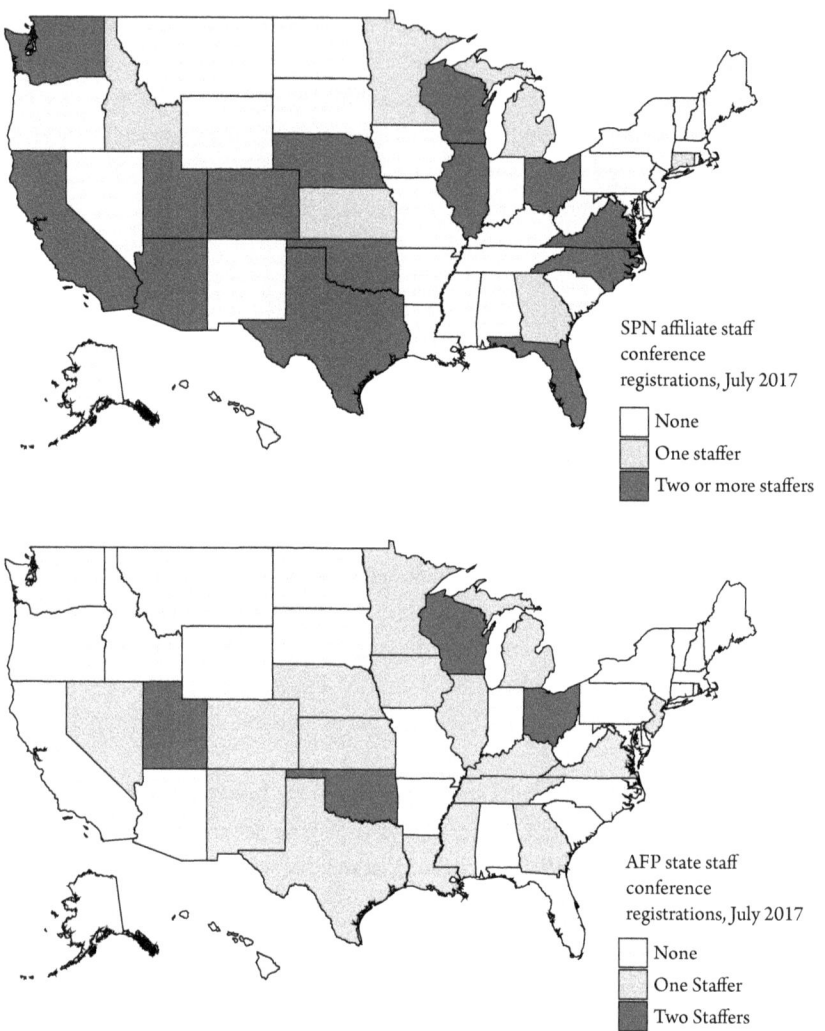

Figure 5.5. ALEC Conference Participation by SPN and AFP by State, 2017. Source is leaked conference materials.

has lobbied for involve business-friendly forms of spending or regulation, like pushing for more favorable public contracting to private service providers. In contrast, the ideologically backed AFP and the Koch network remain staunchly opposed to nearly any public spending or regulation, regardless of whether that spending flows to the private sector. Indeed, on a national level, AFP's anti-government stance has increasingly positioned it to the right of even the US Chamber of Commerce on a range of debates, like the reauthorization of agricultural subsidies, infrastructure spending, and support for US exporters.[156] The US Chamber, though intensely conservative and deeply intertwined with the GOP, still supports these business-friendly expansions of government.[157] As a result, we are less likely to see AFP working together with ALEC and SPN on these narrower, business-friendly policies. (We will examine more of these business-troika tensions in the following chapter.)

Similarly, it is important to recognize that SPN and ALEC are more closely intertwined than AFP is to ALEC. As we saw earlier, many individual SPN affiliates participate on ALEC task forces, responding to the incentives provided by SPN's national office in conjunction with donors. AFP's national headquarters does participate in some ALEC task forces—like the tax and fiscal policy panel—but individual AFP state chapters as a general rule do not. That distinction reflects the fact that AFP state affiliates are not really institutionally separate from their national organization in the same way as SPN affiliates are legally (if not actually in practice).

The SPN, in contrast, has generally offered more opportunities for the participation of individual AFP state chapters, however, and the state directors of many AFP chapters regularly attend SPN national and regional convenings. Of course, even without formal enrollment in ALEC's task forces, AFP still buttresses ALEC's efforts at passing state legislation. AFP state affiliates often provide the grassroots heft to push lawmakers into voting for ALEC priorities. Moreover, by helping to elect very conservative GOPers, AFP creates a friendly audience for ALEC's priorities even before any bills are proposed. The relationship between these three members of the right-wing troika thus varies given the different structures of the three networks, and especially the different composition of their constituent parts.

Having introduced the three members of the right-wing troika, the next chapter turns to documenting how they work together in the pursuit of a common agenda—and what that agenda means for state policy and politics across the country.

6

Transforming the Nation One State at a Time

The Right-Wing Troika and State Policy

Republicans never quite managed to gain full control of Iowa's state government for the nearly two decades spanning 1998 to 2016. While Republicans retained control of the state legislature from the late 1990s through the mid-2000s, Democrats still held the governorship. And when conservative GOPer Terry Branstad replaced Democrat Chet Culver in the governor's mansion, voters still opted to keep Democrats in control of their state's senate. That knife-edge balance of power changed dramatically after the 2016 elections. Republicans picked up six seats in the senate, giving them a nine-seat majority in that chamber and—finally—trifecta control of the whole state. The GOP's margins in both legislative chambers meant that when the 2017 legislative session convened, Democrats would lack any ability to block Republican legislative initiatives. Republican lawmakers were not shy about their plans for capitalizing on their newfound power. "I believe voters gave us a mandate to do business differently," argued Senate Republican leader Bill Dix. "We need to kick the door in on government and how we do business."[1]

What would that mandate look like? In an interview with the *Des Moines Register*, Dix argued that his party would focus primarily on trimming the size of government, ensuring that "the state budget is treated like the family budget," while also taking steps to "grow our state and make our state more attractive for investment and new career opportunities."[2] Most voters and political observers assumed that this would mean a typical Republican agenda of tax cuts and downsizing government programs. But that is not what happened.

Immediately after starting the new legislative session, Republicans announced that their first priority would be pushing major reform of the state's rules governing public-sector labor unions. "Everything is on the table, I'll put it that way," announced the new chair of the senate committee responsible for labor policy, "we're looking at everything."[3] Some Republicans signaled that they would want to restrict the areas over which public-sector unions could bargain with government. Other GOPers called for setting new limits on how contracts were negotiated between unions and governments. And still others discussed eliminating union bargaining rights, established on bipartisan lines forty-some years ago, altogether. Many political observers, especially those in the labor movement, were taken aback by Republicans' choice to prioritize this bill over all other possibilities. "There is not a peoples' mandate for something like this," argued the head of the state teachers union, "I've not heard taxpayers talking about the need to change collective bargaining in Iowa. Maybe that's why they're all over the place and don't know what to do—because this is much more of an attack than something the voters asked for."[4]

Even so, government employee unions and their allies in the Democratic Party were powerless to stop the GOP's push. Without any formal blocking power in the legislature, they were reduced to watching helplessly as Republicans introduced a bill that substantially curtailed the rights of public-sector labor unions—and rammed it through the legislature in just a matter of days. After pulling a marathon all-night legislative session the night after Valentine's Day, Governor Branstad signed the GOP's reform package into law. Inspired by the controversial Wisconsin legislation curtailing public-sector bargaining rights from 2011, Iowa's law goes even further in many respects.[5] Collective bargaining for most public workers would now be limited solely to wages—and even then capped the allowable rate of wage hikes to inflation. Overnight, government employee unions lost the ability to negotiate over all the aspects of working conditions—health insurance, pensions, training, promotion rules, and dismissal guidelines—that are important parts of any job. Unions also must now win the votes of a majority of the workers they represent at the end of every contract, or face decertification. That provision essentially means that unions will need to run continuous campaigns among their members. The bill lastly bars unions from automatically collecting dues from their members, a standard practice for labor organizations in many states.

Remarking on the speed with which the GOP was moving forward with this legislation, one state senate Democrat argued that the Republicans had "cheated Iowans. . . . You cheated people out of the opportunity to pay attention to a really big change that you are ramming in here. You disrespected the people of the state."[6] To many observers of Iowan politics, the fact that the GOP had campaigned on relatively anodyne economic proposals and then ended up pursuing such a hard-right agenda in office seemed puzzling. Even some Republicans were wary of the speed and extremity of the conservative legislative blitz, noting that their constituents were not on board. Reflecting on his decision to buck the party and vote against the public-sector reform bill, one Republican state representative argued that lawmakers "come up here to represent our constituency.... I've heard from hundreds of people back home.... I just feel that I did my duty as a representative."[7]

Public opinion polling, as best we can tell, backs up that Republican's sense that Iowans were not on board with the cuts to public union rights. According to estimates I produced from 2011 polling data that I describe below, only about four in ten Iowans supported cutting back the rights of public workers to collectively bargain with government. That's consistent with a 2018 survey, which found that over 60 percent of Iowan voters thought the legislature should reinstate public-sector collective bargaining.[8] If not voters, what else can explain the aggressive move against public employees?

The legislative text for the bill provides one clue. The language curbing government employee organizing and bargaining rights was very similar to that of the controversial bill passed by Wisconsin's GOP legislature and governor in 2011, which itself drew from ALEC model proposals. That shouldn't come as much of a surprise given that all state lawmakers in Iowa were automatically enrolled as ALEC members during a recent legislative session (GOP chamber leaders made the decision, much to the consternation of Democrats).[9] That included Senate Majority Leader and champion of the public union measure Bill Dix, who had been serving as ALEC's state chair in Iowa, as well as House Speaker Linda Upmeyer, who was serving as a national chairwoman of ALEC.[10] Just as importantly, the state's conservative Republican governor was an early member and founder of ALEC, serving as one of the group's first national directors in the 1970s.[11] Governor Branstad has had nothing but good things to say about the group ever since, noting that he could not "stress enough how unique and important the American Legislative Exchange Council is for our future."[12] "The ALEC Source Books [precursors to model bills] alone are among the most important documents produced in America today," Branstad has concluded glowingly.

Even with the strong support for ALEC in the statehouse, however, ALEC did not have to push the public-sector reforms on its own. Shortly after the legislation was introduced in the legislature, AFP's Iowa chapter announced "the launch of a grassroots campaign mobilizing its base of activists across the state to contact their state legislators to advocate for collective bargaining reform."[13] That campaign included mailers, advertisements, and grassroots outreach—exactly the sort of advocacy we saw in the previous chapter, with AFP activating its volunteer base of over 37,000 Iowans to contact the legislature to push for the bill.[14] "We are calling on our thousands of Iowa activists to urge their legislators to reform Iowa's broken collective bargaining system," AFP's state director proudly announced.[15] That state director was then one of the few representatives to issue testimony in support of the legislation when the bill came up for public discussion—and then he stayed through the marathon all-night session to help whip votes.¹⁶ Once Governor Branstad was ready to sign the bill, he did so in a private ceremony with only one confirmed guest in attendance: the state's AFP director.¹⁷ (The governor claimed others were in attendance, but could not recall their names.¹⁸)

The State Policy Network's (SPN) affiliate in the state, the Public Interest Institute, also got in on the action. Shortly after the election, the Institute sent an update to SPN's national headquarters noting that they were "pleased to see the state election results last November."¹⁹ Facing a friendly legislature, the Institute planned to focus especially closely in the upcoming weeks and months on "changes to the collective bargaining system to eliminate Iowa's Pay Gap between public employees and those in the private sector." Reform of the state's laws governing collective bargaining was a longstanding priority for the Public Interest Institute, just like other SPN affiliates, and the Institute had previously published a number of earlier research reports calling for cuts to public-sector collective bargaining and organizing rights.

Indeed, several of the reports published by the Institute were state-specific versions of a regular publication produced by ALEC.²⁰ And in February, just before the public-sector bargaining bill came up for debate, the Institute released a well-timed report titled "The Wisconsin Miracle: Governor Scott Walker and the Historic Act 10 Reform Measure." As the title suggests, the report extolled the benefits of Wisconsin's cuts to public-sector bargaining rights and detailed the economic gains that could flow to Iowa should the state pursue similar reforms of their own.²¹ "Iowa can learn from Governor Walker and his Act 10 reforms," an Institute analyst concluded, and as Iowa policymakers started deliberation of reforms, they should turn to Walker "for both encouragement and direction."²²

The troika's fingerprints, then, are all over the Iowa public union legislation and suggest the real reason for lawmakers' strong support of that bill and the slew of other measures pursued in the months following the election. With full Republican control of the legislature and governorship and a strong delegation of ALEC members, an SPN affiliate, and an AFP chapter in the state, the troika was able to work together to push a common legislative agenda. In this chapter, I zoom out from the specific case of Iowa to show how the close coordination of the troika members has reshaped legislation across the states, focusing on two policy battles: over public-sector collective bargaining and organizing rights and expansion of the federal–state Medicaid program as part of the Affordable Care Act. This chapter thus provides a richer picture of the coordination between the three members of the right-wing troika that I described in the previous chapter, showing how this coordination plays out in specific policy areas. Together, these two cases represent substantively important policies with implications for the distribution of economic, political, and social resources across the country. They also nicely illustrate how the troika's strategies work in an area where ALEC, AFP, and SPN are actively trying to pass new legislation (union rights) and where the troika members are on the defensive, trying to block legislation from passing (Medicaid expansion).

The One-Two-Three Punch Demobilizing State Public-Sector Labor Unions

In Chapter 1, I explained that ALEC has, since its inception, gone after the right of public unions to organize, bargain collectively, and participate in politics for three reasons, ranging from the philosophical to the pragmatic.[23] ALEC argued that public unions were fundamentally incompatible with democratic government; that those unions contributed to the excess cost of government by driving up public employee wages and benefits and lobbying for new public programs; and that public unions supported liberal candidates and causes, thereby making it harder for ALEC to achieve its own policy agenda. As one state leader wrote in an ALEC magazine in 2011: "Unions often have hoards of money to spend in political campaigns because they can use automatically deducted dues from government employee paychecks. . . . Public employee unions will continue being the [political] 'big dog' as long as they have access to the taxpayer provided salaries of their members. Lawmakers should adopt [ALEC] legislation to block this process."[24]

A survey of sitting state legislators and their staff I fielded in 2017 underscores just how much ALEC legislators—above and beyond their conservative peers—prioritize the defeat of public employee unions (details of this survey appear in the Chapter 6 Appendix). On that survey, I asked a random subsample of legislators about their support for labor union rights for different groups of workers: janitors, teachers, police and firefighters, state and local agency workers, and manufacturing workers (the subsample consisted of 150 lawmakers). For each kind of worker, I asked legislators' support for employee collective bargaining rights, automatic dues collection, agency fees (which permit unions to charge nonmembers for services the union provides to them), the ability of unions to give extra social benefits to their members, as well as the right of unions to make campaign contributions, lobby government, or go on strike. I separately asked whether lawmakers had ever relied on ALEC when drafting legislation.

Lawmakers reliant on ALEC were substantially less likely to indicate support for teachers and state/local worker union rights than were lawmakers not reliant on ALEC. ALEC lawmakers, on average, reported support for 5.1 rights for public-sector workers (out of 14 possible rights), compared with 8.2 rights supported by legislators overall. That difference persisted even after controlling for legislators' self-reported ideology, partisanship, and region (full results appear in the Chapter 6 Appendix). ALEC legislators evidently stand far apart even from their otherwise similar conservative companions in opposing public-sector labor unions.

The other two members of the troika reached similar positions as well, recognizing early on that a strategy of weakening the public-sector labor movement could yield big political dividends in the future. A weaker public-sector labor movement, SPN and AFP have reasoned, would pave the way for the troika to push their own favored candidates and proposals. Tim Phillips, the former grassroots organizer and current head of AFP whom we met in the previous chapter, nicely summed up the troika's perspective on public employee unions in remarks during a 2011 meeting of right-wing activists. Reflecting on why conservative Republicans had failed to gain more political power in the past, Phillips explained that the Democrats "had the public employee unions . . . which have only gotten stronger, have only gotten better-funded, have only gotten better organized."[25] To have a chance of making durable political inroads at either the state or the federal level, AFP and the conservative movement more generally had to push back against the public labor movement. "We go back a long way on this," Phillips summarized on the government union issue.[26]

A recent report from the SPN similarly describes how the group is heavily focused on "taking the kind of dramatic reforms we've seen in recent years in Indiana, Wisconsin, Michigan, and now West Virginia—freeing teachers and other government workers from coercive unionism—and spreading them across the nation."[27] Those reforms, SPN's head emphasized, have the promise of "*permanently depriving* the Left from access to millions of dollars in dues extracted from unwilling union members every election cycle" (original emphasis).[28] Reforms like right to work, cuts to public employee collective bargaining, and efforts to make it harder for government employee unions to collect dues and retain members will "defund and defang one of our freedom movement's most powerful opponents, the government unions" while also "clear[ing] pathways toward passage of so many other pro-freedom initiatives in the states" (original emphasis).[29]

All three networks have thus worked closely with one another to prioritize the defeat of public-sector labor unions, both as a substantive policy objective and as a means of weakening or even removing a political opponent. But does the coordination between the three right-wing state networks matter? And can we see the payoffs of this effort?

To probe the independent effect of the strength and coordination between the three networks on the fate of public employee unions—and state politics more generally—I focus on the period from 2011 to 2012. That is the legislative session in which state battles over the rights of public-sector unions to bargain collectively came to a head.[30] This trend began in Wisconsin, where newly elected conservative GOP Governor Scott Walker signed into law a budget bill that included provisions to end substantive collective bargaining and agency fees for the vast majority of the state's employees. Following Wisconsin's lead, a number of other states began to consider, pass, and enact cuts to public-sector labor unions. A close look at state action in this legislative session thus provides an ideal opportunity to see what—if any—role the troika played in supporting these campaigns above and beyond other political and economic conditions in the states. In all, thirteen states had legislatures that passed such measures, including some reliably conservative states like Indiana, but also some more typically moderate states like Pennsylvania and Illinois.

To measure the presence of, and coordination between, the members of the right-wing troika of AFP, SPN, and ALEC, I have constructed a standardized measure, varying from 0 to 1, consisting of the following components.[31]

AFP

A state received 1 point if AFP had a paid state director in 2011, an important measure of AFP's institutionalized presence in states.[32] A state received an additional point if AFP produced an annual scorecard rating the votes of state lawmakers as of 2011 (based on my review of archived AFP websites). Such scorecards are indicative of attention by AFP state staffers to legislative activities, as we saw with the Arizona and Maine affiliates in the previous chapter. Lastly, states received 1 point for organizing an event or publishing material about public-sector unions and another point for featuring these issues on the AFP website (based again on my review of archived AFP websites). These final indicators should provide a measure of the degree to which AFP chapters were committed to this specific issue in 2011. Each state could thus range from a minimum possible AFP score of zero (as in Massachusetts and Wyoming) to 4 (as in Arizona and Michigan). The median AFP index was 2.

SPN

I measured two aspects of SPN's presence in states. First, I summed the total budgets of all SPN affiliate think tanks in a state as an indicator of SPN's total resources (using data from IRS tax filings). Second, I reviewed each affiliate's website in 2011 to see whether at least one affiliate in a state had published material on public-sector labor unions in that year. If so, the chapter received a single point. Standardizing these two variables, I found the lowest values in South Dakota, which had a relatively underresourced SPN affiliate and also did not publish research on public-sector unions that year. The highest values of SPN strength registered in Michigan and Arizona, where affiliates had larger budgets and had also devoted significant staff time to publishing work attacking public-sector unions.

ALEC

I captured ALEC strength in two ways. First, I counted the number of state lawmakers participating on ALEC's task force responsible for producing model bills related to labor union policy.[33] I expected that states with more lawmakers serving on this task force would be better equipped to move policy related to weakening the labor movement. Second, to gauge coordination between ALEC and state SPN affiliates, I created an indicator counting the total number of ties that SPN affiliates in a given state had with ALEC. So, for instance, Arizona's Goldwater Institute had served on six task forces for ALEC in 2011, setting this indicator at 6. Affiliates with stronger institutional ties with ALEC ought to be better positioned to work together with ALEC's legislative members to pass bills. Thirty-nine percent of states had SPN affiliates that had developed institutional ties with ALEC, and the typical state with ties had an average of three such partnerships. I did not construct indicators for the relationship between AFP and SPN, or AFP and ALEC, as AFP's state-level partnerships are looser than those between SPN and ALEC, as we saw in the previous chapter.

Figure 6.1 summarizes how the index of right-wing troika strength and coordination varies across the fifty states, with darker colors indicating a stronger

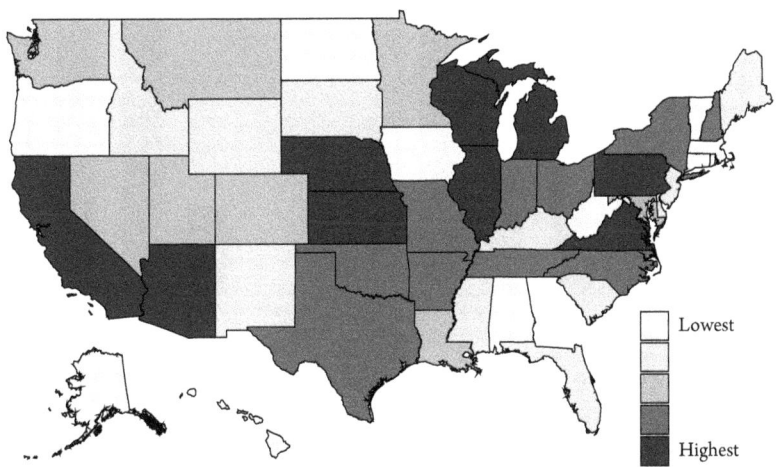

Figure 6.1. RIGHT-WING TROIKA STRENGTH AND COORDINATION ON PUBLIC EMPLOYEE BARGAINING CUTBACKS, 2011–2012. See the text for variable definitions.

presence of ALEC, SPN, and AFP in a state and a more intense focus on cutting public employee bargaining rights. The index registers highest in Wisconsin, Nebraska, Michigan, Kansas, and Arizona, and lowest in Rhode Island, Alaska, Hawaii, Oregon, and Massachusetts.

Was it the case that the states where the troika was more active on this issue were indeed the ones that passed legislative cutbacks to public employee bargaining? The left panel of Figure 6.2 considers this question by grouping the states into five equally sized categories, depending on their ranking of troika strength and coordination, and plotting the proportion of states in each category that passed cutbacks in the 2011 to 2012 legislative session. Sure enough, we see that the number of states passing cutbacks to public-sector collective bargaining steadily increases as we move from states with a weaker presence of the troika to those with a stronger presence. No states in the lowest category of ALEC, SPN, and AFP strength and coordination passed cutbacks to public bargaining—but over half in the highest category did.

Cautious readers might wonder if the troika was simply more active on this issue in Republican-dominated states, which would mean that the positive relationship identified in this plot was simply a story of partisan control of government. This concern turns out to be only half right. It is true that partisan control of government is a very strong explanation for which states ultimately passed cuts to public-sector bargaining. Nine out of the thirteen states passing

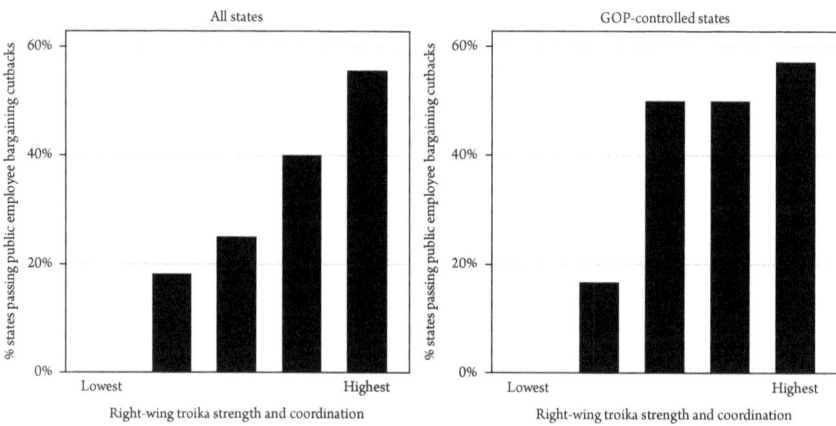

Figure 6.2. RIGHT-WING TROIKA STRENGTH AND COORDINATION AND PUBLIC EMPLOYEE BARGAINING CUTS, 2011–2012. The relationship between the measure of right-wing troika strength and coordination on the public union bargaining issue and the states passing cuts to public-sector bargaining rights. States are divided into five equally sized groups by right-wing strength and coordination index (quintiles). The left panel shows the relationship for all states; the right panel shows the relationship for partially or fully GOP-controlled states.

cutbacks to public employee bargaining rights had full trifecta GOP control. But establishing this fact only begs the question of why those nine states under full GOP control—out of twenty-two such states nationwide—passed cutbacks to public worker collective bargaining. The right panel in Figure 6.2 gives us an answer, showing that within the subset of fully or partially GOP-controlled states, it was the states where ALEC, AFP, and SPN were stronger that cutbacks to public bargaining were more likely to pass legislatures. Even taking into account which party controls state government, then, the strength of the troika predicts where we are more likely to see retrenchment of public union power.[34]

What about the public? Even if public opinion did not appear to drive the recent offensive against public employee bargaining rights in Iowa, it might still be the case that attitudes of ordinary citizens toward government union bargaining could help us to account for the states that did—and did not—legislate cutbacks. To gauge public support for cutting public-sector bargaining, I pooled together four nationally representative surveys fielded in early 2011 to estimate the share of adults in each state that year that favored cutting public-sector labor union bargaining rights (the details are given in the Chapter 6 Appendix).[35] On average, only about 40 percent of American adults supported cuts to public-sector bargaining rights, and support was highest in New Hampshire. The left plot of Figure 6.3 assesses whether there is any relationship between public opinion

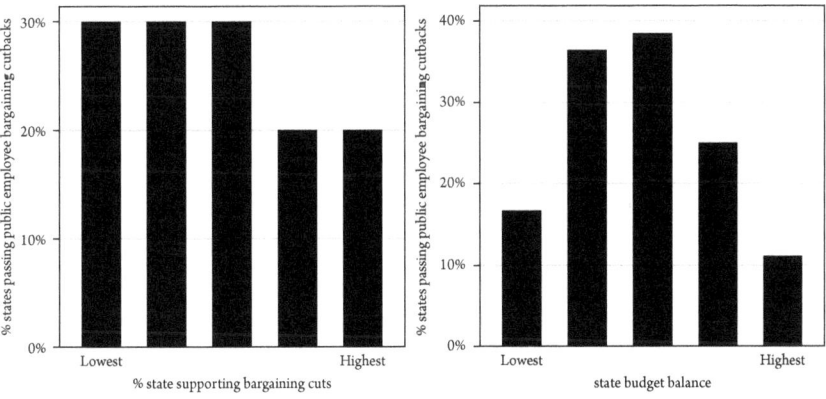

Figure 6.3. PUBLIC OPINION AND STATE BUDGET BALANCE CANNOT EXPLAIN CUTBACKS TO PUBLIC-SECTOR COLLECTIVE BARGAINING, 2011–2012. The relationship between public support for cuts to public bargaining (left panel) and state budget balance (right panel) and the states passing cuts to public bargaining rights. States are divided into five equally sized groups by either public attitudes or budget balance (quintiles). See the Chapter 6 Appendix for the estimation method of support for collective bargaining cuts. State budget balance is the ratio of state revenues to expenditures; higher values indicate better finances. Data from the National Association of State Budget Officers.

toward bargaining retrenchment and where such cutbacks passed legislatures. As is readily apparent, no such relationship exists. Cutbacks were passed just as readily in states with high and low levels of public support for these reforms. Public opinion, then, does not provide us with much help in understanding the landscape of recent public-sector bargaining reform.

If not voters, what about state budgets? Supporters of cutbacks to public-sector bargaining rights often grounded their arguments in budgetary terms. "We must take immediate action to ensure fiscal stability in our state," argued Wisconsin GOP Governor Scott Walker when introducing his measure curbing public-sector bargaining rights.[36] The union bill "will meet the immediate needs of our state and give government the tools to deal with this and future budget crises," he further explained.[37] As a result, we might expect more political support for cutting back public-sector bargaining rights in states that experienced greater fiscal strain. The right plot in Figure 6.3 examines the relationship between state budget balances—the ratio of revenue and expenditures of a state—compared to bargaining cutbacks.[38] (Higher values indicate better state finances.) States with worse budget balances were no more likely than those with better budgets to pass cutbacks. If anything, it tended to be states with middling budget balances that were most likely to try to retrench bargaining rights for government workers. So while budget woes may have been the reason offered by Governor Walker in Wisconsin, it was not the case that states in similar budget straits also turned to bargaining cutbacks.

Figures 6.2 and 6.3 help us to see the importance of the three cross-state, right-wing networks in accounting for the slew of retrenchment efforts against public union rights. But this is a picture across states, not individual lawmakers. Can we see the role of these groups when we drill down to the individual legislator level, as I did in Chapter 3? Such an analysis could show how the right-wing networks mattered above and beyond the effects of legislators' individual ideological commitments and party. Accordingly, I collected all available roll call votes on the measures cutting back public-sector collective bargaining I examined earlier, looking at how each state representative or senator voted on those bills. In all, I was able to compile voting records for nine states: Idaho, Illinois, Indiana, Michigan, New Hampshire, Ohio, Oklahoma, Pennsylvania, and Wisconsin.

For each legislator in those states, I gathered information on their vote, their partisan affiliation, and their ideological orientation (as measured on the standard left-right scale described in Chapter 3).[39] I also reviewed all the internal ALEC records I collected to see if lawmakers were members of the group. Finally, I searched through records of legislative proceedings in each state to see if members referenced the research or work of their state's local SPN affiliate. I combined the ALEC and SPN measures to create an indicator of the extent to which each legislator relied on these two right-wing networks, coded as zero if a lawmaker was neither a member of ALEC nor had relied on SPN think tank work, 1 if a lawmaker was either a member of ALEC or had relied on SPN research, and 2 if a lawmaker was both an ALEC member and had referenced SPN's commentary and analysis in legislative proceedings. Sixteen percent of lawmakers in these states were either ALEC members or had relied on SPN research in the 2011–2012 legislative session. (Since AFP does not work directly with lawmakers as members, it is harder to think of a way to systematically gauge the relationship between AFP and legislative votes on public union cutbacks.)

ALEC and SPN ties certainly seem as though they could shape legislator votes on public bargaining legislation. Looking across all the state lawmakers, I find that just under 70 percent of lawmakers voted for cuts to bargaining for government employees. On the other hand, 92 percent of lawmakers with either a tie to ALEC or SPN voted in favor of curbing government employee bargaining. And all those members with both ALEC and SPN ties voted for bargaining cutbacks. But just as with any look across states, we might wonder if this is simply a partisan story.

Figure 6.4 addresses this concern, documenting how lawmakers relying on either ALEC or SPN (or both) voted on measures to cut back public-sector labor bargaining while also accounting for lawmakers' partisan affiliations. Two characteristics of this plot stand out: first, partisan affiliation indeed goes a long way in accounting for votes on these measures. Republicans were around twice as likely as Democrats to cast votes in favor of cutting public-sector bargaining

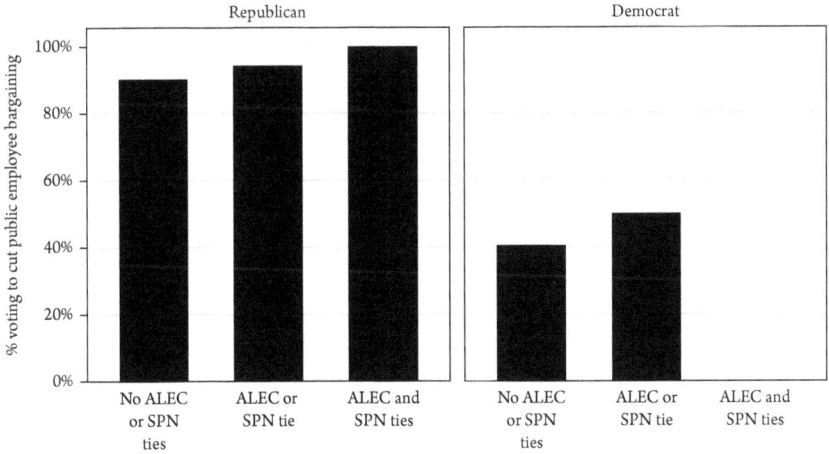

Figure 6.4. ALEC AND SPN RELIANCE AND VOTES ON PUBLIC EMPLOYEE BARGAINING CUTBACKS BY PARTY, 2011–2012. The proportion of lawmakers voting to cut public employee bargaining rights by troika affiliation. States included: Idaho, Illinois, Indiana, Michigan, New Hampshire, Ohio, Oklahoma, Pennsylvania, and Wisconsin.

across all levels of ALEC and SPN membership. But within both Democrats and Republicans, there is still an identifiable relationship between ALEC and SPN ties and final votes on passage of public bargaining cuts. Ninety percent of GOP state lawmakers without any ties to ALEC or SPN voted for final passage of bills cutting public-sector bargaining—but 100 percent of those with both ties did. ALEC- or SPN-reliant Republican lawmakers, then, were about ten percentage points more likely to support public bargaining cuts than their copartisans who did not have such ties. We even see a similar relationship among Democrats: Democrats with no ties to ALEC or SPN voted for public bargaining cuts only about 40 percent of the time, but those with either a relationship to ALEC or SPN voted for cuts 50 percent of the time. (No Democrats in the states I study had ties to both groups.)

Thus, ties to the right-wing troika still matter above and beyond partisanship. As Figure 6.5 shows, the same is also true of lawmakers' ideological orientations. Using the measure of legislative ideology—based on their roll call votes and candidate surveys—I described in Chapter 2, I divided lawmakers into three equally sized groups. We can consider these three groups as representing the liberal state lawmakers, the moderates, and the conservatives. Across all three categories of lawmaker ideological orientation, we see a similar pattern when it comes to ties to ALEC and SPN: the stronger the relationship a lawmaker had to both groups, the more likely that lawmaker was to vote in favor of cuts to government employee union bargaining. This, combined with the results from Figure 6.4, strongly suggests that the SPN and ALEC effect is real—and not simply an artifact of lawmakers' party or left-right leanings. (Results in the

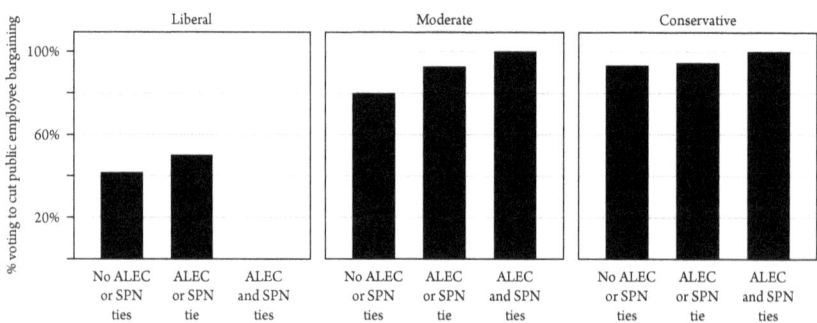

Figure 6.5. ALEC AND SPN RELIANCE AND VOTES ON PUBLIC EMPLOYEE BARGAINING CUTBACKS BY LEGISLATOR IDEOLOGY, 2011–2012. The proportion of lawmakers voting to cut public employee bargaining rights by legislator ideology. States included: Idaho, Illinois, Indiana, Michigan, New Hampshire, Ohio, Oklahoma, Pennsylvania, and Wisconsin. State legislative ideology data from Shor and McCarty 2011.

Chapter 6 Appendix show that the importance of the troika holds up in state- and legislator-level regressions controlling for a variety of other factors.)

Our look at public-sector bargaining cutbacks across the states and individual lawmakers illustrates the broad relationships between right-wing network strength and coordination and legislative action on this issue, but cannot show the specific ways in which the three organizations bolstered one another's efforts. Furthermore, the broad cross-state picture cannot perfectly isolate the pressure that the troika has exerted on state policy debates. In an ideal world, I would be able to draw a comparison between states with otherwise identical political conditions—except for the development of the troika. Yet this world does not exist. In many states, ALEC and SPN have been building ties within the state legislature for at least thirty years, and AFP for up to a decade. The firmly entrenched nature of the troika in many states means that it is hard to speculate about what statehouses would look like *without* the presence of ALEC, SPN, and AFP.

Still, to complement our understanding of the exact mechanisms the troika uses to coordinate with one another and lobby legislatures, as well as to gain a better appreciation of the independent effect of the troika on policy outcomes, we can turn to a case study of one specific state. The advantage of this approach is that we can closely trace the processes the troika deployed, holding other conditions constant. The battle over Wisconsin's controversial Act 10, which among other changes effectively ended most public-sector collective bargaining and agency fees, provides an ideal case for this approach. Act 10 offers a clear illustration of how the three troika members converged in support of common policy goals against public-sector labor unions. It shows how the troika pushed the GOP state government to aggressively tackle public-sector bargaining immediately after Republicans assumed full control of the legislature and governorship in 2011.

Newly elected GOP Governor Walker introduced Act 10, or the Budget Repair Bill, shortly after taking office in early 2011, ostensibly in response to the state's budget gap.[40] The state's Democratic contingent in the legislature, as well as the largest public-sector union, initially signaled that they could negotiate on the budget cuts but not the changes to collective bargaining.[41] Refusing to compromise, Walker pushed ahead with the full proposal, spurring massive protests from union members and sympathetic citizens.[42] Critics of the legislation pointed out that cutting bargaining rights would not directly improve the state's budget situation, and noted that the changes to collective bargaining seemed targeted to Walker's political opponents more than anything else. The restrictions on collective bargaining, for instance, did not apply to public safety officers, workers who tended to lean much more Republican than other public employees.[43]

The troika members were present at every step in the legislative process. As we previously saw, Walker himself was a longtime ALEC participant as a member of the state legislature.[44] Subsequently as governor, several of the initial measures he pushed through the legislature before the budget bill came directly from other ALEC model bills intended to reduce the ability of consumers to bring lawsuits against companies.[45] The budget bill itself contained many provisions from ALEC models, including the legislative language stripping public unions of most bargaining rights. And aside from Walker, the top GOP leaders in both the lower and upper chambers were also longtime ALEC participants and active members in a number of issue areas (recall the Fitzgerald brothers from Chapter 3), as were many of both chambers' more junior members.[46] Indeed, the older Fitzgerald brother (Senate Majority Leader Scott Fitzgerald) had begun floating the idea of curbing union fees at an ALEC meeting a year earlier, in 2010, telling a reporter shortly thereafter that he had "just attended an American Legislative Exchange Council meeting. And I was surprised about how much momentum there was in and around that discussion [around right to work]."[47]

Walker and his legislative allies were further bolstered by AFP's outfit in the state, which had been operating continuously at that point for seven years, making it one of the first chapters installed in the network.[48] Indeed, even before Walker assumed office, AFP had been working with him to craft a legislative agenda for the state that included, at the top of the list, cuts to public-sector collective bargaining rights.[49] Once the union protests were underway at the capitol, AFP organized demonstrations in Madison, paying to bus in hundreds of supporters of Walker's bill from across the state.[50] The legislative battle was such a high priority for the network that it flew out Tim Phillips, AFP's national president, to address one of the group's counterrallies.[51] And apart from grassroots mobilization, AFP also bought at least half a million dollars' worth of TV and radio ads to support Walker and the budget bill during the standoff.[52]

SPN's affiliates in Wisconsin were out in full force as well. The MacIver Institute, one of the two SPN members in the state, published an editorial just weeks after Walker's election in 2010 calling for a repeal of collective bargaining for public employees.[53] MacIver's prescient backing of the measure should not come as a surprise, since the organization had been supporting and working with state Republicans for years (the Institute was in fact co-founded by AFP-Wisconsin's first state director). As one journalist explained, "MacIver not only helped lay the policy groundwork for Act 10, it also helped manage its aftermath."[54]

During the protests at the Capitol, for instance, MacIver dispatched interns to film supporters of Act 10 and clips from that video went viral in the conservative blogosphere. MacIver's work, in turn, was crucial to embattled Republicans in the legislature behind the push for Act 10. "All the naysayers were saying that

Act 10 was the worst thing in the world, that the sky was going to fall, and that there wouldn't be enough teachers to teach classes, school sports would end," explained one Republican senator, Leah Vukmir, who was a champion of the collective bargaining cutbacks (and an active ALEC member). "[MacIver] highlighted the positive things that were happening. Those weren't easy to find in the beginning."[55] Once the governor became the target of a contentious but ultimately unsuccessful recall election, AFP's Wisconsin chapter worked with MacIver to spend at least $4.5 million to run ads proclaiming that the controversial budget bill, including the cuts to public employee bargaining rights, was working.[56] AFP also coordinated with MacIver on grassroots events such as town halls and other rallies to support the governor.[57]

Aside from AFP, MacIver was assisted by the Wisconsin Policy Research Institute, the other in-state SPN affiliate with longstanding ties to Walker and the other members of the troika.[58] The Institute had played a major role in encouraging Walker to deal with the unions as a means of addressing the state's budget crisis. "Some people in the Walker campaign were scratching their heads about how to deal with union health and pension costs, and we supplied the ideas," bragged the Institute's head.[59] Between ALEC, SPN, and AFP, then, Walker was buttressed by a "longstanding conservative alliance against unions," in the words of two *New York Times* reporters.[60]

Seven years after Walker's contentious legislative battle, it looks like the right-wing troika has indeed succeeded in weakening the state's labor movement. With diminished ranks, the unions also have less clout in politics, especially in local and state politics. Lamented one Democratic operative in Madison, "Maybe we can win high-profile races because Wisconsin still leans slightly Democratic, but at the level where Walker has produced the most profound change, it may prove very difficult to turn that around. That's where we pay the price."[61] A public union leader in the state grimly summed up the situation even more succinctly: "Do we have less boots on the ground? Yeah. Do we give the same amounts of money to the candidates? No."[62] Bragged AFP's Tim Phillips in 2017: "We have more grass-roots members in Wisconsin than the Wisconsin teachers' union has members." "That's how you change a state," he explained, referring to his group's role in pushing the public union reform legislation.[63]

Figure 6.6 shows the dramatic effect that Act 10 has had on Wisconsin's public labor movement, tracking the decline in government employee membership (left plot) and revenue of the largest public union in the state, the Wisconsin affiliate of the National Education Association representing public school teachers (right plot). Public union membership in Wisconsin had been relatively stable from 2005 to 2011, but began plummeting right after the passage of Act 10, falling by over 50 percent by 2016.

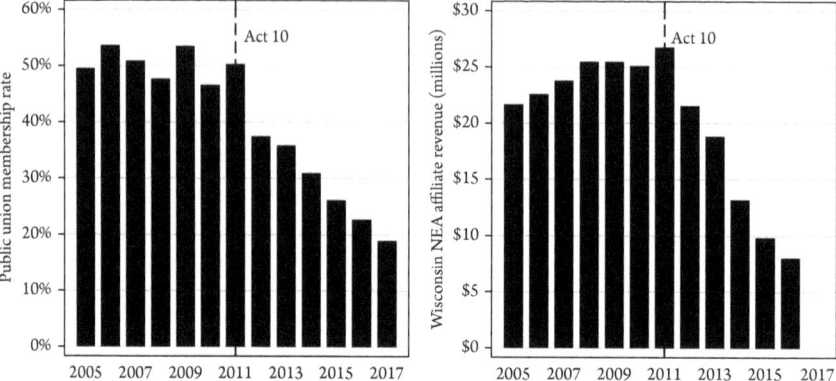

Figure 6.6. THE DECLINE OF WISCONSIN'S PUBLIC LABOR MOVEMENT AFTER ACT 10. Union membership data from UnionStats; Wisconsin NEA affiliate revenue data from IRS tax filings.

With fewer members came fewer dues—and that meant less money for public unions, as the right plot indicates. From 2005 to 2011, the annual budget of Wisconsin's teacher association actually increased from just over $20 million to slightly over $25 million. But following the passage of Act 10, the budget for the union steadily shrunk, standing at well under $10 million by 2016—or over a 60 percent reduction since 2011. And with smaller budgets, teachers unions had less money to invest in state and local elections. Figure 6.7 shows teachers union spending in Wisconsin state and local elections as a proportion of all state and local campaign contributions. After the last-ditch effort to recall Governor Walker in 2011—in which teachers unions accounted for over $1 out of every $20 spent on that race—teachers union spending has steadily declined in both the 2014 and 2016 races to levels not seen in recent years. By the 2016 cycle, Wisconsin teachers unions were spending fewer than $1 out of every $100 made in campaign contributions to state and local races. The story extends to teachers union lobbying in government as well. Government disclosures reveal that the state teachers union was historically one of Wisconsin's most active lobbyists.[64] From 1999 to 2011, the Wisconsin Education Association was consistently in the top 10 most active groups lobbying legislators, often only second or third to the two trade associations representing businesses in the state. But following the 2011 cutbacks in bargaining rights spearheaded by the troika, the Education Association fell from registering about 11,000 hours of lobbying effort in the 2011–2012 legislative session to just over 1,000 hours in the following session, and under 1,000 hours in 2015–2016. With weaker organizational clout and reduced membership rolls, Wisconsin's public-sector unions—and especially the onetime powerhouse teachers unions—are now flat on their backs.

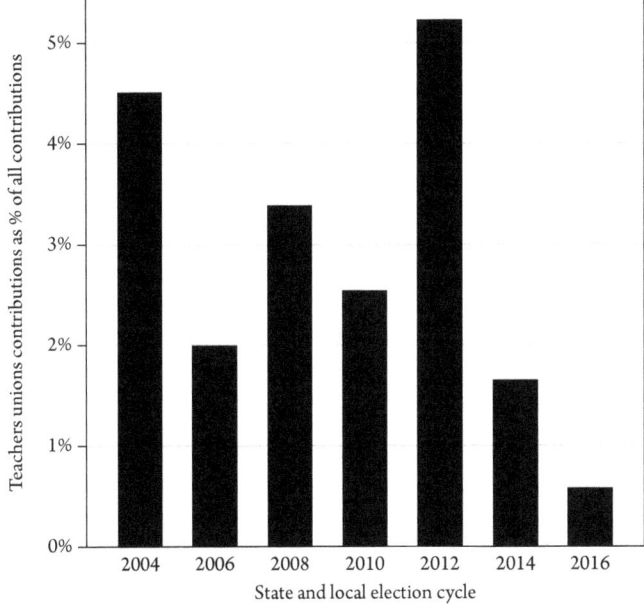

Figure 6.7. WISCONSIN TEACHERS UNION SPENDING IN STATE AND LOCAL ELECTIONS, 2004–2016. State and local campaign contribution data from the National Institute on Money in State Politics.

The Consequences of Public Employee Bargaining Cutbacks: Weaker Unions, Demobilized Workers

The example of Wisconsin shows us the long-run effects of troika-backed legislation on the public-sector labor movement in one state, and suggests that the troika has indeed succeeded in demolishing the organizational and political power of public unions. But is Wisconsin simply the exception? Does troika-backed legislation dampen public union strength in other states? And, by weakening their organizational representation, do the ALEC, SPN, and AFP offensives change the political participation of individual state and local employees?

To answer these questions, we can pan out of Wisconsin and examine the long-run organizational consequences of collective bargaining cutbacks, based on a broader set of troika-drafted and supported bills. My starting point is the plagiarized legislation I identified in Chapter 2 that drew from ALEC-drafted model bills related to public-sector labor unions. In all, I identified eight states in which ALEC legislation related to public-sector labor unions had been enacted into law, and in which either SPN or AFP (or both groups) were involved in promoting the passage of that particular legislation. These include Arizona, Colorado, Georgia, Idaho, North Dakota, Tennessee, Utah, and Wisconsin.

If the ALEC-drafted and SPN- and AFP-supported legislation ended up having an effect on public unions, we can see if, as in Wisconsin, union revenue and membership fell following the passage of those bills. Figure 6.8 tests this idea, showing the change in public union membership (left plot) and revenue, measured as the income of each state affiliate of the National Education Association, per worker in the state (right plot). (Dividing teachers union revenue by the number of workers in each state means that we can compare unions on a more direct apples-to-apples basis.) Each dot on the plot shows, for a particular state, the change in either union membership or revenue in a year either preceding ALEC model bill passage or following it. Note that this plot compares changes *within*, rather than *across*, states—taking into account any stable differences across states, like long-run public opinion or culture.[65]

As the plots suggest, both public-sector union density and revenue fell sharply following the passage of troika-backed legislation, confirming the idea that these bills substantially weaken the government employee labor movement. Equally important, Figure 6.8 also suggests that revenue and membership do not fall in the years immediately *before* troika-backed bills go into effect. That allows us to be more certain that it is the troika legislation—and not other factors changing in the states—that is leading to the weakening of government employee labor unions.

So far, I have documented the relationship between conservative network–backed legislation and measures of the organizational clout of public unions.

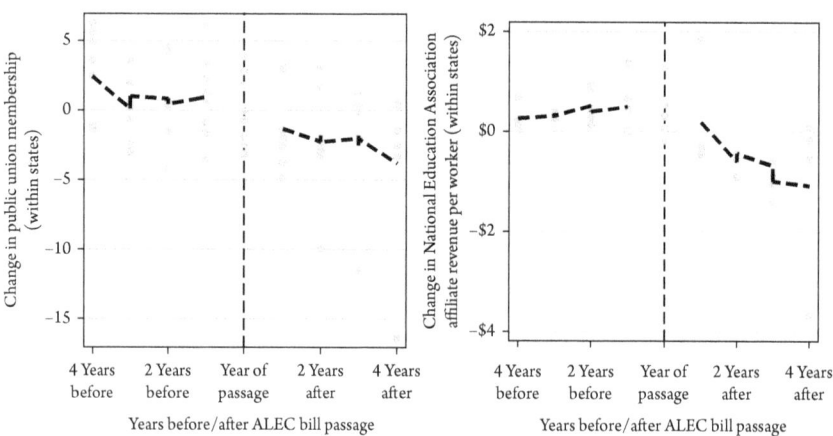

Figure 6.8. PUBLIC UNION MEMBERSHIP AND REVENUE BEFORE AND AFTER TROIKA-BACKED LEGISLATION. The change in public union membership (left plot) and NEA affiliate revenue per worker (right plot) in each year before and after the passage of ALEC model bill–based legislation attacking public employee unions. Both graphs are demeaned by state, so the lines should be interpreted as the average change within states.

But one important reason why unions are powerful is not simply the fact that their organizations have funds to spend on candidates and can boast about large memberships to politicians. Unions are powerful because they foster political action among their members. That means using the social ties unions have developed with their rank-and-file employees to encourage those workers to participate in politics by contacting legislators, donating to campaigns, or volunteering for political causes and candidates.[66] By removing union resources, then, troika-backed legislation might also hamper the political mobilization of individual public employees.

Of course, this dampening effect of conservative network–backed legislation is far from a foregone conclusion. Political participation is often habit-forming and it might be the case that once public-sector unions began mobilizing workers—including teachers—then those workers would become more likely to participate in politics regardless of the presence of a union.[67] It is an open question, then, whether efforts to weaken unions can actually dampen the political participation of union members.

To examine what effect, if any, troika bills have on the participation of government employees, I turn to the American National Election Studies. These national surveys represent the gold standard for public opinion research on elections and political participation. Using data from the 1996 through 2016 election surveys to match the time period for which I have ALEC bills, I look at the political participation of public- and private-sector workers in states that have passed troika bills. If my intuition is correct, then we ought to see the political participation of public employees, but not private workers, fall in states that passed troika legislation. The five political acts I count include if workers: (1) tried to influence the votes of others, (2) worked for a political campaign, (3) displayed a button or sign to support a candidate, (4) donated money to a political campaign, or (5) attended a meeting or rally in support of a candidate.

Before the passage of troika bills, government employees reported participating in more political acts than their private-sector counterparts. Employees of state and local governments reported engaging in nearly twice as many civic acts compared to private-sector workers. That changed following the passage of the anti–public employee legislation. After ALEC model bill passage, the political participation of government workers declined by nearly a third. That put government workers' activism below the participation of private-sector workers. (In the Chapter 6 Appendix, I show that the results generally hold when looking at variation within states, accounting for the demographic characteristics of individual workers and the features of particular time periods.)

In short, the overall picture is one of a decline in the political participation of state and local government workers following the passage of ALEC, AFP, and SPN–backed legislation cutting the organizing and bargaining rights of public employees, even as levels of political participation for private-sector workers remain roughly stable. By weakening the organizational clout of unions, ALEC-written and AFP- and SPN-boosted bills push state and local workers out of politics. Taken with the other findings, the results on government employee political participation suggest that the troika's offensive against public-sector employee unions has indeed succeeded in achieving the goals laid out by ALEC's leaders in the early days of the organization.

Of course, it is important to recognize that the troika has not been successful in retrenching public employee union rights in all states. Although the troika successfully enacted Act 10–like cuts to bargaining and agency fees for government employees in Ohio, a broad-based coalition of unions, community groups, and activists helped to overturn the law through a citizen-initiated referendum.[68] In addition, government unions still remain powerhouses in state and local elections held in states like Illinois, New Jersey, Oregon, Pennsylvania, and Colorado. Nationally, teachers unions represented the fourth-most-generous contributors to state and local elections in 2016, after liberal advocacy groups, conservative advocacy groups, and pharmaceutical manufacturers; other state and local government employee unions represented the fifth-most-generous contributors. Nevertheless, the extent to which troika-backed bills have had such a powerful effect is striking in the states where such legislation has been enacted, which include both red states like Georgia and Tennessee but also traditional union strongholds like Wisconsin.

It is important to note how the troika's ambitions vary by state political context, too. The troika has not attempted the "full monty" of collective bargaining repeal (or near-repeal) in all states. An internal SPN guide for its affiliates contemplating the pursuit of public employee–related legislation stressed the importance of tailoring efforts to the local political climate.[69] SPN leadership pointed out that more expansive curbs to union rights—like right to work or cuts to public union collective bargaining—were only possible in states "with supportive executive branch[es]" *and* "supportive legislative bodies with veto-proof levels of support." That means super-majorities of conservative GOPers in both chambers, plus a governor willing to back the measure in the face of big backlash, like Wisconsin's Scott Walker or Iowa's Terry Branstad did so prominently. In states with less enthusiastic support but still with GOP majorities, SPN recommended pursuing recertification reform for government employee unions. That proposal, which was included in the packages passed in Wisconsin and Iowa, requires government employee unions to hold regular elections at the end of each contract. Unions must win these elections, or else they will lose their right to represent workers.

SPN also had suggestions for their affiliates in Democratically controlled states with strong public employee unions. In these contexts, SPN recommended pursuing union "opt-out" publicity campaigns to teach eligible public workers in non-right-to-work states—typically, home healthcare workers paid through state programs—that they can opt out of paying dues to the union while still taking advantage of the union's benefits.[70] The payoff of this approach, SPN noted, is twofold. Not only can it directly lower public union membership and revenue as workers opt out of dues, but even if workers don't, "public-sector unions must work to prevent their members from resigning and attempt to persuade members . . . causing them to devote additional staff and resources to organizing. This can affect the resources and attention available for union leaders to devote to political action campaigns."[71]

SPN's affiliate in Oregon—a state with especially powerful public unions—calculated that its outreach efforts around the opt-out issue cost public unions in the state at least $8 million from January to August 2016. A more recent memo from SPN made the case that "well run opt-out campaigns can cause public-sector unions to experience 5 to 20% declines in membership, costing hundreds of thousands or even millions of dollars in dues money."[72]

SPN is also gearing up to take such campaigns nationwide in the wake of the landmark 2018 *Janus* v. *AFSCME* Supreme Court case, in which the court's conservative majority barred public-sector unions in all states from collecting dues or fees from non-members who benefit from union-bargained contracts and job protections.[73] The *Janus* decision thus effectively applied a right-to-work law to all public employees across the country, even in previously non–right-to-work states. It is a huge victory for the troika, taking what ALEC, AFP, and SPN were pushing state-by-state to the country as a whole.

SPN in particular played a major role in securing a Court victory in *Janus*. The Freedom Foundation, SPN's affiliate in the Pacific Northwest, helped to build the legal and intellectual case for the Supreme Court's eventual ruling[74] in a series of earlier court cases and legal briefs. Just as importantly, the named plaintiff in the 2018 case, an Illinois child support specialist named Mark Janus, received representation and funding for his case from the Illinois Policy Institute, an SPN member. Janus would in fact leave his government job to join the SPN think tank following the July 2018 court ruling.[75] And in addition, the Freedom Foundation, along with several other SPN affiliates, like the Illinois Policy Institute and the Mackinac Center, have started running tailored opt-out campaigns in a number of blue states to convince government union members to drop their membership now that it is possible to "free ride" off of union benefits without paying dues.[76]

While the exact long-run effects of *Janus* are hard to predict given how unions and state governments may respond, it is clear that in the short run it will deal a major blow to public-sector union clout. Just weeks after the decision came down, the National Education Association announced a 14% projected drop in membership and a corresponding 8% decline in revenue in its upcoming budget.[77] As one labor expert summed up, "In the short-term, labor unions are going to feel the pinch. They will simultaneously have to devote far more resources to keeping their current memberships, while having to adjust to less money coming in from free-riders. This will leave unions with less resources to spend on political issues."[78]

In sum, although the troika's wins have not yet swept across all states, they have been successful in a number of different states with varying political contexts—and ALEC, SPN, and AFP are well positioned to continue dealing "a major blow to the Left's ability to control government at the state and national levels" by "breaking the immense power of the government unions," especially in the wake of *Janus*.[79] Given the close relationship between public-sector unions and the Democratic Party, it is not a stretch to speculate that Democrats will be less likely to win state and local elections—and perhaps even federal elections—with a substantially weakened public employee movement.

SPN head Tracie Sharp agrees, arguing that troika victories in Michigan and Wisconsin may have made a big difference in tilting those "thinly blue" states toward GOP candidate Donald Trump over Democrat Hillary Clinton. In an interview with *The Wall Street Journal* shortly after the 2016 race, Sharp pointed out that Wisconsin union membership fell by 133,000 after the passage of Scott Walker's Act 10 and Michigan's union membership fell by 34,000 after the passage of right to work in that state.[80] Trump's ultimate margins of victory? Less than 23,000 in Wisconsin and 11,000 in Michigan. "When you chip away at one of the power sources that also does a lot of get-out-the-vote, I think that helps—for sure," Sharp summed up.[81]

My research with economist James Feigenbaum and political scientist Vanessa Williamson backs up Sharp's theory.[82] After carefully comparing neighboring counties on either side of a right-to-work state line from 1980 to 2016, we estimate that Democrats did worse up and down the ballot after the passage of right-to-work measures. In presidential elections, for instance, we estimate that Democrats received 3.5 fewer percentage points after right to work went into effect. Voter turnout also dropped sharply, by around 2 points. Those are not trivial effects, especially considering that Democratic candidate Hillary Clinton lost Michigan and Wisconsin in 2016—two relatively recent right-to-work states—by less than one percentage point each.

Aside from changing the landscape of elections, with greater Republican control of legislatures, state governments are much less likely to pursue left-leaning legislation across a range of issues. By making it harder for state and local workers to form unions, fund those unions, bargain collectively with government, and participate in politics, the troika is thus shifting political power away from progressive causes and candidates toward conservative and business-friendly politicians and policies. That's exactly what I found in my study with Feigenbaum and Williamson on right-to-work laws. We observed that state policy moves sharply to the right after the passage of anti-union right-to-work laws—with real consequences for ordinary Americans on issues like minimum wages and labor market standards. We will further see the concrete implications of the troika's legislative advocacy for the lives of citizens by examining state choices around health insurance coverage for the poor as part of the Affordable Care Act.

The Right-Wing Troika and the Offensive against State Medicaid Expansion

A major component of the Affordable Care Act (ACA)—the landmark health reform legislation signed into law by President Obama in 2010—was the extension of health insurance to millions of Americans. Many of these gains in coverage— perhaps half—were anticipated to come from expansions of the federal–state Medicaid programs to cover previously ineligible poor adults.[83] Before the ACA, states were left with broad discretion over the populations they chose to cover as part of their own Medicaid programs. The federal government supported states in the coverage of poor children and their parents, pregnant women, disabled individuals, and elderly Americans needing help paying for Medicare. But beyond those categories, states could choose to cover additional populations—or not. As a result, before the ACA went into effect, only eight states offered childless adults living in poverty full Medicaid benefits, and some of those states had very strict income requirements or limited the number of poor adults who could enroll each year.[84] That left millions of poor adults without affordable health insurance coverage.

To address that gap, the original legislative text of the ACA expanded eligibility for Medicaid to include nearly all nonelderly adults below 138 percent of the federal poverty line (just over $16,000 for an individual in 2015). The ACA also created a streamlined process by which individuals could apply to receive Medicaid benefits, with the hope that the new structure would increase take-up of the program across the pool of potentially eligible enrollees. To encourage states to comply with these new requirements, the federal government promised to cover the full cost of newly eligible enrollees in the first few years of the ACA, and then pledged to pick up 90 percent of the costs thereafter. States that did not expand were threatened with the prospect of losing all their existing federal support for Medicaid, a hefty stick to complement the generous carrot of new federal subsidies. Under such stark terms, policy analysts had expected that all the states would quickly move to participate in Medicaid expansion.

That political calculus changed after the Supreme Court issued its 2012 ruling on the constitutionality of the Affordable Care Act. Although a bare majority of the justices voted to uphold the Act as a whole, they also decided that states had the right to opt out of the Medicaid expansion without losing existing federal funding. The Court's logic was that the federal government's threat of yanking all Medicaid funding would be unconstitutionally coercive. Given the extent to which states rely on federal funding for running their existing Medicaid programs, the threat by Congress to withhold all funding was equivalent to holding a "gun to the head" of the states, in the words of the majority opinion.[85] The Supreme Court thus opened the door for states to choose not to expand their Medicaid programs as envisioned by the Affordable Care Act and still retain their existing federal supports.

At the start of 2017, 31 states had decided to expand their Medicaid programs as part of the ACA, with 19 other states taking advantage of their right of refusal. Figure 6.9 summarizes the decisions made by the states on Medicaid expansion as of January 2017. While expansion was disproportionately concentrated among liberal and Democratic states during the first possible year states could move to expand Medicaid (2012), in the ensuing years, it has been a mix of both

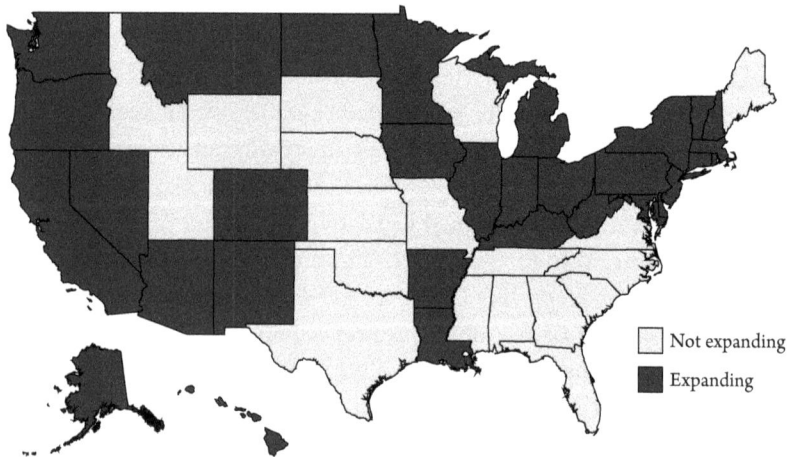

Figure 6.9. STATE DECISIONS ON MEDICAID EXPANSION AS PART OF THE AFFORDABLE CARE ACT, EARLY 2017. Data as of January 2017 from the Kaiser Family Foundation. Note that Maine's expansion, approved by voter referendum in 2017, is still pending.

Democratic and Republican states that have opened their Medicaid programs to the ACA's new enrollees. Seven Republican-controlled states expanded their Medicaid programs from 2013 to 2015.

What explains the decisions made by the states around Medicaid expansion? Certainly, partisan control of government goes a long way in accounting for the reach and timing of expansion. But party control cannot entirely account for these trends, either, given expansion in some conservative and fully GOP-controlled states like Arizona, Indiana, and Michigan. As we will see, the explanation for the puzzling spread of Medicaid expansion lies with the power and advocacy of the right-wing troika.[86]

All three members of the right-wing troika have taken aim at defeating the Affordable Care Act generally, and Medicaid expansion specifically. Consider ALEC first. Since its early years, the group's task force on healthcare has promoted measures that would limit government involvement in health coverage by replacing public health insurance programs with private savings accounts or vouchers. More generally, that task force has taken moves to ensure "that any healthcare reform implemented at the state level would benefit insurance companies far more than policyholders," according to one former health insurance lobbyist.[87] Later, during the start of the Obama administration, ALEC's insurer members were so fearful of health reform under the new Democratic president that they drafted and passed the "Freedom of Choice in Health Care Act," intended to signal state opposition to federal health reform.[88]

After President Obama signed the ACA into law, ALEC urged states to pass model bills it had drafted to undermine the implementation of the health reform program, compiled in the 2011 publication titled *The State Legislators Guide to Repealing Obamacare*.[89] One of those provisions included the call for lawmakers to push for states to "opt out" of Medicaid altogether, arguing that the law forces "cash-strapped states [to] extend their Medicaid programs . . . result[ing] in a near doubling of the Medicaid population."[90] Ending their participation in Medicaid once and for all in an act of protest, the guide argued, could save states nearly $1 trillion.[91]

All across the country, SPN affiliates joined forces with ALEC to oppose the ACA, both during its legislative drafting and during the subsequent battles over implementation. In 2009, for instance, a number of SPN affiliates received grants to work on health reform–related issues, ultimately publishing a series of similarly worded reports attacking the measures that were under consideration by Congress at the time.[92] The report from the Texas Public Policy Foundation sums up the conclusions reached by SPN: "If implemented, . . . President [Obama's] reforms would significantly harm the health care system, patient welfare, and the economy overall."[93] Following passage of the Affordable Care Act, SPN directed similar grants to many state affiliates to oppose the implementation of the law's provisions—and especially Medicaid expansion—once it became clear that the states would be able to opt out without risking their existing federal monies.[94]

For their part, AFP and the Koch political network had targeted Obamacare well before the states were moving to implement the law's various provisions. When Congress was still deliberating over health reform legislation in 2009 and 2010, AFP helped organize "Kill the Bill" rallies outside the US Capitol, and coordinated grassroots protests against lawmakers friendly to the bill in congressional town halls.[95] Once the law passed, AFP pledged to defeat its rollout, especially the Medicaid expansion. "From the very beginning, we turned to a state-by-state effort to stop the expansion of Medicaid," Tim Phillips explained to a journalist.[96] "Medicaid expansion and Obamacare has been the issue we've worked on more than any other single issue."[97] While the group has not disclosed its total spending against Obamacare, one estimate suggests that AFP may have invested millions in mobilization against the law.[98]

Clearly, each of the three members of the right-wing troika has made defeat of the ACA a central priority. But can the strength and coordination of the right-wing networks explain the success or failure of Medicaid expansion across the states above and beyond other factors, like partisanship or state public opinion? To address this question, I took an approach similar to one I had earlier with public-sector bargaining attacks, and constructed an index of troika strength and coordination around the Medicaid expansion issue, consisting of the following measures.

AFP

Unfortunately, chapter-by-chapter information on legislative scorecards is not available in a consistent manner for this time period, as it was for the earlier analysis of public-sector unions. (AFP's individual state chapter websites were no longer archived and searchable, as in the earlier period.) Therefore, I employed a slightly different measure of AFP strength in each state, ranging from 0 to 4. States were assigned a 0 if they had no AFP chapter through 2015. States were assigned a 1 if they had an AFP chapter in the past but it did not survive through the present. States coded with a 2 had a chapter founded between 2012 and 2015, thus operating during the period of the Medicaid expansion debate. States coded as 3 had a chapter founded between 2008 and 2011, also operating during the period of the expansion debate. Lastly, states assigned a 4 had a chapter already in operation by 2007. This measure thus reflects how long an AFP chapter had to build a presence in their state.

SPN

I measured SPN activities in two ways. First, I measured the total budgets of affiliates in each state, as before. SPN budgets were lowest in North Dakota and highest in Virginia. Second, I captured the ways in which the Foundation for Government Accountability (FGA), an especially active SPN affiliate in Florida, worked across state lines to stop Medicaid expansion. FGA played an important role in helping other SPN affiliates to coordinate with ALEC, and its staffers often flew out to other states to help organize opposition to Medicaid expansion.[99] (In fact, FGA's barnstorming Medicaid expert was none other than Christie Herrera, the former ALEC staffer who wrote the legislators' guide to blocking implementation of the ACA.) States received a point on this index if they hosted an FGA staffer giving a presentation opposing Medicaid expansion, and received another point on this index if FGA conducted a public opinion poll within the state intended to show opposition to expansion. Finally, states received another point if FGA staffers wrote media commentary related to the expansion debate in a particular state. The SPN coordination index was lowest in states like Rhode Island, Vermont, and Delaware, and highest in North Carolina, South Carolina, and Idaho.

ALEC

The measure of ALEC strength for the ACA analysis differs somewhat as well from the public union analysis, incorporating leaked information on the share of a state's legislative body participating in ALEC, as well as the number of a state's top four legislative leaders in both chambers with verified ties to ALEC, including task force membership or regular attendance at ALEC events.[100] I focused here on top legislative leaders, rather than rank-and-file members, because these more senior members are critical for squelching the passage of bills in their respective chambers, like the Medicaid expansion. That represents an important contrast between issues like public union cutbacks, where the troika is on the offensive, and where it is on the defensive, as with Medicaid expansion. California registers as a state with the lowest ALEC strength, while I assigned the highest score to Arizona.

Figure 6.10 plots states by their scores on the troika index around the Medicaid expansion, showing how these scores vary across the states. Considering all three troika members at once, the index registers weakest in the

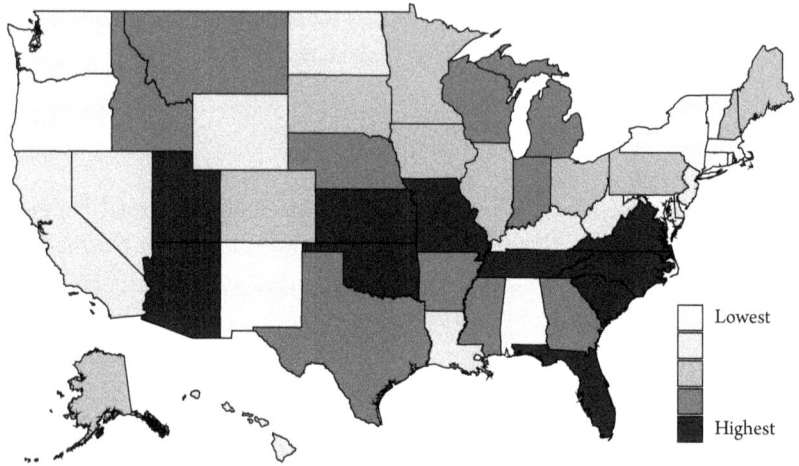

Figure 6.10. RIGHT-WING TROIKA STRENGTH AND COORDINATION ON MEDICAID EXPANSION, 2013–2015. See the text for variable definitions.

Northeast, especially Vermont, Massachusetts, Rhode Island, and New York. AFP, ALEC, and SPN were more active and organized on the Medicaid issue in the Southeast and Midwest, including Virginia, Kansas, South Carolina, Florida, and Tennessee.

Can the activity and coordination of the troika help to account for the variation across the states in decisions about Medicaid expansion? Figure 6.11 divides states into five equally sized groups based on their levels on the troika index and plots the proportion of states in each group that expanded Medicaid from 2013 to 2015. It shows a very strong relationship between levels of troika strength and coordination and Medicaid expansion; as right-wing strength and coordination around Medicaid expansion increases, the proportion of states expanding Medicaid declines.

Equally interesting are the factors beyond partisanship and troika strength that do not help us account for state choices in the expansion debate. Just as with the cross-state examination of public employee bargaining cutbacks, I find that public attitudes toward Medicaid expansion do not help to account for state decisions one way or the other (see the Chapter 6 Appendix).[101] Still, we should be cautious in writing off any role for public opinion. Health policy researchers Colleen Grogan and Ethan Park have found that whites' attitudes—but not minority opinions—were predictive of Medicaid expansion decisions over the same period I examine here.[102]

Another potential explanation might be what states stand to gain or lose from Medicaid expansion. States that had a relatively larger population to be covered by the changes in the Affordable Care Act—because their states were relatively

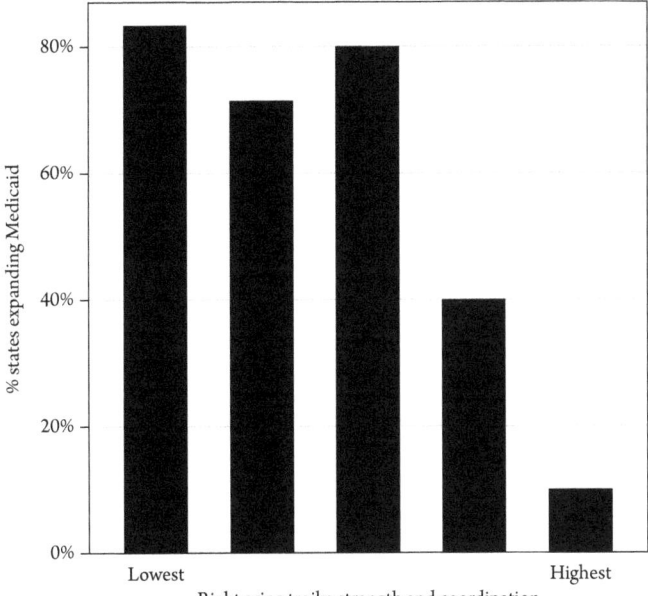

Figure 6.11. RIGHT-WING TROIKA STRENGTH AND COORDINATION AND MEDICAID EXPANSION DECISIONS, 2013–2015. The relationship between the strength and coordination of the right-wing troika on Medicaid expansion and the proportion of states expanding Medicaid as part of the Affordable Care Act.

stingier with their Medicaid programs—might have been more skeptical of the expansion given the greater cost it implied for their budgets.[103] That budgetary cost was indeed a factor repeatedly cited by opponents of the expansion. As he vetoed a bill expanding his state's Medicaid program, Kansas GOP Governor Sam Brownback argued that the cost of expanding health insurance coverage for poor childless adults would be "irresponsible and unsustainable."[104]

Yet although conservative lawmaker after lawmaker cited the cost of an expansion as being the primary driver of their opposition to covering the uninsured in their states, it was not the case that states that stood to spend more on the expansion were more likely to oppose it. There is little relationship between the generosity of a state's Medicaid eligibility requirements (measured as the average income threshold needed to qualify as an adult in 2010) and the number of states expanding Medicaid from 2013 to 2015. State lawmakers were not responding to their citizens or potential budgetary impacts in opposing Medicaid expansion (see the Chapter 6 Appendix). (Note that the appendix shows the importance of the troika strength and coordination index does not change when I simultaneously also control for the party in control of state governments, public opinion, and initial state generosity.)

Still, the evidence I have presented so far can only provide an indication of a broad relationship, not necessarily the specific mechanisms through which the troika is actually shaping state Medicaid decisions. And like our look at cuts to public-sector bargaining rights, the cross-state Medicaid picture cannot entirely isolate the independent effect of the troika on policy decisions. For a closer look at the troika's strategies within one particular state holding all else constant, we can turn to Missouri, a case that nicely illustrates how the members of the right-wing troika worked together to stymie expansion.

During the period when Medicaid expansion was up for debate, Republicans enjoyed majorities in the legislature—certainly cutting against the likelihood of an expansion. But at the same time, Missouri Governor Jay Nixon, a moderate Democrat, had supported the Affordable Care Act and its various provisions, including Medicaid expansion. In addition, expansion had attracted the predictable endorsement of a number of public interest advocates, including labor unions, social service providers, and religious institutions.[105] More surprisingly, the state's business community had come out strongly in favor of expanding Medicaid, led by the state Chamber of Commerce, as well as allied trade associations representing the state's hospitals and medical providers.[106] The state Chamber went so far as to hire former US Republican Senator Christopher Bond to lobby state GOPers to support an expansion.[107] For these pro-expansion business interests, the logic behind their position was relatively straightforward: expansion would mean billions of new federal dollars flowing into the state's local communities and boosted payments for hospitals and medical providers. The work of this strange-bedfellows pro-expansion coalition, however, fell on deaf ears. Time after time, Democrats—and even moderate Republicans—in the state legislature introduced expansion bills only to have them blocked by conservative GOP chamber leaders. When we look to the sources of this opposition, we can see the work of the right-wing troika.

AFP, for its part, was highly active in the state, running ads against pro-expansion bills and mobilizing its some 60,000 Missourian supporters to contact their lawmakers to oppose those measures.[108] As an AFP national press release proudly explained about one of its ads unveiled in early 2014, "As the state legislature debates over Medicaid expansion, Americans for Prosperity-Missouri has released a new radio ad reminding legislators of the high cost to taxpayers. The ad, which opens with the roar of a chainsaw, explains how expanding the state Medicaid program as called for under Obamacare . . . could entail cuts to other state program [sic], higher taxes, or both."[109] AFP also used its legislative scorecards to single out votes for and against Medicaid expansion, praising those GOPers who stood firm and voted against expansion while threatening electoral retribution against those who did not.[110]

Lawmakers hoping to prevent Medicaid expansion could also draw support from the state's local SPN affiliate, the Show-Me Institute. Health policy analysts at Show-Me released a series of reports and commentaries in local media decrying expansion, including criticisms of an analysis authored by the pro-expansion coalition claiming to show job growth associated with the new federal Medicaid funds.[111] Show-Me even testified in the legislature against expansion, reminding lawmakers that the state's citizens rejected Obamacare in a symbolic 2010 ballot initiative.[112] The bottom line, Show-Me argued, was that expansion as envisioned by the legislature would not be a "good deal, especially for future Americans and Missourians."[113]

The longstanding presence of ALEC-affiliated lawmakers within the state's two legislative chambers rounded out the troika's opposition campaign. Missouri is a state with above-average membership in ALEC and nearly a third of its lawmakers participated in the group as dues-paying members in 2013—no surprise given the state's relatively low levels of policy capacity.[114] Missouri was also one of the first states to adopt an ALEC model bill developed to hamper the implementation of the Affordable Care Act. That measure's champion was a state senator who fully admitted that she had taken up the idea after hearing about it at an ALEC meeting. "It's really no secret," Senator Jane Cunningham told a state reporter quite frankly, "I learned about the idea from ALEC and brought it back to Missouri."[115] Looking at the state's lower legislative chamber, I found that GOP lawmakers who were ALEC members were substantially less likely to support expansion, even after controlling for the ideological orientation of the constituents in members' districts.[116] ALEC-affiliated house Republicans were about 20 percent less likely to support Medicaid expansion than non-ALEC members (18 percent if I also account for their districts' underlying ideological orientations).[117] ALEC membership thus may have exerted independent influence as Missouri legislators were voting on Medicaid expansion—above and beyond the behavior we would have expected based on the liberalism or conservatism of their constituents.

The Troika against Big Business?

One curious detail from Missouri that surprised me when reconstructing the narrative around the expansion battle was that the troika was not only going head-to-head against the Democratic governor and moderate Republicans, but also the state business community. As we saw, the state's medical providers—including both the hospital association and many individual healthcare companies—were vocally supportive of the expansion. Those providers understood quite well that the expansion would provide a valuable infusion of financial support to their facilities, especially those in poorer regions that treated Medicaid-dependent patients. These companies thus lobbied the legislature aggressively through new grassroots coalitions and with their own government affairs staff.

But, even more unusually, it was not only the medical providers most immediately invested in the expansion participating in the pro-Medicaid push: the state's Chamber of Commerce and Industry made Medicaid expansion one of its top priorities. The Chamber's main lobbyist said that this was the only issue he was working on in 2014, and that his plan was to make the Chamber's support for the expansion the most "balls out" push "of any state."[118] What makes that support so fascinating is that the Chamber is ordinarily no friend of liberal initiatives. A quick look through the Chamber's legislative priorities handbook reveals many areas of agreement between the group and the troika. The Chamber, for instance, pledges to protect its members against increases in the minimum wage, new labor market regulations, faster union elections, and easy union dues collection, and also indicates strong support for cutting state corporate income taxes. Those goals all place the Chamber squarely on the same side as the troika. So where did the push for expansion come from?

At a basic level, the Chamber understood the huge economic stakes at play. In an interview with me, the Chamber's top lobbyist explained that although he wasn't "huge on Keynesian economics . . . that is $2.2 billion [the estimate for federal Medicaid expansion payments to Missouri] that wouldn't be in our economy otherwise."[119] The money was simply too much to turn down, especially since it would mean direct support for struggling hospitals that "are often economic engines in their communities," dealing with a "disproportionately uninsured population."[120] And beyond the support that the expansion would provide to the medical care industry, the lobbyist also explained to me that he was persuaded by a University of Missouri study showing the potential job-creating effects of the new federal monies. Every dollar spent on Medicaid would help generate new jobs.

As it turns out, the case of the Missouri Chamber, while surprising, is not exceptional. The normally business-friendly, pro-market, and conservative-leaning Chambers of Commerce in twenty-three other states had come out publicly and vocally in favor of the expansion during the heat of the state battles in 2014, based on a survey of those Chambers I did in April of that year.[121] Not all state Chambers approached expansion with the same fervor as Missouri's, however. Aggressive business association support for expansion was crucial in states like Arizona and Arkansas, where Chambers were quite active on this issue. In contrast, the Florida Chamber of Commerce had also come out in favor of expansion—but only if the bill came with more comprehensive reforms to the medical malpractice system, among other changes. Those requirements in some ways put the expansion even further out of reach.[122]

Looking across the states, I found that these strange bedfellow coalitions were a powerful force supporting expansion. States where the main umbrella business association—typically, the Chamber of Commerce—had come out strongly in favor of the proposal and also backed up that endorsement with staff heft were more likely to expand Medicaid, even if the troika was very active in their state.[123] Strong support from the mainstream business community can thus help us account for the puzzling expansions of Medicaid in states like Arizona, Arkansas, Montana, Michigan, and Indiana—all GOP-leaning or GOP-controlled states with substantially above-average levels of troika coordination and activity opposing Medicaid. Figure 6.12 documents this pattern clearly, showing the proportion of states expanding Medicaid by the support offered for the initiative by their state's Chamber.

I consider the combination of two ways in which a Chamber could have supported expansion: first, if a Chamber had come out with a public statement in favor of the proposal, and second, if a Chamber had hired a dedicated health policy staffer who could advise the organization on the intricacies of Medicaid legislation—and just as importantly—on the best ways of lobbying the state

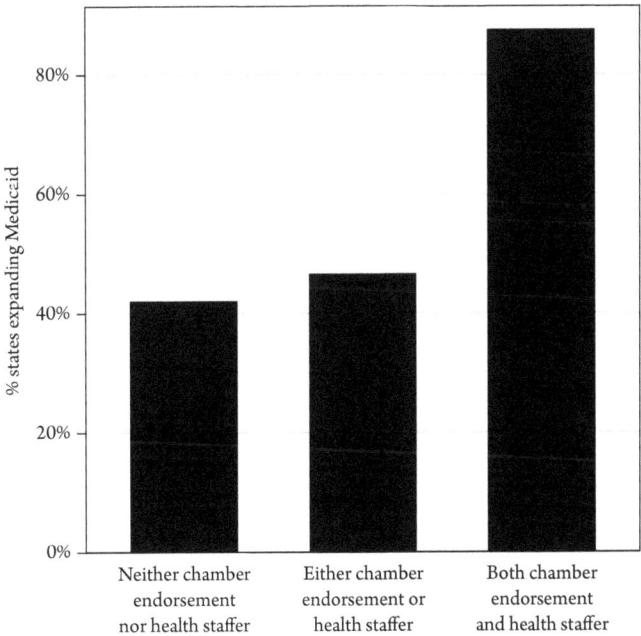

Figure 6.12. STATE CHAMBER OF COMMERCE SUPPORT FOR EXPANSION AND MEDICAID EXPANSION DECISIONS, 2013–2015. The relationship between state Chamber of Commerce support for Medicaid expansion and the proportion of states expanding Medicaid as part of the Affordable Care Act. State Chamber of Commerce endorsement and staff data based on author's survey from April 2014.

legislature on this issue. Just shy of 40 percent of states where a Chamber had taken no supportive action expanded Medicaid, a figure that was similar to those states where a Chamber had either endorsed Medicaid expansion or had a dedicated health policy staffer. But well over twice as many states (nearly 90 percent) in which a Chamber both endorsed the expansion and had a dedicated health policy staffer on board ultimately expanded Medicaid.

The case of Medicaid expansion, then, does not only capture the ways in which the troika lobbies across the states to change policy. It also provides a clear delineation of where the troika's legislative priorities depart from those of mainstream—and even center-right—businesses. For much of the local and state business community, Medicaid expansion was simply too much money to pass up, putting the program in the same category as initiatives like education spending, infrastructure investment, and public promotion of research and development—government spending and intervention that bolsters, rather than undermines, the profit-maximizing efforts of American business. The troika, in contrast, was unwilling to consider that there would be a business case for expansion, instead rooting their opposition to the program in their ideological commitment to smaller government at any and all costs. This, it is safe to say, is an example of where the conservative activist constituents of the troika—especially in ALEC and SPN—won out over any potential Medicaid support from business.

How common are business-troika splits like the Medicaid expansion? Coming up with a picture of all troika and state Chamber of Commerce policy stands across all states is near-impossible. But we can make some headway by closely examining one state—Wisconsin—where the troika has been especially active. Wisconsin also has the added virtue of maintaining one of the most transparent and accessible lobbying disclosure systems of any state in the country. We can thus use Wisconsin's lobbying data to investigate all the bills that the state's main Chamber of Commerce—Wisconsin Manufacturers and Commerce—supported and opposed and how those stances line up against the stances of the troika, represented in this case by Americans for Prosperity (AFP). (AFP is the only troika member within Wisconsin that registered as a lobbyist; neither ALEC nor SPN's affiliates appear in the lobbying database.) Of course, AFP is not perfectly representative of ALEC or SPN, nor is Wisconsin perfectly representative of all states across the country. Still, by sacrificing breadth for depth, we can get a richer picture of the tensions between the troika and mainstream or center-right businesses. And because AFP tends to be oriented toward ideological activist objectives over corporate-friendly ones (as compared with SPN and especially with ALEC), this case study should provide the upper bound for conflicts between the troika and big business.

Between 2005 and 2017, the Wisconsin Chamber and AFP registered positions on about half of the same bills (49 percent). Looking at those pieces of legislation that both the Chamber and AFP actively lobbied for, the two groups were aligned and held the same position in more than eight out of ten bills (84 percent). In short, when AFP and the Chamber both care about a policy, they tend to be aligned with one another in what they want.

The Wisconsin data also permit us to see the policy issues on which the Chamber and AFP were more or less likely to be aligned with one another. Alignment was most common on bills related to the environment (both groups tended to be against greater regulation), the public sector (both groups tended to be supportive of cuts to public employee unions and programs), private-sector labor market and union policy (both groups tended to be supportive of weakening labor market regulations and private unions), and budget and taxes (both groups supported tax cuts). The few cases where divisions existed between the AFP and the Chamber tended to come on legislation related to education and training (with the Chamber supportive of new programs to bolster the workforce but AFP opposed) and business-friendly tax credits or subsidies (with the Chamber supportive of those favorable tax provisions and AFP opposed).

In sum, the sort of divisions we saw between business groups and the troika over Medicaid are likely outliers when considering the full set of policies pursued by mainstream business groups and ALEC, AFP, and SPN. In most cases, the troika is on the same page as umbrella business groups and in favor of loosening environment and labor regulations, cutting taxes, and weakening both public and private employee unions. Divisions tend to come only in the small area of government programs—like healthcare spending or workforce training initiatives—that appeal to corporate managers' bottom lines.

Over the past six chapters, we have seen how ALEC became an incredibly effective lobbying force across the states throughout the 1990s and 2000s, packaging its model bills with other valuable services for underresourced and inexperienced state lawmakers. But especially since the 2000s, ALEC has not been operating alone. First joined by a bolstered SPN flush with new think tank affiliates and cash from wealthy individual and corporate donors, then by a muscular grassroots movement directed by the Koch-led AFP, ALEC could count on powerful allies as it promoted its policy agenda across the states.

While the issues pursued by SPN and ALEC are more closely aligned given their closer affiliations and overlapping donor bases of large, for-profit businesses, ALEC and AFP have more divergent priorities, given that the former has stronger corporate backing than the latter. And on some issues, like Medicaid expansion, all three members of the troika have run up against opposition from mainstream business interests, represented most clearly by state and local Chambers of Commerce. However, on regulations, taxes, and union rights—issues on which the libertarian Koch network and the more business-friendly ALEC see eye-to-eye—these groups work quite closely with one another.

The two cases in this chapter also show that the troika's advocacy carries with it deep and far-reaching implications for future political battles in the states and for the lives of ordinary Americans. In the case of public union organizing and bargaining, for instance, the troika's advocacy has weakened a once-important interest group, making it substantially harder for government employees to build organizational and political power. That aggressive, no-holds-barred approach to tackling public-sector labor unions represents a deliberate political strategy on the part of the troika, which saw public policy not just as a means to achieve technical goals—but also a tool with which ALEC, AFP, and SPN could reshape the political terrain in ways that durably disadvantaged their political opponents. For the troika, policy was a means of building and retaining political power.[124]

But the troika's legacy for the US states is not only one of power-building. The battles over Medicaid expansion illustrate how the legislative priorities pursued by ALEC, AFP, and SPN can fundamentally alter the life chances of citizens, depending on the states where they live. As we have seen, the all-out opposition of the troika to Medicaid expansion has meant that millions of poor Americans do not have access to health insurance coverage.

A final implication of the two case studies in this chapter is that the troika has operated in many states without much in the way of significant opposition, especially once the groups have been able to defund and demobilize unions. In some cases, as with the Medicaid expansion, mainstream business might oppose the troika. But this is not always—or even often—the case, as we saw from the Wisconsin lobbying records. That raises another question: Where is the organized resistance to the troika from the left?

7

"Feisty Chihuahuas versus a Big Gorilla"

Why Left-Wing Efforts to Counter the Troika Have Floundered

Decades of aggressive institution-building have meant that conservatives and businesses can count on a well-developed infrastructure of organizations to promote a coordinated national policy agenda. In light of these successes, one might well wonder: Where has the left been? The answer, as I spell out in this chapter, is that liberals have faltered in similar efforts to build lobbying capacity across the states. As one union official begrudgingly acknowledged recently, conservatives and their affiliated organizations deserve credit since "they made a sound strategic decision to prioritize activity at the state level and they beat us to the punch. They were smarter than we were."[1] *Politico* has described the differences between the left and right in even starker terms, writing that "past efforts to boost Democratic prospects at the state level have floundered. In recent years, liberal groups and academic think tanks have failed to mount a unified push across states, struggling to gain traction in the states or raise the funds necessary to sustain organizations of any heft and often cannibalizing one another."[2]

We can see the imbalance between left and right cross-state networks in stark terms in Figure 7.1, which plots the development, over time, of the three troika members alongside various efforts by progressive activists to construct counterweights of their own. Two things immediately stand out from the figure. The first is how long the troika members have been continuously operating across the states, while the second is how many groups on the left have, at various times, attempted to occupy the same terrain as ALEC, SPN, and AFP—yet eventually faded from the political landscape. Out of the ten organizations I have identified that aimed to take on the right-wing troika since 1970, only five remain in operation as of 2018. Figure 7.1 thus shows that progressives have been

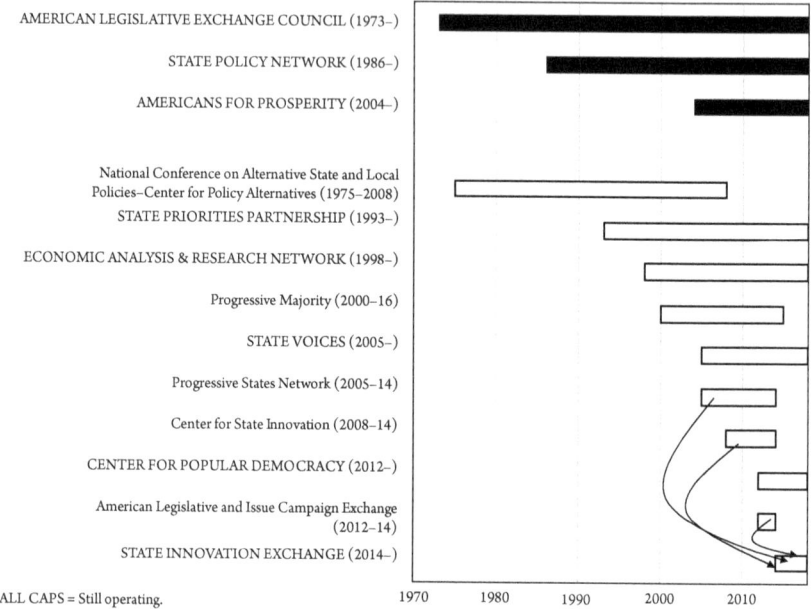

Figure 7.1. CROSS-STATE NETWORKS ON THE LEFT AND RIGHT, 1970–2018. Solid bars indicate conservative networks; hollow bars indicate center-left networks.

more prolific in constructing organizations than the right, yet those center-left organizations have not tended to survive over time.

Why is it that so many groups on the left have fizzled out—while those that remain have not amassed the same clout as the troika? This chapter explores the history behind Figure 7.1 and reveals that liberal state policy activists were hampered by two important factors. To begin with, liberals had taken for granted the participation of conservatives in early-century bipartisan, national networks of government officials. By the 1970s, however, conservative political entrepreneurs realized that they could be more effective advancing their increasingly ideological agenda by building their own set of alternative state networks, rather than working within the existing good government reform groups. It took liberals at least a decade after ALEC had launched before they attempted to construct serious explicit alternatives of their own, still holding out for bipartisan, or at least nonpartisan, collaboration.

Even when liberal political leaders realized that they needed to bolster their presence in the states through networks of their own, they found themselves stymied by a lack of consistent funding for their projects. Time after time, left-wing political entrepreneurs pitched the idea of a serious liberal response to ALEC only to discover that they could not find a sustained financial backer for their efforts. Left-leaning foundations and deep-pocketed individual donors were simply not interested in funding advocacy work in a coordinated manner across the states, preferring to focus their more politically charged giving at the national level while contributing to direct service activities at the state and local levels.

This was further exacerbated by stop-and-start attention to the states on the left, which tended to follow Democratic control of the federal government. When Democrats were in power in Washington, D.C., attention (and funding) for state organizing faltered, only to return anew when Democrats lost control of Congress and the White House. In the few instances when philanthropic patrons funded left state networks, such efforts tended to be fragmented, with different initiatives dueling with one another for scarce dollars, concentrated in the most liberal states where left-wing forces were already powerful, and supported through sporadic and inconsistent grantmaking.

Progressives and the Rise of Good Government State Networks

At the turn of the twentieth century, state legislatures were widely viewed as being "not only bad, but steadily growing worse."[3] As one political scientist summed up, almost anyone at the time "will tell you that our legislatures are filled with 'ward heelers,' 'petty politicians,' and 'yokels,' or even worse, who are more or less equally engaged in clowning and enacting laws designed to 'loot the public treasury' or to favor some special interest at the expense of the common weal."[4] An *Atlantic Monthly* report on the state legislatures in 1904 was even more scathing, stating plainly:

> We have grown to distrust our State Legislatures. Their convening is not hailed with joy, and a universal sigh of relief follows their adjournment. The utterances of the press, the opinions of publicists and scholars, and the sentiments of the street and the market place are quite at one in their denunciation of the Legislature. Our representatives are the subject of jest and ridicule, of anger and fear.[5]

Why did the public distrust state legislatures so much? Writings at the time highlighted perceptions of corruption, ineptitude, and a lack of responsiveness to the pressing social and economic needs of the day.[6] One small group of legislators, led by Colorado State Senator Henry W. Toll, believed that the answer to the woes of the states did not lie with popular solutions of the time. Those proposals included cutting back the pay of lawmakers and shortening sessions from annual to biennial meetings. Rather, while concurring "in the statement which is continually reiterated by all thinking Americans that our legislatures contain many members who lack the mentality, the training, and the disinterested motives which should characterize legislators," Toll believed that state legislatures needed more—not fewer—resources with which to make policy.[7] If anyone was well equipped to fight for a lost progressive cause like this one, it was Toll, who had made a name for himself in Colorado by standing up to his colleagues in opposition to the powerful Ku Klux Klan.[8]

Argued Toll: "No state can hope to induce a large number of capable, educated, responsible men to offer their services for legislative work unless the state is prepared to do its part as any other employer must do, by offering each man who will serve adequate pay [and] adequate assistance in the performance of his task."[9] Part of that support could, Toll believed, come from a new professional association of state legislators, and in December 1925, Toll sent out invitations to all 7,500 legislators serving in state government to join a new "American Legislators' Association" (ALA). The ALA, as Toll and his colleagues envisioned it, would provide the support to state legislators that they otherwise lacked to produce rational, scientifically grounded, and effective policy. This, Toll believed, could overcome the lack of professionalism that characterized legislatures at the time.

Supported by philanthropic funds, member contributions, and appropriations from a handful of state governments, the ALA engaged in five main activities.[10] These included a division that would help states to establish legislative reference bureaus to give nonpartisan research and legal drafting assistance to legislators; an "informational switch-board" through which legislators or their staff could "plug in" and "at once be connected with the best source of information in the United States concerning [their] current problem"; a publication sent to every legislator with information about recommended state laws, the activities of major national associations, new research and writing on relevant issues, and descriptions of exemplary state legislation; an annual meeting of legislators that would coincide with the meeting of the American Bar Association; and a legislative assembly, including committees and advisory boards, that would consider and promote model legislation for the states.[11]

Toll envisioned that the group would complement the work of existing organizations that were promoting interstate cooperation and developing model bills for state lawmakers to consider. Toll noted that the main alternative organization, the Commission on Uniform State Laws, was an expert-led group, rather than a "sales organization," and thus could not actively promote its proposals.[12] The ALA, in contrast, could do just that. Moreover, the ALA, unlike the Commission, could offer general legal and research assistance to lawmakers and their staffs.

Right from its start, the ALA was assiduously nonpartisan, prioritizing expert judgment over particularistic or partisan agendas. The language used in the original documents and transcripts emphasized the value of research and careful study to "improve the quality of the law making process."[13] Above all, Toll desired to "establish a line of communication between specialists and legislators—between those who know best what the laws should be and those who decide what the laws are."[14]

The group's commitment to Progressive Era ideals of expertise over partisanship is exemplified by its close relationship with academia. Five years after its launch in Denver, the ALA opened a Chicago office, which soon after established ties to the University of Chicago and its experts in political science, law, and economics.[15] Some of the early staff of the organization were appointed to the university faculty, and a number of the faculty joined the organization as advisers.[16] Similarly indicative of the group's priorities were its first two major initiatives: to establish nonpartisan legislative reference bureaus in all the states and to reconcile conflicting federal and state tax law.[17]

Perhaps the surest sign of the ALA's bipartisanship was simply the party affiliations of its early founders. Toll, for his part, was a Republican, as was the group's first vice president, Senator George Woodward of Pennsylvania. Senator Alfred Thwing of Minnesota, the group's second vice president, did not have a partisan affiliation, and the group's auditor, Reece A. Caudle of Arkansas, was a Democrat. The group's subsequent presidents after Toll were a Republican (from California) and a Democrat (from Kentucky).

The ALA's good government impulse had strong roots in a longer tradition of progressive activism in the United States. These reformers, first embodied by the Mugwumps of the late 1800s, and then the progressive activists of the early 1900s, sought to rationalize the public sector with nonpartisan, technocratic reforms.[18] Their legacy of blending civic action with government reform fits well with Toll's vision of the ALA both as an instrument for voluntary cooperation, and as a force that could press policy demands on state governments in contrast to less assertive groups like the Commission on Uniform State Laws.[19]

Following the gradual success of the ALA in its first decade, some of its participants began pondering the creation of a second organization that would include not only legislators but also members of the burgeoning state administrative agencies. At the start of 1935, nearly ten years after the founding of the ALA, government officials convened the Council of State Governments (CSG) to accomplish exactly that goal. The Council would "devise and promote means by which the states could better cooperate with one another and with the federal government."[20] The ALA was eventually folded into the new CSG, now with a narrower focus on improving the quality of the legislative process, rather than promoting broader issues of public policy.[21] In a similar vein, national associations of governors, attorneys general, and secretaries of state were eventually incorporated into the CSG as well. CSG's primary activities now included a series of commissions discussing aspects of interstate cooperation and federalism, annual convenings of state and federal officials, and publication of regular volumes summarizing a variety of indicators on state activities.

Toll's goal of bipartisan and expert-driven infrastructure to unite state governments continued through the work of the CSG, and later, several new organizations. In the mid-1950s, CSG expanded to attract more legislative members through a revamped National Legislative Conference.[22] Senior lawmakers from several of the larger states formed their own group, the National Conference of State Legislative Leaders, shortly thereafter. The Conference of State Legislative Leaders would provide many of the same informational resources as the ALA but would operate outside the orbit of CSG, which many senior legislators now viewed as being too beholden to governors and legislative staff.[23] And a third organization, the National Society of State Legislators, emerged in the mid-1960s to represent rank-and-file legislative members, though it never grew as large as either of the other older groups.[24] By the early 1970s, these various associations began discussing a possible merger, and in 1974 the CSG facilitated the successful dissolution of the three groups and the formation of a new National Conference of State Legislatures (NCSL), which continues to the present day.[25] As with its antecedents, the NCSL places a heavy emphasis on accurate and bipartisan responses to legislative inquiries in the spirit of Henry Toll, as well as support for greater professionalization.[26]

The growth of the cross-state associations during the 1930s, and again in the 1960s, was driven just as much by the rapid expansion of government during these two eras as it was by entrepreneurial reformers. It is no coincidence that the ALA and CSG enjoyed growing membership rolls during the New Deal era. State officials flocked to these cross-state associations as a means of preserving state autonomy as the federal government assumed roles, like social welfare provision and labor regulation, that were once the exclusive domain of the states.[27] At the same time, state legislators and executives also sought assistance as they implemented the many provisions of the New Deal that were explicitly delegated to the states, like unemployment insurance, grant-in-aid programs, and public works projects—what were collectively referred to as the "little New Deals."[28] The CSG, for instance, issued important reports that provided extensive comparisons of the various approaches to unemployment insurance pursued by the states, as well as recommendations for reforms "expanding and perfecting" these state programs.[29]

Three decades later, Lyndon Johnson's Great Society initiatives spurred similar moves by state and local officials to organize into networks that could both share knowledge and represent state interests in the federal government. This was especially important because even more than the New Deal, the Great Society relied on state and local governments to implement various new initiatives to aid vulnerable populations, including cash welfare to poor families with children, assistance for disabled adults who did not meet the requirements of the Social Security program, medical insurance for the needy, and aid to struggling public schools.

The Conservative Secession: From Henry Toll to Charlie Duke

Despite the careful efforts of the ALA, CSG, and later, the NCSL to remain staunchly bipartisan, a burgeoning conservative movement in the 1960s and 1970s began to reject the staid trio of associations as being too liberal. Though avowedly ideologically neutral, the associations were still committed to improving the functioning of state government. That, in turn, often required new revenue and increased staff. For instance, the CSG and NCSL had long prioritized increases in the professionalization of state legislatures, which conservatives opposed.[30]

The cross-state groups also favored increased federal responsibility for certain state programs, especially those related to income maintenance, which was anathema to conservatives and business leaders who viewed federalization of social programs as promoting bigger government. And more generally, the good government associations were seen as having facilitated the expansions of economic programs and social rights during the New Deal, and later, the Great Society. In short, every existing organization for state legislators "appeared to be under the dominion of big-government types."[31] "Most of the suggested legislation discussed and recommended [by NCSL] was generally liberal in the sense of more government involvement than I basically supported," summed up one conservative member of the Missouri legislature who formerly attended NCSL meetings.[32]

Conservatives thus abandoned the bipartisan associations that were previously widely embraced by Republicans and Democrats alike, especially after ALEC gave them a new alternative. As one political observer noted, "A few years after NCSL was formed . . . it suffered a secession when a group of conservative legislators left to create their own organization—ALEC."[33] Another journalist interviewed one conservative lawmaker who left the NCSL, finding that the legislator attended one NCSL meeting and then never went back after discovering ALEC: "I just felt more at home at ALEC. I was around legislators who had the same philosophy as I had on running government," that lawmaker concluded.[34]

An ALEC publication discussing President Reagan's negotiations over his "New Federalism" plan in the 1980s summarizes the right's scorn for the NCSL. ALEC's staff argued that while "the Reagan Administration has negotiated with NCSL . . . in the good faith that it shared a mutual interest in sorting out the responsibilities of government," the NCSL was not, in fact, acting in good faith because of the group's "long-standing political persuasion . . . and both the Administration and state legislators should be aware of the fact."[35] The NCSL's "partisan character," according to ALEC, was exemplified by NCSL's new president, William F. Passannante, who as a legislator voted "*against* the death penalty; *for* increases in welfare grants; *for* taxpayer financing of election campaigns; *for* pay increases for legislators; *for* the D.C. amendments; and *for* a gross receipts tax on oil companies. . . . But the piece of legislation Mr. Passannante is most noted for sponsoring is his 'Consensual Sodomy Bill'—one of the nation's pioneer gay rights bills" (original emphasis).[36] With such liberal leadership, ALEC soberly concluded, "It is a grave mistake for the Administration to assume the NCSL represents a consensus in the thinking of State Legislators."[37]

Perhaps no contrast captures the conservative rejection of the previously broadly respected cross-state legislative associations as much as Charlie Duke and Henry Toll. Both men were Republicans representing constituencies in the Colorado State Senate that were a mere 75 miles from each other. But while Toll embraced nonpartisan efforts to professionalize the states in the 1920s, Duke would later describe the NCSL—the descendant of Toll's ALA—as a "liberal left-wing, commie, pinko" organization.[38]

NCSL and CSG continued to provide the same services to their members even as conservatives rejected their organizations. And for the most part, progressives continued to participate in the good government institutions that they had helped to assemble over the past century, even as ALEC grew in size and scope, eventually rivaling the size of NCSL's annual meeting by 1995.[39] As we will see, it was not until the 1990s that liberal efforts to counter ALEC began in earnest. Until that point, the group was seen as playing a role complementary to the other state associations, fostering a pluralist interest group environment.[40] But by the 1990s, it was in many ways too late for liberals to easily catch up with the infrastructure that conservatives had assembled between ALEC and SPN.

There is an irony to conservatives' backlash against NCSL. In part, the preponderance of liberal perspectives at the NCSL is a result of the conservative rejection of those associations. Had conservatives remained committed to the good government associations, the leadership of these groups would have been more equally divided between ideological perspectives in recent times. But, of course, the bottom line is that the NCSL is no direct counterweight for ALEC. Though the group has espoused more liberal positions, especially in the mid- to late 2000s, NCSL remains committed to providing nonpartisan technical capacity to the states. The NCSL, for instance, rotates its leadership between the two parties, and rarely writes model bills, let alone actively promotes particular legislative initiatives.[41] Liberals would need to create other organizations that could more directly counter ALEC's growing reach across the states.

Bread, Roses, ... and State Politics?

One such set of groups that might have been able to counter ALEC's (and later, SPN's and AFP's) cross-state reach is the labor movement. Recalling ALEC's founding from Chapter 1, we saw that it was the spread of public-sector labor unions that stoked conservative fears of left-wing cross-state dominance and inspired Paul Weyrich, among others, to organize state legislators. The 1960s and 1970s were indeed a major turning point for the public labor movement, especially for teachers associations, which began fighting for collective bargaining rights, centralizing their operations within state and national organizations, and ramping up their political involvement across the states and in the federal government.

The political rise of public unions was a remarkably rapid transformation. As late as 1956, a poll conducted by the National Education Association's (NEA) research division revealed that only a fourth of its members answered affirmatively to the question "Do you believe that other than registering and voting, teachers should participate in politics?"[42] Buoyed by new collective bargaining laws that expanded its membership rolls and coffers, the NEA set out to change those perceptions by launching a new "Citizenship Committee" with the charge of persuading its members of the importance of participating in the political process as an organized bloc.[43] That included initiatives to repeal laws banning political activity among teachers, trainings to get educators engaged in politics, and a fellowship program for especially interested individuals to develop advanced political skills and serve as a "reserve corp" of teacher-activists.[44]

All those efforts culminated with a revamped legislative affairs division in 1969 that began issuing regular "scores" to elected officials and then the creation of a national NEA PAC to supplement existing state-level efforts three years later.[45] As one *Washington Post* political reporter put it, over the 1960s and 1970s, the NEA was "increasingly taking on the attributes of a militant labor union"—and was well positioned to have a significant political impact given its "1.8 million educated, articulate, generally well respected members, all of them with unusually intimate access to their own communities" and over $15 million (in present-day dollars) to invest in politics.[46] By 1980, *The Washington Post* political sage David Broder and a colleague opined that teachers unions had become a "powerful force in party politics" as "part of the rising tide of public employee activism."[47]

Public unions continued to direct that heft toward national-level politics—in congressional and presidential races—as well as state politics. In fact, compared to private-sector unions, public-sector employee associations, especially teachers, became the labor unions most involved in state-level politics. State-level data on lobbying, as we have seen, are limited, but examining the 19 states with disclosed lobbying data from 2012 to 2016, I found that public employee unions outspent their private-sector counterparts in 17 states.[48] On average, in the states where public unions outspent private unions, public union spending averaged four times more than private union spending.

Finer-grained lobbying data from Wisconsin, which has unusually rich records, allow us to clearly see the dominance of public unions—especially teachers unions—as compared to either the state AFL-CIO council or the Service Employees International Union (SEIU), the country's largest private-sector union (see Figure 7.2). For comparison, I have also included the state's main business association, Wisconsin Manufacturers and Commerce. Figure 7.2 plots the total hours each of the four groups registered in lobbying the Wisconsin state legislature from 1999 to 2010. From 1999 to 2010, the NEA easily outstripped lobbying by both the AFL-CIO and the SEIU. The Wisconsin teachers union spent an average of nine times as much effort lobbying the state legislature as did the AFL-CIO, and more than five times as much effort as the

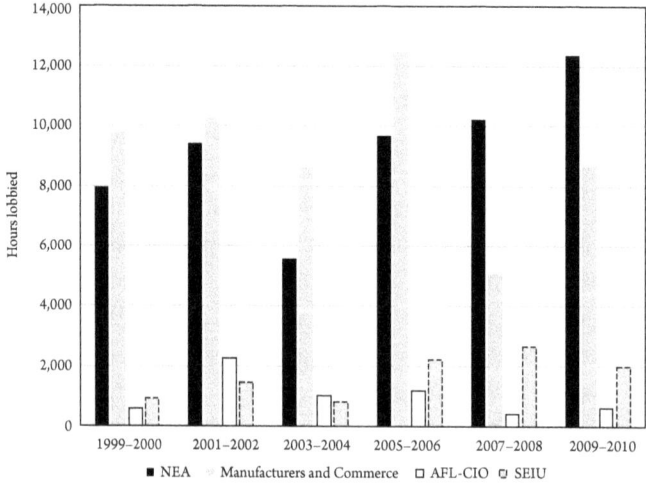

Figure 7.2. TEACHER-DOMINATED LABOR LOBBYING IN THE WISCONSIN LEGISLATURE. Hours of registered lobbying for the Wisconsin NEA affiliate, Wisconsin Manufacturers and Commerce (the state chamber of commerce), AFL-CIO state affiliate, and SEIU state affiliate. Data from the Wisconsin Ethics Commission.

SEIU. Indeed, the Wisconsin NEA affiliate was the only one of the three labor unions to approach the power of the Wisconsin state chamber of commerce, coming close to matching Wisconsin Manufacturers and Commerce in two legislative sessions and outstripping the business association in two other sessions.

Private-sector unions were simply ill-equipped to engage in extensive within- or cross-state lobbying, caught between a historical structure that emphasized power at the local, shop-floor level and leadership at the international federation level. Although the AFL-CIO and other private-sector unions envisioned central labor councils (intended to consolidate labor power at the city or regional level) and state federations (intended to consolidate power at the state level) as "vital links" to bolster their political and organizing clout between locals and internationals, labor leaders struggled to make those links truly meaningful.[49] The AFL-CIO embarked on a campaign to strengthen vertical integration throughout the 1960s without much success, leading the union's President George Meany to lament that "far too many local unions stand apart from their brothers at the state . . . levels and do not bear their share of labor's efforts to make the American community a better place."[50] That weakness of vertical integration led to a weakness in state politics, with one labor leader in California describing the situation in his state as a "political crisis."[51] And even when state labor federations managed to amass political clout, they were more likely than not to prioritize the narrow issues of their members—and not a broader social and economic agenda. As labor scholar Margaret Weir has documented, "Most state labor federations were prepared to weigh in on issues directly related to labor interests . . . [but] were far less well equipped to press for a broad social agenda designed to secure social benefits to be shared by non-union members."[52]

By contrast, public employee unions were well positioned to engage in politics at the state level given that it was state governments—and not the federal government—that set the laws governing their collective bargaining rights; with whom unions negotiated pay, benefits, and working conditions; and that set tax and spending policies affecting their agencies and programs.[53] In addition, the fact that public employee unions depended on government tax and spending policies for their livelihood made alliances with broader social and economic causes easier. Unlike their private-sector counterparts, public employee unions could be reliable and powerful allies in supporting tax hikes and expansions of social programs.[54] Indeed, using Wisconsin as a case study once again, we can see that the Wisconsin teachers union has historically dedicated about as much lobbying effort to non-education policy as to narrower education-related issues. About 48 percent of the Wisconsin teachers union's lobbying efforts from 1999 to 2016 were directed toward education and schooling issues, with the remaining efforts focused on broader measures related to the public sector, local government, budget and taxes, and healthcare—all of importance to many other liberal constituencies.

Public unions, then, with their state-level clout and broad legislative agenda, were perhaps the best-positioned organizations to counter the troika from the left. And with some of the deepest coffers in the labor movement, public unions also had the potential to be generous funders of other liberal cross-state efforts. Still, this network was incomplete at best, given that the strength of public unions in some states, especially in the South and Southwest, was much weaker than in the western, northeastern, or mid-Atlantic states. These geographic constraints on public employee union clout meant that public employee unions would never reach the full scope that the troika has enjoyed across red, blue, and purple states alike.

In addition, public unions are on the defensive in many states as a result of the troika's own advocacy, as we saw in the last chapter. Public-sector union membership dropped in 37 states between 1996 and 2016, averaging a decline of about four percentage points in those states. Strikingly, 15 states saw declines of at least five percentage points and 4 states saw declines of at least ten percentage points. We see a similar picture looking at teachers unions' political spending across the states as well, with teachers unions in 27 states spending less on state and local politics over the period from 2007 to 2016 than from 2000 to 2006.[55]

Even independently of the troika's state-by-state efforts, all those downward trends are likely to accelerate in the face of the Supreme Court's 2018 *Janus* v. *AFSCME* decision. That case, in which the conservative majority ruled against public unions, permits all public employees to opt out of paying any dues to unions, even where unions must represent opt-out workers and negotiate contracts on their behalf.[56] In essence, the decision applies right-to-work to all public-sector employees, even in previously non-right-to-work states like New York and California. *The New York Times*' legal correspondent anticipated that the case would deal a "crushing blow" to public unions—and one that will cause unions to "lose a substantial source of revenue."[57] Indeed, shortly after the *Janus* decision was announced, the National Education Association projected a big decline in its revenue and membership over the coming years.[58]

At the time of this book's writing in 2018, there were some hints that the public-sector labor movement, and especially teachers, might be reaching a breaking point. Facing declining pay and working conditions—often as a result of troika-backed cuts to state taxes and education spending—teachers in Arizona, Colorado, Kentucky, Oklahoma, North Carolina, and West Virginia have gone on strike.[59] On its own, that is impressive given that strikes in most of those states are illegal, carrying the threat of hefty fines and penalties like the loss of teaching licenses. But even more impressive is the fact that the strikes appear to be working: the GOP governments in those states are now reluctantly approving increases in pay and school spending.

Nevertheless, these strikes have not yet secured greater legal rights for teachers—and the overall challenges faced by the movement remain quite large. In short, the labor movement—at least in its present state—cannot be counted on to be a viable alternative to the troika in either the public or private sectors, nor did it ever enjoy the same cross-state projection of power as AFP, ALEC, and SPN did even in public-sector unions' heyday. That may yet change if teachers can build on the momentum from recent strikes to push for broader cross-state institutional reforms—but it is by no means a given.[60]

Nonlabor Left-Wing Efforts Flounder Again and Again

Thus far, we have seen that one important reason for the left–right imbalance in the states is that liberals stuck with the good government infrastructure, like the NCSL, while conservatives abandoned those once broadly accepted institutions to develop their own more ideologically charged organizations, like ALEC and SPN, that ended up outflanking the left. Unions, especially in the public sector, acted as a cross-state lobby for broader left-wing causes for several decades in public union stronghold states. But that lobby was geographically constrained and has weakened considerably in recent years. What happened when liberals attempted to construct more direct analogues to the troika outside of the labor movement?

One such early but tentative effort was the National Conference on Alternative State and Local Policies (CASLP). Formed in 1975 after a meeting of the same name in Madison, Wisconsin, CASLP aimed to "provide a forum and a meeting place for local officials and others to exchange ideas, bills, and proposals through a wide ranging program of publications, newsletters, and regional and national conferences"—in short, much like ALEC in principle, but operating on the left.[61] The group received modest funding and administrative support primarily through the Institute for Policy Studies, a left-wing think tank based in Washington, D.C.

Like ALEC, CASLP recognized that many local and state lawmakers lacked the resources to design policy, and thus CASLP aimed to help draft and disseminate a variety of model bills for city and state governments covering issues as diverse as "land use, tax reform, consumer protection, agricultural policy, minority employment, public power, community and state-owned enterprises, control of natural resources, women's issues, public employees, and many others."[62]

But, despite strong initial interest in the group from lawmakers, CASLP slowly disappeared from the political scene by the 1980s. The last annual conference was held in 1980, and by the mid-1980s, Lee Webb, the group's founder, had moved on to other projects.[63] A key obstacle facing CASLP, and the reason for the group's demise, according to one leader in the organization, was "a constant lack of funding."[64] Part of the problem was that CASLP was not able to successfully differentiate itself from existing membership associations of legislators like the CSG and NCSL. As we will see, insufficient funding and competition with existing associations will characterize the left-wing response to ALEC time and again, ultimately going a long way in explaining the lack of a more robust progressive infrastructure in the states.

Some of the participants in CASLP later attempted to reinvigorate the initiative in the 1990s with the Center for Policy Alternatives (CPA). CPA aimed to create a network of state and local lawmakers to disseminate progressive ideas and bills and to compete directly on the same terrain as ALEC. While the Center did produce and compile annual books of policy ideas—like ALEC's model bills—major funders were mostly interested in leadership training, not legislative advocacy.[65] CPA recognized this imbalance, with a former director bemoaning an "overall absence of focus on ideology" from their backers.[66] Explained the director: "What we're lacking is a framework and a strategy"; at the state level, there are "these single-issue groups out there flailing away. But we are at least two decades behind in understanding how to move policy through the states and to the national level"—in direct contrast to the conservative movement.[67]

Still, at its peak, CPA briefly approached the size and scope of ALEC.[68] In the late 1990s and early 2000s, ALEC claimed around 2,400 legislative members, while CPA was not too far behind with 2,000 members.[69] Just as with ALEC, moreover, CPA was holding annual convenings of those members, and boasted around 100 model bills it was promoting across the states, compared to around 300 for ALEC.[70] And importantly, CPA's budget was approaching around $6 million per year, compared to around $8 million for ALEC, according to tax filings.

Yet just as CPA was about to emerge as a serious counterweight to ALEC, funders began to lose interest in the project and it became harder and harder to sustain general support for CPA's initiatives beyond its narrow leadership training program. Declining funder interest meant declining revenue, and by the mid-2000s, CPA's budget was cut by two-thirds to around $2 million. The Center eventually went under by the mid-2000s.

Though the group never quite managed to sustain a legislative reach on a par with ALEC, the impact of its Flemming Leadership Institute—CPA's leadership development program—did endure over time as its graduates went on to serve in higher office. Many of those graduates would serve in Congress and other national positions, and include prominent Democratic politicians such as

Gabby Giffords (former congresswoman from Arizona), Chellie Pingree (congresswoman from Maine), Jackie Speier (congresswoman from California), Debbie Wasserman Schultz (congresswoman from Florida and past head of the Democratic National Committee), Keith Ellison (congressman from Minnesota and leader in the Democratic National Committee), and Jon Tester (senator from Montana).[71]

With the untimely demise of the CPA, a progressive political entrepreneur attempted to develop a more robust and direct counterweight to ALEC, and sought funding from both unions and foundations. That leader was unable to get "a dollar of funding" for the new state network.[72] Separately, the leaders of a welter of progressive policy groups—including the Economic Policy Institute, a left-wing, labor-backed think tank in Washington, D.C.; a former head of the CPA; a leader of the NAACP's National Voter Fund; the head of Demos, another left-leaning think tank and advocacy group; and the head of Progressive Majority, a political training and campaign support group for progressive candidates—put together a comprehensive proposal for a "State Action Collaborative."[73]

Recognizing that "the Right has an organizational head start in the states . . . the Right can point to massively increased influence over state politics," the Collaborative intended to build "progressive political power in the states" by creating a "progressive state policy platform and program," "a leadership support network among state progressive elected officials and candidates," "targeted support in important legislative policy campaigns," "recruitment and training of a large number of new progressive candidates for state office," and "coordination among significant progressive organizations."[74] Envisioning both a non-profit arm and a PAC, the Collaborative proposed ramping up from around $2.5 million in its first year to $6 million in five years.[75] Despite its persuasive argument that the "progressive opportunity [to invest in the states] is enormous" given years of neglect, the Collaborative was unable to get any significant support from funders—and thus never got off the ground, even with a significantly scaled-back proposal it modestly called a "starter" investment.[76]

Another group, dubbed the Progressive Legislative Action Network (PLAN), attempted to fill this void as well. In the wake of the failure of the Collaborative, PLAN formed in 2005 with the aim of providing "solid public policy research to progressive state legislators," as well as "assistance to legislators, their staffs and grassroots advocacy organizations to ensure that progressives achieve success at the state level."[77] Explained PLAN Co-director David Sirota, a progressive activist and former aide to congressional Democrats: "No one argues that we progressives need to be doing a better job of countering right-wing organizations like the American Legislative Exchange Council. . . . The key to this is getting outside of Washington, D.C., and really starting to use our state leaders. . . . For too long, progressives have been marginalized by the insulated Beltway establishment that says the only place where action happens is in Washington, D.C."[78]

But, right from the start, PLAN faced the same two obstacles that would continue to hamper left-wing efforts in the states: insufficient funding and competition with existing piecemeal efforts.[79] Progressive leaders who were involved in the last years of the CPA immediately questioned the logic of launching a new organization that encroached on their older territory. "[CPA was] such a good organization, my first reaction is why would we start another one?," questioned Wisconsin State Representative Mark Pocan, a leader of CPA. "The bottom line is we have lots of networks. These are feisty Chihuahuas. I don't know if having six feisty Chihuahuas against one big gorilla does much," Pocan colorfully concluded.[80]

Another liberal activist who wasn't involved in either PLAN or CPA voiced similar concerns: "It troubles me that they may be reinventing the wheel."[81] And aside from the competition with existing groups, PLAN struggled to find donors. As *Roll Call* summarized: "PLAN is entering a world in which ALEC's budget outpaces CPA's 3-1, mainly because ALEC's conservative message resonates strongly with corporations with deep pockets. This revenue base has allowed ALEC, with an annual budget of $6 million and a staff of 30, to assemble top-notch materials and put on first-rate events for lawmakers."[82]

PLAN later morphed into the Progressive States Network (PSN), in part a result of PLAN's "long-term financial challenges."[83] While at its peak PSN could claim around 1,000 left-leaning state legislators as members, it was narrowly focused on short-term labor-related issues given that it relied heavily on union backing. The group did not prioritize a long-term political strategy, which ultimately spelled its demise.[84] Indeed, the history of PSN was mentioned to me in several interviews as a cautionary tale of relying too heavily on labor unions for donations—precisely the same problem that plagued private union state federations, as we saw in the previous section.[85]

Yet another initiative was then launched in the form of ALICE, or the American Legislative and Issue Campaign Exchange. A cheekily named solution to the lack of an ALEC for the left, the project was spearheaded by Joel Rogers, a professor at the University of Wisconsin. Rogers had been affiliated with much of the past left-wing organization-building, including the State Action Collaborative. Still, according to interviews with ALICE staff, the group soon realized it was never going to be a direct copy of ALEC on the left, as the organization was unable to secure sufficient funding for the full range of services and activities that ALEC offered its state legislative members.[86] Instead, ALICE shifted to providing a clearinghouse of progressive policy research and proposals that lawmakers could use to help develop their own bills—a "library," rather than an aggressive "lobby."[87] Tellingly, Rogers had attempted to build a previous version of ALICE in 2006 that flopped given a lack of funding from traditional left-wing sources. Separately, Rogers had also started another initiative at the University of Wisconsin, the Center for State Innovation (CSI), which aimed to provide resources to state executives to develop progressive public policy.[88]

Facing the implosion of the PSN, a scaled-back ALICE and CSI, as well as record GOP gains in control of statehouses following the 2010 elections, progressive leaders recognized that something needed to change. After a series of talks with the heads of each of those three groups, ALICE, PSN, and the CSI agreed to join forces to create the State Innovation Exchange, or SIX, in 2014. Initial interviews with SIX's inaugural head, Nick Rathod, an Obama White House alum, indicated lofty goals. SIX aimed to "raise as much as $10 million a year to boost progressive state lawmakers and their causes—partly by drafting model legislation in state capitols to increase environmental protections, expand voting rights, and raise the minimum wage—while also using bare-knuckle tactics like opposition research and video tracking to derail Republicans and their initiatives."[89] Much was made of the fact that SIX was approved for funding from the Democracy Alliance, a consortium of wealthy individual liberal donors who coordinate their giving to political advocacy groups and raise around $150 million each electoral cycle.[90]

Three years in, SIX is a long way off from its original goals. The group has a budget of around $3 million, and an initial look at the states where it has claimed the most legislative activity indicates most are already-liberal enclaves. Figure 7.3 draws on a report of SIX's activities from 2015 to 2016 to map where SIX described the most connections with state lawmakers, relying on a simple tally of whether SIX staff reported visiting a state, offered "policy support" to lawmakers, issued state-specific model legislation, briefed a caucus, or mentioned a state as an explicit priority for 2016.

As Figure 7.3 indicates, SIX reported the most effort in Washington, Colorado, Massachusetts, Minnesota, Oregon, and California—mostly a group of states with already-strong labor movements, strong Democratic parties, and relatively liberal constituents. This spread of efforts thus suggests that SIX is unlikely to expand the reach of progressive policy activists beyond pockets of traditional left-wing strength—at least with its present model of organization. That, of course, may yet change. Still, according to the 2017 survey of state legislators and staffers I described in the previous chapter, a mere 11 percent of state lawmakers and their staff reported relying on SIX very frequently or frequently in their work. (The question text was "How frequently have you relied on the following organizations when considering, drafting, or evaluating legislation?" and possible responses included very frequently, frequently, rarely, or not at all.) By comparison, about four times as many survey respondents reported relying frequently

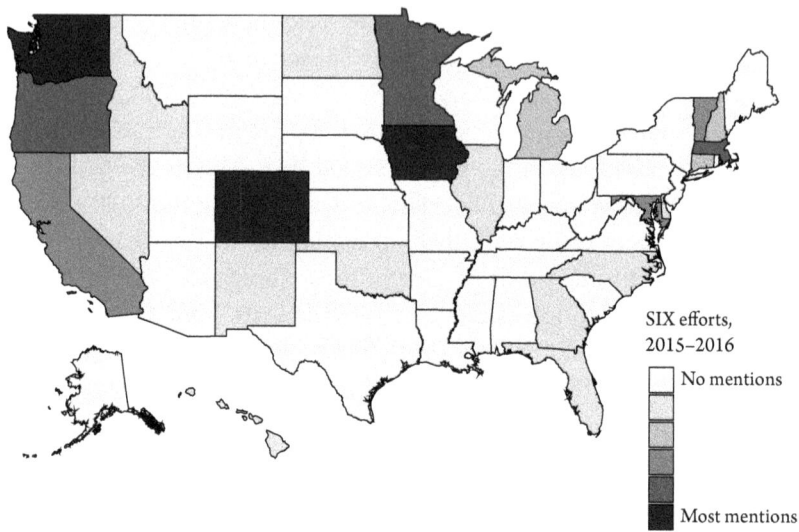

Figure 7.3. ORGANIZING EFFORTS BY THE STATE INNOVATION EXCHANGE, 2015–2016. Organizing effort is a tally of whether SIX staff reported visiting a state, offered "policy support" to lawmakers, issued state-specific model legislation, briefed a caucus, or mentioned a state as an explicit priority for 2016.

or very frequently on their state's chamber of commerce and six times as many reported relying very frequently or frequently on the NCSL.

In addition, there are some signs that SIX may be moving away from legislative advocacy to more electoral activities. Following big down-ballot Democratic losses in 2016, SIX created a new electoral campaign arm dubbed SIX Action, bringing on Democratic operative David Brock and several other experienced campaign strategists to help elect Democrats to state and local office in the coming years.[91]

The history of progressive state networks, then, might best be characterized by repeated cycles of panic, as left-wing advocates recognize the ever-broadening gap between their own efforts and those of the conservative troika, the formation of grand plans for collaboration and investment in new infrastructure, and dashed hopes as progressive leaders find themselves with inadequate, spotty funding competing against the array of other groups supported by left-wing donors. Figure 7.4 captures the essence of these boom and bust cycles, showing trends in the budgets of the CPA, Progressive Majority, PSN, and SIX against ALEC. The picture of a pack of "feisty Chihuahuas" against "one big gorilla" could not be clearer. Even with ALEC's decline in revenue following its publicity crisis, it remains far ahead of its liberal foes.

One pattern that stands out from the fits and starts of left-wing cross-state mobilizing is this: the three major bursts of organization-building occurred

Why Left-Wing Efforts to Counter the Troika Have Floundered 229

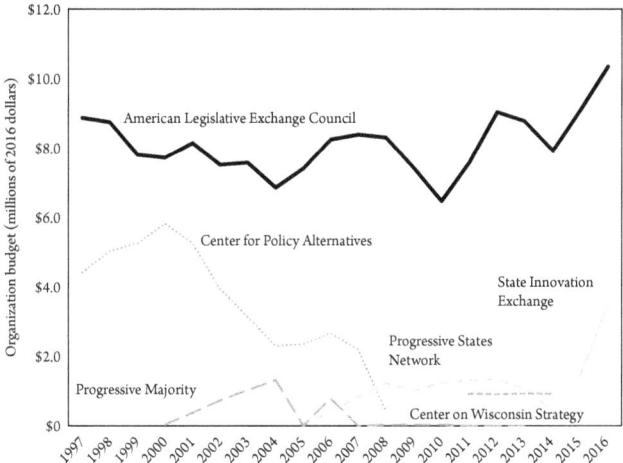

Figure 7.4. BUDGETS OF ALEC AND LEFT-WING COUNTERWEIGHTS, 1997–2017. Data from various IRS tax filings and group annual reports.

when Democrats were out of power in Washington, D.C. The CPA was built up during the first Bush presidency. The next major push happened in the mid-2000s, especially after Democrats endured a second loss to George W. Bush in 2004. That was when the State Action Collaborative, PLAN, and PSN were all trying to get off the ground. Explained one NPR reporter when looking at the flurry of activity in 2005, though "progressives have been talking about doing this literally for years," there was an easy reason to explain why they hadn't.[92] Except for the years from 1953 to 1955, Democrats controlled at least one part of the federal government—White House, Senate, or House—from the New Deal to 2003. So "when a liberal policy needed to be hatched and popularized, powerful Democratic lawmakers or even a Democratic president would do it."[93] The losses Democrats endured under the Bush presidency thus focused the center-left on the states in a way that they had not before.

But just four years later, Democrats abandoned the states by the wayside once more after enjoying big gains in Congress and the election of Barack Obama in 2008. Organizing faltered, and it was not until the GOP's rout of the Democrats in 2010 and again in 2014 and 2016 that there was any renewed interest in building cross-state progressive power. Similar to the fact that repeated victories in presidential elections discouraged serious investment in national Democratic Party committees, sustained national control of government (even partial control) made the hard work of cross-state network-building less appealing to liberal donors and advocates and contributed to the stop-and-start efforts we have seen over time.[94]

Yet against this graveyard of progressive groups, two organizations stand out as enduring success stories. If we return to the vast array of left-wing efforts to counter the troika that I laid out in Figure 7.1, we can discern two liberal cross-state organizations that have operated continuously for approximately two decades: the Economic Analysis and Research Network (EARN) and State Priorities Partnership (SPP). As we will see, these two networks have succeeded in achieving important progressive policy goals across the United States in red and blue states alike. Their success hints at broader lessons for the left to consider in building cross-state power.

Two Progressive Successes in the States: The Economic Analysis and Research Network and State Priorities Partnership

SPP and EARN are both networks of state-level, center-left think tanks focused on economic policy. Started in 1993 by the D.C.-based Center on Budget and Policy Priorities, the State Fiscal Analysis Initiative (now rebranded as the State Priorities Partnership) provides support for some 41 state groups doing research on budgets and public programs for low-income Americans. With a somewhat broader mission, EARN includes about 60 policy organizations overseen by the D.C.-based, union-connected Economic Policy Institute. It would be a mistake to think of these networks as entirely separate entities, however. While they are institutionally distinct at the top, there is a substantial degree of overlap in their membership across the states. Around 60 state-level think tanks participate in either network, and of those, nearly two-thirds participate in both SPP and EARN.

Think tank membership in the two networks means slightly different things. SPP—the older of the two initiatives—has always had a more formal structure, with strict rules on what membership in the network entails, as well as opportunities to apply for grants directly from the network or in partnership with the group's convener, the Center on Budget and Policy Priorities. To join SPP, groups need to meet a relatively strict set of criteria related to their policy focus, their analytical capacity, and their staff resources. One early document detailing those requirements mentioned the following items needed to join the network: a focus on a "broad spectrum of tax and budget issues," the production of timely information and analysis, work products that were "accurate, transparent and free from bias," advancing the needs of diverse populations, securing a diverse portfolio of funding streams, and a commitment to help the other members of the SPP network. In contrast, EARN is a much looser confederation of organizations with no formal requirements for membership—but also (typically) no direct funding opportunities.

Why would state think tanks belong to both groups? Interviews with leaders of the affiliates indicate that the two networks offer different benefits. While SPP gives affiliates more institutional resources in the form of grants and capacity-building, EARN connects its members to a broader set of political advocates and has a more explicitly left-wing and progressive focus. So a state think tank interested in forging ties with the labor movement or other more political activists might use the EARN network for those needs, while participating in SPP to bolster their organization's infrastructure. These differences in the two networks also help to explain why it may not make sense to merge them together, as some have argued in the past.

Despite these differences, SPP and EARN do share a number of activities and approaches. Both networks take advantage of the expertise of their national staffs to help state organizations with policy analysis and outreach. That could include more technical help, such as providing cleaned versions of important datasets, like the Current Population Survey, communications assistance in drafting reports or interacting with the press and elected officials, or advice on crafting grant proposals to foundations. Both networks also facilitate horizontal connections between their participants so that member think tanks with a particular strength in one policy area can help their peers with a demand for information about that policy issue. And both SPP and EARN hold regular convenings of their members each year that disseminate key priorities for the coming legislative sessions, share strategies and war stories, and introduce members to outside experts who might serve as additional resources for their work.

Figure 7.5 compares the spread of SPP (earlier, SFAI) and EARN across the states against SPN—the member of the troika that is closest in form and function to the two left-wing networks. EARN, with its more informal membership, reaches affiliates in more states than does SPP, and together the two networks have a presence in 45 states, against SPN's coverage in all 50 states (the center-left networks lacked a presence in Alaska, Delaware, Hawaii, North Dakota, South Carolina, and Tennessee at the time of this book's writing).

Another way of comparing SPN against the two left-wing networks is to look at the most recent budgets of each of their affiliates. Doing this, I find that the center-left networks tended to be outspent by SPN more often than not (see Figure 7.6). SPP and EARN affiliates have combined budgets larger than SPN members in only 13 out of the 50 states. In the average state, SPP and EARN affiliates had revenues that were about half a million dollars less than those of SPN think tanks. SPP and EARN were most badly outspent in some blue

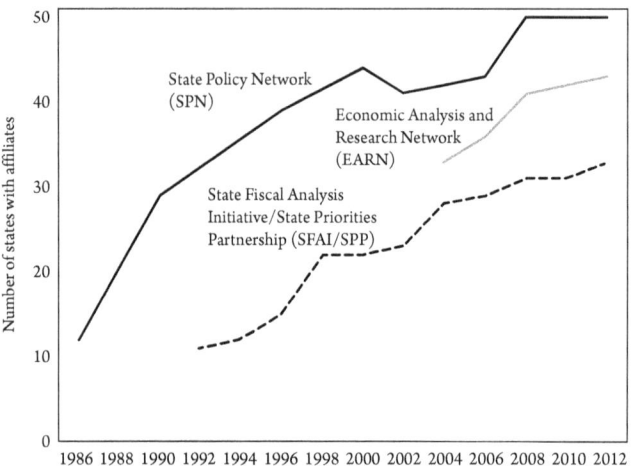

Figure 7.5. THE SPREAD OF SPN, EARN, AND SFAI/SPP ACROSS THE STATES, 1986–2012. Data from archived websites and group annual reports.

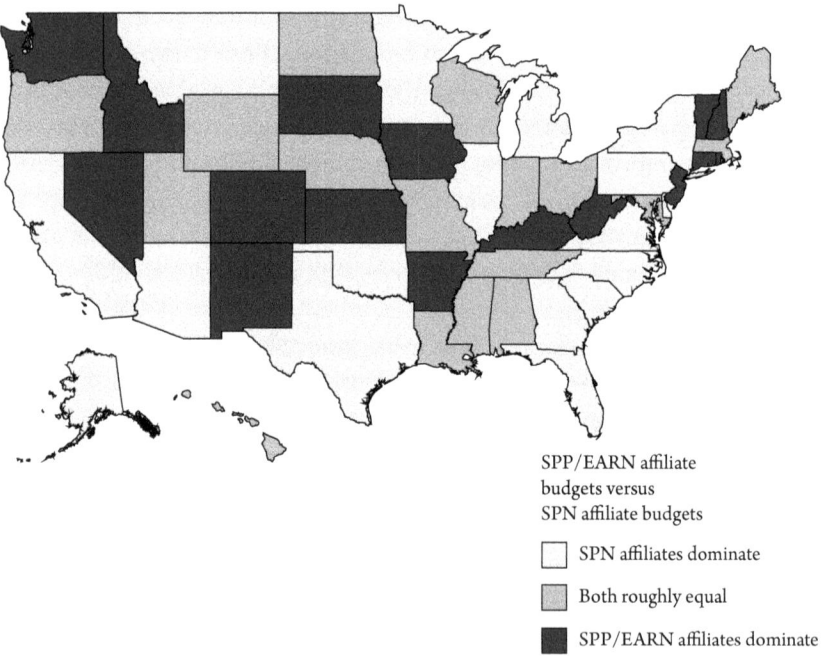

Figure 7.6. COMPARING SPN VERSUS SPP AND EARN BUDGETS BY STATE, 2014. This map divides states by the comparison of SPP/EARN affiliate budgets with SPN affiliate budgets (divided into three equally sized groups, or terciles). Budget data from IRS tax filings, generally for 2014 or the last available filing.

states—like California, Illinois, and New York—but also a number of battleground and traditionally conservative states, like Virginia, Michigan, Texas, and Georgia.

Even in the face of SPN's financial dominance across the states, however, SPP and EARN affiliates have succeeded in engineering a number of important policy victories—including in partially or fully GOP-controlled states. It was SPP and EARN state affiliates, for instance, that helped to convince a number of states to enact earned income tax credits for working poor families through the 1990s and early 2000s.[95] It was also SPP and EARN affiliates that pushed for more generous state welfare programs in the wake of federal welfare reform in the 1990s.[96] The secrets to these successes are affiliates' well-earned reputations for honest numbers and analysis—reputations that can carry weight even with conservative lawmakers. Also important is SPP and EARN's willingness to reach out to unconventional partners, especially businesses, to find political support for programs that help low-income families and workers. Without nudges—and hard data—from SPP and EARN affiliates, those partners, and particularly corporate managers, might not otherwise have waded into politics to defend state and local social programs.

Take one recent victory reported to me by an affiliate in a deeply conservative state with a GOP governor.[97] The SPP/EARN affiliate in that state managed to boost subsidies for poor families to buy childcare services by building on partnerships with childcare providers, who lobbied the legislature from the outside, as well as inside lobbying by the affiliate itself. Those paired strategies managed to convince even conservative lawmakers that the childcare subsidies could be a tool for workforce development by permitting low-income parents to spend more time on the job. In another GOP state, a SPP/EARN affiliate worked with county-level leaders to boost local minimum wages in the face of resistance from the state's Republican legislature and governor. And in a third very conservative state, the affiliate stopped a tax cut package that would have represented a significant loss in state revenue, working in collaboration with business partners from the healthcare and education industries who were successfully persuaded of the downside risks of the tax cut for their bottom lines. Less state revenue meant fewer opportunities for doing business with public schools and the state healthcare system.

EARN and SPP's bipartisan reach is further underscored in the 2017 survey of state legislators and legislative staffs that I described earlier. In that survey, I asked respondents if they had relied on the EARN or SPP affiliate in their state.[98] (Recall the question was "How frequently have you relied on the following organizations when considering, drafting, or evaluating legislation?" and possible responses included very frequently, frequently, rarely, or not at all.) In all, 34 percent of staffers and legislators reported very frequent or frequent reliance on their state's EARN or SPP affiliate (contrast that with the comparable figure of 11 percent for SIX). Sixty-four percent of staffers and legislators reported *any* reliance on EARN or SPP affiliates. Unsurprisingly, EARN and SPP reliance was substantially higher among Democratic lawmakers and staffers than Republicans, with nearly half of Democratic respondents reporting very frequent or frequent reliance. But remarkably, 17 percent of Republican legislators and their staffs still reported very frequent or frequent EARN or SPP reliance. Republicans who said that teachers and large businesses were important groups in their districts were especially likely to report using EARN and SPP, in line with the interviews I conducted above.

Notwithstanding these important victories, SPP and EARN affiliates note that funding remains a big obstacle to their work. In a 2016 online survey I conducted of those two networks along with Theda Skocpol, the most commonly reported impediment aside from opposing partisan control was "insufficient financial resources."[99] Echoing the conclusions from our earlier tour of the various left-wing efforts at countering ALEC, SPP and EARN affiliates were just as likely to say that they needed consistency in funding from year to year as much as generous grants from their financial backers.[100] The story of center-left funding flows to the states, then, is as much of a failure to provide consistent support as it is a case of providing stingy grants to cross-state organizers. But this finding raises its own set of questions, namely, why have major center-left funders tended to ignore the states in their philanthropic giving?

Why Have Center-Left Funders Ignored State Politics and Policy?

One easy argument to dismiss right from the start is that there is simply not enough money on the left to sustain a liberal version of the troika. Between large center-left foundations, unions, and wealthy individual donors, there is certainly enough money to support groups resembling ALEC, AFP, and SPN on the left. It is difficult to pin down a single estimate of the total pool of potential monies that would be available to fund left-wing cross-state political organizing, so instead of looking at potential donations, we can look at actual spending on major center-left and progressive groups in recent years and compare that spending to expenditures on the right. In other work with Theda Skocpol, I have tried to do just that by constructing lists of the conservative and liberal "universes" of major political groups. These lists thus include the political party committees (including the separate organizations responsible for fundraising for House, Senate, and state races), major think tanks, cross-state advocacy organizations, unions (on the left) and business trade groups (on the right), constituency mobilizing groups (like AFP), single-issue groups (like Planned Parenthood on the left and the National Rifle Association on the right), and outside campaign spending groups like Priorities USA (on the left) and the Club for Growth (on the right).[101]

All told, we came up with 37 of these major groups on the right and 44 on the left. These universes are necessarily limited—but together, they provide a rough picture of the major organizations on both sides of the political spectrum and their combined resources. Summing up the budgets of these organizations from 2013 to 2014, we found that all the liberal groups had a pool of resources of just under $4 billion, while the conservative ones commanded resources of over $2 billion. To be clear, I do not interpret these figures as showing that liberals have more money to invest in politics than do conservatives. Instead, I take this comparison as simply illustrating that liberals do indeed have a vast pool of resources—from unions, individual donors, and charitable foundations—that they could tap into to fund cross-state organizing. The issue is that liberals are simply not directing this money to the states, while conservatives have been doing so for decades.

Why is that the case? An important reason that stood out in interview after interview was the culture of traditional center-left and progressive foundations, which have historically been reluctant to finance partisan policy development and lobbying, at least since the 1970s.[102] Reported one foundation leader in response to an interview in the early 1990s asking if his organization would attempt to counter the rising influence of the right in state governments through ALEC and SPN: "We tend to fund national organizations in the mainstream with moderate views," and his philanthropy would not fund think tanks at either end of the political spectrum.[103]

Another liberal foundation head echoed the same distaste for engaging in partisan politics: "The way to make good local government is to clean up the political process, not try to skew things from a particular point of view."[104] Similarly, one liberal observer noted that in the early 2000s, while "large, mainstream foundations like Ford and Carnegie have come to understand the need for new investments in policy organizations geared toward doing battle in the states," it is "less clear . . . whether such foundations are willing to pony up the kind of serious money that is needed to make a real difference"—especially since state groups need donors "who are comfortable with an agenda that often can be quite partisan."[105]

Even when left-wing funders have been willing to finance more explicitly political activities, especially promoting the development of legislation, it has largely been at the national level for both cultural and pragmatic reasons. As one report from a left-leaning philanthropy, the George Soros–funded Open Society Institute, summarized: "For years, progressives—and especially

Liberals—fought against devolution and stressed the belief that major social issues must be addressed nationally."[106] According to one political organizer, major center-left foundations are defined by a "national elitism," run by highly educated individuals who feel that the real talent and opportunities for political change lie in Washington, D.C., not in far-flung state capitals.[107] Another progressive activist put it more bluntly: state policy work simply "wasn't sexy to donors."[108] Thus, the lack of professionalization of state and local politics—which has been a key comparative advantage for ALEC—has also ironically meant that progressive donors do not believe the possibility exists for major reform at the state level.

Aside from a cultural preference for national politics, there are also more substantive political justifications for a lack of investment in state and local policy groups.[109] Major progressive initiatives have frequently come at the national, not state, level given budget constraints faced by state and local governments, state lawmakers' fears of losing capital to other states or becoming "welfare magnets," and the legacy of institutionalized racial oppression in many states and localities.[110] As federalism scholar Heather Gerken has remarked, many progressives "think 'federalism' is just a code word for letting racists be racist. Progressives also associate federalism—and its less prominent companion, localism, which simply means decentralization within a state—with parochialism and the suppression of dissent."[111]

The result of these cultural and political calculations is that most of the major left-leaning foundations have invested little in broad-based cross-state policy initiatives. A similar historical bias against the states can be found with wealthy individual donors on the left as well. This is perhaps best represented by the Democracy Alliance, the club of liberal millionaires and billionaires that coordinates political giving to progressive political advocacy groups. Founded in 2005 after the reelection of President George W. Bush the year before, the Alliance brings together around 100 wealthy donors twice yearly to introduce them to potential grantees and to share political strategies and agendas.[112]

At the core of the Alliance is a list of progressive organizations that are "approved" for donations from Alliance members, who, in turn, must pledge a certain amount of giving each year to organizations appearing on the official list (recently, this minimum has been around $200,000 per year).[113] Appearing on "the list" is thus a necessary step for progressive advocacy groups to secure Alliance donations—but by no means guarantees support for an organization. Groups jockey intensely for inclusion on this roster, and there is significant turnover with regard to who is in and who is out depending on the vision of the Alliance's leadership, lobbying by individual donors, and national political trends.[114]

Examining the core approved lists for the Alliance from 2005, 2007, 2009, 2012, 2014, and 2015, I could only identify three organizations that had been consistently recommended for funding in three or more years and had a significant cross-state policy advocacy focus. That represents just 20 percent of all the groups that had been recommended for funding in three or more donation cycles.

The Alliance's focus is shifting, however. In very recent years, the Alliance explicitly recognized the lack of progressive investment in the states—and made a concerted effort to redirect new flows of funding to both older and newer groups involved in cross-state policy and electoral activities. The need for state-level advocacy has featured prominently on the agendas of recent Alliance convenings, and the Alliance has set up new portfolios for donors to give funds earmarked toward "strategic states."[115]

In fact, the Alliance supported the spin-off of a new group, the Committee on the States, which aims to construct state-level Democracy Alliances—"donor tables"—to jump-start the construction of progressive infrastructure in key battleground states.[116] As the Democracy Alliance puts it, the Committee "is committed to the creation and success of networks that work to advance progressive causes and produce progressive change within individual states."[117] The model for the Committee is Colorado, where a small group of wealthy donors (nicknamed the Four Horsemen) worked with unions, left-wing foundations, and political strategists to fund an infrastructure to retake the state's legislature and governorship and prepare an agenda of progressive legislation to enact when that happened.[118]

With twenty-one national donors in 2014, the Committee on the States coordinated funding flows of around $50 million in the 2013–2014 electoral cycle, and hopes to double that total by 2020.[119] Those are large sums—but the Committee still has yet to move major political outcomes. The states that were targeted for Committee investments in 2013–2014 were no more likely to see bigger Democratic gains than states that were not targeted by the Committee, nor were those targeted states any less likely to pass ALEC-plagiarized model bills.[120] This is not to say that the Committee's investments are failures—but rather, it is too soon for us to evaluate its effects.

The reinvigorated focus on the states has only deepened as the GOP continues to make record gains in control of state legislatures and governorships, and as progressives seek to push back against the Trump administration and a Republican-controlled Congress. "People have gotten a wake-up call," explained Gara LaMarche, the Democracy Alliance's new president, in an interview with *The Washington Post*.[121] "The right is focused on the state level, and even down-ballot, and has made enormous gains. We can't have the kind of long-term progressive future we want if we don't take power in the states."[122]

At long last, then, the states are front and center in the minds of wealthy liberal and progressive donors. But whether this renewed focus can result in durable changes in the landscape of left-wing organizations—such as the construction of a real progressive alternative to AFP, a bolstered SIX or other ALEC counterweight, and renewed funding flows to the successful SPP and EARN networks—remains to be seen.

Are Cities the Progressive Future?

In the meantime, many progressives have increasingly set their sights on large metropolitan areas in the pursuit of policy change. Unlike with state-level advocacy, left-leaning policy activists have natural advantages in urban politics. Over the past sixty years, cities have become much more reliably Democratic and liberal.[123] The causes of this transition are varied, and include the creation of suburbs that enabled more conservative voters to flee cities, the emergence of moral and social issues as major political cleavages, racial tensions in the 1960s and 1970s, and the changing mix of businesses drawn to cities.[124]

The upshot of these transformations, however, is clear: denser areas, especially cities, have become blue strongholds, while more sparsely populated areas are now reliably red country. That distribution of political support has meant that Democrats, and often especially liberal Democrats, are in full control of city government. Looking at the 100 largest cities by population in 2017, for instance, 62 had Democratic mayors, while only 29 had Republicans in charge.[125] "With a group of new, progressive mayors in office . . . the era of big-city liberalism has just begun. . . . Though the right controls most of the statehouses and large swaths of the federal government, the city, increasingly, belongs to progressives," proclaimed the liberal magazine *The Nation* in bold terms.[126]

One policy area where progressives have used that urban-based influence in recent times involves raising the minimum wage. For decades, Congress reliably passed legislation boosting the minimum wage to ensure that its value matched, or even exceeded, rates of inflation. In the 1960s and 1970s, the federal minimum wage averaged over $9 an hour, expressed in 2016 dollars.[127] But by the 1980s, increasing resistance from the Republican Party meant that it became harder and harder to pass congressional increases in the minimum wage, and so its value fell to just under $8 an hour, and dropped even further to just over $7 an hour in the 1990s. Currently, the minimum wage stands at $7.25 an hour. That level seems unlikely to change given full GOP control of Congress and the White House at the time of this book's writing. Given GOP control of so many state governments, too, the possibilities for state action on minimum wage hikes beyond the federal floor have fallen by the wayside.

In response, progressive activists have taken their energies to Democratically controlled cities willing to increase their own minimum wages. The move to the cities received a big boost from "Fight for $15," a movement of low-wage workers in the fast-food industry, home healthcare, and other similar lines of service work seeking increased pay—minimum wage hikes up to $15 an hour— better working conditions, and union representation.[128] Launched with a round of strikes and rallies in 2012, the movement received significant financial support from SEIU, the union representing service-sector workers, and has successfully pushed for minimum wage hikes across the country.[129]

Figure 7.7 documents the rapid increase of city and municipal action on the minimum wage in both blue states under full Democratic control (left-hand plot), but also in an increasing number of states under split or full Republican control (right-hand plot). Minimum wage activists have also pushed concurrently for local measures to extend paid sick leave to workers as a condition of employment, given that many workers—and disproportionately low-wage, service-sector employees—lack paid sick or family leave.[130] (The United States is one of the only rich democracies without such a national policy for paid leave.)

If the story ended here, it might well provide a strong justification for progressives to abandon cross-state organization in favor of a city-based approach. But in their enthusiastic urban turn, liberal activists have overlooked a major barrier: most state legislatures can simply overrule (or "preempt") city action with which they disagree. As progressives have tried

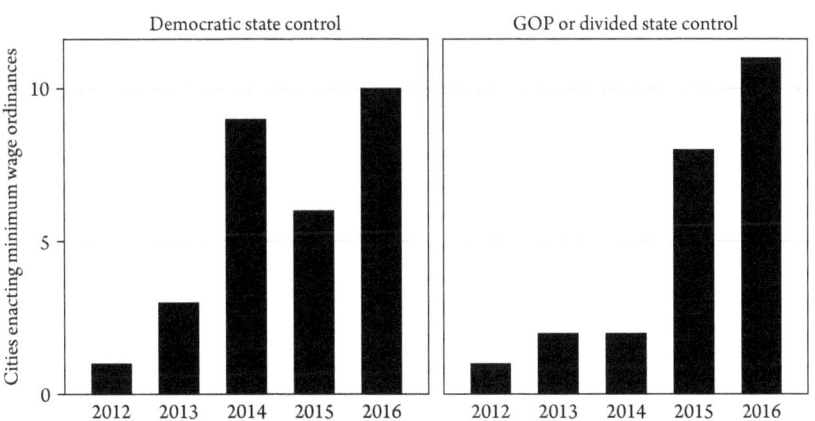

Figure 7.7. THE SPREAD OF LOCAL MINIMUM WAGES ACROSS THE UNITED STATES, 2012–2016. Local minimum wage ordinances from the University of California, Berkeley Labor Center's Inventory of US City and County Minimum Wage Ordinances. Figure divided by partisan control over 2012 to 2016.

to pursue more liberal urban initiatives, the troika has responded by vigorously embracing preemption. Take the example of minimum wage and paid sick leave initiatives. The spread of these laws did not go unnoticed by employers. The fast-food sector in particular began worrying about the cost of these measures for their bottom lines. Sensing the possibility of a wave of action in 2011, YUM! Brands—the parent company of fast-food giants Kentucky Fried Chicken, Pizza Hut, and Taco Bell and a longtime ALEC participant—brought up the issue at an ALEC meeting that year.[131] In the convening of ALEC's business regulation subcommittee of the commerce, insurance, and economic development task force, fast-food lobbyists handed out a map to the gathered participants of local paid sick leave initiatives that had already passed, as well as the cities in which activists were preparing for a push in the coming months.[132]

Fast-food representatives also offered a potential solution to the threat, engineered by Wisconsin's newly elected GOP governor and longstanding ally of ALEC, Scott Walker. Facing the prospect of a paid sick leave program in Milwaukee, Walker and the state's GOP legislature—alongside the Wisconsin chamber of commerce and the local chapter of the National Restaurant Association—enacted a law barring any Wisconsin locality from passing labor market regulations exceeding the state's provisions.[133] That meant no Wisconsin city could enact its own paid sick leave program (since the state lacked such a program), nor could cities raise their minimum wages beyond what the state had done already. YUM! distributed printouts of the Wisconsin law to the ALEC task force, recommending that ALEC lawmakers introduce similar measures across the states. It was not the first time that ALEC had used preemption to stop cities from imposing onerous regulations on business. In the 1990s, ALEC, prompted by the tobacco industry, promoted model bills that would prevent cities from enacting anti-smoking laws that exceeded the standards set by states.[134] By 2000, a majority of states had enacted versions of that ALEC-drafted tobacco regulation preemption.[135] (Some states—though not all—have rescinded those tobacco preemption laws.[136])

Preemption of city labor standards followed a similar path, with ALEC legislators introducing and enacting Wisconsin-like legislation all across the country. Figure 7.8 plots the share of the US population living in a state with either preemption of local minimum wage rates or local paid sick and family leave programs. It also indicates with a dashed vertical line the year in which ALEC began focusing on preempting local labor market programs (2011). Figure 7.8 shows that an increasing proportion of the US population lives in states with both kinds of preemption—with an especially big increase after ALEC began focusing on these issues in 2011. In 2000, fewer than 2 percent of Americans

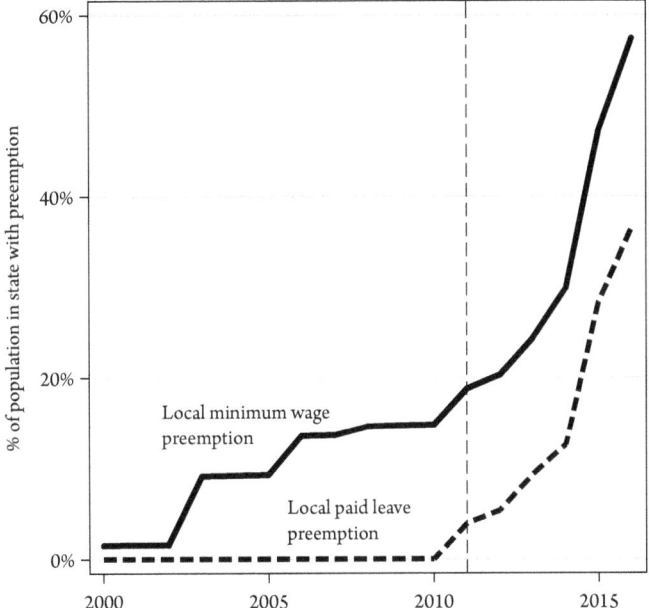

Figure 7.8. THE SPREAD OF LOCAL LABOR LAW PREEMPTION, 2000–2016. This graph shows the share of the US population living in states with local minimum wage preemption or local paid or family leave preemption. Dashed vertical line indicates 2011, the year in which ALEC began distributing local labor policy preemption bills to its members. Source is author's review of state legislation and the US Census Bureau.

lived in a state preempting local minimum wage hikes. By 2016, that share had increased to nearly six in ten Americans. The trend for preemption of citywide paid leave initiatives is similarly striking. No state had paid leave preemption on the books in 2000, but by 2016 nearly four in ten Americans lived in a state barring local paid sick leave initiatives unless the state had already created a leave program.

In short, the combination of state power over preemption, coupled with the troika's cross-state reach, severely curtails the ability of blue cities located within red states to take action on their own. While in some cases states have had to back off of preemption drives—as when North Carolina barred cities from prohibiting discrimination against LGBT people, including the use of bathrooms consistent with individuals' gender identities—more run-of-the-mill preemption of city efforts to raise working standards, improve the environment and deal with climate change, and address obesity and sugar consumption have generally been harder to reverse.[137] Given the distribution of political power across America's states and cities, then, progressives cannot retreat to their city strongholds and neglect the states.[138]

Throughout this chapter, we have observed the persistent imbalance in the capacity of liberals to construct durable and effective networks of legislators, experts, and advocates to press policy demands across the states. Part of the explanation rested with the surprising secession of conservative lawmakers from once broadly accepted, bipartisan associations. Progressives initially continued to channel their legislative activities through the bipartisan associations, ultimately falling behind as conservatives built up ALEC, SPN, and later, AFP. It is only in facing a major loss of control in Washington, D.C., that center-left attention, including donor attention, shifts to the states in any meaningful way.

Political organizers have thus found themselves stymied by a lack of consistent and generous funding and energy. Progressive entrepreneurs were often forced to compete for scarce dollars from foundations and wealthy donors that were reluctant to spend money on explicitly ideological or partisan advocacy across the states. Contemporary center-left donors, as we saw, tended to think in terms of national action, rather than focusing on the potential for cumulative state and local activities to promote coordinated policy change, as exemplified by the conservative movement and progressive New Deal–era activists at the turn of the twentieth century. Unions—the group that could perhaps provide the most natural funding for left-wing networks to counter corporate funding on the right and that formed the basis for a cross-state lobby in the public sector— are in steep decline, in part as a result of the strategic offensive staged by the right-wing troika, as we saw in previous chapters. And progressives tended to duplicate efforts, first forming the CPA, then PLAN, PSN, Progressive Majority, CSI, and ALICE (not to mention the efforts that never got off the ground)— a veritable alphabet soup of individual small initiatives that together formed a pack of "feisty Chihuahuas," rather than a true counterweight to the "one big gorilla" of ALEC. While more recent enthusiasm about the cities may be well founded for urban areas located in already-blue states, it is no replacement for vigorous cross-state mobilization.

All told, the early reluctance of liberal donors to support large-scale, well-coordinated state-by-state efforts across the country has meant that the task of combating ALEC and SPN has only grown over time, magnifying small initial differences between the organizing capacities of the left and the right. Lamented one staffer at a left-wing philanthropy in 2001, "The disconnect between what is spent now and what it would cost [progressives] to become a long-term opposition force is considerable"—and that assessment has only gotten worse in the ensuing years.[139] In the Conclusion section that follows, I draw from the successes and missteps of the troika to spell out the concrete steps that progressive donors and activists could take to rebuild cross-state power, as well as broader lessons for our understanding of US politics.

Conclusion

State Capture and American Democracy

From Hillary Clinton's campaign emails to Donald Trump's infamous *Access Hollywood* tape with Billy Bush, 2016 was a year of big leaks. You would thus be in good company if you missed the news about hackers breaking into the computer files of a Wisconsin-based foundation in the fall of that year.[1] Initially, most of the news coverage focused on the question of whether the organization—the Bradley Foundation, which I introduced in Chapter 1 as a longtime funder of ALEC—had been hacked by the Russians or not. But slowly, over the next six months, investigative journalists began pouring over the leaked records themselves. Those journalists eventually pieced together a picture of a very politically active philanthropy channeling money to right-wing advocacy groups all over the country.[2]

The Bradley Foundation, these documents revealed, had already succeeded in paving the way for conservative reforms on welfare, education, and union policy in its home state of Wisconsin. It now sought to replicate these victories in other states. The best bang for Bradley's buck, an internal evaluation concluded, would involve supporting conservative "state infrastructure"—sets of organizations "that work well together to advance the Foundation's mission and grantmaking program in their respective states."[3] Key characteristics of this infrastructure that the Bradley Foundation highlighted involved state-level think tanks, opposition research, receptive policymakers in state legislatures, and a symbiotic relationship with grassroots groups.[4] Singled out for top support from the Foundation were national groups with a cross-state presence. By now, you should be able to guess the top-funded groups on Bradley's list for state-based infrastructure: the American Legislative Exchange Council (ALEC), Americans for Prosperity (AFP), and the State Policy Network (SPN).[5]

As part of the new state infrastructure initiative that Bradley launched, the Mackinac Center for Public Policy—the Michigan-based SPN affiliate we met during our look at cross-state advocacy against public employee unions—received a doubling of support for a new education policy project that would be "replicable by other state think tanks" participating in SPN and working through ALEC.[6] The Arizona-based Goldwater Institute, which we met during our tour of SPN affiliates, similarly received a huge boost in funding to create a cross-state "litigation alliance."[7] That effort would help other SPN affiliates to construct legal centers, exactly like the Goldwater Institute's own, very successful litigation initiative that had brought winning cases in a number of states curbing public union rights. Bradley also gave expanded support to the Florida-headquartered Foundation for Government Accountability. The Foundation is another SPN affiliate that, as we saw in Chapter 6, was instrumental in working with ALEC to lobby across the states to oppose Medicaid expansion.[8] Bradley was supporting the Foundation to continue to "provide public-education resources to state think tanks and allies about Medicaid expansion."[9] Bradley planned large grants directly to ALEC and AFP's 501c3 foundation arm, too.

The lesson that Bradley had learned was that the "only way to compete on the battlefield of ideas" and win was to invest in political organizations that could establish ties within and across the states that built enduring relationships with lawmakers, shared resources across multiple levels of government, and developed a formidable presence outside of the legislature through think tanks and grassroots organizations. That meant, in turn, investing in ALEC, AFP, and SPN, which have all built up the capacity to do exactly those things across the whole country.

With increased support from institutional donors, like Bradley, the ever-more generous support from the wealthy individuals participating in the Koch seminars, and corporate interest from businesses realizing the gains from cross-state lobbying, the troika of ALEC, AFP, and SPN looks to be on sure footing for years to come. We are a long way from the days of conservative leaders like Paul Weyrich or Sam Brunelli bemoaning the ways that local conservative activists "were on their own in each state and . . . overwhelmed." Looking across the states in 2013, Bradley rightly concluded that the possibilities for "meaningful conservative policy advancement"—like further cuts to government employee union law, dismantling the Affordable Care Act, and moves to undermine environmental regulations—never looked brighter.

The lessons that the Bradley Foundation learned about the power of cross-state organizing provide a good opportunity for us to take stock of what we have learned about American politics in the last seven chapters. After reviewing those broader implications, I discuss what my analysis means for those concerned about the troika's effects on American public policy and democracy, spelling out the reasons why we ought to worry about the troika's monopoly on cross-state lobbying. In light of those concerns, I conclude with some concrete steps that citizens and political activists should take to check the power of the troika in the coming years.

What Can the Right-Wing Troika Teach Us about American Politics?

The outsized role of organized interests in American politics generally—and cross-state advocacy in particular. In *Winner-Take-All Politics*, an insightful book examining the dramatic rise of inequality in the United States, political scientists Jacob Hacker and Paul Pierson argue that their discipline has missed out on the political causes of economic concentration by treating government as "electoral spectacle"—thus missing out on the real action of politics, which they dub "organizational combat."[10]

By "electoral spectacle," Hacker and Pierson mean an overly narrow focus on individual voters and elections, treating policy as the direct product of politicians' electoral promises and voters' preferences. While elegant and reassuring, that picture of politics excludes organized interest groups, above all well-resourced actors like businesses and wealthy individual donors. Yet those organized interests are often deeply involved in elections, and even more importantly, they step in once the dust from elections has settled to change public policy. As Hacker and Pierson explain, policy battles are typically "long, hard slogs" that involve "drawn-out conflicts in multiple arenas, extremely complicated issues where only full-time, well-trained participants are likely to be effective, and stakes that can easily reach hundreds of billions of dollars."[11] To explain why American policy changes, Hacker and Pierson argue, we need to look to organized interests just as much, if not more than, individual voters and politicians.[12]

My close examination of the troika's development and growth across the country resonates strongly with Hacker and Pierson's call for a renewed focus on politics as "organized combat"—and even goes beyond their original formulation to show new ways in which organizations matter in American politics. The businesses, donors, and activists behind the troika members recognized that the best way they could start retaking the states would involve building organizations that would not necessarily intervene in individual elections or invest in specific politicians, but would instead focus on changing policy in durable ways over time.

Notably, only one of the troika members—AFP—is significantly involved in state elections, and even then AFP makes its electoral advocacy only one part of a broader strategy of moving public policy toward the libertarian, hard-right agenda pursued by the Koch political network. The Kochs have never viewed individual politicians as being central, considering them to be mere "actors" reading off of the scripts provided to them—ideally by groups directed by the Kochs. Similarly, recall from Chapter 1 that ALEC's leaders believed a natural extension of their success in the late 1980s meant starting a political action committee to elect business- and conservative-friendly politicians but then eventually realized that they could be far more effective staying behind the scenes and providing already elected lawmakers with the policy resources they would otherwise lack.

Clearly, the troika has itself grasped the reality of politics as organized combat. Instead of electoral spectacle, the troika—and especially ALEC—has focused on reshaping the policy positions of individual state politicians, and eventually, the Republican Party. By providing easy-to-use model bill ideas, research assistance, and political advice to otherwise harried, understaffed, and inexperienced politicians, ALEC discovered that it could define what it meant to be a pro-business, conservative official in state government. ALEC became, in the parlance of political scientists, a policy-demanding interest group squarely part of the Republican Party coalition.[13] ALEC was aided in these efforts by the creation of SPN, and later, AFP, which could provide even more resources in support of ALEC's policy ideas.

The histories of ALEC, AFP, and SPN also carry an even broader message about the importance of organized interests in the American political system. In our fragmented government divided across the fifty states, well-resourced organizations become an especially important tool for actors who want to carry out sustained policy change that bypasses the federal government. With an increasingly gridlocked Congress, national cross-state organizations like the troika can make a big difference by pushing for the same policies across multiple states at once. Conservatives might not be able to pass right to work, an overhaul of the country's educational system, or a complete repeal of the Affordable Care Act in Congress, but they can advance exactly those same policies on a state-by-state basis, making it harder for unions to organize, promoting privatization of public schools, and stymieing expansion of Medicaid.

In fact, cross-state advocacy that plays the entire field of states has advantages over efforts that focus exclusively on Congress. As we saw in Chapter 1, the model of multistate lobbying means that groups get many bites at the same apple. ALEC, SPN, and AFP can afford to lose some battles as long as they still succeed in other states. And that also opens the window for well-organized cross-state networks to push the boundaries of the possible.

With more opportunities to win, groups like ALEC have pursued fairly ambitious proposals, knowing full well that some of those bills would have no chance of adoption in most states. But some states would take the most extreme versions of their proposals, creating a precedent for ALEC to build on in subsequent legislative battles. In this way, the range of the possible slowly expands over time. (That process—known as moving the "Overton Window"—was actually coined by an analyst affiliated with the Mackinac Center in Michigan.[14]) Labor union policy offers an instructive example: although ALEC had been pushing right-to-work laws since its creation, the group often had to settle for smaller cutbacks to union rights—like making it harder for unions to collect dues or participate in politics. All those more modest measures, however, helped to build gradual support for the more aggressive union retrenchment that would come in later years. Summed up one progressive state legislator who has been tracking ALEC's efforts closely for years: ALEC encourages legislators to "introduce a fourteen-point platform, so that you can make it harder for [the left] to focus and for the press to cover fourteen different planks . . . You do it drip by drip."[15]

State legislatures and governors increasingly matter—as do the parties in control of those institutions. The importance of cross-state advocacy in the current era of gridlocked federal government also raises a second lesson, which is to remind us of the central role of the states as sites of major policy action. Stressing that the states matter is not exactly a new insight. The American Founders certainly envisioned a robust role for the states in developing and administering major policies in our country.[16]

Yet political observers in recent years have all too often continued writing off the states. Some of that tendency comes from the same impulse we observed in progressive political funders in the previous chapter, who believed that major policy change could not come from the states given the complicated legacies of Jim Crow, pressures to appease business out of fears of interstate competition, and a lack of policy capacity and resources. For many other political analysts or citizens, states are simply not on their radar given limited news coverage of statehouse politics—a situation that has only worsened with further cuts to traditional news media outlets.[17] As a result, around 40 percent of American adults say that they do not know which political party controls their state's legislative chambers.[18]

And for a third set of political observers in my own academic home of political science, battles over partisan control of state government are often a sideshow. According to this view, states will generally trend in the same directions in terms of policy, regardless of which party is in control of the legislature or governorship at any given point in time. While noting that the importance of partisan control has risen since the 1980s, Devin Caughey, Christopher Warshaw, and Yiqing Xu still argue, "Democrats and Republicans may disagree consistently and even violently, but the policy consequences of electing one over the other pales in comparison to the policy differences across states."[19]

The findings in the last seven chapters call for revisiting these perspectives. As ALEC's founders recognized early on, the states are responsible for a wide range of decisions over taxes, labor market protections, voting rights, healthcare, subsidies, labor union rights, education, and criminal justice—decisions that conservative activists, donors, and businesses all saw as valuable and worthy of attention.

Against the argument that partisan control of the states matters only a little, we have seen that the party in control of state government has come to matter a great deal in explaining the adoption of ALEC, SPN, and AFP's priorities. Party control, coupled with troika infrastructure, was one of the best predictors of policy enactments for both battles over public-sector labor unions and Medicaid expansion. And, more generally, partisan control of state government has become an ever-stronger predictor of where ALEC-drafted bills are plagiarized into law as ALEC came to define evermore closely what policies GOP politicians would pursue. Not only do the states increasingly matter given barriers to significant policy change at the federal level, but *who* controls state government does, too, when zooming in on individual policy areas. While it may be true that partisan control is only a modest predictor of state policies when looking at a very broad array of issues, the picture changes when we examine the policies in which the troika is most involved.[20]

Businesses have conflicted preferences for federalism—but cross-state networks like the troika can help managers get the best of both worlds. Apart from illustrating the changing role of the states, my analysis of cross-state advocacy organizations shows the complicated relationship that American businesses have with federalism—and how savvy businesses can get the best of both worlds.

On the one hand, businesses have good reasons to prefer that important decisions over taxes and regulation be made at the state, rather than the national, level. That is because states face pressures to keep their policies favorable to businesses that are mobile and can easily threaten to move from state to state—well-recognized "race to the bottom" effects.[21] In addition, state legislatures are often more strapped for the sort of resources that the troika, especially ALEC, can offer. And given that state politics typically receives less scrutiny than does national politics, businesses can more easily influence state politicians without backlash from the public.[22]

But on the other hand, large businesses that cross state lines have a competing interest in passing tax and regulatory legislation through Congress instead of each and every state, as managers would much rather deal with one single set of rules about doing business than fifty different ones. As we saw, ALEC—and the troika more generally—helped businesses to bridge these two competing interests, permitting managers to keep policymaking in the states while ensuring that many (if not most) of the states played by the same set of rules preferred by their companies.

The importance of wealthy donors for constructing and coordinating political advocacy. Corporate America was not the only backer of the troika's growth; we saw that wealthy individual donors (like the Koch brothers) and charitable philanthropies (like those associated with the Bradley, Coors, and Scaife families) were essential in supporting the creation and expansion of ALEC, AFP, and SPN.

That fits with a more general trend since the 1970s and 1980s whereby an evermore economically advantaged set of individuals and families invest their gains not just in traditional charitable works, but also in more explicitly political efforts.[23] To riff off the apocryphal exchange between Ernest Hemingway and F. Scott Fitzgerald, the very rich are different from you and me not only because they have money—and much more of it since the meteoric rise in income and wealth concentration—but also because they can direct that money into politics.

The historical evolution of the troika as traced in Chapter 5 reaffirmed the increasing role that wealthy individuals are playing in political organizations. It also showed how funders can work closely with political advocacy groups to develop ties between disparate organizations, to align agendas within a network of different affiliates, and to shape the messages that those affiliates produce. The reason why ALEC and SPN have become so closely intertwined is that donors worked with the leadership of both groups to give hefty incentives for otherwise institutionally separate state think tanks to join ALEC task forces and pursue a common legislative agenda, like coordinating attacks on Medicaid expansion.

Even before that point, the reason that SPN became a full-fledged member of the troika was that one of ALEC's early executive directors realized the value of creating a network of state-level think tanks to bolster his group's work. He thus reached out to donors about supporting precisely that initiative. The broader lesson is that donors play a central role in establishing and reconfiguring the landscape of interest groups operating in American politics.[24] Funder decisions can mean the creation of new reserves of political power, as with the example of the troika, or the absence of such power, as with the case of the liberal donors who were reluctant to support the creation of organizations that could counter the troika.

Political coalitions on the right are not necessarily automatic and require organizational mechanisms to mediate conflicts. There is a strong urge among many political observers—especially on the left—to assume that big businesses and conservative activists share a natural and automatic affinity for each other. The Center for Media and Democracy, which has compiled perhaps the most extensive records on ALEC, for instance, has argued that ALEC seamlessly merges far-right activists with corporate lobbyists and state legislators.[25] Similarly, in his book on corporate advocacy across the states, labor scholar Gordon Lafer makes the different—but related—case that lobbies like the US Chamber of

Commerce, ALEC, and AFP are interchangeable forces pushing for the same business-friendly legislation.[26] Neither of these characterizations of ALEC—and the troika more generally—is quite right and indeed misses out on two important conclusions that emerge from this book.

The troika, and especially ALEC, is not simply a front for big business. While companies do support all three organizations, and especially ALEC and SPN, they are not the only voices in those groups. Also present, as we have seen, are conservative activists and wealthy donors whose interests may often be aligned with companies—but sometimes are not. As Chapter 1 illustrated so vividly, social conservatives argued quite vigorously about the need for ALEC to pursue a culture war agenda. Corporate managers, in contrast, either cared little about those proposals, or worse, believed that they distracted lawmakers and the public from the sort of pro-business policies their companies wanted ALEC to promote. Later in the 2000s, staunchly conservative lawmakers and activists helped to push ALEC toward voter ID and expansive gun laws that were not necessarily in the direct interest of ALEC's corporate members—and ended up driving many companies out of the group. And as Chapter 6 reveals, in some cases, the troika goes toe-to-toe against big business, as in the case of the Medicaid expansion battles or infrastructure spending.

Managing coalitions between conservative activists, donors, and for-profit businesses, then, is no easy task, and required creative organizational mechanisms that adjudicate between these competing interests. ALEC, for instance, created a system of delegated governance through issue-specific task forces. Those would ensure that the political actors most invested in a given area would produce policy recommendations in that area alone. Within each task force, moreover, ALEC's use of the "pay to play" model created a system that dampened conflicts between members involved in the same issues. If a company wanted to push its proposals over the complaints of other ALEC task force members, its representatives knew that they could simply contribute a higher amount to the group to ensure that their voice would be heard. And aside from the task force structure, ALEC also needed to shield its private-sector members from the backlash that they might receive from their connections to ideological activists and donors.

Of course, ALEC did not arrive at these organizational structures immediately, and it took at least a decade for its leaders to come up with these means of reconciling the diverse preferences and priorities of its members. That delay should remind us that political coalitions are not automatic, and are often underwritten by specific institutions and organizational designs. Those designs are, in turn, often the products of leaders who do not have perfect foresight.[27] It also should give pause to the conclusion that conservative elites necessarily have an easier time creating durable alliances because of the inherent nature of their ideology or the ways in which conservatives think about politics.[28] ALEC—and the broader set of troika members—are successful not necessarily because they are ideologically conservative, but because they have designed organizations in ways that can consolidate and represent a diverse set of views and perspectives. These lessons also encourage us to question how easily interest groups, donors, and activists can form enduring coalitions with one another to support political parties. While it is true that groups, donors, and activists have much to gain from allying with one another and with politicians, it is important to recognize the costs to such an approach—and the specific mechanisms needed to ensure that those coalitions persist over time.[29]

The troika thinks about policy not just as a means of achieving substantive goals but as a way of explicitly reshaping power relations. The final implication of my examination of the troika is perhaps the most striking, and captures a fundamental divide in the way in which liberal and conservative cross-state advocacy networks have approached the policymaking process.

For many of the left-leaning cross-state networks described in the previous chapter, the goal of policy advocacy was to develop proposals that would achieve carefully delineated goals addressing specific policy problems. Reviewing the Center for Policy Alternatives model bill catalogue, for instance, it is obvious that each policy proposal is motivated by a clear progressive policy problem.[30] Under civil rights and liberties, for instance, the Center noted the discrimination faced by lesbian, gay, bisexual, and transgender Americans, and thus recommended new state-level protections for those communities. Similarly, the Center bemoaned exploitative payday lending practices and put forward legislation that would prohibit payday lending or cap the rates that those lenders could charge borrowers.

The troika has certainly advanced policies motivated in a similar way by conservative perspectives on policy problems, like reducing taxes on businesses. But there is another set of policies that ALEC, SPN, and AFP have pursued that is less focused on addressing specific problems and much more on reshaping the political landscape to provide political benefits to the troika. One example of this strategy came up in Chapter 1, where we saw ALEC seeking limits on the ability of individuals to bring tort suits against businesses. This not only addressed a policy problem for businesses—like manufacturers or healthcare providers— worried about lawsuits from consumers and patients. It also weakened the political position of the trial lawyer bench, a major funder of ALEC's liberal opponents. But an even more striking example was offered in Chapter 6, where we saw how the troika's offensive against public-sector unions demobilized those organizations and their members. That, in turn, paved the way for ALEC, SPN, and AFP to further entrench their political position across the states.

The practice of using policy as a means of reshaping political power fits well with a phenomenon that political scientists dub "policy feedback," or the way that once in place policies can reshape the political landscape, with implications for future rounds of policymaking. The best example of such feedback effects is the Social Security program, whose generous benefits to the elderly create a powerful political constituency of retired individuals who pressure politicians to maintain and expand the program.[31] Without those benefits, retired Americans would be far less active in politics. In a similar way, the troika's cutbacks to public-sector collective bargaining rights *demobilize* government employees, with implications for future elections and policy battles. The difference between what I describe in this book and the sort of effects described by policy feedback scholars is that the troika *deliberately engineers the demobilizing consequences of policy change.*

The idea of using policy in this very deliberate—and sometimes demobilizing—way is one that merits far more attention, especially because it suggests that political power may be path-dependent over time as political scientist Paul Pierson has proposed.[32] After gaining political control of government, the politicians aligned with the troika pursue policies like collective bargaining cuts, voter ID laws, and redistricting that all make it more likely that those politicians will win future policy battles and elections by weakening their opponents. The degree to which this strategy has succeeded—and its implications for democratic accountability and representation—all deserve a sustained focus by my colleagues interested in American politics.

Having taken stock of what my findings mean for our understanding of American political development, we can now consider what the past chapters imply for citizens, activists, and politicians on the left and right. Should we welcome the troika's expansion across the states? Or should we be concerned? And if so, what can be done?

Is the Troika Good for Democracy?

Reasonable Americans can and should disagree about the substance of public policies and the interest groups that promote those policies. Conservatives may applaud the troika's work because they agree with many of the ideas it promotes. Liberals, on the other hand, can and do criticize the troika on the basis of those very same ideas. Yet even independently of concerns about the troika's effects on social and economic life, I believe there are reasons to be worried about how the troika has reshaped the democratic process.

We can start with the benefits of the three conservative cross-state networks for the functioning of American government. Perhaps most clearly, the troika, and especially ALEC, provide valuable resources to lawmakers that they would lack otherwise. As we saw so vividly from the stories of lawmakers like Gene

Whisnant from Oregon, many state politicians simply do not have the experience, staff, or time to seriously develop and promote legislation on their own. ALEC fills that role. To the extent that ALEC's benefits and resources help legislators pass bills that they could not have passed otherwise, we can view the group as improving the democratic process of representation. And in addition to helping lawmakers, the troika provides an important opportunity for businesses and activists to participate in the political process. Corporate managers and political activists—like other American citizens—enjoy the constitutional right to petition their government, and the troika offers them an avenue to do just that.

If those are the reasons to celebrate the troika's contributions to US government, what are the concerns with ALEC, SPN, and AFP? The most fundamental one involves representation of ordinary Americans in government. There are any number of ways to judge the health of a representative democracy, but surely one persuasive test would involve asking whether the decisions made by a government represent some semblance of the preferences of majorities of its citizens.[33] If the policy outcomes preferred by majorities of citizens are consistently ignored in favor of proposals boosted by small subsets of the population, then we might be concerned that the government is no longer responsive to its constituents. A new wave of scholarship from political scientists indicates just such a lack of responsiveness to the mass public in the United States.[34] Looking at the policy views of low-, middle-, and high-income Americans, political scientists Martin Gilens and Benjamin Page have concluded that the policies enacted by the federal government are much more likely to represent the preferences of high-income Americans and business groups than poorer or middle-class Americans. If this is indeed the case, it casts serious doubt on the health of American democracy.[35]

There is good reason to think that the troika has contributed to this elite skew of representation across the states given that many of the policies it has pursued run against the preferences of majorities of Americans. As we saw in Chapter 6, two of the most significant legislative pushes of ALEC, SPN, and AFP—cutting union rights and stopping Medicaid expansion—were not very popular at the national level, and even more strikingly, public attitudes about these policies were not determinative of which states actually took action on troika ideas.

Indeed, looking across an even broader range of issues where we have readily available polling data, the troika's stances are generally opposed by majorities of citizens. Table C.1 examines recent national polling on seven important redistributive policies that ALEC, AFP, and SPN have pursued across the states and indicates the proportion of American adults aligned with the troika's stance. Even on the issue that tends to attract the most support from the general public—providing school vouchers for low-income households—nearly 60 percent of Americans still opposed the troika position in 2017. Even larger proportions of citizens are opposed to efforts to cut taxes on private-sector companies, a

Table C.1. **The Troika's Priorities and Public Opinion.**

Policy	% Against Troika	Poll Date	Poll Source
Offer school vouchers for low-income parents	57%	April 2017	AP-NORC
Raise minimum wage to $15/hour	60%	September 2016	PRRI/Atlantic
Reduce collective bargaining rights and pay of state employees	60%	March 2011	NBC/WSJ
Eliminate ACA Medicaid expansion	63%	March 2017	CNN/ORC
Believe companies pay too little in taxes	65%	January 2015	ABC News/Washington Post
Require utilities to rely on renewable energy sources, even if it costs $100/year, on average	67%	February 2015	Yale/George Mason
Offer paid sick leave to employees	85%	May 2015	CBS/NYT

longstanding priority of ALEC, SPN, and AFP, and to end renewable energy standards, as the troika has attempted to do in many states. And a whopping 85 percent of Americans support requiring employers to offer paid sick leave to their employees—something ALEC has fought tooth and nail to stop, as we saw in Chapter 7. In sum, across many of the troika's priorities, when ALEC, AFP, and SPN succeed, they are doing so *against*, not *in line with*, what majorities of American citizens say they want from government. The troika may thus be pulling government policy away from the preferences held by most Americans and toward those of a smaller group of businesses, activists, and donors. In each and every one of the cases highlighted in Table C.1, the troika is pushing in the pro-market, pro-business direction generally favored by very wealthy Americans and businesses—and away from the stated preferences of lower- and middle-income Americans.[36]

We can go even further in testing whether the troika contributes to inequalities in political representation by looking at the survey of legislators and legislative staff that I fielded in the fall of 2017 (see the Chapter 6 Appendix for more details). In that survey, I asked legislators and their staffs if they had relied on ALEC, with four possible responses: very frequently, frequently, rarely, or not at all. Nearly 40 percent of legislators said that they never relied on ALEC and 14 percent said that they relied on ALEC very frequently or frequently.

On the same survey, I also asked lawmakers what they believed public opinion was in their district on a variety of major policy issues: raising the minimum wage to $12 an hour; eliminating mandatory minimum sentences for nonviolent drug offenders; mandating background checks for all gun sales; making abortion illegal in all circumstances; increasing spending on highways, bridges, and infrastructure; repealing the Affordable Care Act; setting limits on carbon dioxide emissions from coal-fired power plants to reduce global warming and improve public health; and granting legal status to undocumented children brought to the United States illegally but who have graduated from high school (see the Appendix to Chapter 6 for exact language). Respondents indicated the proportion of people living in their district who agreed with each of those proposals. I then used data from mass public opinion surveys in 2016 to estimate the *true* proportion of people in legislators' districts agreeing with those policy ideas—and compared the accuracy of legislators' guesses to actual public opinion.[37] The idea is that I can see how well legislators perceive the attitudes of people in their constituencies.

Two other researchers using this method—David Broockman and Christopher Skovron—have shown that state legislators have only a limited understanding of their constituents' political views, and my results confirm this dim assessment.[38] Looking across all the policy issues, legislators were off of actual public opinion by an enormous twenty-three percentage points, on average. As with this past research, moreover, I found that lawmakers tended to systematically overestimate the conservatism of their constituents. Out of eight policy issues, the average legislator overestimated constituent conservatism on six (the two issues where legislators overestimated constituent *liberalism* were immigration and repeal of the ACA). One example: on average, legislators thought that slightly less than 50 percent of their constituents supported emissions limits on coal-fired power plants. In practice, fully 62 percent of their constituents actually supported such environmental regulation. The gap is even more striking for gun policy. Legislators *thought* that only 52 percent of their constituents wanted universal background checks for gun sales. The reality? Fully 85 percent of their constituents wanted to see those background checks implemented.

Legislators, then, have a skewed understanding of what their constituents want. Can this gap be explained by the troika's advocacy given that the troika tends to push policies that run against public opinion on many issues? To answer this question, we can see if legislators were more likely to be off in guessing their constituents' preferences when they were more reliant on ALEC. I test this idea in Figure C.1, which shows the average amount by which legislators were off of their constituents' actual opinions (averaging across all eight of the policy issues) plotted against legislators' self-reported reliance on ALEC. Of course, legislators likely have a strong reason to understate their reliance on ALEC, especially given its negative portrayal in the media in recent years. But this underreporting should make it harder to find a relationship.

Figure C.1 reveals a striking relationship: the more that lawmakers reported relying on ALEC, the less likely legislators were to correctly perceive their constituents' preferences. On average, legislators who reported relying on ALEC very frequently or frequently were about 10 percentage points off in their estimates of public opinion than legislators who did not rely on ALEC at all. That is no trivial difference given that the average state legislator was off by 23 percentage points. While this relationship merits far more research, it provides evidence suggesting that the troika—and especially ALEC—may be contributing to gaps in representation between ordinary Americans and their elected officials. One reason why lawmakers think their constituents are so much

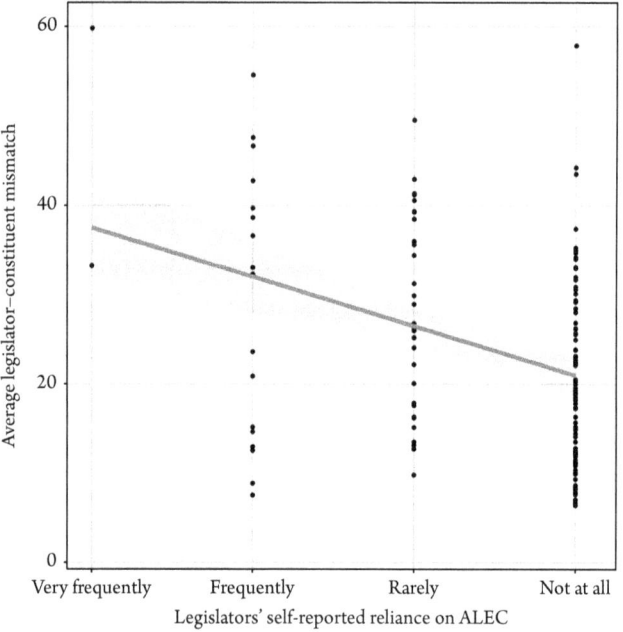

Figure C.1. LEGISLATORS' RELIANCE ON ALEC AND BIAS IN PERCEPTIONS OF CONSTITUENT OPINION. This graph shows the average mismatch between legislators' perceptions of their constituents' preferences and constituents' actual preferences across eight policy areas by self-reported reliance on ALEC (see the text and Chapter 6 Appendix for more details). Source for district-level public opinion is Kalla and Porter 2018. Source of data on legislators is 2017 state legislative survey. Line indicates linear regression best fit; gray bars indicate 95 percent confidence intervals.

more conservative than they are in practice is that lawmakers are participating in, and relying on, very conservative groups affiliated with the troika.

In addition to the concern that the troika is pursuing policy opposed to the preferences of majorities of Americans, a worry is that the troika also promotes policies that restrict the range of voices that are heard in the political process—and especially the voices of economically disadvantaged citizens. Most notably, by weakening the labor movement, ALEC, SPN, and AFP are taking out groups that might otherwise represent the interests of working-class Americans. Regardless of what one thinks about the economic consequences of unions for employers or state governments, there is clear evidence that unions boost the political representation of low-income Americans.[39]

A final concern with the troika, and especially ALEC, is the way that much of its influence depends on obscuring its relationship with lawmakers and businesses. The fact that politicians might be getting legislative ideas and support from the activists, donors, and businesses affiliated with ALEC but are not always required to disclose that support makes it substantially harder for citizens to hold their elected officials accountable. Citizens ought to have a right to know to whom their legislators are turning to write bills—and who else might have deep and vested interests in passing that legislation. Similarly, while companies are required to disclose the direct campaign contributions they make to political candidates, they are typically not required to do the same for ALEC or SPN—and in many cases, that is a direct appeal of the troika. All this obfuscates the role of private interests in American democracy.

Un-Capturing the States

Together, these issues with the troika's advocacy would be troubling at any point in American history, but they are even more concerning now given that they are occurring against a backdrop of high and rising inequality of income, wealth, and political voice. Given these concerns that the troika presents for American democracy, what should be done?

We can think about potential responses as falling into several broad categories: proposals that would restrict the ability of companies and donors to invest in politics—what we might term as *money in politics reform*; measures to increase state policy capacity—*boosting legislative resources*; efforts to put public or financial pressure on businesses and donors to stop investing in groups like ALEC, SPN, and AFP—what we might term a *public pressure* strategy; and lastly, efforts to build organizations that would oppose the troika on its own terms—what I dub a *countervailing power* approach.

Of the four reform alternatives, money in politics is perhaps the most widely embraced. Politicians from across the political spectrum—from progressive hero Elizabeth Warren to Tea Party firebrand Dave Brat—may not agree on much, but they do manage to come to a consensus that there is far too much money in politics.[40] The exact content of money in politics reform proposals varies considerably, but the gist is simple: set and enforce strict limits on what political donors can spend to elect candidates. Of particular interest are limits on corporate giving, given the oversized voice that businesses have in the political process across all levels of government.[41]

Such curbs on corporate political participation are appealing in their underlying logic—if there is too much money in politics, especially corporate money, then we should get it out. It should thus come as no surprise that large majorities of Americans support these bills. More than 80 percent of the public in recent polls, regardless of party, think that campaign contributions directly influence political decisions.[42] Over 60 percent of the public, in turn, supports either curbing corporate political giving or banning it altogether.[43] Indeed, money in politics reform proposals involving limits on corporate participation have even attracted considerable backing from reform-oriented wealthy donors and many private-sector business managers.[44] Notwithstanding this broad support, we should be skeptical about their possibilities for seriously curtailing the troika's power.

Throughout the twentieth century, a number of states implemented bans on corporate campaign contributions and independent expenditures. (Independent expenditure is spending intended to support the election or defeat of a candidate that is not coordinated with a campaign.) Is it the case that by limiting corporate money in elections, these bans reduced the troika's influence in state legislatures, as measured by ALEC model bill plagiarism? Money-in-politics reformers certainly would argue that they should—yet my findings in Chapter 3 suggest that corporate electoral spending does not make much of a difference for ALEC's success. Figure C.2 tests this idea directly by plotting the proportion of ALEC bill enactments for states with and without corporate spending bans in place. (Note that I only look at ALEC bill shares for 1996 to 2010 for corporate independent expenditure bans, because the Supreme Court's 2010 *Citizens United v. Federal Election Commission* decision overturned these state laws.[45])

Whether looking at bans on corporate contributions (in the left plot) or corporate independent expenditures (right plot), states with such limits in place actually have slightly *higher*, not lower, reliance on ALEC model bills than states without bans in place. It is simply not the case that these bans eliminate legislative reliance on the troika.

My look at corporate contribution and spending bans and ALEC reliance should *not* be interpreted as direct evidence that money in politics reforms are

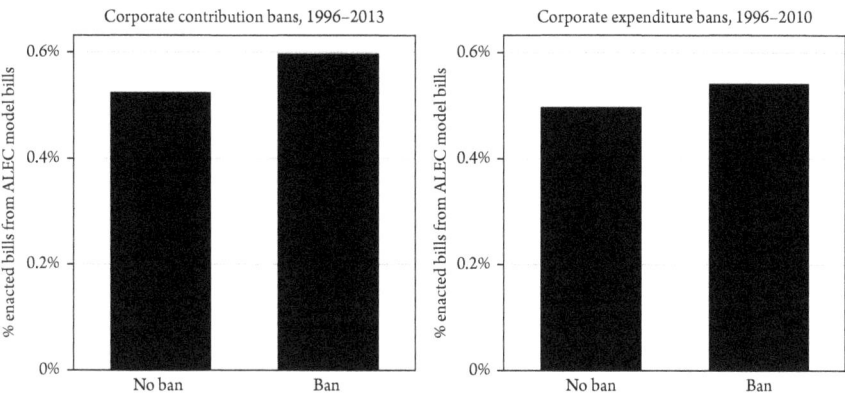

Figure C.2. STATE CORPORATE POLITICAL SPENDING BANS AND ALEC BILL RELIANCE. These graphs show the average share of enacted bills from ALEC model bills in states with and without bans on corporate electoral contributions (left panel) and corporate independent expenditures (right panel). Corporate spending ban data from the National Conference of State Legislatures.

fruitless.[46] (And in addition, greater disclosure of more forms of contributions and spending, especially dark money spending, could help researchers and investigative journalists hold donors to account.) Rather, my argument is that, on their own, measures to try and limit corporate spending in politics are unlikely to end the troika's influence in politics. Similarly, efforts to change, ban, or limit other forms of campaign spending without broader changes to the political system are unlikely to affect the troika. Much of the troika's spending is not directly related to elections and therefore any changes to election financing are unlikely to significantly alter the clout that these three groups enjoy in state politics.

If money in politics reform—at least on its own—cannot weaken the reliance of state legislatures on the troika, what can? One good place to start are the findings from Chapter 3 on the states and lawmakers that have been most likely to introduce and enact ALEC model bills. Given that state legislative capacity— the time, staff, and experience that lawmakers can bring to bear on developing legislation—is such an important factor in explaining ALEC's reach across the states, bolstering these resources ought to be a central priority of reformers looking to limit the troika's influence.[47]

Any measures that would provide lawmakers access to more (and more experienced) staff members, lengthen legislative sessions so that lawmakers could spend more time considering bills, and—most controversially—increasing the pay of legislators so that they do not need to hold outside employment, could help reduce lawmakers' demand for ALEC's services. A back-of-the-envelope calculation based on the relationships between legislative capacity and ALEC bill reliance from Chapter 2 suggests that moving underresourced states to the level of professionalization in Illinois—around the 90th percentile of capacity—might lower the proportion of enacted bills that lawmakers copy from ALEC by about 40 percent.

Improving policy capacity and resources in state legislatures will, of course, cost money. I estimate that to provide at least three permanent staffers for each lawmaker, state legislatures would need to hire around 6,000 new policy aides. (Twenty-two states currently provide fewer than three permanent staffers for each of their legislators, on average.) I further estimate that it would cost the states with currently low levels of staffing about $19 per resident per year, on average, to pay for the salaries of these new staffers. So professionalizing the twenty-two or so underresourced states will certainly require new sources of funding—but not necessarily insurmountable sums. Similar back-of-the-envelope calculations for boosting legislative pay reveal modest and reasonable increases in state spending that could be shouldered easily by residents of currently underprofessionalized states.

Nevertheless, these proposals are likely to be a hard sell to a public that views elected officials with mistrust. The arguments in favor of a "citizen" legislature resonate powerfully in this context: Why should the public have to subsidize a bloated legislature filled with "professional" politicians? Isn't it fairer and more efficient to keep the legislature as lean as possible? And if many workers have not seen raises themselves for decades, why should politicians' pay be any different? Those are exactly the same arguments that Michigan Republicans have made recently in support of moving Michigan from a full-time to part-time legislature: "In this time of declining trust in government, we cannot be afraid to hit the 'refresh' button in Lansing and move Michigan to a part-time legislature," argued Michigan's Attorney General Bill Schuette in a 2017 op-ed.[48] Such a move would go far in "saving taxpayers' money," he added.[49] One proposal offered by Michigan's lieutenant governor tellingly would tie legislative compensation to teacher pay—if teachers have not received raises, the logic goes, why should lawmakers?[50]

Fifty-state surveys on attitudes about state legislative pay and resources are limited, but we can glean some sense of public support for state policy resources from a survey fielded by researchers at the University of Missouri that asked a nationally representative sample of Americans about their preferences for state legislative resources.[51] Respondents to the survey were asked whether they preferred more or less legislative staff, higher or lower legislative salaries, and shorter or longer sessions.[52]

Consistent with Americans' relatively pessimistic view of government, there are no outright majorities in favor of moving toward more professional state legislatures. Still, perhaps surprisingly, nontrivial proportions of Americans (nearly 40 percent in some cases) *do* support granting lawmakers higher salaries, increasing the length of legislative sessions, and giving lawmakers more staffers. So while many Americans may be skeptical of professional politicians, there is still a reservoir of support for boosting legislative resources. In any case, dedicated political reformers could—and should—work to shift Americans' understanding of this issue. Most Americans do believe, often quite strongly, that the wealthy and big businesses have too much of a say in politics, and so explaining how low levels of legislative resources open the door to more influence-peddling by the troika could help nudge up public support for boosting legislative resources.

Even as greater levels of policy resources will help lawmakers to resist the grip that ALEC has on many legislatures, it cannot be the only solution reformers pursue. Another alternative would build on the success of the scrutiny and pressure that activists put on ALEC (and, to a lesser degree, SPN and AFP) following the Trayvon Martin shooting in 2012. As I explained in Chapters 1 and 4, center-left activists sought to draw and maintain attention on ALEC and the organizations with which it worked to weaken the group's funding base and influence in state government.

This anti-troika strategy entailed mobilization across multiple fronts. First, liberal activists relied on leaks of internal materials, including model bills, conference programs, and task force discussion notes to highlight the ways in which ALEC facilitated corporate influence in politics. Activists then used those internal documents to produce lists of the companies and philanthropies participating in ALEC and SPN in an effort to pressure managers to leave the groups, building on consumer and investor boycotts.

As we saw in Chapter 4, these measures achieved some degree of success: about a third of ALEC's corporate membership dropped their ties in the wake of the protests. As we would expect if the consumer and investor pressure was working, it was companies that had the most to lose from consumer backlash, as well as those owned by public-sector employee retirement funds, which were most likely to sever their ties to ALEC.

Yet at the same time, the fact remains that a majority of companies—including even a majority of consumer-facing companies and those held by government employee pension funds—did not leave ALEC. Many of the companies that did remain, as Chapter 4 indicated, were some of the most politically active and pushed the most sweeping changes to public policy—such as the extractive energy companies discouraging efforts to address climate change. And some companies have even *restarted* their ALEC participation after leaving in the wake of the PR crisis, like health insurer Blue Cross Blue Shield, online rating platform Yelp, and ridesharing giant Uber.[53]

Perhaps even more relevant, there is little evidence that ALEC has suffered in the long run from the work of progressive activists. Although its legislative membership and bill enactments fell in the years following the boycotts, its budget has bounced back, and the group has since expanded to new political arenas through its City-County Exchange arm. All these trends suggest that public scrutiny and financial pressure can only play a modest role in countering the troika's influence. This conclusion is further bolstered by the fact that it took a very high-profile focusing event—in the form of the Trayvon Martin shooting—to draw sufficient attention to ALEC (and, by extension, to SPN) and inspire widespread outrage and attention. Recall that progressive activists had tried a similar campaign in the early 2000s that went nowhere as organizers found that it was challenging to draw attention to the otherwise obscure topics of state legislatures and model bills.

The final potential line of opposition to the troika is the one that I judge to be most realistic and most likely to be effective: investing in the creation of cross-state networks that can counter the troika on its own terrain. Political reformers concerned about the role of ALEC, SPN, and AFP ought to construct their own cross-state networks. As we saw in the last chapter, such efforts have stalled to date, but there is no reason why this has to remain so. Though meager and spotty funding and duplication have hindered efforts at constructing a real alternative to the troika, center-left donors are now much more attuned to the states than they were in the past. What is more, the major source of the troika's success— exploiting the fact that so many state legislatures are underresourced—is one that need not be confined to the right.

Moving forward, progressives seeking their own versions of the troika ought to learn from the troika's successes, and just as importantly, the troika's failures. Although center-left reformers are starting from behind, there is no need for them to repeat the same errors that the conservative leaders of ALEC, SPN, and AFP committed. In fact, progressive reformers may have the "advantage of backwardness" in that they can borrow from conservative reformers' past experiences. Eight lessons emerge from the troika's evolution over the past forty years that progressive organization-builders should heed.[54]

It's not the federal government or bust. The feast-then-famine cycles of progressive attention to state organizing have tended to follow Democratic majorities in Congress and control of the White House. When Democrats lost their razor-thin control of the Senate in 2002, leaving them without any formal power in Washington, D.C., their attention shifted back to the states. But Democratic supermajorities in Congress and the election of Barack Obama made state-based organizing less relevant as Democrats were posed to enact a long-awaited national agenda, including an economic stimulus, financial regulation, national healthcare reform, and climate change mitigation. Now, with full Republican control of Congress and a Trump presidency, Democrats have rediscovered the importance of the states once more. If progressives are going to build sustained cross-state power, then they need to pay attention to the states even when they have control of the federal government. Otherwise, they will be forced to start all over again the next time that they inevitably lose a chamber of Congress or the White House.

One reason conservatives did not fall prey to this kind of D.C.-or-bust thinking is that they did not have the luxury of as much sustained control of the federal government as Democrats did. Conservative organizers like Paul Weyrich and Sam Brunelli realized that the states could be an important start to regaining national political power. Even so, after ALEC and the State Policy Network got off the ground, both networks continued to grow even during periods of Republican control in Washington. Indeed, far from discouraging cross-state organizing, Republican White Houses (and especially the Reagan administration) worked closely with ALEC to build the group's membership and coordinate on policy initiatives. Progressives should learn from the close relationship between the troika and Republican presidents, using Democratic administrations in a similar way to bolster—rather than ignore—cross-state organizing.

Don't reinvent the wheel (again). In trying to defeat the troika, and especially ALEC, center-left organization builders have all too often abandoned older efforts and simply created new and competing groups vying for the same members and grants (consider, for instance, the dueling Center for Policy Alternatives and the Progressive Legislative Action Network in the mid-2000s). Not only are such efforts wasteful, sapping scarce donor funds and activist energy, but ultimately they are also self-defeating, preventing any one organization from building the scale necessary to seriously challenge the troika.

One reason that ALEC, AFP, and SPN have been so successful is that they reinforce one another's efforts without duplicating them. ALEC creates a legislative agenda and presses it on lawmakers, SPN makes the policy case for those bills, and AFP offers the muscle to get that legislation passed. When thinking about investing in new cross-state organizations, progressive donors need to consider how those groups are going to fit together. Center-left organizations may well combine functions that exist separately in the troika, but progressives still need groups that will complement, not compete with, each other in the service of the same agenda.

It's not just about the model bills. ALEC's model bills are an important part of its lobbying strategy, as we saw in Chapter 2. But it would be a mistake for progressive organizers to think that they can replicate the troika's success simply by drafting a long list of legislative proposals and expecting them to fly off the shelves on their own. ALEC's model bills are attractive, as we observed in Chapter 3, because ALEC also provides extensive research assistance and support to its lawmakers that make it easy to take the bills from introduction to final passage. That means offering legislators policy briefs, talking points, polling, expert witnesses, and help with drafting specific provisions—not just legislative text.

In addition, ALEC also relies heavily on social ties and networking to build relationships with state legislatures over years. Through its multiple convenings in desirable locations, ALEC makes it very appealing for legislators to keep coming back and building bonds with ALEC staff, corporate representatives, and conservative policy experts. Though harder to measure quantitatively, the interview evidence I presented in Chapter 3 strongly suggests that these networks are just as important to ALEC's continued influence as the model bills. What this means for progressives is that a real "anti-ALEC" will require more than just coming up with a policy library, as several past efforts have done. It will mean providing lawmakers with the other resources they need to craft policy and establishing valuable social networks of lawmakers, activists, and policy experts.

Establish membership that means something. Of course, to build those social networks, you need members. Here, ALEC, AFP, and SPN benefit from a deep and highly engaged membership base assembled over decades. ALEC has legislators, private businesses, and activist organizations as enrolled members; AFP has citizen-activists on state-by-state lists; and SPN uses newsletters, meetings, and surveys to keep in close contact with state-level think tanks. Although the meaning of membership varies across the three networks, a common theme is the identity that membership conveys and benefits that the networks offer to their affiliates.

Any effort to advance progressive organization-building beyond the usual liberal enclaves will require offering practical and useful benefits to potential members. ALEC, for its part, learned the hard way that listening only to hardcore social conservatives would alienate its other potential corporate members. It gained clout only after it figured out how to offer specific benefits that a wide range of legislators and companies could really use—and then required participants to become dues-paying members to receive those perks. Similarly, SPN did better once it started conducting surveys of its affiliates to understand their desire for services, such as training or regional convenings tailored to state political conditions. And AFP has attracted volunteers to its lists by offering opportunities to become a more effective grassroots activist and to meet with prominent political leaders.

To build membership, turn to preexisting networks within states. Spreading benefits is not the only way to build a presence in states, especially not at first with an unknown group. Successful political organizations leverage existing social relationships, rather than just trying to attract participants from afar to attend national meetings or follow communications from national headquarters on mailing lists. As this underscores, it is going to be a challenge for countervailing center-left organizations to build credibility in states where Democrats or progressives do not control government. That may explain why SIX chose to focus its initial organizing efforts on states where progressives were already well established, as we saw in the last chapter.

The best way to make progress may be to copy ALEC's move in the 1980s of instituting in-state chairs, respected local legislators who can gradually spread the word and connect others to practical benefits useful even in relatively conservative states. (Recall that ALEC's leader during these early years even set up friendly competitions, modeled on the NFL, to get chairs to recruit a diversity of members in terms of party, geographic constituencies, and policy expertise.) Another obvious strategy would be to work with existing state-level think tanks participating in the SPP or EARN networks, which in many states have an established track record of working with a range of legislators, not just those who already think of themselves as very liberal or progressive.

Establish organizational structures for adjudicating between conflicting policies or priorities. On both sides of the political spectrum, organizers struggle with how to reconcile and prioritize diverse goals and perspectives. Should a new cross-state, center-left network stress middle-class economics for workers? Help for the poor? Racism or sexism? Rights for immigrants? The fight for access to the ballot box? Reproductive rights? LGBT rights? Saving the planet from global warming? Left-leaning coalitions could spend endless hours debating such questions, and usually end up just adding everything up into long lists to satisfy advocates from every cause. (This tendency is nothing new: sociologist Francesca Polletta tellingly titled her book on 1960s-era left-wing social movements *Freedom Is an Endless Meeting*). At best, such aggregation curbs the influence of a group on any one particular issue, and at worst, it alienates potential coalition members and lawmakers.

Of course, as we now know from Chapter 1, ALEC faced an identical problem in its early years, when it realized that companies had competing policy preferences and found that the interests of major corporations are not always aligned with those of right-wing activists and donors. To address these challenges, ALEC created task forces with strict rules over how policy stands would be issued and promoted. The ALEC members most invested in a particular policy area are put in charge of that domain, and within each task force, members who contribute the most in dues get the most say.

Americans for Prosperity, run from the center, offers a different model. AFP ensures that state directors and activists stress issues within clear boundaries—matters of taxes, regulations, social spending, voting and union rights, but not religious or social causes. And SPN uses a third strategy, leveraging generous grants and other resources to prod its members into tackling particular issues and working with specific partners, especially ALEC.

Liberal cross-state networks cannot always copy the institutional arrangements ALEC, AFP, and SPN have devised, but they can think of ways to avoid the collective-action problems inherent in assembling coalitions that just add up diverse interests into one big list. New cross-state groups could create national task forces in some key areas of interest and ask organizational and legislator members to choose only one or two to join at a time, depending on where their priorities lie in any given period. In turn, these task forces should develop sensible and transparent rules about whose interests will prevail in within-task-force conflicts.

Find better sources and structures for funding. Although conservative organizations are staunch proponents of market competition, ironically it is liberal-leaning donors who encourage advocacy leaders to compete for limited, short-run funding. And even though leftists stress the value of participants controlling their own organizations, it is ALEC that has institutionalized membership rights and duties, including obligations to pay regular dues in return for benefits, participation on task forces, and say on agendas.

New organizations on the center-left would be smart to move toward sustained funding from dues-paying individuals and organizations, even if the flows would not be as generous or as steady as corporate payments to ALEC. Overreliance on foundation funding and contributions from unions and wealthy donors makes liberal ventures, including cross-state networks, vulnerable to shifting donor fads or shrinking donor resources, as we saw in the last chapter. ALEC charges state legislators only modest dues, and there is no reason that new groups, once they leverage social ties and offer up concrete benefits, could not do the same.

Furthermore, although there is no left equivalent of rich corporations to pay high levels of dues, new organizations could charge specialized institutional dues to foundations, policy organizations, advocacy groups, unions, and other entities that want to join relevant task forces. Having these organizations provide dues, rather than simply grants, changes their relationship from one of being simply a funder to a member, as ALEC learned. (The Democracy Alliance offers another example of this model on the left by permitting foundations and unions to "join" alongside individual households on a different schedule of dues.)

Use policy as a means to advance both substantive and political goals. Perhaps the most important conclusion is one that we have already covered in this chapter: the left needs to think about policy in terms of political power just as the troika has already done for so many years. Of course, it would be a mistake for liberals to use policy to demobilize groups in the political process or to shut organizations out of politics altogether (as the troika has done). Nor should liberals abandon their use of policy to respond to well-defined and specific problems. Yet much more could be done to push proposals that *both* solve important social and economic issues *and* build power on the center-left.

Strengthening the labor movement is a clear example, but so too are measures to expand access to the franchise, especially among disadvantaged citizens, or to make clear the role that government plays in improving the lives of ordinary citizens. The implementation of health reform, especially pushing for the expansion of Medicaid coverage for poor adults, is an ideal example in this regard. Not only would such a measure directly improve the health and economic standing of vulnerable Americans, but it would also empower these individuals to participate in politics.[55]

Nearly a century ago, progressive reformers looked at the states with a similar degree of frustration as many on the left do today. When Henry W. Farnam, a professor of political economy at Yale, characterized the picture of state legislatures in 1910, he remarked with bitter frustration on how state legislation was "prodigious in its mass [but] mainly the product of unskilled labor."[56] Even worse, lawmakers were highly sensitive to the demands of big business and fearful of doing anything that might be seen as disrupting the free market. "Rather than run the risk of doing harm," Farnam concluded about state legislatures' hesitancy to enact new social programs, "it is better, we are told, not to do anything at all."[57]

Yet Farnam also thought he had a solution. Together with a number of leading social scientists in political science, law, and economics, he founded the American Association for Labor Legislation (AALL). The AALL was intended to provide what we would call today policy-relevant research and data to support the development of state social insurance and labor market protections. Unusual for other groups of academics at the time, the AALL explicitly focused on what it called the "art of legislative midwifery" in order to learn from what business lobbies had done so effectively in the past and apply those lessons to the public interest.[58] Through regular publications, partnerships with other national associations, and model bills, the AALL attempted to push state governments to adopt workmen's and unemployment compensation schemes, safety regulations for factories, and health insurance programs.

Despite these lofty aims, Farnam's AALL never quite managed to achieve the legislative influence to which it aspired. The AALL avoided building a federated network of grassroots advocates who could push for policy change from the ground up across the United States, staying mainly in enclaves already favorable to their proposals—not at all dissimilar to the decisions made by more recent center-left advocacy groups since the 1970s.[59] The AALL also eschewed partnerships with other grassroots groups rooted in local communities that might have helped to promote the AALL's vision. As a result, the AALL went from a promising start to quietly fading from the American political scene.

Now, as then, to avoid the AALL's fate, progressive reformers seeking to change the balance of power across the states need to learn from the successes of their right-leaning foes to develop reinforcing, federated networks of organizations that not only count academics and policy experts as members—but also lawmakers, organizers, and citizen-activists. And these organizations must have a real reach across the whole country. Conservative activists, businesses, and wealthy right-wing donors realized that goal after decades of trial and error—and have been reaping the policy gains ever since. If they are to have any influence in the coming years, the center-left will need to finally learn from those lessons.

Appendices

CHAPTER 3 APPENDIX

Details on the 2014 National Candidate Survey

In the analysis of legislators' reliance on ALEC, I use data from the 2014 National Candidate Survey, a combined online and mail instrument fielded by David Broockman, Nicholas Carnes, Melody Crowder-Meyer, and Christopher Skovron in October 2014. The survey was delivered to state political candidates from major parties whose contact information was listed on Project Vote Smart, a comprehensive database of political candidates (8,965 candidates were listed as running in total). 8,858 candidates had mailing addresses listed in Project Vote Smart and 4,775 candidates had email addresses on file. In early October 2014, all candidates with an identified mailing address on file received a mailing announcing the survey. All candidates with email addresses listed on Project Vote Smart subsequently received three email invitations over a period of about three weeks. In mid-October 2014, all candidates with listed mailing addresses who had not already taken the online version of the survey received a paper copy of the survey that they had the opportunity to return by mail or online. 1,187 candidates responded to the email solicitation, 84 responded online after receiving the mail version, and 616 candidates returned the paper version of the survey, for a total sample size of 1,887 candidates. The overall response rate was 21 percent. The survey was designed to reduce the possibilities of staffers, rather than candidates themselves, responding to the survey through screener questions on both the online and paper instruments. Additionally, where multiple email or mailing addresses were listed in Project Vote Smart, survey administrators chose the options most likely to be the candidate's home address or personal email. The survey is described in greater detail in Broockman and Skovron 2018.

Legislative Professionalism and ALEC Bill Introductions and Enactments

The regressions in Table A.3.1 show that state legislative professionalism continues to predict ALEC bill introductions and enactments (as a share of all introductions and enactments) while controlling for a variety of other state characteristics and examining variation within states over time (using state and biennium fixed effects). Unit of analysis is the state-biennium.

Legislative Professionalism: Standardized index of state legislative compensation, length of legislative sessions, and spending on the state legislature. Data from the Council of State Government's *Book of the States*. Ranges from 0 to 1.

Union Density: State-level union membership rate. Data from UnionStats. Expressed in percentage points (0–100).

Table A.3.1. **Legislative professionalism and ALEC bill introductions and enactments.**

	Introduced ALEC Bill Share	Enacted ALEC Bill Share
	Model 1	*Model 2*
Legislative professionalism	−1.24**	−1.56**
	(0.57)	(0.73)
Union density	−0.00	0.01
	(0.04)	(0.03)
Democratic control (0–3 Index)	−0.06*	−0.13***
	(0.04)	(0.04)
State unemployment	0.04	0.03
	(0.05)	(0.05)
State mass economic liberalism	−0.69	−0.14
	(0.47)	(0.73)
State fixed effects	Y	Y
Biennium fixed effects	Y	Y
R-squared	0.75	0.61
N	369	307

OLS models; robust errors clustered by state.

Significance levels: * $p < 0.10$, ** $p < 0.05$, *** $p < 0.01$.

Democratic Control: Count of institutions held by Democrats: lower legislative chamber, upper legislative chamber, and governorship. Data from Carl Klarner's state partisan database. Ranges from 0 to 3.

State Unemployment: State unemployment rate. Data from the Bureau of Labor Statistics. Expressed in percentage points (0–100).

State Mass Economic Liberalism: Estimate of state mass liberalism on economic policy from Devin Caughey and Christopher Warshaw, "Policy Preferences and Policy Change: Dynamic Responsiveness in the American States, 1936–2014," *American Political Science Review*, 2017.

Individual-Level ALEC Bill Authorship

The regressions in Table A.3.2 use individual-level legislator data to show that lawmakers with more years of experience were less likely to author or sponsor ALEC model bills from 2003 to 2013. Unit of analysis is a state legislator-year.

Table A.3.2. **Individual-level ALEC bill authorship.**

	Authored ALEC Bill	
	Model 1	*Model 2*
Years of service	−0.03**	−0.03*
	(0.02)	(0.02)
Democrat		−0.54
		(0.41)
Public administration share of district		−5.71***
		(2.19)
Manufacturing/extractive resource share of district		−1.17
		(1.07)
State fixed effects	Y	Y
Year fixed effects	Y	Y
Pseudo-R-squared	0.26	0.20
N	4,503	2,373
Logistic models; robust errors clustered by state.		
Significance levels: * $p < 0.10$, ** $p < 0.05$, *** $p < 0.01$.		

Authored ALEC Bill: Legislator authored or sponsored an ALEC model bill in a given year, as determined by text reuse analysis (0/1).

Democrat: Binary variable for Democratic lawmaker (0/1); Republican or other is excluded category.

Public Administration Share of District: Share of a lawmaker's district employed in public administration, using data from the American Community Survey, rolling five-year samples (proxy for pressure from public-sector labor unions).

Manufacturing/Extractive Resource Share of District: Share of a lawmaker's district employed in manufacturing or extractive resources, using data from the American Community Survey, rolling five-year samples (proxy for pressure from businesses that stand to lose from tighter environmental regulations).

Analysis of ALEC Legislative Reliance and State Chairs in 2014

The regressions in Table A.3.3 use data from the 2014 state legislative candidate survey to show that states with installed ALEC state chairs have a greater

Table A.3.3. **Analysis of ALEC legislative reliance and state chairs in 2014.**

	Reported ALEC Reliance	
	Model 1	Model 2
1 ALEC state chair	0.09***	0.01
	(0.03)	(0.02)
2 or more ALEC state chairs	0.15***	0.03*
	(0.03)	(0.02)
Moderate		−0.14**
		(0.05)
Liberal		−0.08
		(0.05)
Republican		0.23***
		(0.05)
Support from business		0.13***
		(0.02)
R-Squared	0.01	0.27
N	708	663
OLS models; robust errors clustered by state.		
Significance levels: * $p < 0.10$, ** $p < 0.05$, *** $p < 0.01$.		

proportion of state legislators reporting reliance on ALEC, even controlling for individual legislator ideology, partisanship, and self-reported reliance on business for political support. Unit of analysis is a state legislative candidate who previously served in the state legislature.

ALEC Reliance: Self-reported reliance on ALEC for bill ideas and resources as defined in the text (0/1).

ALEC State Chairs: Number of installed ALEC state chairs in 2014, as reported by ALEC. Variable coded as 0 (reference category), 1, or 2 or more.

Ideology: Self-reported legislator ideology (0/1), recoded as liberal, moderate, or conservative (reference category).

Partisanship: Self-reported legislator partisanship (0/1), recoded as Democrat/other (reference category) or Republican.

Support from Business: Self-reported reliance on business as an early political supporter (0/1).

CHAPTER 4 APPENDIX

Coding State Regulatory Threats Facing Industries

Table A.4.1 summarizes the industries, search strings, counts, and standard deviation of legislation used to code the regulatory threat facing companies from 1996 to 2013 using the text of state legislation.

Table A.4.1. **Coding state regulatory threats facing industries.**

Industry	Avg. Count	Std. Dev. Count	Search Strings
Household and personal products	0.3	0.7	("personal" OR "household") AND "products"
IT services	1.8	1.7	"information technology"
Publishing	2.1	1.7	"publisher"
Scientific equipment	2.9	2.3	"scientific equipment"
Semiconductors	2.9	2.3	"semiconductors"
Home equipment, furnishings	3.8	2.3	"home" AND "furnishing"
Industrial machinery	3.9	3.2	"machinery" AND "industrial"
Diversified outsourcing services	8.5	6.3	"outsourcing" AND "diversified"
Temporary help	8.5	6.3	"temporary" AND ("help" OR "employment")
Advertising/marketing	8.6	3.4	"advertising" OR "marketing"
Motor vehicles	9.4	5.3	("cars" OR "motor vehicles") AND "manufacturing"

Table A.4.1. **Continued**

Industry	Avg. Count	Std. Dev. Count	Search Strings
Aerospace/defense	10.7	3.1	"aerospace"
Computer peripherals, software, equipment	10.7	6.2	"computer" AND ("software" OR "equipment")
Forest and paper products	12.7	5.6	"forest" OR "paper"
Communications	13.2	4.8	"communications"
Wholesalers	13.7	5.8	"wholesale"
Apparel	13.9	5.4	"apparel"
Engineering, construction	22.7	10.0	"engineering" OR "construction"
Metals	22.8	8.0	"metals"
Medical equipment	23.0	9.6	"medical" AND ("equipment" OR "devices")
Oil and gas equipment	23.2	9.5	("oil" OR "gas") AND "equipment"
Retailers	24.8	7.0	"retail"
Financial data services	26.4	15.1	"financial data" AND "services"
Pharmaceuticals	28.6	8.9	"pharmaceutical"
Packaging	33.4	6.1	"packaging"
Entertainment	36.3	13.0	"entertainment"
Pipelines	38.4	6.1	"pipeline"
Electronics, electrical equipment	39.6	11.8	("electronics" OR "electrical") AND "equipment"
Waste management	51.4	27.3	"waste management"
Mail	52.8	14.3	"mail"
Transportation	53.8	24.5	"transportation"
Trucking	53.8	24.5	"trucking"
Automotive retailing, services	55.8	20.7	"automotive" AND "retail"
Healthcare: Medical facilities	60.9	21.7	"medical facility" OR "medical facilities" OR "clinic" OR "hospital"

(*continued*)

Table A.4.1. **Continued**

Industry	Avg. Count	Std. Dev. Count	Search Strings
Prepared food	63.9	15.2	"prepared food"
Chemicals	76.9	18.1	"chemical" AND "manufacturing"
Healthcare: Pharmacy and other services	96.4	27.3	"pharmacy" OR "pharmacies"
Food production	114.3	56.5	"food" AND ("production" OR "manufacturing")
Airlines	127.3	34.0	"airline"
Railroads	133.1	26.5	"railroad"
Mining, crude oil	179.6	55.5	"mining" AND "oil"
Construction	182.6	50.3	"construction" OR "constructors"
Internet services	193.3	86.0	"Internet service provider"
Telecommunications	231.4	61.8	"telecommunications"
Commercial banks	337.7	151.6	"banks" OR "banking"
Diversified financials	387.1	81.7	"financial" AND "diversified"
Energy	621.9	225.8	"energy"
Securities	646.8	248.2	"securities"
Beverages	760.2	104.8	"beverages"
Insurance: Life, mutual, stock	771.7	107.8	"insurance" AND ("life" OR "mutual" OR "stock")
Food stores	855.4	127.4	"grocer" OR "groceries"
Tobacco	890.3	166.2	"tobacco"
Hotels and resorts	929.6	91.4	"hotel" OR "resort"
Utilities: Gas and electric	996.7	14.1	("utility" OR "utilities") AND ("gas" OR "electric")
Healthcare: Insurance and managed care	>1,000	0.0	"health insurance" OR "managed care" OR "health insurer"
Petroleum	>1,000	0.0	"petroleum"

Regressions Predicting Corporate Membership and Departures from ALEC

The regressions in Table A.4.2 show the predictors of ALEC participation over the period 1996 to 2013, as well as the predictors of which companies severed their ties to ALEC following 2011. Because corporate political spending and other business association participation are plausibly posttreatment to the other corporate characteristics, I run models without and with these variables. The results are generally similar to those presented in the text.

Variables are defined in the main text.

Table A.4.2. **Predicting corporate membership and departures from ALEC.**

	Any ALEC Participation		Left ALEC Following 2011	
	Model 1	Model 2	Model 3	Model 4
State regulatory threat (quintiles)	0.24**	0.22**	−0.02	−0.10
	(0.10)	(0.10)	(0.20)	(0.19)
National regulatory threat (quintiles)	0.01	0.00	−0.09	−0.06
	(0.08)	(0.09)	(0.17)	(0.16)
Logged revenue	0.79***	0.67***	0.95***	0.52**
	(0.13)	(0.14)	(0.31)	(0.23)
Industrial concentration	0.91	0.96	2.63	2.59
	(1.23)	(1.30)	(2.20)	(2.12)
Industrial unionization	0.03***	0.02	−0.08**	−0.07**
	(0.01)	(0.01)	(0.03)	(0.03)
Political spending as % of revenue		263.76***	43.92	
		(69.01)	(127.49)	
Other business association participation		0.84***	−1.64***	
		(0.26)	(0.57)	
Consumer-facing company			1.37**	1.41**
			(0.62)	(0.57)
Public employee retirement fund–held			1.63	1.83*
			(1.20)	(1.10)
Pseudo-R-squared	0.15	0.22	0.31	0.23
N	418	415	103	105

Logistic models.

Significance levels: * $p < 0.10$, ** $p < 0.05$, *** $p < 0.01$.

CHAPTER 6 APPENDIX

Details on 2017 State Legislative Survey

The 2017 state legislative survey was conducted jointly with Matto Mildenberger and Leah Stokes at the University of California, Santa Barbara. We fielded the survey using an online instrument from September to November 2017. The survey targeted all sitting legislators with available contact information as of the fall of 2017, plus top policy staffers for those lawmakers, for a total of 11,524 possible respondents. We obtained email and mailing address contact information from the National Conference of State Legislatures. We only included legislative staffers with job titles that contained one or more of the following string words, suggesting substantive policy responsibilities: Chief of Staff, COS, Legislat, Policy, Administrative Assistant, Executive Assistant, Communications Director, Research Assistant, District, Constituent, or Press Secretary. Legislators and staffers received an invitation and three follow-up emails, as well as a mailed postcard reminder, over the course of about a month and a half. In all, 314 legislators and 437 staffers completed 90 percent of the survey or more, for an average response rate of about 7 percent. Fortunately, the legislators and staffers who responded to the survey were not too different from the broader population of legislators and staffers in terms of region, rank, or party.

The question about legislator and staffer support for union rights appears in Table A.6.1.

The question about ALEC reliance appears in Table A.6.2. The SPP/EARN affiliate and SIX items were identical, with the name of the respondent's in-state SPP or EARN affiliate piped into the survey. In states with multiple SPP or EARN affiliates, we randomly selected which affiliate to display to respondents.

The questions asking about respondents' perceptions of their constituents' preferences appear in Table A.6.3. Note that only legislative staffers who

Table A.6.1. **2017 state legislative survey item on support for union rights.**

Regardless of your state's current law, do you think it should be legal for unions or labor associations of the following kinds of workers to . . .

	Janitors	Teachers	Police and Firefighters	State/local workers	Manufacturing workers
Collectively bargain for wages and benefits	☐	☐	☐	☐	☐
Automatically collect dues from members' paychecks	☐	☐	☐	☐	☐
Require all workers at unionized shops to pay dues (except political contributions)	☐	☐	☐	☐	☐
Provide extra unemployment benefits to members	☐	☐	☐	☐	☐
Make campaign contributions to candidates	☐	☐	☐	☐	☐
Lobby government	☐	☐	☐	☐	☐
Go on strike	☐	☐	☐	☐	☐

reported working for a single legislator were included in this item, along with legislators. We selected issues that would be available on the 2016 Cooperative Congressional Election Survey, a large-scale, nationally representative survey, so that we could use multilevel regression and post-stratification (MRP) to estimate public opinion in legislative districts. MRP has been successfully applied

Table A.6.2. **2017 state legislative survey item on reliance on outside groups.**

How frequently have you relied on the following organization when considering, drafting, or evaluating legislation?

	Very frequently	*Frequently*	*Rarely*	*Not at all*
American Legislative Exchange Council	○	○	○	○

to studies estimating a range of subnational policy attitudes, including gay rights and support for health reform (e.g., Kastellec et al. 2010). Two other political scientists, Joshua Kalla and Ethan Porter, had already estimated public opinion at the state legislative district level for these items using this method for a separate project, and so we used their estimates in our final analyses (see Kalla and Porter 2018 for more details).

In Table A.6.4, I show OLS regression results documenting the correlation between ALEC reliance (measured on a scale of 1–4 from "not at all" to "very frequently") and support for public-sector union rights. Support for public-sector union rights adds up union rights for teachers and state/local workers and ranges from 0 to 14 (see Table A.6.1 for a full set of union rights). Sample only includes state legislators and controls for legislative party (Democrat or Republican), ideology (on a 1–7 scale), and US Census division.

Estimation of Public Attitudes toward Public-Sector Collective Bargaining Cuts

To analyze the role of public opinion in the 2011–2012 efforts to restrict public-sector union bargaining rights, I estimated state-by-state public attitudes toward collective bargaining in the public sector using multilevel regression and poststratification (see the preceding discussion).

I first searched the Roper Center for Public Opinion Research database for nationally representative surveys that included at least one question about respondents' attitudes toward the right of public-sector workers to collectively bargain with state governments. In all, I identified four such surveys fielded on nationally representative samples of adult Americans between February and March of 2011. There were 4,007 valid responses to public-sector union questions in the merged dataset. The surveys and questions are summarized in

Table A.6.3. **2017 state legislative survey item on constituent preference perceptions.**

	% of **People Living in District** Agreeing with Statement
Eliminate mandatory minimum sentences for nonviolent drug offenders (1)	
Mandate background checks for all gun sales, including at gun shows and over the Internet (3)	
Make abortions illegal in all circumstances (4)	
Increase minimum wage to $12 an hour by 2020 (5)	
Authorize $305 billion to repair and expand highways, bridges, and transit over the next 5 years (6)	
Repeal the Affordable Care Act of 2010 (also known as Obamacare) (7)	
Set strict carbon dioxide emission limits on existing coal-fired power plants to reduce global warming and improve public health (8)	
Give states the option of expanding their existing Medicaid program to cover more low-income, uninsured adults (9)	
Grant legal status to people who were brought to the US illegally as children, but who have graduated from a US high school (10)	

Table A.6.4. **ALEC reliance on state legislative support for public-sector union rights.**

	Support for Public-Sector Union Rights (0–14)
ALEC: Rarely rely	−0.253
	(0.824)
ALEC: Frequently rely	−2.405**
	(1.133)
ALEC: Very frequently rely	−4.029*
	(2.04)
Republican	−0.156
	(1.037)
Ideology: Liberal	−0.234
	(1.073)
Ideology: Somewhat liberal	−0.494
	(1.199)
Ideology: Moderate	−2.768**
	(1.093)
Ideology: Somewhat conservative	−8.58***
	(1.676)
Ideology: Conservative	−6.416***
	(1.326)
Ideology: Very conservative	−7.308***
	(1.474)
Region fixed effects	Y
R-squared	0.62
N	135

OLS regression results.

Statistical significance levels: * $p < 0.10$, ** $p < 0.05$, *** $p < 0.01$.

Table A.6.5. The main variable of interest is a binary indicator if a survey respondent expressed a desire to eliminate the right of public-sector labor unions to bargain collectively with state governments.

Pooling the four polls together, I next modeled public opinion about public-sector labor unions as a function of various individual and state-level

Table A.6.5. **Surveys used to estimate 2011 state-level public support for collective bargaining cutbacks.**

Date	Survey	Size	Question Text
February 2011	NBC/WSJ	1,000	Do you support eliminating public employees' right to collectively bargain over healthcare, pensions, and other benefits when negotiating a union contract?
February 2011	CBS/NYT	984	Do you favor or oppose taking away some of the collective bargaining rights of these unions? (If favor/oppose, ask:) Do you favor/oppose that strongly or somewhat?
February 2011	Gallup/USA	1,000	As you may know, one way the legislature in Wisconsin is seeking to reduce its budget deficit is by passing a bill that would take away some of the collective bargaining rights of most public unions, including the state teachers union. Would you favor or oppose such a bill in your state?
March 2011	Gallup	1,027	As you may know, Wisconsin and other states have been in the news because of disputes between the governors and state employee labor unions over collective bargaining policies and the state's budget. In states where there are such disputes, with whom would you say you agree more?

characteristics. I then weighted each type of respondent (varying across the individual and state predictors) by the known shares of each respondent type from Census data.

For the individual model, I estimated public-sector union attitudes as a function of respondent income, education, race, Hispanic ethnicity, race, age, sex, union membership, state, and state-by-income groups. I also included Obama's 2008 vote share and public union density as state-level predictors. The proportion of adults who supported restricting the ability of public-sector unions to bargain with the state ranged from 31 to 46 percent, with a median and mean of 40 percent.

Analysis of State-Level Cutbacks in Public-Sector Collective Bargaining

The logistic regression in Table A.6.6 shows that the conservative network strength and coordination index remains a strong predictor of which states passed cutbacks to public-sector bargaining in 2011 to 2012 while controlling for a variety of other factors, including Democratic control of government, private-sector union density, state budget balance, public attitudes, an indicator for whether states introduced a bargaining cutback bill in the previous legislative session, and fixed effects for Census regions.

Variables are defined in the main text, except for any introduced bargaining cutback bill in the last session, which is a binary indicator for whether a state introduced a bargaining cutback bill in the previous legislative session, based on my review of

Table A.6.6. **Analysis of state-level cutbacks in public sector collective bargaining.**

	Passed Cutback to Public-Sector Bargaining Model 1
Troika strength and coordination	1.20**
	(0.50)
Democratic control (0–3 index)	−0.95*
	(0.52)
Private union density	−0.11
	(0.21)
State budget balance	0.004
	(0.03)
% Public supporting cuts	−0.22
	(0.26)
Introduced bargaining cut bill last session	−0.20
	(0.31)
Region fixed effects	Y
Pseudo-R-squared	0.46
States	45

Logistic regression model.
Statistical significance levels: * $p < 0.10$, ** $p < 0.05$, *** $p < 0.01$.

the National Conference of State Legislatures database on public union legislation. Only states with collective bargaining in place are included in analysis.

Analysis of Individual Legislator Votes for Cutbacks to Public-Sector Collective Bargaining

The logistic regression in Table A.6.7 shows that affiliations with ALEC and SPN remain a strong predictor of which lawmakers voted in favor of cutbacks to public-sector bargaining in 2011 to 2012 while controlling for a variety of other factors, including partisanship (Democrat/Republican), legislator conservatism (NP Score; Shor and McCarty 2011, see the text for more details), the share of lawmakers' districts employed in local and state government (using data from the American Community Survey, 2009–2011 sample), and state fixed effects.

Variables are defined in the main text.

Table A.6.7. **Analysis of individual legislator votes for cutbacks to public-sector collective bargaining.**

	Voted in Favor of Cutbacks to Public-Sector Bargaining
ALEC and SPN affiliation	0.86**
	(0.37)
Democrat	−0.45
	(0.71)
Legislator conservatism (NP Score)	2.72***
	(0.47)
Local and state government employment share	2.24
	(2.89)
State fixed effects	Y
Pseudo-R-squared	0.59
Legislators	1,112
States	7

Logistic regression model.
Statistical significance levels: * $p < 0.10$, ** $p < 0.05$, *** $p < 0.01$.
Standard errors clustered by state.

Analysis of Troika Model Bills and Public Union Strength

Tables A.6.8 and A.6.9 summarize a variety of regression results documenting the relationship between troika model bills and reductions in public union membership and NEA state affiliate revenue (expressed on a per worker basis). Covariates include Democratic control of state government, private-sector union density, and state unemployment. "Treated" sample only includes states that passed ALEC legislation relating to public-sector unions.

Private Union Density: State-level private-sector union membership rate. Data from UnionStats. Expressed in percentage points (0–100).

Democratic Control: Count of institutions held by Democrats: lower legislative chamber, upper legislative chamber, and governorship. Data from Carl Klarner's state partisan database. Ranges from 0 to 3.

State Unemployment: State unemployment rate. Data from the Bureau of Labor Statistics. Expressed in percentage points (0–100).

Table A.6.8. **Analysis of troika model bills and public union membership.**

	Public Union Density (Percentage Points)				
ALEC bill passed	−4.56**	−4.51**	−2.74**	−4.48**	−5.27*
	(2.11)	(1.84)	(1.08)	(1.75)	(2.30)
Sample	All	All	All	All	Treated
State fixed effects	Y	Y	Y	Y	Y
Year fixed effects	Y	Y	Y	Y	N
Covariates	N	Y	Y	Y	N
Lagged dependent variable	N	N	Y	N	N
Region trends	N	N	N	Y	N
R-squared	0.11	0.18	0.33	0.17	0.87
N	1,050	1,031	982	982	168

Notes: OLS regressions; standard errors clustered by state; * $p < 0.10$, ** $p < 0.05$, *** $p < 0.01$. Outcome is public-sector union density, in percentage points (0–100).

Table A.6.9. **Analysis of troika model bills and teachers union revenue.**

	NEA Affiliate Revenue (Revenue/All Wage and Salary Workers)				
ALEC bill passed	−1.67***	−1.51***	−1.03***	−1.18***	−1.08***
	(0.30)	(0.40)	(0.35)	(0.43)	(0.21)
Sample	All	All	All	All	Treated
State fixed effects	Y	Y	Y	Y	Y
Year fixed effects	Y	Y	Y	Y	N
Covariates	N	Y	Y	Y	N
Lagged dependent variable	N	N	Y	N	N
Region trends	N	N	N	Y	N
R-squared	0.29	0.32	0.33	0.45	0.94
N	512	504	453	504	80

Notes: OLS regressions; standard errors clustered by state; * $p < 0.10$, ** $p < 0.05$, *** $p < 0.01$. Outcome is NEA state affiliate revenue expressed as a proportion of all wage and salary workers in a state.

Analysis of Troika Model Bills and Government Worker Political Participation

Here, I append the full question text from the American National Election Study items I used as outcomes in the analysis of the effect of troika-backed legislation on public employee political participation:

Political Participation (0–5 additive index of each item)

- *Persuade others about voting*: We would like to find out about some of the things people do to help a party or a candidate win an election. During the campaign, did you talk to any people and try to show them why they should vote for or against one of the parties or candidates?
  ○ Yes
  ○ No

- *Political meetings or events*: Did you go to any political meetings, rallies, speeches, dinners, or things like that in support of a particular candidate?
  - Yes
  - No
- *Button/sign/stickers*: Did you wear a campaign button, put a campaign sticker on your car, or place a sign in your window or in front of your house?
  - Yes
  - No
- *Work for candidates*: Did you do any (other) work for one of the parties or candidates?
  - Yes
  - No
- *Contribute to campaign*: During an election year, people are often asked to make a contribution to support campaigns. Did you give money to an individual candidate running for public office?
  - Yes
  - No

In Table A.6.10, I present the full regression results of the effect of conservative network-backed legislation on public employee participation using negative binomial count models.

Table A.6.10. **Analysis of troika model bills and government worker political participation.**

	Participation Index (0–5 Scale)	
	Private Workers	Public Workers
ALEC model bill enacted	−0.01	−0.53*
	(0.08)	(0.27)
Union member	0.10	0.04
	(0.06)	(0.07)
Age	−0.01*	−0.03***
	(0.01)	(0.01)
Age squared	0.00*	0.00***
	(0.00)	(0.00)
Male	0.08**	0.05
	(0.04)	(0.05)
White	−0.07	0.14
	(0.05)	(0.10)

Table A.6.10. **Continued**

	Participation Index (0–5 Scale)	
	Private Workers	Public Workers
Black	−0.06	0.18
	(0.06)	(0.12)
Hispanic	−0.12*	−0.07
	(0.07)	(0.09)
Some college	0.25***	0.21**
	(0.05)	(0.09)
College or graduate/doctoral level	0.27***	0.29***
	(0.06)	(0.08)
Family income (deciles)	0.02***	−0.02
	(0.01)	(0.02)
Interest in politics	0.69***	0.74***
	(0.03)	(0.05)
Strong partisan	0.38***	0.51***
	(0.04)	(0.07)
State fixed effects	Y	Y
Year fixed effects	Y	Y
Pseudo-R-squared	0.09	0.11
N	6,809	1,811

Analysis of Troika Strength and Coordination and Medicaid Expansion Decisions, 2013–2015

In Table A.6.11, I show the logistic regression results testing the relationship between the right-wing strength and coordination index and Medicaid expansion decisions in 2013–2015, while controlling for public support for Medicaid expansion, cumulative partisan control from 2013 to 2015 (the number of Democratic veto points in each year, summed across all years), and the initial generosity of state Medicaid programs during the passage of the Affordable Care Act (in 2010).

Variables are defined in the main text.

Table A.6.11. **Analysis of troika strength and coordination and Medicaid expansion decisions.**

	Outcome Is Expansion of Medicaid as Part of ACA 2013–2015
	Model 1
Troika network strength and coordination	−0.43*
	(0.23)
Public support for Medicaid expansion	−0.04
	(0.06)
Cumulative Democratic control, 2013–2015	0.53**
	(0.23)
Medicaid eligibility generosity	−0.49
(average income threshold in 2010)	(0.97)
Pseudo-R-squared	0.41
States	43

Logistic regression model.

Statistical significance levels: * $p < 0.10$, ** $p < 0.05$, *** $p < 0.01$.

CHAPTER 7 APPENDIX

Liberal and Conservative Organizational Universe Lists

Table A.7.1 lists the organizations included in the liberal universe. See Skocpol and Hertel-Fernandez 2016b for more details.

Table A.7.1. **Liberal Organization Universe.**

Type of Organization	Name
Constituency mobilization	Center for Community Change
Constituency mobilization	ACORN
Constituency mobilization	USAction
Constituency mobilization	AFL-CIO
Constituency mobilization	SEIU
Constituency mobilization	AFGE
Constituency mobilization	AFSCME
Constituency mobilization	NEA
Constituency mobilization	AFT
Constituency mobilization	NAACP
Constituency mobilization	NCLR
Constituency mobilization	CWA
Constituency mobilization	IBEW
Extra party funder	MoveOn
Issue advocacy	Sierra Club

(*continued*)

Table A.7.1. **Continued**

Type of Organization	Name
Issue advocacy	League of Conservation Voters
Issue advocacy	National Resources Defense Council
Issue advocacy	NARAL
Issue advocacy	Planned Parenthood of America
Issue advocacy	Human Rights Campaign
Issue advocacy	National Organization for Women
Party committees	Democratic national committees
Think tank	Center on Budget and Policy Priorities
Think tank	Economic Policy Institute
Think tank	Campaign for America's Future
Think tank	Demos
Think tank	Center for Economic Policy Research
Think tank	Institute for Women's Policy Research
Think tank	Institute for Policy Studies
Think tank	The Century Foundation
Think tank	Democratic Leadership Council
Media monitoring	Media Matters for America
Media monitoring	ProgressNow
Constituency mobilization	Organizing for Action
Constituency mobilization	Change to Win
Extra party funder	ActBlue
Extra party funder	Democracy Alliance (only primary groups)
Extra party funder	American Bridge (Super PAC)
Extra party funder	NextGen (Super PAC)
Extra party funder	Senate Majority PAC
Extra party funder	House Majority PAC
Issue advocacy	America Votes/Action Fund
Think tank	Center for American Progress/Action Fund
Think tank	Third Way

Table A.7.2 enumerates the organizations included in the conservative universe.

Table A.7.2. **Conservative Organization Universe.**

Type of Organization	Name
Party committees	GOP national committees
Think tank	Heritage Foundation
Think tank	American Enterprise Institute
Think tank	Cato Institute
Think tank	Mercatus Center
Think tank	Council for National Policy
Extra party funder	Club for Growth
Extra party funder	Chamber of Commerce
Constituency mobilization	National Rifle Association
Constituency mobilization	National Federation of Independent Business
Constituency mobilization	Christian Coalition of America
Constituency mobilization	National Right to Life Committee/Education Fund
Constituency mobilization	Republican Jewish Coalition
Issue advocacy	Citizens for a Sound Economy/Foundation
Issue advocacy	Americans for Tax Reform/Foundation
Issue advocacy	Focus on the Family
Issue advocacy	National Organization for Marriage
Issue advocacy	National Pro-Life Alliance
Issue advocacy	National Right to Work Committee/Foundation
Issue advocacy	60 Plus Association
Issue advocacy	Gun Owners of America
Extra party funder	American Crossroads/Crossroads GPS
Extra party funder	Koch Seminars
Extra party funder	Freedom Partners Chamber of Commerce
Extra party funder	Heritage Action
Extra party funder	Congressional Leadership Fund
Extra party funder	Senate Conservatives Action
Constituency mobilization	FreedomWorks/Foundation
Constituency mobilization	Americans for Prosperity/Foundation

(*continued*)

Table A.7.2. **Continued**

Type of Organization	Name
Constituency mobilization	Libre Trust/Institute
Constituency mobilization	Faith and Freedom Coalition (Ralph Reed)
Constituency mobilization	Concerned Veterans of America
Constituency mobilization	Generation Opportunity
Constituency mobilization	Tea Party Patriots
Issue advocacy	American Energy Alliance/Institute for Energy Research
Issue advocacy	Center to Protect Patient Rights/American Encore
Think tank	American Action Network/Forum

NOTES

Preface

1. This biographical information is from Whisnant's interview with Travis H. Brown at the 2013 annual ALEC meeting. Available online: https://www.youtube.com/watch?v=-RPdSvabMsk.
2. Reported in Cole 2012.
3. Author's analysis of Council of State Governments' Book of the States dataset.
4. Author's analysis of National Conference of State Legislatures' total staff dataset.
5. Whisnant 2011.
6. Pilkington and Goldenberg 2013.
7. See Chapter 2 for a more systematic analysis. By ALEC's own scorekeeping, it succeeds in enacting about 100 bills per year, and introducing about 800 to 1,000.
8. Ismail 2003.
9. Wayne 2002.
10. ALEC 1996b. Indeed, ALEC was one of the first lobbying groups to produce model legislation introducing greater competition into state electricity markets; Burkhart 1996.
11. ALEC 1997a, 22–23.
12. ALEC 1997a, 50–51.
13. Wayne 2002.
14. Wayne 2002.
15. Wayne 2002.
16. Peirce and Guskind 1984.
17. Peterson 1995.
18. Tabulations from the 2016 Cooperative Congressional Election Survey, Columbia module.
19. See Culpepper 2010 on this concept of business power in spaces of "quiet politics." See also Rogers 2017 on electoral unaccountability in state politics.
20. This is consistent with Grant McConnell's argument that decentralization through federalism has "served to maintain and enhance a variety of systems of private power" (McConnell 1966, 166).
21. ALEC budget data from IRS tax returns.
22. See http://www.bobwilliamshome.net/bob-s-bio.
23. See http://www.bobwilliamshome.net/articles/building-tomorrow-today.
24. See, for example, Williams 2012.
25. ALEC 1993b, 16.
26. Natelson 2011.
27. Kogan 2017.
28. Wines 2016a. But see Bottari 2017 for disputes within ALEC over this issue.
29. Peirce and Guskind 1984.
30. For one excellent history, see Martin 2013, Chapter 7.

31. See https://www.youtube.com/watch?v=-RPdSvabMsk.
32. To be clear, I do not mean to imply that the activities of the groups that I study are illegal or corrupt. Indeed, as I emphasize in the conclusion, opponents of conservative cross-state networks like ALEC would be far more effective constructing organizations of their own, rather than trying to ban the conservative mobilization I document in the pages that follow.

Introduction

1. Branigin 2010.
2. Obama 2010.
3. Baker and Hulse 2010; Balz and Branigin 2010.
4. Balz 2010, citing National Conference of State Legislatures data.
5. Balz 2010.
6. See, for example, Schwartz 2015.
7. Follman and Williams 2013.
8. Ellwood and Fine 1987; Feigenbaum et al. 2018.
9. Berman 2015, especially Chapters 8–10. For a detailed discussion on the effects of voter ID laws, see Highton 2017.
10. See, for example, Bouie 2013; Wines 2016b.
11. Magoc 2012.
12. Berman 2015, 261.
13. Magoc 2012.
14. Tempus 2012.
15. Tempus 2012.
16. Tempus 2012.
17. First quote from Berman 2015, 261. Second quote from Magoc 2012.
18. For the original report, see Herrick 2015. For evidence of the coordination between affiliates, see Mayer 2013a.
19. See, for example, SPN 2013a. See also SPN's state affiliate "toolkit": Bauman 2016.
20. Cunningham 2015.
21. Garfield and Damico 2016.
22. See, for instance, Cray 2011; MacLean 2017; Nichols and McChesney 2013. For one interpretation of the troika as being seemingly all-powerful, see especially Lafer 2017. For a similar argument against the myth of diabolical conservative competence generally and obstacles to coalition-building between business conservatives and ideological conservatives in the context of the law, see Teles 2010. On the need to "read history forward," see especially Pierson 2004.
23. Perhaps most canonically, see Downs 1957; see also Schlesinger 1991.
24. Aldrich 1995.
25. In more recent formulations of his theoretical framework, John Aldrich includes activists and organized groups, but the focus is still largely on the politicians themselves. Donation data from the Center for Responsive Politics.
26. Bawn et al. 2012. See also Hacker and Pierson 2010a, 2014.
27. See especially Karol 2009; Noel 2013.
28. Achen and Bartels 2016; Lenz 2012; Zaller 1992; Converse 1964. But see Page and Shapiro 1992.
29. Schlozman et al. 2012; Hacker and Pierson 2010a; Drutman 2015.
30. Krimmel 2017; McCarty and Rothenberg 2000, 1996; Schickler 2016; McCarty and Schickler 2018.
31. Skinner 2006; see also Krimmel 2017 on the informational importance of these networks that interest groups can offer.
32. These pressures are especially acute in a two-party, majoritarian political system; see, for example, Martin and Swank 2012.
33. We will see that ALEC's task forces bear remarkable similarity to the structure of legislative committees within Congress and are designed to address similar problems; see, for example, Shepsle and Weingast 1987.

34. On the cost–benefit analysis of corporate political involvement, see, for example, Mitchell et al. 1997.
35. Bawn et al. 2012, 575.
36. See Chapter 5, and also Skocpol and Hertel-Fernandez 2016b.
37. 2002 State Legislative Survey, conducted by John M. Carey, Richard G. Niemi, Lynda W. Powell, and Gary Moncrief. Extracted from the Inter-University Consortium for Political and Social Research. ICPSR 20960.
38. Campaign website for Mike Breitbach (http://www.friendsforbreitbach.com/issues.html); campaign website for Craig Johnson (http://johnsonforsenate.net/index.php); and campaign website for Rene Gadelha (https://web.archive.org/web/20161018031256/http://renegadelha.com/index.php).
39. For similar evidence on the importance of interest groups in defining state legislative candidate policy positions, see Frendreis et al. 2003.
40. But see also Karol 2009. For a similar account of how African American activists, industrial unionists, Jewish groups, and urban liberals refined the Democratic party's positions on civil rights from the bottom up, see, for example, Schickler 2016. On growing partisan polarization in the states, see Shor and McCarty 2011. On the nationalization of state politics, see Hopkins 2017 and Hopkins 2018.
41. The canonical theoretical framework of lobbying as subsidizing allies who already agree with an interest group comes from Hall and Wayman 1990; Hall and Deardorff 2006.
42. For some of these works, see Phillips-Fein 2009; Ferguson and Rogers 1986; Vogel 1989; Hacker and Pierson 2010a; Edsall 1984; Schulman and Zelizer 2008; McGirr 2001.
43. See also McConnell 1966, Chapter 6.
44. Bragdon n.d., 4.
45. See, for example, Winston 2002; Kincaid 1990.
46. See, for example, Caughey et al. 2016; Erikson et al. 1989; Holbein and Dynes 2018. Caughey et al. 2016 do argue that the effect of partisan control on policy outcomes has increased over time. That is consistent with Grumbach 2017.
47. For one intellectual history, see, for example, Gerken 2012. See also the discussion in Chapter 7.
48. Mayer 2016; Schulman 2014; Doherty 2007. See also MacLean 2017.
49. Ansolabehere et al. 2003. More generally, see also Tullock 2001.
50. For a discussion of these methodological issues, see Schlozman et al. 2012, Chapter 10. See also Baumgartner and Leech 1998, Chapter 2, and Carpenter 2013.
51. See, for example, Ansolabehere et al. 2003; Smith 2000. See also many of the case studies in Carpenter and Moss 2013.
52. Baumgartner et al. 2009 report that they "find virtually no linkage between [interest group] resources and outcomes" (204). They hypothesize that this finding indicates that the policy status quo already embodies past victories from well-resourced groups.
53. Hall and Deardorff 2006; Hall and Wayman 1990. For empirical evidence of one example, see Kalla and Broockman 2016.
54. This is consistent with recent work on corporate lobbying in the states; for example, Hall 2016; Fouirnaies and Hall 2018; Fouirnaies 2018.
55. On this point, see especially Hansen 1991.
56. See, for example, Raja and Schaffner 2015; Bonica 2016.
57. Grumbach and Pierson 2018.
58. See canonically Peterson 1995 on race-to-the-bottom effects and Culpepper 2010 on low salience politics and business influence. In the context of historical social welfare spending and tax policy, see also Robertson 1989; Hacker and Pierson 2002. See Rogers 2017 on electoral unaccountability in the states.
59. Here, I build on the concept of policy feedback effects; for example, Pierson 1993; Skocpol 1992.
60. But see Lafer 2017; Williams and Johnson 2013 for two examples of such efforts.
61. On the connection between racial politics, voter ID laws, and ALEC, see Berman 2015.

Chapter 1

1. Greeley and Fitzgerald 2011.
2. Rogers and Dresser 2011.
3. Nichols 2011.
4. Lafer 2017, 12.
5. Scola 2012.
6. Graves 2011.
7. Graves 2011.
8. On this distinction, see, for example, Skocpol and Hertel-Fernandez 2016b.
9. Smith 2000; Martin 2000; Wilson 1986; Schmitter and Streeck 1999 [1981].
10. Waterhouse 2013; Mizruchi 2013; Judis 2001; Akard 1992.
11. Mizruchi 2013, 199.
12. Schmitter and Streeck 1999 [1981]; Olson 1965.
13. See the quotes in Greenblatt 2011.
14. Tønnessen 2014.
15. Weber 2008.
16. This history draws from Tønnessen 2014, 2009.
17. Tønnessen 2009, 29.
18. These decisions were *Engel v. Vitale* (1962) and *Griswold v. Connecticut* (1965), respectively.
19. See also Grann 1997.
20. Tønnessen 2009, 32.
21. Stahl 2016, 72–73.
22. Stahl 2016, 73.
23. The heavy involvement of politicians (and former politicians) in forming ALEC is consistent with most other business associations in the United States and elsewhere. As Cathie Jo Martin and Duane Swank have argued, individual firms are often too disorganized to form their own associations without the direction of elected officials, who themselves often have strong electoral motivations for the establishment of business groups (Martin and Swank 2012).
24. Rubin 1996; Human Events 1975. See also Bishop 2008, 223–224.
25. Bishop 2008, 223–224.
26. Crawford 1980; Tønnessen 2009, 69.
27. Human Events 1973.
28. Human Events 1973.
29. Rubin 1996.
30. Clymer 2007.
31. ALEC 1998b, 14; on the history of the NCSL, see Kurtz 1999.
32. Kielsgard 2008, 5.
33. Brunelli 1990, 2.
34. Brunelli 1990, 2. On the rise of teachers unions, see especially Anzia and Moe 2016; Walker 2014a and also Chapter 7.
35. ALEC 1998b, 14.
36. US Chamber of Commerce 1965.
37. Quoted in Conservative Digest 1985, 7.
38. Conservative Digest 1985, 7.
39. Omang 1979.
40. Shotts 1976, 3 and 27. See also Flavin and Hartney 2015; Hartney 2014; Anzia and Moe 2016; Levi 1977; Walker 2014a. But see Paglayan (forthcoming) on the limits of teacher collective bargaining without strike rights.
41. ALEC 2007b.
42. Baker 1978; Hunter 1980. ALEC had strong ties at its inception to the American Conservative Union (ACU), and its early directors included Stanton Evans of the Union, and Edward Feulner of the Heritage Foundation. Similarly, ALEC's initial executive director, Kathy Teague, was a leader of Paul Weyrich's Free Congress Research and Education Foundation (Hunter 1980, 63–64). The defeat of the DC voting rights amendment was an important victory for ALEC, which was credited as having an important role to play in the opposition

NOTES   299

movement (see, e.g., Hunter 1980). It would use many of the same tactics it developed to defeat the amendment in later legislative campaigns (see, e.g., Baker 1978; Natural Resources Defense Council 2002).
43. ALEC 1985.
44. Hunter 1980, 68.
45. Author interview with former Tennessee state legislator, September 15, 2015.
46. ALEC 1976, 1977, 1979b, 1980b.
47. Hunter 1980, 20.
48. ALEC 1982.
49. John M. Olin Foundation Inc. 1985, 1989.
50. ALEC 1998b, 8.
51. Bryant 1982, 4.
52. Hunter 1980; Natural Resources Defense Council 2002.
53. Of course, this tax-exempt status also prohibited ALEC from engaging in significant lobbying or other overt political activities, a distinction that ALEC certainly would stretch to its limits.
54. On the history of tort reform in the states in the 1980s, see CBO 2004.
55. Hunter 1986.
56. Rosenbaum 1986.
57. ALEC 1986a, 1.
58. Landis 1986.
59. Brinkley 1986; Zegart 2004.
60. Kristof 1986.
61. ALEC 1986a, 1.
62. ALEC 1986c, 4.
63. CBO 2004, ix.
64. ALEC 1986d; "Private Sector Coordinating Council on Civil Justice."
65. Edsall 2003.
66. Edsall 2003.
67. See https://www.youtube.com/watch?v=8GBAsFwPglw.
68. See https://www.youtube.com/watch?v=8GBAsFwPglw.
69. Conservative Digest 1985, 7.
70. ALEC 1979a, 1984. 1983–1984 is the first year I could identify where the Tobacco Institute, the tobacco industry's main policy lobbying group, donated to ALEC.
71. ALEC 1986b, 1 and 9.
72. See http://archive.tobacco.org/History/Tobacco_History.html.
73. ALEC 1986b.
74. Farney 1985; Peirce and Guskind 1984.
75. Peirce and Guskind 1984.
76. Malott 1990, 4.
77. Peirce and Guskind 1984.
78. Peirce and Guskind 1984.
79. National Committee for Responsive Philanthropy 1991, 12.
80. ALEC 1990b, 1994b; Biewen 2002. In recent years, ALEC has moved toward alternatives to incarceration as part of the prison reform movement (Silver 2013; Dagan and Teles 2012).
81. ALEC 1998b, 17–18.
82. Author interview with Sam Brunelli, September 30, 2015.
83. See http://www.nfl.com/player/sambrunelli/2510514/profile.
84. See http://www.nfl.com/player/sambrunelli/2510514/profile.
85. Author interview with Sam Brunelli, September 30, 2015.
86. Author interview with Sam Brunelli, September 30, 2015.
87. Author interview with Sam Brunelli, September 30, 2015.
88. Author interview with Sam Brunelli, September 30, 2015.
89. Author interview with Sam Brunelli, September 30, 2015.
90. Author interview with Sam Brunelli, September 30, 2015.
91. ALEC 1981a, 1983a.
92. ALEC n.d.-c.

93. Farney 1985.
94. Farney 1985.
95. In very recent years, ALEC has begun experimenting with more grassroots mobilization to buttress its proposals in a 501c4 partner group dubbed the "Jeffersonian Project." A 2016 strategic plan described a future goal as establishing "the Jeffersonian Project as a standalone powerful entity and hire a fulltime director that does serious voter education and outreach work" (ALEC 2016, 7). As of 2016, however, the project does not seem to have much of a presence. Its 2016 tax return reported only $22,500 in revenue.
96. ALEC 1992b.
97. ALEC 1992b, 28–29. On the importance of these foundations in funding the conservative movement more generally, see O'Connor 2008. ALEC relied on conservative foundations to fund policy initiatives that were not of interest to private-sector firms, like welfare reforms. Internal ALEC documents indicate that ALEC lost the support of conservative foundations during the late 1980s and early 1990s and that it tried to reestablish those connections in the mid-1990s. One business plan from 1996 argued that ALEC needed to "rebuild [its] credibility with conservative foundations," ALEC 1996d, 9.
98. ALEC 1996c.
99. Noye 1991.
100. National Committee for Responsive Philanthropy 1991, 6.
101. ALEC 1996d, 1996c.
102. ALEC 1996c, 6.
103. ALEC 1996c; ALEC 1997b, 2.
104. ALEC 1996d, 2.
105. ALEC's controller, for example, recommended to the board of directors that ALEC emphasize "policy, the main product" (ALEC 1996c).
106. ALEC 1997b, 6.
107. ALEC 1996d, 1997b.
108. Author interview with former ALEC leader, September 30, 2015.
109. Author interview with former ALEC leader, September 30, 2015.
110. ALEC 1995a, 3.
111. ALEC 1998a, 1–2.
112. For instance, see the group's task force operating procedures: ALEC 2009a.
113. See Bottari 2017 on the internally controversial issue of Article V conventions in ALEC.
114. ALEC 1990b, 1994b; Biewen 2002. However, in recent years, ALEC has sharply changed its direction on crime, seeking to move toward alternatives to incarceration. This is consistent with a broader shift by conservatives on criminal justice policy (Silver 2013; Dagan and Teles 2012).
115. Johnson 2013.
116. Author interview with Sam Brunelli, September 30, 2015.
117. Author interview with Sam Brunelli, September 30, 2015.
118. ALEC 1998a.
119. ALEC 1995a, 11.
120. See, for example, ALEC 1998a, 19.
121. Smith 2000; Martin 2000.
122. Berlau 2003, 44.
123. Wilce 2012.
124. Greenblatt 2003; Natural Resources Defense Council 2002.
125. For instance, ALEC 1996b.
126. Natural Resources Defense Council 2002, 12.
127. Berlau 2003, 44.
128. Skocpol 2003.
129. Author interview with Sam Brunelli, September 30, 2015.
130. Author interview with Sam Brunelli, September 30, 2015.
131. Author interview with Sam Brunelli, September 30, 2015.
132. Author interview with Sam Brunelli, September 30, 2015.
133. ALEC 2002.

134. ALEC 2000, 13.
135. On Marion Hammer's role in Florida, see especially Spies 2018. See more specifically https://www.nraila.org/articles/20050812/nra-presents-alec-model-legislation-in.
136. See http://web.archive.org/web/20071012150725/http://alec.org/2/criminal-justice.html.
137. ALEC 2007a.
138. ALEC 2008, 14.
139. ALEC Taxpayer and Citizen Protection Act.
140. Santos 2016.
141. Stern 2011.
142. Quoted in http://apps.azsos.gov/election/2004/info/PubPamphlet/Sun_Sounds/english/prop200.htm.
143. Quoted in http://apps.azsos.gov/election/2004/info/PubPamphlet/Sun_Sounds/english/prop200.htm.
144. Rau 2012; Steigerwald 2012.
145. For results, see http://www.cnn.com/ELECTION/2004/pages/results/ballot.measures/; Fischer 2013.
146. Fischer 2013.
147. Shor and McCarty 2011. No master membership list of state legislators participating in ALEC exists. I therefore compiled this chart by going through all available records of ALEC publications and searching for state legislative members, which I supplemented with names identified by the Center for Media and Democracy.
148. Note that the ideological scores are assigned to legislators for their entire career, as is ALEC membership. As a result, changes shown in Figure 1.5 come from changes in the composition of legislators (via legislators joining or leaving state legislatures), rather than changes in ALEC membership or ideology within legislators over time.
149. Hacker and Pierson 2005; McCarty et al. 2006; Mann and Ornstein 2012; Theriault 2013.
150. Dagan and Teles 2016, 100.
151. These include Texas Representative Joe Driver, Vermont Representative Margaret Flory, Arkansas Representative Dan Greenberg, Texas Representative Jerry Madden, Arizona Senator Russell Pearce, Indiana Representative Bill Ruppel, Wisconsin Representative Scott Suder, New Hampshire Representative Jordan Ulrey, and Oregon Representative Gene Whisnant. See http://web.archive.org/web/20100713032752/http://www.alec.org/AM/Template.cfm?Section=Public_Sector_Executive_Committee2.
152. Jones and Moody 2009, 18.
153. Jones and Moody 2009, 19.
154. See http://web.archive.org/web/20110501164057/http://www.alec.org/AM/Template.cfm?Section=PublicSafetyandElectionsModelLegislation&TEMPLATE=/CM/ContentDisplay.cfm&CONTENTID=11602.
155. See http://web.archive.org/web/20100710123627/http://www.alec.org/AM/Template.cfm?Section=Cracking_ACORN.
156. Magoc 2012.
157. See http://web.archive.org/web/20100710123627/http://www.alec.org/AM/Template.cfm?Section=Cracking_ACORN; Berman 2015, 261.
158. See Graves 2012a; Sullivan 2010.
159. For a more extensive comparison between ALEC and NCSL, see Powell and Colleluori 2012.
160. For example, Hawkins 2013; Abowd 2012.
161. Abowd 2012.
162. ALEC 1998c, 12.
163. ALEC 1997b, 5.
164. See http://www.commoncause.org/policy-and-litigation/letters-to-government-officials/joint-letter-to-irs-alec-tax-status.pdf.
165. Phillips 2014.
166. Barry et al. 2012.
167. Graves 2012a.
168. Weiner 2012.

169. Hoffman 2012.
170. Progress Now Colorado 2013.
171. Stone et al. 2003.
172. Stone et al. 2003.
173. Wohl 2012.
174. ALEC 2013.
175. ALEC 2013.
176. Pilkington and Goldenberg 2013.
177. Lichtblau 2012.
178. McIntire 2012; NYT 2012.
179. Nichols 2012.
180. Greeley 2012b.
181. Weiner 2012.
182. Shiner 2013.
183. NYT 2012.
184. Bykowicz 2014.
185. Taylor 2013.
186. Greeley 2012a.
187. Pilkington 2014.
188. See http://www.prwatch.org/files/private-sector-acce-final-web.pdf.
189. See http://www.prwatch.org/files/public-sector-acce-final-web.pdf.
190. Greenblatt 2014.
191. Arnold 2015.
192. See http://www.ncsl.org/research/environment-and-natural-resources/plastic-bag-legislation.aspx.
193. See http://www.ncsl.org/research/environment-and-natural-resources/plastic-bag-legislation.aspx.
194. Arnold 2015; http://www.ncsl.org/research/environment-and-natural-resources/plastic-bag-legislation.aspx.
195. Riccardi 2017.
196. Fischer and Bottari 2015; Bottari and Fischer 2015.
197. Parker 2016.
198. Greenblatt 2014.
199. Greenblatt 2014.
200. 2013 total of incorporated places from https://www.census.gov/content/dam/Census/library/publications/2015/demo/p25-1142.pdf. Membership estimate from Parker 2016.

Chapter 2

1. See http://www.house.mo.gov/billtracking/bills141/sumpdf/SB0508t.pdf.
2. See https://www.alec.org/model-policy/navigator-background-check-act/.
3. Fischer 2014a.
4. Seitz-Wald 2012.
5. See https://www.youtube.com/watch?v=aIMgfBZrrZ8.
6. See https://www.youtube.com/watch?v=aIMgfBZrrZ8.
7. For a more formal definition of a smoking gun test, see Bennett 2010.
8. This means that I am also assuming that in the absence of ALEC, legislators would have written different legislation without ALEC-influenced language, potentially even on different policy issues—holding other characteristics of lawmakers, like their ideology, their constituents, and their partisanship, constant. This is, of course, ultimately a problem of causal inference (Morgan and Winship 2014), since we cannot observe this alternate world without ALEC.
9. Readers interested in the technical implementation of these methods can consult a supplemental methodological paper (Hertel-Fernandez and Kashin 2015) posted on the author's website.
10. See https://www.prwatch.org/news/2011/07/10883/about-alec-exposed.

NOTES 303

11. For access to state legislative libraries, I relied on the very helpful staff at the Harvard Widener Library. At UCSF, I relied on the Legacy Tobacco Archives. At Berkeley, I relied on the People for the American Way Collection of Conservative Political Ephemera, 1980–2004.
12. Data from the Council of State Governments' Book of the States dataset.
13. Center on Budget and Policy Priorities 2017.

Chapter 3

1. Greenblatt 2013.
2. Council of State Governments 2012.
3. Scolforo 2011.
4. See http://knowledgecenter.csg.org/kc/system/files/3.21%202016.pdf.
5. See http://knowledgecenter.csg.org/kc/system/files/3.21%202016.pdf.
6. Author interview with Jeremy Nordquist, February 13, 2014.
7. See http://nebraskalegislature.gov/senators/senators.php.
8. See http://nebraskalegislature.gov/senators/senators.php.
9. Question text: "What groups do you regard as among your strongest supporters—Business?" 2002 State Legislative Survey. John M Carey, Richard G. Niemi, Lynda Powell, and Gary Moncrief. ICPSR 20960.
10. Virginia Delegate Patrick A. Hope at "The Legislative Attack on American Wages and Labor Standards," a panel discussion at the Economic Policy Institute in Washington, D.C., October 31, 2013; remarks transcribed by the author.
11. Biewen 2002.
12. ALEC 1987.
13. See, for example, the "State Testimony Highlights" in ALEC 2002.
14. See, for example, the "2012 Tax and Fiscal Policy Task Force Meeting" schedule in Common Cause's leaked ALEC document archives (Williams 2012).
15. ALEC 2002.
16. ALEC 1981b.
17. ALEC n.d.-a.
18. Conservative Digest 1985, 5–6.
19. Conservative Digest 1985, 6.
20. ALEC 1983b, 2.
21. Natural Resources Defense Council 2002, 5.
22. Cole 2012.
23. This description is from ALEC 1997a.
24. ALEC 1997a, 2.
25. Graves 2012b.
26. ALEC 1989b, 15.
27. ALEC 1989b, 15.
28. ALEC 1989b, 7.
29. ALEC 1991.
30. Graves 2012, 14.
31. ALEC 1989c, 2.
32. ALEC 1991, 3.
33. Graves 2012b.
34. Author interview with Wisconsin state representative, September 25, 2013.
35. See http://www.prwatch.org/files/AT&T.pdf.
36. See http://knowledgecenter.csg.org/kc/system/files/3.9%202016.pdf.
37. See http://knowledgecenter.csg.org/kc/system/files/3.9%202016.pdf.
38. See http://www.ncsl.org/research/about-state-legislatures/legislative-session-length.aspx.
39. See http://www.ncsl.org/research/about-state-legislatures/legislative-session-length.aspx.
40. See http://www.ncsl.org/research/about-state-legislatures/legislative-session-length.aspx.
41. Data from http://www.ncsl.org/research/about-state-legislatures/legislatures/staff-change-chart-1979-1988-1996-2003-2009.aspx.

42. For discussions of the measurement of legislative professionalism and its development over time across the states, see Squire 2007, 2012. Data on legislative pay and length of legislative sessions are from the Council of State Governments' Book of the States, while data on spending on legislative support come from the US Census Bureau. I combine these three standardized variables into a single summary index, which is highly correlated with Squire's index for the years in which that measure is available (R-squared: 0.90).
43. Both estimates significant at $p < 0.05$, a two-tailed test.
44. 2014 National Candidate Study. David Broockman, Nicholas Carnes, Melody Crowder-Meyer, and Christopher Skovron. See the Appendices for more details on the methodology.
45. For more details, see, for example, Broockman and Skovron 2018.
46. 2002 State Legislative Survey. John M Carey, Richard G. Niemi, Lynda Powell, and Gary Moncrief. ICPSR 20960.
47. Results presented in the Chapter 3 Appendix show years of service remains a strong predictor of individual-level ALEC bill authorship controlling for legislator party and interest group pressure (public employment and manufacturing/extractive employment in district), as well as state and year fixed effects.
48. For evidence, see especially Grumbach 2017; Rose and Bowling 2015. Of course, as I explained in the Introduction, not all political scientists support this argument—and so finding a strong and growing partisan effect to ALEC enactments provides an important addition to this debate.
49. Moe 2011; McGuinn 2006.
50. See canonically Downs 1957; Aldrich 1995.
51. For this theory, see especially Bawn et al. 2012. See also Schlozman 2015; Anzia and Moe 2016.
52. Although I do not present these results, I find a similar story dividing lawmakers by legislative experience—regardless of their seniority, lawmakers were more likely to turn to ALEC when they had fewer public employees in their district.
53. See, for instance, https://www.epa.gov/ghgemissions/global-greenhouse-gas-emissions-data.
54. For other examples and discussions of this distributive conflict, see Cheon and Urpelainen 2013; Aklin and Urpelainen 2013; Mildenberger 2015.
55. For a discussion of ALEC's stances and activities on climate change, see, for example, Hamburger et al. 2015.
56. Again, I find a similar story looking across legislative experience instead of party.
57. Recall that the survey question text was "Thinking about your run for office this year, were there any groups that were especially important early supporters?" and one of the answer choices was "Businesses."
58. Common Cause 2011.
59. Common Cause 2011.
60. Moyers 2012.
61. See, for example, Porter 2015.
62. This is consistent with the first versus the second faces of power; see, for example, Lukes 2005; Pierson 2015. See also Finger 2017 for similar evidence as applied to teachers unions.
63. This hypothesis is consistent with Powell 2012, who shows how the value of a legislative seat is worth more in a professionalized legislature and therefore contributions carry more weight in these states.
64. Pilkington 2015.
65. Biewen 2002.
66. Doherty 2011.
67. Doherty 2011.
68. Fischer 2012b, 7 (see also the general discussion on pp. 5–10).
69. Sinovic et al. n.d.
70. Glauber 2011.
71. ALEC 1995c, 12. See also ALEC 1995b.
72. ALEC 2000, 5.
73. See https://www.alec.org/about/alumni/.

74. For a similar argument in Congress, see Drutman 2015; Drutman and Teles 2015.
75. See https://legislature.idaho.gov/resources/citizenlegislature/.

Chapter 4

1. Rabe 2007; Stokes 2015.
2. See http://www.ncsl.org/research/energy/renewable-portfolio-standards.aspx; http://www.ncsl.org/research/energy/net-metering-policy-overview-and-state-legislative-updates.aspx for updated state totals.
3. Mills et al. 2015, 1.
4. Mills et al. 2015, 14.
5. For one calculation, see https://www.quora.com/How-many-homes-can-one-gigawatt-in-energy-capacity-provide-for.
6. See http://awea.files.cms-plus.com/FileDownloads/pdfs/Executive%20Summary%20-%20AWEA%20RPS%20Market%20Assessment.pdf.
7. Katakey 2017.
8. Abrams 2015.
9. Mulkern 2010.
10. For ExxonMobil's contributions to Heartland, see http://www.exxonsecrets.org/html/orgfactsheet.php?id=41. For Heartland's fundraising sources in 2012, see Johnson and Israel 2012
11. Eilperin 2012.
12. ALEC 2012.
13. See, for example, the Beacon Hill Institute 2015. More generally, see http://www.beaconhill.org/BHIRPSStudies.html for state-by-state reports from Beacon Hill.
14. See http://www.aeltracker.org/graphics/uploads/2015-Trends-in-Renewable-Portfolio-Standard-Legislation_4_15.pdf.
15. Light 2015.
16. ALEC 1990a, 31.
17. ALEC 1989a.
18. ALEC 1990a, 1989a, 2.
19. ALEC 1989a, 7.
20. ALEC 1990a, 31 and 35.
21. ALEC 1996a.
22. ALEC 1992a, 5 (for LA and MD) and ALEC 1990a, 31 (for GA, MS, TN, and WA).
23. ALEC 1990a, 31.
24. ALEC 1995a, 3.
25. Malott 1990.
26. Malott 1990, 1.
27. Malott 1990, 1 and 4.
28. Malott 1990, 4.
29. Malott 1990, 1.
30. I use data from Compustat to assemble the sample.
31. Fischer 2014b.
32. Industrial sales data from Compustat.
33. Data from the Bureau of Labor Statistics.
34. Drutman 2015; Hillman et al. 2004; Hillman and Hitt 1999; Masters and Keim 1985.
35. Corporate revenue data from Compustat.
36. See, for example, Drutman 2015; Martin 2000.
37. Data from the Center for Responsive Politics, averaged from 1996 to 2013.
38. Data from IRS tax filings for these business associations.
39. National regulation data from the RegData program at the Mercatus Center at George Mason University.
40. For example, ALEC 1986d.
41. Rosenbaum 1992.

42. ALEC 1993c, 4.
43. Blendon and Donelan 1991, 147.
44. ALEC 1993c, 4.
45. ALEC 1993c, 5.
46. ALEC 1993c, 27.
47. ALEC 1993c, 27.
48. Dreyfuss and Stone 1996. See also Hacker 2008, 150.
49. ALEC 1995a, 9.
50. ALEC 1993a. This was part of the group's 1993 "Washington Briefing, June 10–12, 1993."
51. Morris 1993, 1.
52. Chilcote 1993.
53. Morris 1993.
54. Morris 1993, 2.
55. ALEC 1993b, 9.
56. ALEC 1993b, 9.
57. ALEC 1993b, 8 and 14.
58. Vedder and Gallaway 1994. For a more rigorous analysis, see CBO 1994.
59. Grassroots America 1994.
60. See, for instance, Hoberock 1994 in the *Tulsa News*.
61. Hoberock 1994.
62. Hoberock 1994.
63. Hoberock 1994.
64. Grassroots America 1994.
65. ALEC 1994c, 11–13.
66. ALEC 1994c, 11–13.
67. Hacker 2001.
68. ALEC 1994a, 3.
69. ALEC 1995a.
70. Data from the Center for Responsive Politics.
71. Data from the Center for Responsive Politics.
72. Eng 2015; McCabe and Trujillo 2015. But see Broockman et al. 2017 for a detailed discussion of the conflicting social and economic dimensions of technological entrepreneurs' political attitudes.
73. ALEC 2009b.
74. Mazerov 2010.
75. Mazerov 2010.
76. NCSL 2014.
77. Novack 2011.
78. ALEC 2009b, 1.
79. An Amazon Affiliate Blog 2008.
80. For background, see Dolmetsch 2013.
81. ALEC 2009b. On online retailer participation in the group, see, for example, ALEC 2010.
82. Cooper 2008, 10.
83. Supreme Court of the United States Blog 2016.
84. Johnson 2010.
85. Cooper 2008, 15.
86. ALEC 2010, 2.
87. Stephenson 2011, 2.
88. Stephenson 2012.
89. Griffin 2014.
90. Smith 2016.
91. ALEC 2013.
92. As prior work has shown, political consumerism—the practice of consumers selecting products based on their personal political or social considerations—is an important force that shapes corporate decision-making, and a longstanding tradition in American political life (Vogel 2006; Stolle et al. 2005).

93. Specifically, I used summaries of firm activities from *Fortune* and *Hoover's*.
94. See https://corpgov.law.harvard.edu/2015/07/01/public-pension-funds-shareholder-proposal-activism/.
95. See http://www.afscme.org/news/press-room/press-releases/2016/institutional-investors-continue-to-press-companies-for-disclosure-of-lobbying-in-2016.
96. See http://www.afscme.org/news/press-room/press-releases/2016/institutional-investors-continue-to-press-companies-for-disclosure-of-lobbying-in-2016.
97. Data from Thompson Reuters.
98. Drutman 2015.
99. See, for example, https://www.sourcewatch.org/index.php/ALEC_Corporations.
100. ALEC 2013, 48.
101. ALEC 2013, 49.
102. Drutman 2015; Waterhouse 2013.
103. See, for example, Sachs 2012.

Chapter 5

1. Martin 2012b.
2. On the effect of right-to-work laws on union organizing and political activities, see, for example, Ellwood and Fine 1987; Feigenbaum et al. 2018.
3. In 2012, Michigan had a private-sector membership rate of 11.3 percent, compared to 6.6 percent nationwide, according to UnionStats.
4. Weigel 2012a.
5. Jones 2013.
6. Martin 2012a.
7. Eggert 2012.
8. Eggert 2012.
9. Fischer 2012a.
10. Center for Media and Democracy 2015.
11. Manuse 2012.
12. SourceWatch 2017.
13. LaFaive 2012.
14. Fang 2012.
15. Progress Michigan 2013.
16. Skocpol and Hertel-Fernandez 2016a.
17. Gardner 2012.
18. Gardner 2012.
19. Gardner 2012.
20. Kroll 2012; Fang 2012.
21. Oosting 2014.
22. Oosting 2014.
23. On Lund and the AFP, see Egan 2015.
24. SPN 2013b.
25. Recounted in detail in Mayer 2013a.
26. Lopez 2013.
27. Sharp 2016.
28. Sharp 2016.
29. National Committee for Responsive Philanthropy 1991. See also https://spn.org/history/.
30. SourceWatch 2015.
31. National Committee for Responsive Philanthropy 1991.
32. National Committee for Responsive Philanthropy 1991, 4.
33. National Committee for Responsive Philanthropy 1991, 4.
34. Author interview with Sam Brunelli, September 30, 2015.
35. Author interview with Sam Brunelli, September 30, 2015.
36. Author interview with Sam Brunelli, September 30, 2015.
37. SPN 2001a.

38. SPN 2000, 3.
39. SPN 2001b, 3.
40. SPN n.d.
41. SPN n.d.
42. SPN n.d.
43. See https://spn.org/state-policy-network-about/.
44. Dennis 2001, 4.
45. SPN 2002, 6.
46. Parks 2002, 1.
47. Parks 2002, 4.
48. Budget totals from IRS tax filings; media citations from LexisNexis searches of affiliates in state newspapers.
49. Data from IRS tax filings.
50. See https://issuu.com/statepolicynetwork/docs/2016._jan-feb_spn_news_-_final.
51. Only 25 percent of affiliates in fully GOP-controlled states reported the public as a political target, compared to nearly 60 percent of affiliates in Democratically controlled states. This is consistent with efforts at outside lobbying in general; see, for example, Kollman 1998.
52. See the Goldwater Institute's profile on GuideStar: https://www.guidestar.org/profile/86-0597661. See also Goldwater Institute 2015.
53. See the Goldwater Institute's profile on GuideStar: https://www.guidestar.org/profile/86-0597661. See also Goldwater Institute 2015.
54. Goldwater Institute 2015.
55. See http://goldwaterinstitute.org/en/work/topics/unions/release-time/arizona-supreme-court-rules-taxpayers-can-be-force/.
56. See http://goldwaterinstitute.org/en/work/topics/unions/release-time/case/wiley-v-austin/.
57. See http://www.goldwaterinstitute.org/en/work/topics/unions/paycheck-protection/urgent-call-speaker-tobin-and-tell-him-to-bring-hb/.
58. See http://goldwaterinstitute.org/en/work/topics/unions/save-our-secret-ballot/federal-court-upholds-save-our-secret-ballot/.
59. See http://goldwaterinstitute.org/en/work/topics/unions/save-our-secret-ballot/federal-court-upholds-save-our-secret-ballot/.
60. See http://goldwaterinstitute.org/en/work/topics/education/education-savings-accounts/mississippi-governor-phil-bryant-signs-bills-creat/.
61. See http://goldwaterinstitute.org/en/work/topics/education/education-savings-accounts/oklahoma-supreme-court-arizona-education-savings-a/.
62. Arizona Working Families and Center for Media and Democracy 2013.
63. Arizona Working Families and Center for Media and Democracy 2013, 11–12.
64. See the Goldwater Institute's profile on GuideStar: https://www.guidestar.org/profile/86-0597661.
65. Arizona Working Families and Center for Media and Democracy 2013; Sanchez 2016.
66. See the Heritage Policy Center's profile on GuideStar: https://www.guidestar.org/profile/22-3888250.
67. Sun Journal 2005. See also Maine's Majority Education Fund and Center for Media and Democracy 2013.
68. Maine's Majority Education Fund and Center for Media and Democracy 2013; Miller 2009.
69. Dann 2016.
70. Mistler 2015.
71. Mistler 2015.
72. Maine's Majority Education Fund and Center for Media and Democracy 2013, 11.
73. Phillips 2017.
74. Nemitz 2011.
75. Cuzzi 2014.
76. See http://www.themainewire.com/about/.
77. See http://www.themainewire.com/2017/03/lepage-dhhs-call-strict-welfare-reforms/; http://mainepolicy.org/issues/fixing-welfare/the-welfare-problem/.
78. Moretto 2014.

79. Moretto 2014.
80. See http://mainepolicy.org/2010/12/portland-event-obamacare-how-maine-can-fight-back/.
81. SPN 2009, 4.
82. SPN 2009, 4.
83. SPN 2009, 4.
84. SPN 2013a, 9.
85. See http://www.jbartlett.org/about-us.
86. Kopan 2013.
87. Kopan 2013.
88. Forbes 2017.
89. Forbes 2017.
90. Forbes 2016.
91. Forbes 2016.
92. Mayer 2016.
93. This section draws from joint work with Theda Skocpol, especially Skocpol and Hertel-Fernandez 2016a, 2016b.
94. The other two Koch brothers, Fred and Bill, have largely eschewed politics.
95. On the importance of political organizations, see especially Hacker and Pierson 2014, 2010a.
96. Schulman 2015, 99.
97. Doherty 2007, 410.
98. Levinthal 2015; Schulman 2014.
99. Walker 2014b.
100. Citizens for a Sound Economy n.d., 2.
101. Public Citizen 2000, 2.
102. Citizens for a Sound Economy n.d., 2.
103. Citizens for a Sound Economy n.d., 2.
104. Schulman 2014, 270.
105. Mayer 2012.
106. Mayer 2016, 198–199; Schulman 2014, 270.
107. See Hertel-Fernandez et al. 2016a for more information on these seminars.
108. Wilson and Wenzl 2012.
109. Wilson and Wenzl 2012.
110. Skocpol and Hertel-Fernandez 2016b; Hertel-Fernandez et al. 2016a; Hohmann 2017.
111. Skocpol and Hertel-Fernandez 2016b; Hertel-Fernandez et al. 2016a.
112. Vogel 2014a, 14–15.
113. Author correspondence, May 3, 2018.
114. Hertel-Fernandez et al. 2016a.
115. Schouten 2017.
116. See also Bump 2014.
117. Gold 2014b.
118. Hertel-Fernandez et al. 2016a.
119. Hertel-Fernandez et al. 2016a.
120. On the effectiveness of federated political groups, see, for example, Skocpol 2003.
121. Skocpol and Hertel-Fernandez 2016a and 2016b.
122. Skocpol and Hertel-Fernandez 2016a and 2016b.
123. AFP 2017, 23.
124. Skocpol and Hertel-Fernandez 2016b.
125. See https://americansforprosperity.org/volunteer/.
126. See https://americansforprosperity.org/volunteer/.
127. AFP 2017, 2015, 5.
128. For example, Gold 2014a.
129. Skocpol and Hertel-Fernandez 2016a and 2016b.
130. Weigel 2012b.
131. Ward 2012.

132. Ward 2012.
133. Skocpol and Hertel-Fernandez 2016a and 2016b.
134. See, for instance, https://web-beta.archive.org/web/20071003005538/http://aztaxpayers.org:80/.
135. https://web-beta.archive.org/web/20071003005538/http://aztaxpayers.org:80/.
136. https://web-beta.archive.org/web/20071003005538/http://aztaxpayers.org:80/.
137. See https://web-beta.archive.org/web/20090205000906/http://www.americansforprosperity.org/011209-anti-tax-group-releases-guide-2009-legislative-scorecard-arizona-reform-plan.
138. See https://web-beta.archive.org/web/20090204225758/http://www.americansforprosperity.org/011509-its-budget-cutting-time-and-arizonas-legislators-will-need-your-help.
139. See https://web-beta.archive.org/web/20110504023527/http://www.americansforprosperity.org/041811-will-gov-jan-brewer-stand-unions-urgent.
140. See https://web-beta.archive.org/web/20090205012023/http://www.americansforprosperity.org/tentative-schedule-and-confirmed-speakers-dec-6th-summit-and-balloon-launch.
141. See https://web-beta.archive.org/web/20090205012023/http://www.americansforprosperity.org/tentative-schedule-and-confirmed-speakers-dec-6th-summit-and-balloon-launch.
142. See https://web-beta.archive.org/web/20090205012023/http://www.americansforprosperity.org/tentative-schedule-and-confirmed-speakers-dec-6th-summit-and-balloon-launch.
143. https://web-beta.archive.org/web/20110504203032/http://www.americansforprosperity.org/061510-americans-prosperity-launches-maine-chapter#ixzz4dOmYeMAF.
144. https://web-beta.archive.org/web/20110504203016/http://www.americansforprosperity.org/061810-afp-maine-trains-waldo-county-grassroots-activists.
145. See https://web-beta.archive.org/web/20110504202657/http://www.americansforprosperity.org/091310-attend-grassroots-activists-training-your-area.
146. See https://web-beta.archive.org/web/20110504202931/http://www.americansforprosperity.org/073010-bangor-daily-news-afp-maines-workshop-teaches-political-activism-tools.
147. See https://web-beta.archive.org/web/20110504202657/http://www.americansforprosperity.org/091310-attend-grassroots-activists-training-your-area.
148. See http://web.archive.org/web/20131101070031/http://americansforprosperity.org/maine/legislativealerts/030111-testimony-support-tax-cut-provisions-included-20122013-biennial-budget-proposal/.
149. See https://www.memun.org/DesktopModules/Bring2mind/DMX/Download.aspx?Command=Core_Download&EntryId=8550&language=en-US&PortalId=0&TabId=204.
150. See http://web.archive.org/web/20151217180037/http://americansforprosperity.org/maine/carol-weston-afp-maine-state-director/.
151. See http://web.archive.org/web/20151217180037/http://americansforprosperity.org/maine/carol-weston-afp-maine-state-director/.
152. Skocpol and Hertel-Fernandez 2016b.
153. Mayer 2013b.
154. See https://web-beta.archive.org/web/20110504203003/http://www.americansforprosperity.org/071410-gubernatorial-us-house-candidates-%E2%80%93-lepage-levesque-and-scontras-all-sign-no-climate-tax-pled#ixzz4dOwdQVcF.
155. See https://web-beta.archive.org/web/20110504203003/http://www.americansforprosperity.org/071410-gubernatorial-us-house-candidates-%E2%80%93-lepage-levesque-and-scontras-all-sign-no-climate-tax-pled#ixzz4dOwdQVcF.
156. Hertel-Fernandez and Skocpol 2016.
157. See Hacker and Pierson 2016, Chapter 7, on the evolution of the US Chamber of Commerce.

Chapter 6

1. Petroski 2017a.
2. Petroski 2016.
3. Noble 2017.
4. Noble 2017.
5. Petroski and Pfannenstiel 2017.
6. Petroski and Pfannenstiel 2017.

7. Petroski and Pfannenstiel 2017.
8. PPP Poll of 664 Iowan voters, January 3–4, 2018.
9. Sinovic et al. n.d.; for the response of Democrats, see http://iowahouse.org/iowa-lawmakers-to-alec-we-are-not-members/.
10. SourceWatch n.d.
11. ALEC 1979b.
12. ALEC n.d.-c.
13. See https://americansforprosperity.org/afp-iowa-announces-grassroots-campaign-collective-bargaining-reform/.
14. Activist estimate from 2015 AFP Donor Proposal.
15. See https://americansforprosperity.org/afp-iowa-announces-grassroots-campaign-collective-bargaining-reform/.
16. Pfannenstiel 2017; Petroski 2017b.
17. Petroski 2017b.
18. Petroski 2017b.
19. See https://spn.org/public-interest-institute-update-januaryfebruary-2017/.
20. See http://www.limitedgovernment.org/wisdon.html.
21. See http://www.limitedgovernment.org/ps-17-3-p3.html.
22. See http://www.limitedgovernment.org/ps-17-3-p3.html; http://www.limitedgovernment.org/brief24-5.html; https://caffeinatedthoughts.com/2017/02/scott-walker-guide-collective-bargaining-reform-iowa/.
23. ALEC 1980a.
24. Hough 2011, 10.
25. Stan 2011.
26. Vogel 2011.
27. Sharp 2016, 2.
28. Sharp 2016, 2.
29. Sharp 2016, 8.
30. Freeman and Han 2012.
31. Unless otherwise noted, these measures are from 2011 to 2012. I standardized each of the subcomponents and then scaled the final additive measure to run from 0 to 1.
32. Skocpol and Hertel-Fernandez 2016a and 2016b.
33. SourceWatch n.d.
34. It does not appear that states were more likely to pass legislation curbing public-sector labor unions where public unions were more active (either as measured by campaign contributions or membership). Cutbacks were passed just as readily in states with relatively weaker and stronger public-sector unions alike. This is likely because of the strong overlap between strong public employee unions and Democratic control. To fully test this proposition, I would need a three-way interaction between public union strength, troika strength, and partisan control, for which I do not have the statistical power. See also Wade 2018 for similar evidence.
35. These include February 2011 polling from NBC/WSJ, February 2011 polling from CBS/New York Times, February 2011 polling from Gallup/USA Today, and March 2011 polling from Gallup. There were 4,007 responses to the questions that I pooled together.
36. Office of the Governor 2011.
37. Office of the Governor 2011.
38. State budget balance is the ratio of state expenditures to revenue; data from the National Association of State Budget Officers.
39. State legislative ideology data from Shor and McCarty 2011.
40. Hernandez 2011.
41. Walker 2011b.
42. Kroll 2011. For a more detailed treatment, see Kersten 2011.
43. Drum 2011.
44. Fischer 2012b.
45. Fischer 2012b.
46. SourceWatch n.d.
47. Kaufman 2018, chapter 5.

48. Skocpol and Hertel-Fernandez 2016a and 2016b.
49. Lipton 2011.
50. Kroll 2011.
51. Glauber and Walker 2011; for an invitation for one of the AFP events, see http://freerepublic.com/focus/news/2676310/posts.
52. Walker 2011a.
53. Fraley 2010.
54. Woodruff 2015.
55. Woodruff 2015.
56. Hall 2013.
57. Fischer 2012b.
58. Healy and Davey 2015.
59. Healy and Davey 2015.
60. Healy and Davey 2015.
61. Davey 2016.
62. Davey 2016.
63. Hohmann 2017.
64. Data from the State of Wisconsin Ethics Commission.
65. These totals are state-demeaned.
66. Greenstone 1969; Schlozman 2015; Rosenfeld 2014; Leighley and Nagler 2007.
67. On the habit-forming nature of political participation, see, for example, Coppock and Green 2016. On the mobilizing effects of public unions on teacher political participation, see Flavin and Hartney 2015.
68. The example of Ohio's attempt at union cutbacks shows the importance of institutional features like legislative referenda for checks on the troika's strength, especially in a context of full GOP control. On the referenda battle in Ohio, see especially McNay 2013.
69. Bragdon n.d.
70. This is a result of the *Harris v. Quinn* (2014) Supreme Court decision. See Estlund and Forbath 2014.
71. Bragdon n.d., 11.
72. Pilkington 2018. See also Greenhouse 2016a.
73. Abernathy 2018.
74. Armentrout 2018.
75. Fang and Surgey 2018, VanderHart 2018.
76. VanderHart 2018.
77. https://ra.nea.org/wp-content/uploads/2018/06/Strategic_Plan_and_Budget_2018.pdf.
78. Fang and Surgey 2018.
79. Sharp 2016.
80. Peterson 2016.
81. Peterson 2016.
82. Feigenbaum et al. 2018.
83. CBO 2010.
84. Musumeci 2012, 2.
85. *NFIB v. Sebelius* (2012).
86. This section draws from Hertel-Fernandez et al. 2016b.
87. Potter 2011.
88. Potter 2011.
89. Herrera 2011.
90. Herrera 2011.
91. Herrera 2011.
92. SourceWatch 2015.
93. Laffer et al. 2009.
94. SPN 2013a.
95. Mayer 2010.
96. Cunningham 2015.
97. Cunningham 2015.

98. Kessler 2014.
99. FGA 2015.
100. Legislative chamber membership data based on ALEC 2013; top legislative leadership membership data based on SourceWatch n.d.
101. The estimates for Medicaid expansion support come from Rigby and Haselswerdt 2013. Elizabeth Rigby generously shared the state-by-state estimates of public opinion with me.
102. Grogan and Park 2017.
103. Income threshold data from the Kaiser Family Foundation.
104. Goodnough and Smith 2017.
105. See here: https://missourihealthcareforall.org/learn/about/endorsements/. On the importance of public health and public interest lobbyists for Medicaid expansion, see Callaghan and Jacobs 2016.
106. Ferguson 2013; Missouri Scout n.d.; Pfannenstiel 2013.
107. Lieb 2014.
108. Americans for Prosperity-Missouri 2013b, 2014b. AFP volunteer estimate from 2015 AFP Donor Prospectus.
109. Americans for Prosperity-Missouri 2014a and 2014b.
110. Americans for Prosperity-Missouri 2013a, 2014a.
111. Ishmael 2014; Wilson 2012.
112. Ishmael 2013.
113. Ishmael 2013, 3.
114. ALEC 2013.
115. Greenblatt 2011.
116. Hertel-Fernandez et al. 2016.
117. To measure constituent ideologies, I used the measure computed by Tausanovitch and Warshaw 2013.
118. Author's interview with Missouri Chamber of Commerce lobbyist, April 16, 2014.
119. Author's interview with Missouri Chamber of Commerce lobbyist, April 16, 2014.
120. Author's interview with Missouri Chamber of Commerce lobbyist, April 16, 2014.
121. I emailed the head lobbyist or government affairs staffer at each state chamber of commerce in April 2014. For states that did not respond to my inquiry, I searched their website and local and state media for evidence of the chamber's position. I used state chamber websites to look for a dedicated health policy staffer.
122. Galewitz 2014.
123. For more details, see Hertel-Fernandez et al. 2016b.
124. See especially Hacker and Pierson 2014; Pierson 2015; Anzia and Moe 2016.

Chapter 7

1. Vogel 2014b.
2. Vogel 2014b.
3. Shumate 1938, 189.
4. Shumate 1938, 189.
5. Orth 1904.
6. Squire 2012, Chapter 7.
7. Toll 1928, 127.
8. Davis 1965, 96–97.
9. Toll 1928, 128.
10. Toll 1928.
11. Toll 1928, 128–129.
12. Toll 1926, 642.
13. Council of State Governments 1935a, 5.
14. Teaford 2002, 144.
15. Council of State Governments 1935c, 5–8.
16. Council of State Governments 1935c, 8.
17. Council of State Governments 1935b.

18. Tucker 1998; Moss 1995; Rahman 2016.
19. For example, Skocpol 1992, 265–266.
20. Council of State Governments 1937, 10.
21. Council of State Governments 1937, 10.
22. Teaford 2002, 167.
23. Kurtz 1999.
24. Kurtz 1999.
25. Kurtz 1999.
26. Kurtz 1999.
27. Teaford 2002, Chapter 6.
28. Amenta 1998, Chapter 5.
29. CSG 1944.
30. Teaford 2002, 165.
31. Bishop 2008, 224.
32. Rust 2012.
33. Mack 1997, 25–26.
34. Bishop 2008, 222.
35. ALEC n.d.-b, 7.
36. ALEC n.d.-b, 7.
37. ALEC n.d.-b, 7.
38. Brown 1995.
39. Brown 1995.
40. Humphrey 1995.
41. See http://www.ncsl.org/aboutus/mission-and-governance/faqs.aspx on NCSL governance and Graves et al. 2011 for a comparison of ALEC and NCSL.
42. Shotts 1976, 1.
43. Shotts 1976, 2–3.
44. Shotts 1976, 2–3.
45. Shotts 1976, 4.
46. Kaiser 1976.
47. Broder and Sawyer 1980.
48. These states include Arkansas, California, Colorado, Connecticut, Florida, Iowa, Kentucky, Massachusetts, Maine, Michigan, Nebraska, New Jersey, New York, Oregon, South Carolina, Texas, Vermont, Washington, and Wisconsin.
49. Weir 2009.
50. Weir 2009, 13.
51. Weir 2009, 15.
52. Weir 2009, 17.
53. Walker 2014a. See also Skocpol et al. 2000 on the importance of organizations modeling themselves on the structure of American political institutions.
54. DiSalvo 2015.
55. Data from the Institute on Money in State Politics.
56. Liptak 2017.
57. Liptak 2017.
58. https://ra.nea.org/wp-content/uploads/2018/06/Strategic_Plan_and_Budget_2018.pdf.
59. The Economist 2018; Newkirk and Braun 2018.
60. For one critical assessment, see Brooks 2018.
61. Shearer and Webb 1975.
62. Shearer and Webb 1976.
63. Clavel 2010, 25.
64. Clavel 1989, xiii.
65. W.K. Kellogg Foundation n.d., 2004.
66. Kallick 2002, 20.
67. Kallick 2002, 20.
68. Center for Policy Alternatives 2006.
69. Center for Policy Alternatives 2006.

70. Center for Policy Alternatives 2006.
71. See http://www.leadersforprogress.org/flemming/FlemmingFellowsDirectory.htm.
72. Interview with progressive state policy advocate, August 14, 2014.
73. Ettlinger et al. 2005b, 1–2. The group first issued a major planning document two years earlier.
74. Ettlinger et al. 2005b, 1 and 3.
75. Ettlinger et al. 2005b, 14–15.
76. Ettlinger et al. 2005a.
77. Singer 2005.
78. Singer 2005.
79. The repeated competition between various left-wing cross-state efforts is in some ways consistent with the broader account of the fragmentation of liberal interest groups described by Matt Grossmann and David Hopkins (2016). Yet while Grossmann and Hopkins emphasize liberal divisions by issues and constituencies, what I find is duplication of *functions*—like PLAN versus CPA. These were organizations intended to achieve the same purpose— building cross-state progressive political power.
80. Conniff 2006.
81. Jacobson 2005.
82. Jacobson 2005.
83. Jacobson 2005.
84. Interview with progressive state policy advocate, January 15, 2015.
85. August 14, 2015, and January 15, 2015, interviews.
86. Interview with ALICE staffer, December 7, 2013.
87. Interview with ALICE staffer, December 7, 2013.
88. See http://web.archive.org/web/20110707170511/http://www.stateinnovation.org:80/Mission-Statement.aspx.
89. Vogel 2014b.
90. Hertel-Fernandez et al. 2016a.
91. Vogel 2017.
92. Overby 2005.
93. Overby 2005.
94. Galvin 2012. See also Schlozman 2016; Galvin 2016.
95. Schmitt et al. 2014.
96. Schmitt et al. 2014.
97. These were reported to me through the online survey described next. The item, which provided an open-ended response box for survey-takers, was as follows: "Briefly, please describe a recent success your organization achieved in the past two years, including the policy issue involved, what your organization did, the outcome, and important allies/opponents involved in the issue."
98. In states with multiple affiliates, respondents were shown a randomly selected affiliate (see the Chapter 6 Appendix for more details).
99. The online survey was fielded on directors of all SPP and EARN affiliates, who received an invitation to participate via email. We collected responses from November 2016 to March 2017, and obtained a 90 percent response rate. The item mentioned in the text had the following text: "We are interested in understanding whether any of the following items are important obstacles to your organization's work. For each item, please indicate how important of an obstacle it has been to your organization's work in recent years on a scale of never to always." After opposition control of government and narrative, the most frequently cited item was "Insufficient financial resources in your organization."
100. This finding is from an item that asked SPP/EARN directors the following: "Now, we would like you to rank each of these characteristics of funders from (1) most important to (7) least important. Please reorder the characteristics of funders so that they are in descending order of importance to your organization. You can drag and drop the items to reorder them." Directors were just as likely to rank "generous grants" as first or second in importance as they were to rank "consistent funding from year to year."

101. See the Chapter 7 Appendix for a full list of the organizations that appear in both the liberal and conservative universes.
102. On the reluctance of non-profits to engage in politics more generally, see Berry and Arons 2005.
103. National Committee for Responsive Philanthropy 1991, 12.
104. National Committee for Responsive Philanthropy 1991, 12.
105. Callahan 2001.
106. Kallick 2002.
107. Interview with progressive state policy advocate, August 14, 2014.
108. Interview with progressive state policy advocate, January 13, 2015.
109. Interview with progressive state policy advocate, January 13, 2015.
110. Robertson 1989; Peterson 1995; Katznelson et al. 1993; Hacker and Pierson 2002, 2016.
111. Gerken 2012.
112. Hertel-Fernandez et al. 2016a.
113. Hertel-Fernandez et al. 2016a.
114. Hertel-Fernandez et al. 2016a.
115. Author review of Democracy Alliance portfolios.
116. See https://ballotpedia.org/Committee_on_States.
117. See http://democracyalliance.org/organization/committee-on-states/.
118. Kroll 2014b.
119. Kroll 2014a.
120. There was no statistically or substantively significant difference between the change in partisan control of states from 2014 to 2015 in states that were targeted by the Committee for investment (nor by the size of those Committee investments, or when looking from 2014 to 2017). In a similar vein, there was no relationship between states targeted by the Committee for investment and the number of ALEC bills introduced or enacted in 2013 to 2014.
121. Gold 2015.
122. Gold 2015.
123. Badger and Bui 2016.
124. For some discussion of these varied causes, see, for example, Hopkins 2017; Nall 2015; McGirr 2001; Perlstein 2008.
125. See https://ballotpedia.org/List_of_current_mayors_of_the_top_100_cities_in_the_United_States.
126. Goldberg 2014.
127. Cooper 2016.
128. Greenhouse 2016b.
129. Rolf 2016.
130. On the availability of paid leave by worker wages and other characteristics, see https://www.bls.gov/news.release/pdf/ebs2.pdf.
131. Bottari and Fischer 2013.
132. Bottari and Fischer 2013.
133. Pabst 2011; Marley 2011. See testimony by the Wisconsin Restaurant Association at http://docs.legis.wisconsin.gov/2011/related/public_hearing_records/sc_labor_public_safety_and_urban_affairs/bills_resolutions/11hr_sc_lpsua_sb0023_pt01.pdf.
134. Bottari and Fischer 2015.
135. Bottari and Fischer 2015.
136. CDC 2011.
137. Graham 2017.
138. The city-centered progressive strategy might be seen as what Elisabeth Clemens describes as a "misalignment" in political and social geography (Clemens 2017). Although progressives' social bases of support are increasingly concentrated in cities, the political institutions of federalism limit power at that level of government.
139. Callahan 2001.

Conclusion

1. Shannon 2016.
2. See also Mayer 2016.
3. The Lynde and Harry Bradley Foundation. "Request for a proposal to build the capacity of conservative infrastructures in the states." For the documents, see: https://projects.jsonline.com/news/2017/5/5/hacked-records-show-bradley-foundation-taking-wisconsin-model-national.html.
4. Appendix: The Barder Fund, August 19, 2014, Subtab B (capacity-building in the states), B-1 to B-9.
5. Appendix: The Barder Fund, August 19, 2014, Subtab B (capacity-building in the states), B-1 to B-9.
6. Appendix: The Barder Fund, August 19, 2014, Subtab B (capacity-building in the states), B-1 to B-9.
7. Appendix: The Barder Fund, August 19, 2014, Subtab B (capacity-building in the states), B-1 to B-9.
8. Appendix: The Barder Fund, August 19, 2014, Subtab B (capacity-building in the states), B-1 to B-9.
9. Appendix: The Barder Fund, August 19, 2014, Subtab B (capacity -building in the states), B-1 to B-9.
10. Hacker and Pierson 2010a. See also Hacker and Pierson 2014.
11. Hacker and Pierson 2010b, 172.
12. For a similar argument, see Bawn et al. 2012; Krimmel 2017; Karol 2009.
13. Bawn et al. 2012; Schlozman 2015.
14. See http://mackinac.org/overtonwindow.
15. Kaufman 2018, chapter 3.
16. See, for example, Robertson 2018.
17. See http://www.journalism.org/2014/07/10/americas-shifting-statehouse-press/.
18. According to my tabulations of the 2016 Cooperative Congressional Election Survey.
19. Caughey et al. 2016; Holbein and Dynes 2018; for older evidence of the lack of a direct effect of partisan control, see Erikson et al. 1993. But see Grumbach 2017 for evidence of more striking contemporary differences.
20. This helps to account for the differences between the findings reported here and those in Caughey et al. 2016.
21. See, for example, Peterson 1995.
22. See especially Culpepper 2010 on "quiet politics." This finding is consistent with Rogers 2017 on electoral unaccountability in state legislatures.
23. See especially Callahan 2017; Skocpol 2016; Drezner 2017.
24. On the need for scholars to study organized philanthropy in politics, see especially Skocpol 2016. For other arguments in a similar vein: Walker 1991; Wilson 1995; Teles 2010, 2013.
25. See http://www.alecexposed.org/wiki/What_is_ALEC%3F.
26. Lafer 2017.
27. See here the concept of institutions as carriers of common—but diverse—interests detailed in Mahoney and Thelen 2009. See also Teles 2010 for the notion of social learning in political organizations.
28. Grossmann and Hopkins 2015, 2016.
29. See also Krimmel 2017; McCarty and Schickler 2018.
30. Horn 2006.
31. Campbell 2003. See also Skocpol 1992; Pierson 1993; Hacker 2002; Mettler 1998; Mettler and Soss 2004.
32. Pierson 2015. See also Hacker and Pierson 2014.
33. Of course, measuring this relationship is both conceptually and empirically difficult. For one excellent discussion of these issues, see Broockman 2016.
34. Gilens 2012; Gilens and Page 2014; Bartels 2008. For alternative perspectives, see Enns 2015; Branham et al. 2017.

35. Though note that these conclusions and their implications have been debated by some scholars, including Branham et al. 2017; Enns 2015; Erikson 2015.
36. On the alignment of wealthy individuals and businesses with these priorities, see Gilens 2012; Page et al. 2013, 2015. Of course, Table C.1 refers to preferences toward specific policies, not general orientations to government. This is important because longstanding work in American politics has shown that American citizens tend to hold more liberal opinions on specific policies as compared to abstract principles (e.g., Free and Cantril 1967; Grossmann and Hopkins 2016). At the same time, it is these policies that make for the clearest comparison given that they are ultimately the concrete changes in government that the troika is pursuing.
37. Data on actual district opinion from Kalla and Porter 2018.
38. Broockman and Skovron 2018.
39. See, for instance, Freeman and Medoff 1984; Leighley and Nagler 2007; Rosenfeld 2014; Moe 2011; Kim and Margalit 2017; Flavin 2016; Schlozman et al. 2012. For historical perspectives, see Schlozman 2015; Greenstone 1969; Hacker and Pierson 2010a. See also Page and Gilens 2017, Chapter 7.
40. See, for example, Kiely 2016.
41. See, for example, Drutman 2015; Yackee and Yackee 2006; Hacker and Pierson 2010a, 2016.
42. Associated Press-NORC Money in Politics Survey, November 2015.
43. Associated Press-NORC Money in Politics Survey, November 2015.
44. For one assessment of the donors in the money-in-politics space and their activities, see, for example, Novick 2013. For a poll of business managers' attitudes toward campaign finance, see Corrado 2013.
45. See http://www.ncsl.org/research/elections-and-campaigns/citizens-united-and-the-states.aspx.
46. For one excellent summary of a range of reforms, see, for example, Page and Gilens 2017, Chapter 7.
47. For a similar argument in Congress, see Drutman 2015.
48. Schuette 2017.
49. Schuette 2017.
50. Oosting 2017.
51. Richardson and Milyo 2017. I thank the authors for generously providing the data for this analysis, which came from the University of Missouri Cooperative Congressional Election Study module in 2016.
52. Question text: "Next, we would like to ask you a few questions about your state legislature. State legislatures vary in how often they meet, how much state legislators are paid, and how much staff legislators are provided. As you think about your state legislature, do you prefer..."
53. Data from leaked 2017 ALEC conference registrations.
54. These recommendations draw from Hertel-Fernandez and Skocpol 2015.
55. See Campbell 2003; Mettler and Soss 2004 for such effects generally and Clinton and Sances 2017 for effects in the Medicaid program specifically. But see also Michener 2018.
56. Farnam 1911, 7.
57. Farnam 1911, 9.
58. Farnam 1911, 14.
59. Skocpol 1992, 182–183.

WORKS CITED

Abernathy, James. 2018. "Freedom Foundation Influences Janus Decision." *Freedom Foundation – Litigation*, July 9.
Abowd, Paul. 2012. "ALEC Gets a Break From State Lobbying Laws." *Mother Jones*, May 8.
Abrams, Lindsay. 2015. "Exxon CEO Ridicules Green Energy: 'We choose not to lose money on purpose.'" *Salon*, May 28.
Achen, Christopher, and Larry M. Bartels. 2016. *Democracy for Realists: Why Elections Do Not Produce Responsive Government*. Princeton, NJ: Princeton University Press.
AFP. 2015. *Partner Prospectus, Winter 2015*. Arlington, VA: Americans for Prosperity.
———. 2017. *Partner Prospectus, January 2017*. Arlington, VA: Americans for Prosperity.
Akard, Patrick J. 1992. "Corporate Mobilization and Political Power: The Transformation of U.S. Economic Policy in the 1970s." *American Sociological Review* 57 (5): 597–615.
Aklin, Michaël, and Johannes Urpelainen. 2013. "Political Competition, Path Dependence, and the Strategy of Sustainable Energy Transitions." *American Journal of Political Science* 57 (3): 643–658.
Aldrich, John H. 1995. *Why Parties? The Origin and Transformation of Political Parties in America*. Chicago: University of Chicago Press.
ALEC. 1976. *1977 Suggested State Legislation*. Washington, DC: American Legislative Exchange Council.
———. 1977. *1978–79 Suggested State Legislation*. Washington, DC: American Legislative Exchange Council.
———. 1979a. "Letter from Kathleen Teague to Raymond A. Oliverio." University of California, Berkeley, Bancroft Library, People for the American Way Collection, Carton 6, Folder 16.
———. 1979b. *The Source Book of American State Legislation*. Washington, DC: American Legislative Exchange Council.
———. 1980a. *Public Employee Collective Bargaining: The Legislative Issues*. Washington, DC: American Legislative Exchange Council.
———. 1980b. *The Source Book of American State Legislation 1981–82*. Washington, DC: American Legislative Exchange Council.
———. 1981a. *ALEC's Exclusive White House and Cabinet Briefing, II*. Washington, DC: American Legislative Exchange Council.
———. 1981b. "Fundraising Letter from Lawrence D. Pratt for ALEC." University of California, Berkeley, Bancroft Library, People for the American Way Collection, Carton 6, Folder 16.
———. 1982. "American Legislative Exchange Council 1982 Annual Report." University of California, San Francisco, Legacy Tobacco Archives.
———. 1983a. "American Legislative Exchange Council 1983 Annual Report." University of California, San Francisco, Legacy Tobacco Archives.

———. 1983b. "First Reading: Interview with ALEC National Chairman Buz Lukens." University of California, Berkeley, Bancroft Library, People for the American Way Collection, Carton 6, Folder 27.

———. 1984. "Letter from Kathleen Teague to Samuel D. Chilcote, Jr., President, Tobacco Institute." University of California, Berkeley, Bancroft Library, People for the American Way Collection, Carton 6, Folder 16.

———. 1985. "Homosexuals: Just Another Minority Group?" *ALEC State Factor* 11 (3).

———. 1986a. "ALEC's National Project on Risk and Liability: Helping America Come to Grips with the Liability Crisis." *ALEC First Reading* 12 (January).

———. 1986b. "Clearing the Air: The Environmental Tobacco Smoke Debate." In *The State Factor*, vol. 12, no. 5. University of California, San Francisco, Legacy Tobacco Archives.

———. 1986c. "Risk and the Civil Justice System: The Crisis in Tort Law." *ALEC State Factor* 11 (10).

———. 1986d. "Risk and the Civil Justice System: The Crisis in Tort Law." University of California, Berkeley, Bancroft Library, People for the American Way Collection, Carton 6, Folder 16.

———. 1987. "Letter from Constance C. Heckman to Samuel D. Chilcote, Jr., President, Tobacco Institute." University of California, San Francisco, Legacy Tobacco Archives.

———. 1989a. *Environmental Monitor*, vol. 1, no. 9. Washington, DC: American Legislative Exchange Council.

———. 1989b. "Fact Sheet: ALEC's 1989 Annual Meeting." University of California, San Francisco, Legacy Tobacco Archives.

———. 1989c. "Letter from Samuel A. Brunelli to Samuel D. Chilcote, Jr., President, Tobacco Institute." University of California, San Francisco, Legacy Tobacco Archives.

———. 1990a. *American Legislative Exchange Council 17th Annual Meeting in Boston, Massachusetts, July 25–29, 1990*. Washington, DC: American Legislative Exchange Council.

———. 1990b. "Criminal Justice Reporter." University of California, San Francisco, Legacy Tobacco Archives.

———. 1991. "ALEC's 18th Annual Meeting Flyer." University of California, San Francisco, Legacy Tobacco Archives.

———. 1992a. *States and Nations: Special Annual Meeting Edition*. Washington, DC: American Legislative Exchange Council.

———. 1992b. "Winning the Debate in the States: 1992 Annual Report." University of California, San Francisco, Legacy Tobacco Archives.

———. 1993a. "1993 Washington Briefing—Tentative Agenda, Friday June 11." University of California, San Francisco, Legacy Tobacco Archives.

———. 1993b. "ALEC's 20th Anniversary Annual Meeting Program." University of California, San Francisco, Legacy Tobacco Archives.

———. 1993c. "Keeping the Promise: Making Health Care Accessible and Affordable for All Americans." University of California, San Francisco, Legacy Tobacco Archives.

———. 1994a. "Letter from Sam Brunelli to Samuel D. Chilcote, Jr., President, Tobacco Institute." University of California, San Francisco, Legacy Tobacco Archives.

———. 1994b. "Report Card on Crime and Punishment." University of California, San Francisco, Legacy Tobacco Archives.

———. 1994c. "Turning the Tide: ALEC Health Care Campaign." In *FYI: July 9, 1994*. University of California, San Francisco, Legacy Tobacco Archives.

———. 1995a. "Prospectus 1994–5, Guide to Private Sector Membership." University of California, San Francisco, Legacy Tobacco Archives.

———. 1995b. "Sourcebook of American State Legislation, Annotated Index." University of California, San Francisco, Legacy Tobacco Archives.

———. 1995c. *States and Nation: A Remarkable Year!* Washington, DC: American Legislative Exchange Council.

———. 1996a. *Annotated Index 1995–96: A Comprehensive Index to Update '96 and the 1995 Sourcebook of American State Legislation.* Washington, DC: American Legislative Exchange Council.
———. 1996b. "Electric Industry Restructuring." University of California, San Francisco, Legacy Tobacco Archives.
———. 1996c. "Joint Board of Directors Meeting Minutes." University of California, San Francisco, Legacy Tobacco Archives.
———. 1996d. "Meeting the Challenge: Ideas + Action = Results, a Business Plan for the American Legislative Exchange Council." University of California, San Francisco, Legacy Tobacco Archives.
———. 1997a. "24th Annual Meeting." University of California, San Francisco, Legacy Tobacco Archives.
———. 1997b. "Spring Joint Board of Directors Meeting Minutes." University of California, San Francisco, Legacy Tobacco Archives.
———. 1998a. "1998 Business Plan." University of California, San Francisco, Legacy Tobacco Archives.
———. 1998b. "Jeffersonian Principles in Action! 25th Anniversary Annual Meeting." University of California, San Francisco, Legacy Tobacco Archives.
———. 1998c. "Spring Joint Board of Directors Meeting Minutes." University of California, San Francisco, Legacy Tobacco Archives.
———. 2000. *Annual Report.* Washington, DC: American Legislative Exchange Council.
———. 2002. *Annual Report.* Washington, DC: American Legislative Exchange Council.
———. 2007a. *2007 Legislative Scorecard.* Washington, DC: American Legislative Exchange Council.
———. 2007b. "American Legislative Exchange Council Bylaws," Form 990, Part VI, Line 77. American Legislative Exchange Council, Washington, DC.
———. 2008. "New 2008 Spring Task Force Summit Model Bills." *Inside ALEC*, July.
———. 2009a. "American Legislative Exchange Council Task Force Operating Procedure." American Legislative Exchange Council, Washington, DC. Documents leaked by Common Cause.
———. 2009b. Amicus Curiae Brief in *Amazon.com LLC, and Amazon Services, LLC v. New York State Department of Taxation and Finance.* Filed on behalf of ALEC by Charles A. Stewart III, Stewart Occhipinti, LLP, New York.
———. 2010. "Telecommunications and Information Technology Task Force Meeting: Tentative Agenda (as of 10/27/10)." American Legislative Exchange Council, Washington, DC.
———. 2012. *Electricity Freedom Act.* Washington, DC: American Legislative Exchange Council.
———. 2013. "ALEC Board Meeting Notes." American Legislative Council, Washington, DC. Documents leaked by *The Guardian.*
———. 2016. *Strategic Plan: 2016–2018.* Arlington, VA: American Legislative Exchange Council.
———. n.d.-a. "ALEC: A Grant Proposal for Focus on Tax Policy." University of California, San Francisco, Legacy Tobacco Archives.
———. n.d.-b. "Negotiating the New Federalism: Is NCSL the 'Office Voice?'" *ALEC First Reading.*
———. n.d.-c. *What Others Say About ALEC.* Washington, DC: American Legislative Exchange Council.
Amenta, Edwin. 1998. *Bold Relief: Institutional Politics and the Origins of Modern American Social Policy.* Princeton, NJ: Princeton University Press.
Americans for Prosperity-Missouri. 2013a. *2013 Economic Prosperity Report Card.* Americans for Prosperity-Missouri.
———. 2013b. *AFP-Missouri Members Speak Out Against Medicaid Expansion.* Americans for Prosperity-Missouri.
———. 2014a. *2014 Economic Prosperity Report Card.* Americans for Prosperity-Missouri.

———. 2014b. *New AFP Radio Ad: Medicaid Expansion Could Lead to Cuts in Education*. Americans for Prosperity-Missouri.

Amazon Affiliate Blog. 2016. *How Many Affiliates Are Registered With Amazon Associates Program?* Cited 2016, published 2008. https://amazonaffiliate.wordpress.com/2008/07/30/how-many-affiliates-are-registered-with-amazon-associates-program/.

Ansolabehere, Stephen, John M. de Figueiredo, and James M. Snyder, Jr. 2003. "Why Is There So Little Money in U.S. Politics?" *Journal of Economic Perspectives* 17 (1): 105–130.

Anzia, Sarah F., and Terry M. Moe. 2016. "Do Politicians Use Policy to Make Politics? The Case of Public-Sector Labor Laws." *American Political Science Review* 110 (4): 763–777.

Arizona Working Families, and Center for Media and Democracy. 2013. *A Reporter's Guide to the Goldwater Institute*. Arizona Working Families and the Center for Media and Democracy.

Armentrout, Mitchell. 2018. "Mark Janus quits state job for conservative think tank gig after landmark ruling." *The Chicago Sun-Times*, July 20.

Arnold, Steve. 2015. *Undercover at ACCE: ALEC Offshoot Spins City and County Officials on Dirty Energy, Local Control*. Madison, WI: Center for Media and Democracy.

Badger, Emily, and Quoctrung Bui. 2016. "Why Republicans Don't Even Try to Win Cities Anymore." *The New York Times*, November 2.

Baker, Donald P. 1978. "Conservatives Unite to Oppose D.C. Amendment." *The Washington Post*, December 3.

Baker, Peter, and Carl Hulse. 2010. "Deep Rifts Divide Obama and Republicans." *The New York Times*, November 3.

Balz, Dan. 2010. "The GOP Takeover in the States." *The Washington Post*, November 13.

Balz, Dan, and William Branigin. 2010. "After Midterm Wins, GOP Vows to Block Obama's Agenda." *The Washington Post*, November 3.

Barry, Dan, Serge F. Kovaleski, Campbell Robertson, and Lizette Alvarez. 2012. "Race, Tragedy and Outrage Collide After a Shot in Florida." *The New York Times*, April 1.

Bartels, Larry M. 2008. *Unequal Democracy: The Political Economy of the New Gilded Age*. Princeton, NJ: Princeton University Press.

Bauman, Naomi Lopez. 2016. *State Health Care Toolkit: Ten Reforms State Lawmakers Can Implement Now*. Arlington, VA: State Policy Network.

Baumgartner, Frank R., Jeffrey M. Berry, Marie Hojnacki, David C. Kimball, and Beth L. Leech. 2009. *Lobbying and Policy Change: Who Wins, Who Loses, and Why*. Chicago: University of Chicago Press.

Baumgartner, Frank R., and Beth L. Leech. 1998. *Basic Interests: The Importance of Groups in Politics and in Political Science*. Princeton, NJ: Princeton University Press.

Bawn, Kathleen, Martin Cohen, David Karol, Seth Masket, Hans Noel, and John Zaller. 2012. "A Theory of Political Parties: Groups, Policy Demands and Nominations in American Politics." *Perspectives on Politics* 10 (3): 571–597.

Beacon Hill Institute. 2015. *The Economic Impact of New Hampshire's Renewable Portfolio Standard*. Boston, MA: Beacon Hill Institute.

Bennett, Andrew. 2010. "Process Tracing and Causal Inference." In *Rethinking Social Inquiry* (207–19), 2nd ed., ed. H. Brady and D. Collier. New York: Rowman & Littlefield.

Berlau, John. 2003. "States Put Brakes on Big Government." *Insight on the News* 19 (4): 42–44.

Berman, Ari. 2015. *Give Us the Ballot: The Modern Struggle for Voting Rights in America*. New York: Farrar, Straus and Giroux.

Berry, Jeffrey M., and David F. Arons. 2005. *A Voice for Nonprofits*. Washington, DC: Brookings Institution Press.

Biewen, John. 2002. "Corporate-Sponsored Crime Laws." *American RadioWorks*. Cited 2016, published 2002. http://americanradioworks.publicradio.org/features/corrections/laws1.html.

Bishop, Bill. 2008. *The Big Sort: Why the Clustering of Like-Minded America Is Tearing Us Apart*. New York: Houghton Mifflin.

Blendon, Robert J., and Karen Donelan. 1991. "Public Opinion and Efforts to Reform the U.S. Health Care System: Confronting Issues of Cost-Containment and Access to Care." *Stanford Law & Policy Review* 3: 146–54.

Bonica, Adam. 2016. "Avenues of Influence: On the Political Expenditures of Corporations and Their Directors and Executives." *Business and Politics* 18 (4): 367–394.

Bottari, Mary. 2017. *Infighting, Legal Questions Slow ALEC Push for Second Constitutional Convention*. Madison, WI: Center for Media and Democracy.

Bottari, Mary, and Brendan Fischer. 2013. "Efforts to Deliver 'Kill Shot' to Paid Sick Leave Tied to ALEC." *The Huffington Post*, April 3.

———. 2015. "The ALEC-Backed War on Local Democracy." *The Huffington Post*, March 30.

Bouie, Jamelle. 2013. "Republicans Admit Voter ID Laws Are Aimed at Democratic Voters." *The Daily Beast*, August 28.

Bragdon, Trevor. n.d. *State Workplace Freedom Toolkit*. Arlington, VA: State Policy Network.

Branham, J. Alexander, Stuart N. Soroka, and Christopher Wlezien. 2017. "When Do the Rich Win?" *Political Science Quarterly* 132 (1): 43–62.

Branigin, William. 2010. "Obama Reflects on 'Shellacking' in Midterm Elections." *The Washington Post*, November 3.

Brinkley, Joel. 1986. "Doctors v. Lawyers: 'A Real Nasty Fight.'" *The New York Times*, February 14.

Broder, David S., and Kathy Sawyer. 1980. "Teachers' Union Becomes Powerful Force in Party Politics." *The Washington Post*, January 20.

Broockman, David E. 2016. "Approaches to Studying Policy Representation." *Legislative Studies Quarterly* 41 (1): 181–215.

Broockman, David E., Greg F. Ferenstein, and Neil Malhotra. 2017. "Wealthy Elites' Policy Preferences and Economic Inequality: The Case of Technology Entrepreneurs." Working paper, Stanford University Graduate School of Business, Palo Alto, CA.

Broockman, David E., and Christopher Skovron. 2018. "Bias in Perceptions of Public Opinion Among Political Elites." *American Political Science Review* 112 (3): 542–63.

Brooks, Chris. 2018. "After the Wave." *Jacobin Magazine*, May 7.

Brown, Fred. 1995. "Now It's Smart: ALEC." *The Denver Post*.

Brunelli, Sam. 1990. *State Legislatures: The Next Conservative Battleground*. Washington, DC: Heritage Foundation.

Bryant, Gene. 1982. "Profile of a New Right Group: American Legislative Exchange Council." In *TEA PRgram*. University of California, Berkeley, Bancroft Library, People for the American Way Collection, Carton 6, Folder 16.

Bump, Philip. 2014. "Americans for Prosperity May Be America's Third-Biggest Political Party." *The Washington Post*, June 19.

Burkhart, Lori A. 1996. "Electric Industry Splits Over National Choice Bill." *Public Utilities Fortnightly*, September 1.

Bykowicz, Julie. 2014. "The Corporations, and Dentists, That Still Love ALEC." *Bloomberg Politics*, December 5.

Callaghan, Timothy, and Lawrence R. Jacobs. 2016. "Interest Group Conflict Over Medicaid Expansion: The Surprising Impact of Public Advocates." *American Journal of Public Health* 106 (2): 308–313.

Callahan, David. 2001. "Clash in the States." *The American Prospect*, May 29.

———. 2017. *The Givers: Wealth, Power, and Philanthropy in a New Gilded Age*. New York: Random House.

Campbell, Andrea Louise. 2003. *How Policies Make Citizens: Senior Political Activism and the American Welfare State*. Princeton, NJ: Princeton University Press.

Carpenter, Daniel. 2013. "Detecting and Measuring Capture." In *Preventing Regulatory Capture: Special Interest Influence and How to Limit It* (57–68), ed. D. Carpenter and D. Moss. New York: Cambridge University Press.

Carpenter, Daniel, and David Moss, eds. 2013. *Preventing Regulatory Capture: Special Interest Influence and How to Limit It*. New York: Cambridge University Press.

Caughey, Devin, Yiqing Xu, and Chris Warshaw. 2016. "Incremental Democracy: The Policy Effects of Partisan Control of State Government." *Journal of Politics* 79 (4): 1342–1358.

CBO. 1994. *A Preliminary Analysis of the Health Security Act as Reported by the Senate Committee on Finance*. Washington, DC: Congressional Budget Office.

———. 2004. *The Effects of Tort Reform: Evidence from the States*. Washington, DC: Congressional Budget Office.

———. 2010. "Letter from Douglas Elmendorf to House Speaker Nancy Pelosi, March 18 2010." Congressional Budget Office, Washington, DC.

CDC. 2011. "State Preemption of Local Tobacco Control Policies Restricting Smoking, Advertising, and Youth Access—United States, 2000–2010." *Morbidity and Mortality Weekly Report* 60 (33): 1124–27.

Center for Media and Democracy. 2015. *Michigan ALEC Politicians*. Madison, MI: Center for Media and Democracy.

Center for Policy Alternatives. 2006. *Comparing ALEC and CPA*. Washington, DC: Center for Policy Alternatives.

Center on Budget and Policy Priorities. 2017. *Policy Basics: Where Do Our State Tax Dollars Go?* Washington, DC: Center on Budget and Policy Priorities.

Cheon, Andrew, and Johannes Urpelainen. 2013. "How Do Competing Interest Groups Influence Environmental Policy? The Case of Renewable Electricity in Industrialized Democracies, 1989–2007." *Political Studies* 61 (4): 874–897.

Chilcote, Samuel D. 1993. "MEMORANDUM to the Members of the Executive Committee (November 19, 1993)." University of California, San Francisco, Legacy Tobacco Archives.

Citizens for a Sound Economy. n.d. *Mobilizing Grassroots America Behind Ideas*. Washington, DC: Citizens for a Sound Economy.

Clavel, Pierre. 1989. *The Progressive City: Planning and Participation, 1969–1984*. New Brunswick, NJ: Rutgers University Press.

Clemens, Elisabeth S. 2017. "Distrust in Distant Powers: Misalignments of Political and Social Geography in American Democracy." *Items: Insights from the Social Sciences*, August 8. Referenced 2018, published 2017. https://items.ssrc.org/misalignments-of-political-and-social-geography-in-american-democracy/.

Clinton, Joshua D., and Michael W. Sances. 2017. "The Politics of Policy: The Initial Mass Political Effects of Medicaid Expansion in the States." *American Political Science Review* 112 (1): 167–85.

Clymer, Adam. 2007. "Former Rep. Henry Hyde Is Dead at 83." *The New York Times*, November 30.

Cole, Michelle. 2012. "ALEC Gains Foothold in Oregon, with One-Fourth of Legislators as Members." *The Oregonian*, May 26.

Common Cause. 2011. *Legislating Under the Influence: Money, Power, and the American Legislative Exchange Council*. Washington, DC: Common Cause.

Conniff, Ruth. 2006. "Ruth Conniff: Hope Is in the States." *The Progressive*, March 7.

Conservative Digest. 1985. "ALEC—The Most Dangerously Effective Organization." University of California, Berkeley Bancroft Library, People for the American Way Collection, Carton 6, Folder 17.

Converse, Philip. 1964. "The Nature of Belief Systems in Mass Publics." In *Ideology and Discontent* (206–61), ed. D. Apter. New York: Free Press.

Cooper, David. 2016. *Economic Snapshot: The Federal Minimum Wage Has Been Eroded by Decades of Inaction*. Washington, DC: Economic Policy Institute.

Cooper, Seth. 2008. "Government Killed the Internet Star: How State Sales Taxes Threaten the Online Commerce." *Inside ALEC*, July.

Coppock, Alexander and Donald P. Green. 2016. "Is Voting Habit Forming? New Evidence from Experiments and Regression Discontinuities." *American Journal of Political Science* 60 (4): 1044–62.

Corrado, Anthony. 2013. *Hiding in Plain Sight: The Problem of Transparency in Political Finance*. Washington, DC: Committee for Economic Development.

Council of State Governments. 1935a. "Portrait of an Association." In *Book of the States*, Chapter 2. Denver, CO: Council of State Governments.
———. 1935b. "Tax Troubles." In *Book of the States*, Chapter 7. Denver, CO: Council of State Governments.
———. 1935c. "Entente Cordiale." In *Book of the States*, Chapter 8. Denver, CO: Council of State Governments.
———. 1937. *Book of the States*. Denver, CO: Council of State Governments.
———. 2012. *Book of the States*. Lexington, KY: Council of State Governments.
Crawford, Alan. 1980. *Thunder on the Right*. New York: Pantheon.
Cray, Charlie. 2011. *The Lewis Powell Memo: Corporate Blueprint to Dominate Democracy*. Madison, WI: Center for Media and Democracy.
CSG. 1944. *Unemployment Compensation in the Post-War Period*. Chicago: Council of State Governments.
Culpepper, Pepper D. 2010. *Quiet Politics and Business Power: Corporate Control in Europe and Japan*. New York: Cambridge University Press.
Cunningham, Paige Winfield. 2015. "Meet the Group Blocking Obamacare's Medicaid Expansion." *The Washington Examiner*, April 8.
Cuzzi, Michael. 2014. "Michael Cuzzi: Maine Heritage Policy Center Loses Both Its Way and Its Credibility." *Portland Press Herald*, September 21.
Dagan, David, and Steven M. Teles. 2012. "The Conservative War on Prisons." *The Washington Monthly*, November/December.
———. 2016. *Prison Break: Why Conservatives Turned Against Mass Incarceration*. New York: Oxford University Press.
Dann, Carrie. 2016. "Maine Governor: Drug Dealers Often 'Impregnate a Young White Girl,'" *NBC News*, January 7. Referenced 2017, published 2016. https://www.nbcnews.com/politics/politics-news/maine-governor-drug-dealers-often-impregnate-young-white-girl-n492501.
Davey, Monica. 2016. "With Fewer Members, a Diminished Political Role for Wisconsin Unions." *The New York Times*, February 27.
Davis, James H. 1965. "Colorado Under the Klan." *Colorado Magazine* 42 (2): 93–108.
Dennis, William C. 2001. "Funding Liberty." *SPN News*, Spring, 4.
DiSalvo, Daniel. 2015. *Government against Itself: Public Union Power and Its Consequences*. New York: Oxford University Press.
Doherty, Brian. 2007. *Radicals for Capitalism: A Freewheeling History of the Modern American Libertarian Movement*. New York: Public Affairs.
Doherty, Shawn. 2011. "Vital Signs: State GOP Health Bills Mirror Model ALEC Legislation." *The Capital Times*, March 27.
Dolmetsch, Chris. 2013. "Amazon, Overstock Lose Challenge to N.Y. Web Sales Tax." *Bloomberg Technology*, March 28.
Downs, Anthony. 1957. *An Economic Theory of Democracy*. New York: Harper and Row.
Dreyfuss, Robert, and Peter H. Stone. 1996. "MediKill." *Mother Jones*, January–February.
Drezner, Daniel. 2017. *The Ideas Industry: How Pessimists, Partisans, and Plutocrats Are Transforming the Marketplace of Ideas*. New York: Oxford University Press.
Drum, Kevin. 2011. "Defunding the Democratic Party." *Mother Jones*, February 17.
Drutman, Lee. 2015. *The Business of America Is Lobbying*. New York: Oxford University Press.
Drutman, Lee, and Steven M. Teles. 2015. "A New Agenda for Political Reform." *Washington Monthly*, March/April/May.
The Economist. 2018. "Behind the Teacher Strikes That Have Roiled Five States." May 5.
Edsall, Thomas B. 1984. *The New Politics of Inequality*. New York: W.W. Norton.
———. 2003. "Battle Over Damage Awards Takes a More Partisan Turn." *The Washington Post*, August 10.
Egan, Paul. 2015. "Former GOP Lawmaker Lund to Head Anti-Tax Group." *The Detroit Free Press*, May 20.

Eggert, David. 2012. "Gov. Snyder Signs Right-to-Work Law, Calls It 'major day in Michigan's history.'" *MLive*, December 11. Referenced 2017, published 2012. https://www.mlive.com/news/index.ssf/2012/12/gov_snyder_signs_right-to-work.html.

Eilperin, Juliet. 2012. "Climate Skeptic Group Works to Reverse Renewable Energy Mandates." *The Washington Post*, November 24.

Ellwood, David T., and Glenn Fine. 1987. "The Impact of Right-to-Work Laws on Union Organizing." *Journal of Political Economy* 95 (2): 250–273.

Eng, James. 2015. "Google, Apple, Microsoft Join Business Pledge to Fight Climate Change." *NBC News*, July 27. Referenced 2017, published 2015. https://www.nbcnews.com/science/environment/google-apple-microsoft-join-business-pledge-fight-climate-change-n399296.

Enns, Peter K. 2015. "Relative Policy Support and Coincidental Representation." *Perspectives on Politics* 13 (4): 1053–1064.

Erikson, Robert S. 2015. "Income Inequality and Policy Responsiveness." *Annual Review of Political Science* 18: 11–29.

Erikson, Robert S., Gerald C. Wright, and John P. McIver. 1989. "Political Parties, Public Opinion, and State Policy in the United States." *American Political Science Review* 83 (3): 729–750.

———. 1993. *Statehouse Democracy*. New York: Cambridge University Press.

Estlund, Cynthia, and William E. Forbath. 2014. "Op-Ed: The Supreme Court Ruling on *Harris v. Quinn* Is a Blow for Unions." *The New York Times*, July 2.

Ettlinger, Michael, Tim McFeeley, Gregory Moore, Miles Rapoport, Joel Rogers, and Gloria Totten. 2005a. *A Starter SAC?* Washington, DC: State Action Collaborative.

———. 2005b. *Winning in the States: State Action Collaborative (SAC)*. Washington, DC: State Action Collaborative.

Fang, Lee. 2012. "Pro-'Right to Work' Groups in Michigan Outspend Union Counterparts." *The Nation*, December 8.

Fang, Lee, and Nick Surgey. 2018. "Right-Wing, Business-Funded Groups Are Preparing to Use the Janus Decision to Bleed Unions, Internal Documents Show." *The Intercept*, June 30.

Farnam, Henry W. 1911. "Practical Methods in Labor Legislation." *American Labor Legislation Review* 1: 5–16.

Farney, Dennis. 1985. "New Right Group Promotes Reagan Ideology in State Capitals From Boise to Baton Rouge." *The Wall Street Journal*, August 7.

Feigenbaum, James, Alexander Hertel-Fernandez, and Vanessa Williamson. 2018. "From the Bargaining Table to the Ballot Box: Political Effects of Right to Work Laws." Working paper no. 24259, National Bureau of Economic Research, Cambridge, MA.

Ferguson, Mike. 2013. "Business Groups Rate Missouri Legislators' Efforts." *Missouri Viewpoints with Mike Ferguson*, March 25. Referenced 2016, published 2013. http://missouriviewpoints.com/business-groups-rate-missouri-legislators-efforts/.

Ferguson, Thomas, and Joel Rogers. 1986. *Right Turn: The Decline of the Democrats and the Future of American Politics*. New York: Hill & Wang.

FGA. 2015. "Transcript of State Solutions for *King v. Burwell* Conference Call." Foundation for Government Accountability, Naples, FL.

Finger, Leslie. 2018. "Interest Group Influence and the Two Faces of Power." *American Politics Research*. Published Online.

Fischer, Brendan. 2012a. *Michigan Passes "Right to Work" Containing Verbatim Language from ALEC Model Bill*. Madison, WI: Center for Media and Democracy.

———. 2012b. *Wisconsin: The Hijacking of a State*. Madison, WI: Center for Media and Democracy.

———. 2013. *U.S. Supreme Court Strikes Down Another ALEC Voting Bill*. Madison, WI: Center for Media and Democracy.

———. 2014a. *ALEC Politicians Caught Plagiarizing ALEC Bill, Drafting Error and All*. Madison, WI: Center for Media and Democracy.

———. 2014b. *How ALEC Helps Big Telecom Change State Laws for Corporate Gain*. Madison, WI: Center for Media and Democracy.

Fischer, Brendan, and Mary Bottari. 2015. "Meet ALEC's Little Brother, ACCE." *The Nation*, June 23.

Flavin, Patrick. 2016. "Labor Union Strength and the Equality of Political Representation." *British Journal of Political Science*, First View.

Flavin, Patrick, and Michael T. Hartney. 2015. "When Government Subsidizes Its Own: Collective Bargaining Laws as Agents of Political Mobilization." *American Journal of Political Science* 59 (4): 896–911.

Follman, Mark, and Lauren Williams. 2013. "Actually, Stand Your Ground Played a Major Role in the Trayvon Martin Case." *Mother Jones*, July 19.

Forbes. 2016. "America's Largest Private Companies: Koch Industries." *Forbes*. https://www.forbes.com/largest-private-companies/list/.

———. 2017. "The Richest People in America." *Forbes*. https://www.forbes.com/forbes-400/list/.

Fouirnaies, Alexander. 2018. "When Are Agenda Setters Valuable?" *American Journal of Political Science* 62 (1): 176–91.

Fouirnaies, Alexander, and Andrew B. Hall. 2018. "How Do Interest Groups Seek Access to Committees?" *American Journal of Political Science* 62 (1): 132–47.

Fraley, Brian. 2010. *The Time Is Now to Reform Labor Laws Which Threaten Our State's Future*. Madison, WI: John K. MacIver Institute for Public Policy.

Free, Lloyd A., and Hadley Cantril. 1967. *The Political Beliefs of Americans: A Study of Public Opinion*. New Brunswick, NJ: Rutgers University Press.

Freeman, Richard B., and Eunice Han. 2012. "The War Against Public Sector Collective Bargaining in the US." *Journal of Industrial Relations* 54 (3): 386–408.

Freeman, Richard B., and James L. Medoff. 1984. *What Do Unions Do?* New York: Basic Books.

Frendreis, John, Alan R. Gitelson, Shannon Jenkins, and Douglas D. Roscoe. 2003. "Testing Spatial Models of Elections: The Influence of Voters and Elites on Candidate Issue Positions." *Legislative Studies Quarterly* 28 (1): 77–101.

Galewitz, Phil. 2014. "Business Groups Split on Medicaid Expansion." *Kaiser Health News*, March 10.

Galvin, Daniel J. 2012. "The Transformation of Political Institutions: Investments in Institutional Resources and Gradual Change in the National Party Committees." *Studies in American Political Development* 26 (1): 50–70.

———. 2016. "Obama Built a Policy Legacy. But He Didn't Do Enough to Build the Democratic Party." *The Washington Post, Monkey Cage Blog*, November 16. Referenced 2017, published 2016. https://www.washingtonpost.com/news/monkey-cage/wp/2016/11/16/obama-built-a-policy-legacy-but-didnt-do-enough-to-build-the-democratic-party/.

Gardner, Greg. 2012. "Koch Brothers' Americans for Prosperity Are Leading the Charge for Snyder's 'Right-to-Work' Bill." *The Detroit Free Press*, December 6.

Garfield, Rachel, and Anthony Damico. 2016. *The Coverage Gap: Uninsured Poor Adults in States That Do Not Expand Medicaid*. Washington, DC: Kaiser Family Foundation.

Gerken, Heather K. 2012. "A New Progressive Federalism." *Democracy*, Spring (24).

Gilens, Martin. 2012. *Affluence and Influence: Economic Inequality and Political Power in America*. Princeton, NJ: Princeton University Press.

Gilens, Martin, and Benjamin I. Page. 2014. "Testing Theories of American Politics: Elites, Interest Groups, and Average Citizens." *Perspectives on Politics* 12 (3): 564–581.

Glauber, Bill. 2011. "Fitzgerald Brothers a Powerful Force in Wisconsin Politics." *Milwaukee Journal Sentinel*, June 25.

Glauber, Bill, and Don Walker. 2011. "Protests at Capitol Keep Growing." *Milwaukee Journal Sentinel*, February 18.

Gold, Matea. 2014a. "Americans for Prosperity Plows Millions into Building Conservative Ground Force." *The Washington Post*, October 6.

———. 2014b. "Koch-Backed Political Network, Built to Shield Donors, Raised $400 Million in 2012 Elections." *The Washington Post*, January 5.

———. 2015. "Wealthy Donors on Left Launch New Plan to Wrest Back Control in the States." *The Washington Post*, April 12.
Goldberg, Michelle. 2014. "The Rise of the Progressive City." *The Nation*, April 2.
Goldstein, Amy. *Janesville: An American Story*. New York: Simon & Schuster.
Goldwater Institute. 2015. *2015 Annual Report*. Phoenix, AZ: Goldwater Institute.
Goodnough, Abby, and Mitch Smith. 2017. "Kansas Governor Vetoes Medicaid Expansion, Setting Stage for Showdown." *The New York Times*, March 30.
Graham, David A. 2017. "Red State, Blue City." *The Atlantic*, March.
Grann, David. 1997. "Robespierre of the Right." *The New Republic*, October 27.
Grassroots America. 1994. "The Demise of Clintoncare." University of California, San Francisco, Legacy Tobacco Archives.
Graves, Lisa. 2011. "ALEC Exposed: The Koch Connection." *The Nation*, July 12.
———. 2012a. *Backgrounder: The History of the NRA/ALEC Gun Agenda*. Madison, WI: Center for Media and Democracy.
———. 2012b. *Buying Influence: How the American Legislative Exchange Council Uses Corporate-Funded "Scholarships" to Send Lawmakers on Trips with Corporate Lobbyists*. Common Cause, Center for Media and Democracy, and DBA Press.
Graves, Lisa, Jennifer Page, Brendan Fischer, and Mary Bottari. 2011. *A Comparison of ALEC and NCSL*. Madison, WI: Center for Media and Democracy.
Greeley, Brendan. 2012a. "ALEC's Secrets Revealed; Corporations Flee." *Bloomberg Businessweek*, May 3.
———. 2012b. "What Occupy Wall Street Gets Wrong About ALEC." *Bloomberg Businessweek*, March 1.
Greeley, Brendan, and Alison Fitzgerald. 2011. "Pssst . . . Wanna Buy a Law?" *Bloomberg Businessweek*, December 1.
Greenblatt, Alan. 2003. "What Makes Alec Smart?" *Governing the States and Localities*, October.
———. 2011. "ALEC Enjoys a New Wave of Influence and Criticism." *Governing the States and Localities*, December.
———. 2013. "Newbies Infiltrate State Legislative Chambers." *Governing the States and Localities*, January.
———. 2014. "ALEC Goes Local." *Governing the States and Localities*, June.
Greenhouse, Steven. 2016a. "The Door-to-Door Union Killers: Rightwing Foundation Takes Labor Fight to the Streets." *The Guardian*, March 10.
———. 2016b. "How the $15 Minimum Wage Went From Laughable to Viable." *The New York Times*, April 1.
Greenstone, J. David. 1969. *Labor in American Politics*. New York: Knopf.
Griffin, Mark. 2016. "RE: Question from Reporter about Overstock.com Funding of ALEC." Center for Media and Democracy. Cited 2016, published 2014.http://www.prwatch.org/files/appendix.pdf.
Grogan, Colleen M., and Sunggeun (Ethan) Park. 2017. "The Racial Divide in State Medicaid Expansions." *Journal of Health Politics, Policy and Law* 42 (3): 539–572.
Grossmann, Matt, and David A. Hopkins. 2015. "Ideological Republicans and Group Interest Democrats: The Asymmetry of American Party Politics." *Perspectives on Politics* 13 (1): 119–139.
———. 2016. *Asymmetric Politics: Ideological Republicans and Group Interest Democrats*. New York: Oxford University Press.
Grumbach, Jake, and Paul Pierson. 2018. "Are Large Corporations Politically Moderate? Using Money in Politics to Infer the Preferences of Business." Unpublished manuscript, University of California, Berkeley, Travers Department of Political Science.
Grumbach, Jake M. 2017. "From Backwaters to Major Policymakers: Policy Polarization in the States, 1970–2014." Unpublished manuscript, University of California, Berkeley, Travers Department of Political Science.

Hacker, Jacob S. 2001. "Learning from Defeat? Political Analysis and the Failure of Health Care Reform in the United States." *British Journal of Political Science* 31 (1): 61–94.
———. 2002. *The Divided Welfare State*. New York: Cambridge University Press.
———. 2008. *The Great Risk Shift: The New Economic Insecurity and the Decline of the American Dream*. New York: Oxford University Press.
Hacker, Jacob S., and Paul Pierson. 2002. "Business Power and Social Policy: Employers and the Formation of the American Welfare State." *Politics and Society* 30 (2): 277–325.
———. 2005. *Off Center: The Republican Revolution and the Erosion of American Democracy*. New Haven, CT: Yale University Press.
———. 2010a. *Winner-Take-All Politics: How Washington Made the Rich Richer—and Turned Its Back on the Middle Class*. New York: Simon & Schuster.
———. 2010b. "Winner-Take-All Politics: Public Policy, Political Organization, and the Precipitous Rise of Top Incomes in the United States." *Politics and Society* 38 (2): 152–204.
———. 2014. "After the "Master Theory": Downs, Schattschneider, and the Rebirth of Policy-Focused Analysis." *Perspectives on Politics* 12 (3): 643–662.
———. 2016. *American Amnesia: How the War on Government Led Us to Forget What Made America Prosper*. New York: Simon & Schuster.
Hall, Andrew B. 2016. "Systemic Effects of Campaign Spending: Evidence from Corporate Contribution Bans in US State Legislatures." *Political Science Research and Methods* 4 (2): 343–359.
Hall, Dee. 2013. "Report: Investigation Targets Scott Walker Recall Campaign, Political Groups." *Wisconsin State Journal*, November 18.
Hall, Richard L., and Alan V. Deardorff. 2006. "Lobbying as Legislative Subsidy." *American Political Science Review* 100 (1): 69–84.
Hall, Richard L., and Frank W. Wayman. 1990. "Buying Time: Moneyed Interests and the Mobilization of Bias in Congressional Committees." *American Political Science Review* 84 (3): 797–820.
Hamburger, Tom, Joby Warrick, and Chris Mooney. 2015. "This Conservative Group Is Tired of Being Accused of Climate Denial—and Is Fighting Back." *The Washington Post*, April 5.
Hansen, John Mark. 1991. *Gaining Access: Congress and the Farm Lobby, 1919–1981*. Chicago: University of Chicago Press.
Hartney, Michael T. 2014. "Turning Out Teachers: The Causes and Consequences of Teacher Political Activism in the Postwar United States." PhD diss., University of Notre Dame, Dept. of Political Science, South Bend, IN.
Hawkins, Beth. 2013. "ALEC Declares Itself Exempt from Public-Disclosure Laws, and Is Challenged." *The Minnesota Post*, August 22.
Healy, Patrick, and Monica Davey. 2015. "Behind Scott Walker, a Longstanding Conservative Alliance Against Unions." *The New York Times*, June 8.
Hernandez, Sergio. 2011. "Cheat Sheet: What's Really Going On With Wisconsin's Budget." *ProPublica*, February 22.
Herrera, Christie. 2011. *The State Legislators Guide to Repealing Obamacare*. Washington, DC: American Legislative Exchange Council.
Herrick, Devon M. 2015. *Medicaid Expansion: Texas Should Chart Its Own Course*. Dallas, TX: National Center for Policy Analysis.
Hertel-Fernandez, Alexander, and Konstantin Kashin. 2015. "Capturing Business Power Across the States with Text Reuse." Unpublished working paper. Harvard University, Dept. of Government, Cambridge, MA.
Hertel-Fernandez, Alexander, Jason Sclar, and Theda Skocpol. 2016a. "When Wealthy Political Contributors Join Forces: U.S. Donor Consortia on the Left And Right." Paper presented at Annual Meeting of American Political Science Association, Philadelphia, PA.
Hertel-Fernandez, Alexander, and Theda Skocpol. 2015. "How the Right Trounced Liberals in the States." *Democracy: A Journal of Ideas*, Winter (39).

———. 2016. "Billionaires Against Big Business." Unpublished working paper. Harvard University, Dept. of Government, Cambridge, MA.

Hertel-Fernandez, Alexander, Theda Skocpol, and Daniel Lynch. 2016b. "Business Associations, Conservative Networks, and the Ongoing Republican War over Medicaid Expansion." *Journal of Health Politics, Policy and Law* 41 (2): 239–286.

Highton, Benjamin. 2017. "Voter Identification Laws and Turnout in the United States." *Annual Review of Political Science* 20: 149–167.

Hillman, Amy J., and Michael A. Hitt. 1999. "Corporate Political Strategy Formulation: A Model of Approach, Participation, and Strategy Decisions." *Academy of Management Review* 24 (4): 825–842.

Hillman, Amy J., Gerald D. Keim, and Douglas Schuler. 2004. "Corporate Political Activity: A Review and Research Agenda." *Journal of Management* 30 (6): 837–857.

Hoberock, Barbara. 1994. "Rallies Held for, Against Clinton's Health Proposal." *Tulsa World*, April 7.

Hoffman, John. 2012. "ColorofChange.org and Advocacy: The ALEC Campaign." *Nonprofit Quarterly*, May 1.

Hohmann, James. 2017. "The Daily 202: Koch Network Laying Groundwork to Fundamentally Transform America's Education System." *The Washington Post*, January 30.

Holbein, John B., and Adam Dynes. 2018. "Noisy Retrospection: The Effect of Party Control on Policy Outcomes." Unpublished working paper.

Hopkins, David A. 2017. *Red Fighting Blue: How Geography and Electoral Rules Polarize American Politics*. New York: Cambridge University Press.

Hopkins, Daniel J. 2018. *The Increasingly United States: How and Why American Political Behavior Nationalized*. Chicago: University of Chicago Press.

Horn, Bernie, ed. 2006. *Progressive Agenda for the States 2006: State Policy Leading America*. Washington, DC: Center for Policy Alternatives.

Hough, Michael. 2011. "Public Employee Unions: Pushing Government to Bankruptcy." *Inside ALEC*, January.

Human Events. 1973. "Capital Briefs." *Human Events*, November 24, 2.

———. 1975. "Vital Role of the American Conservative Union." *Human Events*, December 6, 10–13.

Humphrey, Theresa. 1995. "National Organizations Provide Basics and Background for Legislators." *The Associated Press*, April 15.

Hunter, Robert. 1986. "Reform Insurance, Not Liability Law; Taming the Latest Insurance 'Crisis.'" *The New York Times*, April 13.

Hunter, William A. 1980. *The "New Right": A Growing Force in State Politics*. Edited by T. W. Bonnett. Washington, DC: Conference on Alternative State and Local Policies and the Center to Protect Workers' Rights.

Ishmael, Patrick. 2013. *Medicaid Expansion Under Obamacare Is Wrong for Missouri*. Saint Louis, MO: Show-Me Institute.

———. 2014. *Obamacare's Medicaid Expansion as "Job Creator"? Not So Fast*. Saint Louis, MO: Show-Me Institute.

Ismail, M. Asif. 2003. *Enron's Deregulation Fight*." Center for Public Integrity. Referenced 2017, published 2003. https://www.publicintegrity.org/2003/01/06/3161/enrons-deregulation-fight.

Jacobson, Louis. 2005. "New Organization to Push Liberal Measures in State Legislatures." *Roll Call*, June 23.

John M. Olin Foundation. 1985. "1985 Annual Report." University of California, Berkeley, Bancroft Library, People for the American Way Collection, Container 50.

———. 1989. "1989 Annual Report." University of California, Berkeley, Bancroft Library, People for the American Way Collection, Container 50.

Johnson, Brad, and Josh Israel. 2012. "EXPOSED: The 19 Public Corporations Funding the Climate Denier Think Tank Heartland Institute." *ThinkProgress*, February 17. Referenced

2017, published 2012. https://thinkprogress.org/exposed-the-19-public-corporations-funding-the-climate-denier-think-tank-heartland-institute-2b4a345ab636/.
Johnson, M. Alex. 2010. "States Working Harder to Collect Online Sales Taxes." *NBC News*, September 17. Referenced 2017, published 2010. http://www.nbcnews.com/id/39159604/ns/business-personal_finance/t/states-working-harder-collect-online-sales-taxes.
Jones, Andy, and Jonathan Moody. 2009. "Integrity in Elections: Proactively Combating Voter Fraud in the States." *Inside ALEC*, Special Report, July.
Jones, David K. 2013. "Michigan Battle over 'Obamacare' Becomes Fight for Soul of GOP." *Al Jazeera*, October 6.
Judis, John. 2001. *The Paradox of American Democracy: Elites, Special Interests, and the Betrayal of the Public Trust*. New York: Routledge Press.
Kaiser, Robert G. 1976. "NEA 'Awakening' Politically for '76." *The Washington Post*, March 16.
Kalla, Joshua L., and David Broockman. 2016. "Campaign Contributions Facilitate Access to Congressional Officials: A Randomized Field Experiment." *American Journal of Political Science* 60 (3): 545–558.
Kalla, Joshua L., and Ethan Porter. 2018. "Correcting Bias in Perceptions of Public Opinion Among American Elected Officials: Results from a Randomized Field Experiment." Unpublished working paper.
Kallick, David Dyssegaard. 2002. *Progressive Think Tanks: What Exists, What's Missing?* Washington, DC: Open Society Institute.
Karol, David. 2009. *Party Position Change in American Politics*. New York: Cambridge University Press.
Katakey, Rakteem. 2017. "Shell Plans to Spend $1 Billion a Year on Clean Energy by 2020." *Bloomberg*, July 10.
Katznelson, Ira, Kim Geiger, and Daniel Kryder. 1993. "Limiting Liberalism: The Southern Veto in Congress, 1933–1950." *Political Science Quarterly* 108 (2): 283–306.
Kaufman, Dan. 2018. *The Fall of Wisconsin*. New York: W. W. Norton.
Kersten, Andrew E. 2011. *The Battle for Wisconsin: Scott Walker and the Attack on the Progressive Tradition*. New York: Farrar, Straus and Giroux.
Kessler, Glenn. 2014. "'Billions' Spent on Attacking Obamacare?" *The Washington Post*, April 4.
Kielsgard, Kirsten. 2008. "35 Years of Serving State Legislators: The American Legislative Exchange Council, Then and Now." *Inside ALEC*, July.
Kiely, Kathy. 2016. "A Bipartisan Campaign Finance Reform Bill?" *Mother Jones*, September 12.
Kim, Sung Eun, and Yotam Margalit. 2017. "Informed Preferences? The Impact of Unions on Workers' Policy Views." *American Journal of Political Science* 61 (3): 728–743.
Kincaid, John. 1990. "From Cooperative to Coercive Federalism." *Annals of the American Academy of Political and Social Sciences* 509 (1): 139–152.
Kogan, Richard. 2017. *Constitutional Balanced Budget Amendment Poses Serious Risks*. Washington, DC: Center on Budget and Policy Priorities.
Kollman, Ken. 1998. *Outside Lobbying: Public Opinion and Interest Group Strategies*. Princeton, NJ: Princeton University Press.
Kopan, Tal. 2013. "Report: Think Tanks Tied to Kochs." *Politico*, November 13.
Krimmel, Katherine. 2017. "The Efficiencies and Pathologies of Special Interest Partisanship." *Studies in American Political Development* 31 (2): 149–69.
Kristof, Nicholas D. 1986. "Insurance Woes Spur Many States to Amend Law on Liability Suits." *The New York Times*, March 31.
Kroll, Andy. 2011. "What's Happening in Wisconsin Explained." *Mother Jones*, March 17.
———. 2012. "Americans for Prosperity Lures Michigan Right-to-Work Fans With Gas Cards, Free Food." *Mother Jones*, December 11.
———. 2014a. "This Is the Left's Confidential $100 Million Plan to Win Back the States." *Mother Jones*, November 14.
———. 2014b. "This Machine Turned Colorado Blue. Now It May Be Dems' Best Hope to Save the Senate." *Mother Jones*, October 29.

Kurtz, Karl T. 1999. "The History of Us." *State Legislatures*, July/August.
La Raja, Raymond J., and Brian F. Schaffner. 2015. *Campaign Finance and Political Polarization: When Purists Prevail*. Ann Arbor: University of Michigan Press.
LaFaive, Michael D. 2012. *Right-to-Work and the Mackinac Center*. Midland, MI: Mackinac Center for Public Policy.
Lafer, Gordon. 2017. *The One Percent Solution*. Ithaca, NY: Cornell University Press.
Laffer, Arthur, Donna Arduin, and Wayne Winegarden. 2009. *The Prognosis for National Health Insurance: A Texas Perspective*. Austin, TX: Texas Public Policy Foundation.
Landis, Diane M. 1986. "Associations: January 27th." *The Washington Post*, January 27.
Leighley, Jan E., and Jonathan Nagler. 2007. "Unions, Voter Turnout, and Class Bias in the U.S. Electorate, 1964–2004." *Journal of Politics* 69 (2): 430–441.
Lenz, Gabriel S. 2012. *Follow the Leader? How Voters Respond to Politicians' Policies and Performance*. Chicago: University of Chicago Press.
Levi, Margaret. 1977. *Bureaucratic Insurgency: The Case of Police Unions*. Lexington, MA: Lexington Books.
Levinthal, Dave. 2015. *Koch Brothers Supersize Higher-Ed Spending*. Center for Public Integrity. Referenced 2017, published 2015. https://www.publicintegrity.org/2015/12/15/19007/koch-brothers-supersize-higher-ed-spending.
Lichtblau, Eric. 2012. "Martin Death Spurs Group to Readjust Policy Focus." *The New York Times*, April 17.
Lieb, David A. 2014. "Ex–GOP Senator Now Lobbying for Medicaid Expansion." *HuffPost Politics*, January 24.
Light, John. 2015. "Score One for ALEC: West Virginia Is First State to Repeal a Renewable Energy Standard." *Grist*, February 5.
Liptak, Adam. 2017. "Supreme Court Will Hear Case on Mandatory Fees to Unions." *The New York Times*, September 28.
Lipton, Eric. 2011. "Billionaire Brothers' Money Plays Role in Wisconsin Dispute." *The New York Times*, February 21.
Lopez, Manny. 2013. "Mackinac Center President Honored for Leadership." *Michigan Capitol Confidential*, October 1.
Lukes, Steven. 2005. *Power: A Radical View*, 2nd ed. London: Palgrave.
Mack, Charles. 1997. *Business, Politics, and the Practice of Government Relations*. Westport, CT: Quorum Books.
MacLean, Nancy. 2017. *Democracy in Chains: The Deep History of the Radical Right's Stealth Plan for America*. New York: Viking Press.
Magoc, Ethan. 2012. "Flurry of Photo ID Laws Tied to Conservative ALEC Group." *News21*, August 20.
Mahoney, James, and Kathleen Thelen, eds. 2009. *Explaining Institutional Change: Ambiguity, Agency, and Power*. New York: Cambridge University Press.
Maine's Majority Education Fund, and Center for Media and Democracy. 2013. *Fooling Maine*. Maine's Majority Education Fund and the Center for Media and Democracy.
Malott, Robert H. 1990. "The Emerging Importance of State Legislation." Paper presented at National Orientation Conference for New State Legislators, American Legislative Exchange Council, Washington, DC, November 30.
Mann, Thomas E., and Norman J. Ornstein. 2012. *It's Even Worse Than It Looks: How the American Constitutional System Collided With the New Politics of Extremism*. New York: Basic Books.
Manuse, Andrew. 2016. *What I Learned from the ALEC 2012 Spring Task Force Summit: My Trip to the ALEC Conference in Charlotte, N.C., Part II*. Referenced January 2016, published 2012. http://amanuse.rlcnh.org/2012/05/13/what-i-learned-from-the-alec-2012-spring-task-force-summit-my-trip-to-the-alec-conference-in-charlotte-n-c-part-ii/.
Marley, Patrick. 2011. "Bill Voiding Sick Leave Law Sent to Walker." *Milwaukee Journal Sentinel*, April 12.

Martin, Cathie Jo. 2000. *Stuck in Neutral: Business and the Politics of Human Capital Investment Policy*. Princeton, NJ: Princeton University Press.

Martin, Cathie Jo, and Duane Swank. 2012. *The Political Construction of Business Interests: Coordination, Growth, and Equality*. New York: Cambridge University Press.

Martin, Isaac. 2013. *Rich People's Movements: Grassroots Campaigns to Untax the One Percent*. New York: Oxford University Press.

Martin, Tim. 2012a. "Michigan Gov. Rick Snyder: Right to Work 'on the agenda' But No Decisions Made." *MLive*, December 4. Referenced 2017, published 2012. https://www.mlive.com/politics/index.ssf/2012/12/michigan_gov_ricksnyder_right.html.

———. 2012b. "Michigan Legislature: House Republicans Hang On to Slim Majority over Democrats." *MLive*, November 7. Referenced 2017, published 2012. https://www.mlive.com/politics/index.ssf/2012/11/michigan_legislature_republica.html.

Masters, Marick F., and Gerald D. Keim. 1985. "Determinants of PAC Participation Among Large Corporations." *Journal of Politics* 47 (4): 1158–1173.

Mayer, Jane. 2010. "Covert Operations: The Billionaire Brothers Who Are Waging a War Against Obama." *The New Yorker*, August 30.

———. 2012. "The Kochs vs. Cato." *The New Yorker*, March 1.

———. 2013a. "Is IKEA the New Model for the Conservative Movement?" *The New Yorker*, November 15.

———. 2013b. "Koch Pledge Tied to Congressional Climate Inaction." *The New Yorker*, June 30.

———. 2016. *Dark Money: The Hidden History of the Billionaires Behind the Rise of the Radical Right*. New York: Doubleday Press.

Mazerov, Michael. 2010. *Amazon's Arguments Against Collecting Sales Taxes Do Not Withstand Scrutiny*. Washington, DC: Center on Budget and Policy Priorities.

McCabe, David, and Mario Trujillo. 2015. "Overnight Tech: Zuckerberg Group Rolls Out Next Part of Immigration Push." *The Hill*, December 10.

McCarty, Nolan, Keith T. Poole, and Howard Rosenthal. 2006. *Polarized America: The Dance of Ideology and Unequal Riches*. Cambridge, MA: MIT Press.

McCarty, Nolan, and Lawrence Rothenberg. 1996. "Commitment and the Campaign Contribution Contract." *American Journal of Political Science* 40 (3): 872–904.

———. 2000. "Coalitional Maintenance: Politicians, Parties, and Organized Groups." *American Politics Research* 28 (3): 291–308.

McCarty, Nolan, and Eric Schickler. 2018. "On the Theory of Parties." *Annual Review of Political Science* 21: 175–93.

McConnell, Grant. 1966. *Private Power and American Democracy*. New York: Alfred Knopf.

McGirr, Lisa. 2001. *Suburban Warriors: The Origins of the New American Right*. Princeton, NJ: Princeton University Press.

McGuinn, Patrick. 2006. *No Child Left Behind and the Transformation of Federal Education Policy, 1965–2005*. Lawrence: University Press of Kansas.

McIntire, Mike. 2012. "Conservative Nonprofit Acts as a Stealth Business Lobbyist." *The New York Times*, April 21.

McNay, John T. 2013. *Collective Bargaining and the Battle of Ohio: The Defeat of Senate Bill 5 and the Struggle to Defend the Middle Class*. New York: Palgrave Macmillan.

Mettler, Suzanne. 1998. *Dividing Citizens: Gender and Federalism in New Deal Public Policy*. Ithaca, NY: Cornell University Press.

Mettler, Suzanne, and Joe Soss. 2004. "The Consequences of Public Policy for Democratic Citizenship: Bridging Policy Studies and Mass Politics." *Perspectives on Politics* 2 (1): 55–73.

Michener, Jamila. 2018. *Fragmented Democracy: Medicaid, Federalism, and Unequal Politics*. New York, NY: Cambridge University Press.

Mildenberger, Matto. 2015. "Fiddling While the World Burns: The Logic of Double Representation in Comparative Climate Policymaking." PhD thesis, Yale University, New Haven, CT.

Miller, Kevin. 2009. "Is Maine Ready for TABOR?" *The Bangor Daily News*, October 16.

Mills, Sarah B., Barry G. Rabe, and Christopher Borick. 2015. "Widespread Public Support for Renewable Energy Mandates Despite Proposed Rollbacks." *National Surveys on Energy and Environment* Number 22. Ann Arbor, MI: Center for Local, State, and Urban Policy, Gerald R. Ford School of Public Policy.

Missouri Scout. n.d. "Medicaid Expansion Coalition Continues to Grow." *Missouri Scout*. Referenced 2017. http://moscout.com/medicaid-expansion-coalition-continues-to-grow/.

Mistler, Steve. 2015. "Cut Maine's Income Tax? Not Without Anguish." *Portland Press Herald*, January 4.

Mitchell, Neil J., Wendy L. Hansen, and Eric M. Jepsen. 1997. "The Determinants of Domestic and Foreign Corporate Political Activity." *Journal of Politics* 59 (4): 1096–1113.

Mizruchi, Mark S. 2013. *The Fracturing of the American Corporate Elite*. Cambridge, MA: Harvard University Press.

Moe, Terry M. 2011. *Special Interest: Teachers Unions and America's Public Schools*. Washington, DC: Brookings Institution Press.

Moretto, Mario. 2014. "New Leader of Maine Conservative Group Aims to Build Upon Election Day Wins." *Bagnor Daily News*, November 20.

Morgan, Stephen L., and Christopher Winship. 2014. *Counterfactuals and Causal Inference*. New York: Cambridge University Press.

Morris, Randy C. 1993. "MEMORANDUM RE: The American Legislative Exchange Council Meeting: Denver, Colorado." University of California, San Francisco, Legacy Tobacco Archives.

Moss, David A. 1995. *Socializing Security: Progressive-Era Economists and the Origins of American Social Policy*. Cambridge, MA: Harvard University Press.

Moyers, Bill. 2012. "Bill Moyers: More Money, Less Democracy." *Moyers & Company*, video and transcript, September 21.

Mulkern, Anne C. 2010. "Oil and Gas Interests Set Spending Record for Lobbying in 2009." *The New York Times*, February 2.

Musumeci, MaryBeth. 2012. *A Guide to the Supreme Court's Decision on the ACA's Medicaid Expansion*. Washington, DC: Kaiser Family Foundation.

Nall, Clayton. 2015. "The Political Consequences of Spatial Policies: How Interstate Highways Facilitated Geographic Polarization." *Journal of Politics* 77 (2): 394–406.

Natelson, Rob. 2011. *Proposing Constitutional Amendments by a Convention of the States: A Handbook for State Lawmakers*. Washington, DC: American Legislative Exchange Council.

National Committee for Responsive Philanthropy. 1991. "Special Report: Burgeoning Conservative Think-Tanks (Spring)." Enclosed in ALEC Letter from Sam Brunelli to Tobacco Institute, University of California, San Francisco, Legacy Tobacco Archives.

Natural Resources Defense Council. 2002. *Corporate America's Trojan Horse in the States: The Untold Story Behind the American Legislative Exchange Council*. Washington, DC: National Resources Defense Council and Defenders of Wildlife.

NCSL. 2014. *Collecting E-Commerce Taxes; E-Fairness Legislation*. Washington, DC: National Conference of State Legislatures.

Nemitz, Bill. 2011. "Bill Nemitz: Taking Stock as Chief of Maine Conservative Think Tank Suddenly Rises to Power." *Portland Press Herald*, March 2.

Newkirk, Margaret, and Martin Z. Braun. 2018. "The Kochs Helped Slash State Taxes. Now Teachers Are in the Streets." *Bloomberg*, May 16.

Nichols, John. 2011. "ALEC Exposed." *The Nation*, July 12.

———. 2012. "How Scott Walker and ALEC Plotted the Attack on Arizona's Unions." *The Nation*, February 2.

Nichols, John, and Robert W. McChesney. 2013. *Dollarocracy: How the Money and Media Election Complex Is Destroying America*. New York: PublicAffairs.

Noble, Jason. 2017. "'Everything is on the table' for Collective Bargaining Debate in Iowa." *The Des Moines Register*, January 3.

Noel, Hans. 2013. *Political Ideologies and Political Parties in America*. New York: Cambridge University Press.
Novack, Janet. 2011. "Are Amazon.com's Days of Tax Free Selling Numbered?" *Forbes*, February 27.
Novick, Tom. 2013. *Rockefeller Brothers Fund: Money-in-Politics Grantmaking Impact Assessment*. New York: M+R Strategic Services.
Noye, Fred C. 1991. *Why the 1990s Will Be the Decade of the States*. Washington, DC: Heritage Foundation, November 7.
NYT. 2012. "The Big Money Behind State Laws." *The New York Times*, February 12.
O'Connor, Alice. 2008. "Financing the Counterrevolution." In *Rightward Bound: Making America Conservative in The 1970s* (158–170), ed. B. J. Schulman and J. E. Zelizer. Cambridge, MA: Harvard University Press.
Obama, Barack. 2010. "The President's News Conference: November 3, 2010." In *The American Presidency Project*, ed. G. Peters and J. T. Woolley. http://www.presidency.ucsb.edu/ws/index.php?pid=88668.
Office of the Governor. 2011. "Governor Walker Introduces Budget Repair." *Office of Wisconsin Governor Scott Walker*, February 11.
Olson, Mancur. 1965. *The Logic of Collective Action*. Cambridge, MA: Harvard University Press.
Omang, Joanne. 1979. "'New Right' Figure Sees McCarthyism in NEA's Conference on Conservatives." *The Washington Post*, February 24.
Oosting, Jonathan. 2014. "Michigan Political Points: Americans for Prosperity Touts Common Ground with Gov. Rick Snyder." *MLive*, November 1. Referenced 2017, published 2014. https://www.mlive.com/lansing-news/index.ssf/2014/11/michigan_political_points_amer_1.html.
———. 2017. "Part-Time Legislature Efforts Ramp Up in Michigan." *The Detroit News*, May 31.
Orth, Samuel P. 1904. "Our State Legislatures." *The Atlantic Monthly*.
Overby, Peter. 2005. "Progressives Take a Page from Conservative Networks." *NPR Morning Edition*, August 18. Referenced 2017, published 2005. https://www.npr.org/templates/story/story.php?storyId=4804915.
Pabst, Georgia. 2011. "Walker Signs Law Pre-Empting Sick Day Ordinance." *Milwaukee Journal Sentinel*, May 5.
Page, Benjamin I., Larry M. Bartels, and Jason Seawright. 2013. "Democracy and the Policy Preferences of Wealthy Americans." *Perspectives on Politics* 11 (1): 51–73.
Page, Benjamin I., and Martin Gilens. 2017. *Democracy in America?* Chicago: University of Chicago Press.
Page, Benjamin I., Jason Seawright, and Matthew J. Lacombe. 2015. "Stealth Politics by U.S. Billionaires." Paper presented at Annual Meeting of the American Political Science Association, San Francisco, Sept. 2–6, 2015.
Page, Benjamin I., and Robert Y. Shapiro. 1992. *The Rational Public*. Chicago: University of Chicago Press.
Paglayan, Agustina. Forthcoming. "Public-Sector Unions and the Size of Government." *American Journal of Political Science*.
Parker, Bruce. 2016. "City, County Officials from Across Nation Gather at ALEC." *Watchdog.org*, July 29. Referenced 2017, published 2016. https://www.watchdog.org/indiana/city-county-officials-from-across-nation-gather-at-alec/article_b7ebef6c-c087-5130-88ad-3239fecd2245.html.
Parks, Mariana. 2002. "Marketing Think Tank Ideas to Corporate America." *SPN News*, Spring.
Peirce, Neal R., and Robert Guskind. 1984. "The New Right Takes Its Political Show on the Road to Win Power in the States." *The National Journal*, October 13.
Perlstein, Rick. 2008. *Nixonland: The Rise of a President and the Fracturing of America*. New York: Simon & Schuster.
Peterson, Kyle. 2016. "The Spoils of the Republican State Conquest." *The Wall Street Journal*, December 9.
Peterson, Paul E. 1995. *The Price of Federalism*. Washington, DC: Brookings Institution Press.

Petroski, William. 2016. "New Iowa Senate GOP Majority Chooses Dix, Whitver for Top Posts." *The Des Moines Register*, November 11.
———. 2017a. "GOP Will Exercise Muscle in 2017 Iowa Legislature." *The Des Moines Register*, January 4.
———. 2017b. "Lobbyist Attending Bargaining Bill Signing Brings Criticism." *The Des Moines Register*, February 20.
Petroski, William, and Brianne Pfannenstiel. 2017. "Iowa House, Senate Approve Sweeping Collective Bargaining Changes." *The Des Moines Register*, February 16.
Pfannenstiel, Brianne. 2013. "Missouri Chamber of Commerce Backs Medicaid Expansion." *Kansas City Business Journal*, March 13.
———. 2017. "House Ethics Committee Admonishes Americans for Prosperity Lobbyist." *The Des Moines Register*, March 22.
Phillips, Amber. 2017. "Maine Voters Just Resoundingly Approved a Medicaid Expansion. Their Governor Is Trying to Stop It from Going into Effect." *The Washington Post*, November 8.
Phillips, Ari. 2014. "Inside, and Kicked Out of, ALEC's Secretive Policy Summit." *ThinkProgress*, December 5. Referenced 2017, published 2014. https://thinkprogress.org/inside-and-kicked-out-of-alecs-secretive-policy-summit-e05dbb900318/.
Phillips-Fein, Kim. 2009. *Invisible Hands: The Making of the Conservative Movement from the New Deal to Reagan*. New York: W.W. Norton.
Pierson, Paul. 1993. "Review: When Effect Becomes Cause: Policy Feedback and Political Change." *World Politics* 45 (4): 595–628.
———. 2004. *Politics in Time*. Princeton, NJ: Princeton University Press.
———. 2015. "Power and Path Dependence." In *Advances in Comparative-Historical Analysis* (123–46), ed. J. Mahoney and K. Thelen. New York: Cambridge University Press.
Pilkington, Ed. 2014. "Conservative Group Alec Trains Sights on City and Local Government." *The Guardian*, March 6.
———. 2015. "Scott Walker, First Alec President? Long Ties to Controversial Lobby Raise Concern." *The Guardian*, July 22.
———. 2018. "Exclusive: How Rightwing Groups Wield Secret 'Toolkit' to Plot against US Unions." *The Guardian*, May 15.
Pilkington, Ed. and Suzanne Goldenberg. 2013. "ALEC Facing Funding Crisis from Donor Exodus in Wake of Trayvon Martin Row." *The Guardian*, December 3.
Polletta, Francesca. 2002. *Freedom Is an Endless Meeting*. Chicago: University of Chicago Press.
Porter, Eduardo. 2015. "Corporations Open Up About Political Spending." *The New York Times*, June 9.
Potter, Wendell. 2011. "ALEC Exposed: Sabotaging Healthcare." *The Nation*, July 12.
Powell, Brian, and Salvatore Colleluori. 2012. "Breitbart.com's Fool's Errand: Comparing ALEC to NCSL." *Media Matters*, June 5. https://www.mediamatters.org/research/2012/06/05/breitbartcoms-fools-errand-comparing-alec-to-nc/184068.
Powell, Lynda W. 2012. *The Influence of Campaign Contributions in State Legislatures: The Effects of Institutions and Politics*. Ann Arbor: University of Michigan Press.
Progress Michigan. 2013. "Mackinac Center Admits to Lobbying Lawmakers." January 29. Referenced 2017, published 2013. http://www.progressmichigan.org/2013/01/mackinac-center-admits-to-lobbying-lawmakers/.
Progress Now Colorado. 2013. "The United States of ALEC Screening Event Panel Discussion." *Progress Now Colorado*. Available from author on request.
Public Citizen. 2000. "A Public Citizen Report on Citizens for a Sound Economy: A Corporate Lobbying Front Group." *Public Citizen's Congress Watch*. https://www.citizen.org/sites/default/files/citizens_for_a_sound_economy_report.pdf.
Rabe, Barry. 2007. "Race to the Top: The Expanding Role of U.S State Renewable Portfolio Standards." *Sustainable Development Law & Policy* 7 (3): 10–17.
Rahman, K. Sabeel. 2016. *Democracy Against Domination*. New York: Oxford University Press.

Rau, Alia Beard. 2012. "ACLU: Pearce E-mails Prove SB 1070 Was Racially Motivated." *The Arizona Republic*, July 19.

Riccardi, Nicholas. 2017. "US Conservatism Expands to Final Frontier: City Hall." *U.S. News & World Report*, July 27.

Richardson, Lilliard, and Jeff Milyo. 2017. "Public Attitudes on State Legislative Professionalism." Paper presented at 2017 State Politics and Policy Conference, St. Louis, MO.

Rigby, Elizabeth, and Jake Haselswerdt. 2013. "Hybrid Federalism, Partisan Politics, and Early Implementation of State Health Insurance Exchanges." *Publius* 43 (3): 368–391.

Robertson, David Brian. 1989. "The Bias of American Federalism." *Journal of Policy History* 1 (3): 261–291.

———. 2018. *Federalism and the Making of America*. New York: Routledge Press.

Rogers, Joel, and Laura Dresser. 2011. "ALEC Exposed: Business Domination Inc." *The Nation*, July 12.

Rogers, Steven. 2017. "Electoral Accountability for State Legislative Roll Calls and Ideological Representation." *American Political Science Review* 111 (3): 555–571.

Rolf, David. 2016. *The Fight for Fifteen: The Right Wage for a Working America*. New York: The New Press.

Rose, Shanna, and Cynthia J. Bowling. 2015. "The State of American Federalism 2014–15: Pathways to Policy in an Era of Party Polarization." *Publius* 45 (3): 351–379.

Rosenbaum, David E. 1992. "The 1992 Campaign; Difference Among the Democratic Candidates." *The New York Times*, February 16.

Rosenbaum, Marcus D. 1986. "The Liability Crisis, and How to Cool It." *The New York Times*, May 27.

Rosenfeld, Jake. 2014. *What Unions No Longer Do*. Cambridge, MA: Harvard University Press.

Rubin, Steve. 1996. "Conservative Spotlight: American Legislative Exchange Council." *Human Events*, July 26.

Rust, Gary. 2012. "Opinion: A Historical Perspective on ALEC and NCSL." *Southeast Missourian*, April 29.

Sachs, Benjamin I. 2012. "Unions, Corporations, and Political Opt-Out Rights after Citizens United." *Columbia Law Review* 112 (4): 800–869.

Sanchez, Yvonne Wingett. 2016. "Ducey Appoints Independent to Supreme Court." *The Republic*, January 6.

Santos, Fernanda. 2016. "Sheriff Joe Arpaio, Accused of Targeting Latinos, Is Charged With Contempt." *The New York Times*, October 17.

Schickler, Eric. 2016. *Racial Realignment: The Transformation of American Liberalism, 1932–1965*. Princeton, NJ: Princeton University Press.

Schlesinger, Joseph A. 1991. *Political Parties and the Winning of Office*. Ann Arbor: University of Michigan Press.

Schlozman, Daniel. 2015. *When Movements Anchor Parties*. Princeton, NJ: Princeton University Press.

———. 2016. "The Lists Told Us Otherwise: The Democratic Collapse and the Ascent of Trumpism." *n+1 Magazine*, December 24.

Schlozman, Kay Lehman, Sidney Verba, and Henry E. Brady. 2012. *The Unheavenly Chorus: Unequal Political Voice and the Broken Promise of American Democracy*. Princeton, NJ: Princeton University Press.

Schmitt, Mark, Shelley Waters Boots, and Karen Murrell. 2014. *The State Priorities Partnership: Creating Opportunity through Smart Policy*. Washington, DC: State Priorities Partnership and the Center on Budget and Policy Priorities.

Schmitter, Philippe C., and Wolfgang Streeck. 1999 [1981]. *The Organization of Business Interests: Studying the Associative Action of Business in Advanced Industrial Societies*. Cologne, Germany: Max Planck Institute for the Study of Societies.

Schouten, Fredreka. 2017. "Koch Brothers Network Aims to Raise $300M to $400M for Conservative Causes." *USA Today*, January 28.

Schuette, Bill. 2017. "Schuette: Make Lansing Transparent." *The Detroit News*, May 24.
Schulman, Bruce J., and Julian E. Zelizer, eds. 2008. *Rightward Bound: Making America Conservative in the 1970s*. Cambridge, MA: Harvard University Press.
Schulman, Daniel. 2014. *Sons of Wichita: How the Koch Brothers Became America's Most Powerful and Private Dynasty*. New York: Grand Central Publishing.
———. 2015. "The Koch Brothers Just Launched a Lobbying Campaign to Eliminate an Obscure Government Agency. Here's Why." *Mother Jones*, March 3.
Schwartz, Herman. 2015. "One Party System: What Total Republican Control of a State Really Means." *Reuters: The Great Debate*, August 19. http://blogs.reuters.com/great-debate/2015/08/19/one-party-system-what-total-republican-control-of-a-state-really-means/.
Scola, Nancy. 2012. "Exposing ALEC: How Conservative-Backed State Laws Are All Connected." *The Atlantic*, April 14.
Scolforo, Mark. 2011. "Pennsylvania Legislative Staff Is Among the Largest in the Country." *The Associated Press*, April 10. Referenced 2017, published 2011. https://www.pennlive.com/midstate/index.ssf/2011/04/pennsylvania_legislative_staff_1.html.
Seitz-Wald, Alex. 2012. "Oops: Florida Republican Forgets to Remove ALEC Mission Statement From Boilerplate Anti-Tax Bill." *ThinkProgress*, February 2. Referenced 2017, published 2012. https://thinkprogress.org/oops-florida-republican-forgets-to-remove-alec-mission-statement-from-boilerplate-anti-tax-bill-f595c95a844/.
Shannon, Brittany. 2016. "'Really bizarre': Milwaukee's Charitable Bradley Foundation Network Hacked by Anonymous Group." *Fox6 Now*, November 3. Referenced 2017, published 2016. https://fox6now.com/2016/11/03/really-bizarre-milwaukees-charitable-bradley-foundation-network-hacked-by-anonymous-group/.
Sharp, Tracie. 2016. "Letter re: Breakthrough 2016 Campaign." State Policy Network, Arlington, VA.
Shearer, Derek, and Lee Webb, eds. 1975. *Reader on Alternative Public Policies for the Conference on Alternative State & Local Public Policies*. Ithaca, NY: Cornell University Library Division of Rare and Manuscript Collections.
———, eds. 1976. *Second Annual Public Policy READER for the Conference on Alternative State & Local Public Policies*. Ithaca, NY: Cornell University Library Division of Rare and Manuscript Collections.
Shepsle, Kenneth A., and Barry R. Weingast. 1987. "The Institutional Foundations of Committee Power." *American Political Science Review* 81 (1): 85–104.
Shiner, Meredith. 2013. "After Trayvon Martin Verdict, Durbin Pushes 300 Companies on 'Stand Your Ground' Laws." *Roll Call*, August 6.
Shor, Boris, and Nolan McCarty. 2011. "The Ideological Mapping of American Legislatures." *American Political Science Review* 105 (3): 530–551.
Shotts, Constance Trisler. 1976. "The Origin and Development of the National Education Association Political Action Committee, 1969–1976." Ed.D. diss., Indiana University School of Education, Bloomington, IN.
Shumate, Roger V. 1938. "A Reappraisal of State Legislatures." *Annals of the American Academy of Political and Social Sciences* 195: 189–197.
Silver, Charlotte. 2013. "US Criminal Justice System: Turning a Profit on Prison Reform?" *Al Jareeza America*, September 27. Referenced 2017, published 2013. https://www.aljazeera.com/indepth/opinion/2013/09/us-criminal-justice-system-turning-a-profit-prison-reform-201392514144860917.html.
Singer, Matt. 2005. "Man with the PLAN." *In These Times*, July 15.
Sinovic, Matt, Trish Nelson, and Dave Bradley. n.d. "ALEC Exposed in Iowa." *Center for Media and Democracy, Common Cause, People for the American Way, and Progress Now*. https://www.sourcewatch.org/images/b/be/Iowa.ALEC.report.pdf.
Skinner, Richard M. 2006. *More Than Money: Interest Group Action in Congressional Elections*. New York: Rowman & Littlefield.

Skocpol, Theda. 1992. *Protecting Soldiers and Mothers: The Political Origins of Social Policy in the United States*. Cambridge, MA: Belknap Press.
———. 2003. *Diminished Democracy: From Membership to Management in American Civic Life*. Norman: University of Oklahoma Press.
———. 2016. "Why Political Scientists Should Study Organized Philanthropy." *PS: Political Science* 49 (3): 433–436.
Skocpol, Theda, Marshall Ganz, and Ziad Munson. 2000. "A Nation of Organizers: The Institutional Origins of Civic Voluntarism in the United States." *American Political Science Review* 94 (3): 527–546.
Skocpol, Theda, and Alexander Hertel-Fernandez. 2016a. "The Koch Effect: The Impact of a Cadre-Led Network on American Politics." Paper presented at Annual Southwest Political Science Association Meetings in San Juan, Puerto Rico, January 8.
———. 2016b. "The Koch Network and Republican Party Extremism." *Perspectives on Politics* 14 (3): 681–699.
Smith, Mark. 2000. *American Business and Political Power: Public Opinion, Elections, and Democracy*. Chicago: University of Chicago Press.
SourceWatch. 2015. *State Policy Network*. Madison, WI: Center for Media and Democracy.
———. 2017. *Mackinac Center for Public Policy*. Madison, WI: Center for Media and Democracy.
———. n.d. *ALEC Politicians*. Madison, WI: Center for Media and Democracy.
Spies, Mike. 2018. "The N.R.A. Lobbyist Behind Florida's Pro-Gun Policies." *The New Yorker*, March 5.
SPN. 2000. "SPN Western Regional Meeting: Record Turnout at the Silicon Valley Conference." *SPN News*, Fall.
———. 2001a. *2000 Summary and Goals for 2001*. Arlington, VA: State Policy Network.
———. 2001b. "SPN Southern Regional Meeting: Birmingham Event Attracts Numerous Think Tank Leaders." *SPN News*, Spring.
———. 2002. "Industry Experts, SPN Members Strategize Health Care Policy Ideas." *SPN News*, Spring.
———. 2009. *SPN & ALEC: A Model Relationship*. Arlington, VA: State Policy Network.
———. 2013a. "Searle Tax and Budget Grant Proposals." *State Policy Network*. https://www.documentcloud.org/documents/842271-spn-budget-proposals-state-by-state.html.
———. 2013b. *SPN Annual Meeting: Schedule*. Arlington, VA: State Policy Network.
———. n.d. *SPN Survey: A Comprehensive Survey of Market-Oriented State Think Tank in the United States*. Arlington, VA: State Policy Network.
Squire, Peverill. 2007. "Measuring State Legislative Professionalism: The Squire Index Revisited." *State Politics & Policy Quarterly* 7 (2): 211–227.
———. 2012. *The Evolution of American Legislatures*. Ann Arbor: University of Michigan Press.
Stahl, Jason. 2016. *Right Moves: The Conservative Think Tank in American Political Culture since 1945*. Chapel Hill: University of North Carolina Press.
Stan, Adele M. 2011. "Wall Street Journal Honcho Shills for Secret Worker 'Education' Program Linked to Koch Group." *AlterNet: The Investigative Fund at The Nation*, June 3. Referenced 2017, published 2011. https://www.alternet.org/story/151182/wall_street_journal_honcho_shills_for_secret_worker_%27education%27_program_linked_to_koch_group.
Steigerwald, Laura. 2012. *Emails from ALEC Member Russell Pearce Show Anti-Immigrant Law May Have Been Racially Motivated*. Madison, WI: Center for Media and Democracy.
Stephenson, John. 2011. "Memorandum to Telecommunications and Information Technology Task Force Members RE: 35-Day Mailing-States and Nation Policy Summit." American Legislative Exchange Council, Washington, DC, documents leaked by Common Cause.
———. 2012. "Memorandum to Telecommunications and Information Technology Task Force Members RE: 2012 Spring Task Force Summit." American Legislative Exchange Council, Washington, DC, documents leaked by Common Cause.
Stern, Ray. 2011. "Sheriff Joe Arpaio's Office Commits Worst Racial Profiling in U.S. History, Concludes DOJ Investigation." *Phoenix New Times*, December 15.

Stokes, Leah C. 2015. "Power Politics: Renewable Energy Policy Change in the US States." PhD diss., Massachusetts Institute of Technology, Cambridge, MA.

Stolle, Dietlind, Marc Hooghe, and Michele Micheletti. 2005. "Politics in the Supermarket: Political Consumerism as a Form of Political Participation." *International Political Science Review* 26 (3): 245–269.

Stone, Peter H., Bara Vaida, and Louis Jacobson. 2003. "From the K Street Corridor: The Left Challenges ALEC." *The National Journal*, August 2.

Sullivan, Laura. 2010. "Prison Economics Help Drive Ariz. Immigration Law." *NPR Morning Edition*, October 28. Referenced 2017, published 2010. https://www.npr.org/2010/10/28/130833741/prison-economics-help-drive-ariz-immigration-law.

Sun Journal. 2005. "Think Tank Draws Praise and Pans." *Sun Journal*, July 11.

Supreme Court of the United States Blog. 2016. *Amazon.com, LLC v. New York State Department of Taxation and Finance*. Referenced 2016, published 2013. http://www.scotusblog.com/case-files/cases/amazon-com-llc-v-new-york-state-department-of-taxation-and-finance/.

Tausanovitch, Chris, and Christopher Warshaw. 2013. "Measuring Constituent Policy Preferences in Congress, State Legislatures, and Cities." *Journal of Politics* 75 (2): 330–342.

Taylor, Chris. 2013. "The Rise and Fall of ALEC Nation." *Milwaukee Journal Sentinel*, September 19.

Teaford, Jon C. 2002. *The Rise of the States: Evolution of American State Government*. Baltimore, MD: Johns Hopkins University Press.

Teles, Steven M. 2010. *The Rise of the Conservative Legal Movement: The Battle for Control of the Law*. Princeton, NJ: Princeton University Press.

———. 2013. "Organizational Maintenance, The Funder-Grantee Nexus, and the Trajectory of American Political Development." Paper presented at Conference Honoring the Life and Work of James Q. Wilson, Harvard University, Cambridge, MA.

Tempus, Alexandra. 2012. "Voter ID Drive Part of Quiet, Well-Funded National Conservative Effort." *MPR News*, March 5. Referenced 2017, published 2012. https://www.mprnews.org/story/2012/03/04/voter-id-alec.

Theriault, Sean M. 2013. *The Gingrich Senators: The Roots of Partisan Warfare in Congress*. New York: Oxford University Press.

Toll, Henry W. 1926. "The American Legislators' Association." *American Bar Association Journal* 12 (9): 642–643.

———. 1928. "The Work of the American Legislators' Association." *American Political Science Review* 22 (1): 127–129.

Tønnessen, Alf Tomas. 2009. *How Two Political Entrepreneurs Helped Create the American Conservative Movement, 1973–1981*. Lewiston, NY: Edwin Mellen Press.

———. 2014. "Paul Michael Weyrich." In *American National Biography Online*. American Council of Learned Societies, Oxford University Press.

Tucker, David M. 1998. *Mugwumps: Public Moralists of the Gilded Age*. Columbia: University of Missouri Press.

Tullock, Gordon. 2001. "Efficient Rent-Seeking." In *Efficient Rent-Seeking* (3–16), ed. A. Lockard and G. Tullock. Boston: Springer Press.

US Chamber of Commerce. 1965. *Members Appraise Associations*. Washington, DC: Association Service Department, Chamber of Commerce of the United States.

Valletta, Robert G., and Richard B. Freeman. 1988. "The NBER Public Sector Collective Bargaining Law Data Set." In *When Public Employees Unionize*, ed. R. B. Freeman and C. Ichniowski. Chicago: NBER and University of Chicago Press.

VanderHart, Dirk. 2018. "How a Fight Over Unions Could Change the Direction of Oregon Politics." *Oregon Public Broadcasting*, July 29.

Vedder, Richard, and Lowell Gallaway. 1994. *Concealed Costs: The Real Impact of the Administration's Health Care Plan on the Economy: A State-by-State Analysis*. Washington, DC: American Legislative Exchange Council.

Vogel, David. 1989. *Fluctuating Fortunes: The Political Power of Business in America*. New York: Basic Books.

———. 2006. "Tracing the American Roots of the Political Consumerism Movement." In *Politics, Products and Markets: Exploring Political Consumerism Past and Present* (83–101), ed. M. Micheletti, A. Follesdal and D. Stolle. New Brunswick, NJ: Transaction.

Vogel, Kenneth P. 2011. "For Right, Wis. Was Years in Making." *Politico*, February 28.

———. 2014a. *Big Money: 2.5 Billion Dollars, One Suspicious Vehicle, and a Pimp—on the Trail of the Ultra-Rich Hijacking American Politics*. New York: Public Affairs.

———. 2014b. "Democrats Create an ALEC-Killer." *Politico*, November 9.

———. 2017. "David Brock, Donors Wade into State Fights." *Politico*, February 22.

Wade, Magic M. 2018. "Targeting Teachers While Shielding Cops? The Politics of Punishing Enemies and Rewarding Friends in American State Collective Bargaining Reform Agendas." *Journal of Labor and Society* 21 (2): 137–57.

Walker, Alexis N. 2014a. "Labor's Enduring Divide: The Distinct Path of Public Sector Unions in the United States." *Studies in American Political Development* 28 (2): 175–200.

Walker, Don. 2011a. "Koch Group Americans for Prosperity Campaigning in Wisconsin." *Milwaukee Journal Sentinel*, February 28.

———. 2011b. "Walker Rejects Union Offer on Bargaining Rights." *Milwaukee Journal Sentinel*, February 18.

Walker, Edward. 2014b. *Grassroots for Hire: Public Affairs Consultants in American Democracy*. New York: Cambridge University Press.

Walker, Jack. 1991. *Mobilizing Interest Groups in America: Patrons, Professions, and Social Movements*. Ann Arbor: University of Michigan Press.

Ward, Kenric. 2012. "Americans for Prosperity Taps Tea Party Volunteers for Tuesday." *Sunshine State News*, January 28.

Waterhouse, Benjamin C. 2013. *Lobbying America: The Politics of Business from Nixon to NAFTA*. Princeton, NJ: Princeton University Press.

Wayne, Leslie. 2002. "Enron, Preaching Deregulation, Worked the Statehouse Circuit." *The New York Times*, February 9.

Weber, Bruce. 2008. "Paul Weyrich, 66, a Conservative Strategist, Dies." *The New York Times*, December 18.

Weigel, David. 2012a. "Rick Snyder Didn't Want to Sign Right-to-Work Legislation Until He Signed It." *Slate*, December 11.

———. 2012b. "The Tea Party Is Outside Your House." *Slate*, September 24.

Weiner, Rachel. 2012. "How ALEC Became a Political Liability." *The Washington Post*, April 24.

Weir, Margaret. 2009. *"Beyond the Plant Gates": Postwar Labor and the Organizational Substructure of Liberalism*. Berkeley: Institute for Research on Labor and Employment, University of California, Berkeley.

Whisnant, Gene. 2011. "State Budget Reform Toolkit Bills in Oregon: An In-Depth Look at the State's Budget Reform." *Inside ALEC*, April.

Wilce, Rebekah. 2012. *Solar Energy Industries Association (SEIA) Cuts Ties to ALEC*. Madison, WI: Center for Media and Democracy.

Williams, Erica, and Nicholas Johnson. 2013. *ALEC Tax and Budget Proposals Would Slash Public Services and Jeopardize Economic Growth*. Washington, DC: Center on Budget and Policy Priorities.

Williams, Jonathan. 2012. "Memorandum to Tax and Fiscal Policy Task Force Members RE: 35 Day Mailing-ALEC's Spring Task Force Summit." American Legislative Exchange Council, Washington, DC. Documents leaked by Common Cause.

Wilson, Andrew B. 2012. It Is Time to Reform Medicaid, Not Expand It. Saint Louis, MO: Show-Me Institute.

Wilson, Bill, and Roy Wenzl. 2012. "The Kochs' Quest to Save America." *The Witchita Eagle*, October 13.

Wilson, Graham. 1986. "American Business and Politics." In *Interest Group Politics* (227–31), ed. A. Cigler and B. Loomis. Washington, DC: CQ Press.

Wilson, James Q. 1995. *Political Organizations*. Updated ed. Princeton, NJ: Princeton University Press.

Wines, Michael. 2016a. "Inside the Conservative Push for States to Amend the Constitution." *The New York Times*, August 22.

———. 2016b. "Some Republicans Acknowledge Leveraging Voter ID Laws for Political Gain." *The New York Times*, September 16.

Winston, Pamela. 2002. *Welfare Policymaking in the States: The Devil in Devolution*. Washington, DC: Georgetown University Press.

W.K. Kellogg Foundation. 2004. *A Legacy of Innovation: 2004 Annual Report*. Battle Creek, MI: W.K. Kellogg Foundation.

———. n.d. *Devolution Partner: Center for Policy Alternatives*. Battle Creek, MI: W.K. Kellogg Foundation.

Wohl, Jessica. 2012. "Wal-Mart Ending Membership in Conservative Group." *Reuters*, May 31. Referenced 2017, published 2012. https://www.reuters.com/article/us-walmart-alec/wal-mart-ending-membership-in-conservative-group-idUSBRE84U05N20120531.

Woodruff, Betsy. 2015. "Inside Scott Walker's Secret Brain Trust." *The Daily Beast*, April 16.

Yackee, Jason Webb, and Susan Webb Yackee. 2006. "A Bias Towards Business? Assessing Interest Group Influence on the U.S. Bureaucracy." *Journal of Politics* 68 (1): 128–139.

Zaller, John. 1992. *The Nature and Origins of Mass Opinion*. New York: Cambridge University Press.

Zegart, Dan. 2004. "The Right Wing's Drive for 'Tort Reform.'" *The Nation*, October 7.

INDEX

60 Plus Association 162–3

Adams, John (state legislator from Ohio) 88
Adelson, Sheldon 7
Affordable Care Act (ACA):
   American Legislative Exchange Council and 4, 16, 199, 201–3, 205, 207–10, 253, 289–90
   Americans for Prosperity and 4–5, 16, 166, 200–204, 207–10, 253
   healthcare insurance coverage increased under 197
   healthcare navigators and 64
   Medicaid expansion and 4–5, 16, 152, 177–8, 197–210, 244, 246, 253, 267, 289–90
   public opinion regarding 253–5
   Republican efforts to repeal 4, 144, 199
   State Policy Network and 4, 16, 146, 152, 156–7, 199–203, 205, 207–10, 253, 289–90
   Supreme Court ruling (2012) on 198
Alabama 52, 93, 109
Alaska 74, 182
ALCOA 114
Alinsky, Saul 60
Alliance of American Insurers 35
Allott, Gordon 28
Altria 87
Amazon 58, 130–2
American Association for Labor Legislation (AALL) 267–8
American Bail Coalition 49
American City County Exchange (ACCE) 60–2
American Conservative Union 29
American Electric Power Company 137
American Federation of Labor and Congress of Industrial Organizations (AFL-CIO) 58, 220–1
American Federation of State, County and Municipal Employees (AFSCME) 58, 134, 195, 222
American Legislative and Issue Campaign Exchange (ALICE) 226–7, 242
American Legislative Exchange Council (ALEC), *see also* policy plagiarism of American Legislative Exchange Council model bills
   abortion and xiii, 32, 37
   Affordable Care Act and 4, 16, 199, 201–3, 205, 207–10, 253, 289–90
   agricultural policies and 69, 75–6, 99
   American City County Exchange and 60–2
   Americans for Prosperity and 16, 171, 173
   analysis of probability of individual legislators' authoring bills and 271–2
   analysis of probability of individual legislators' votes on collective bargaining and 285
   analysis of regulatory threats addressed by 274–6
   Article V Constitutional Convention proposal and xiii–xiv
   Association of Community Organizations for Reform Now and 54–5
   backlash against 27, 56–60, 115, 133–4, 137–8, 261
   balanced budget amendment proposals and xiv, 75
   budget of 26, 41, 59, 226, 229
   bylaws of 32
   climate change legislation and 43–4, 75, 113, 261
   Clinton health care plan and 126–8

American Legislative Exchange Council (*cont.*)
  collective bargaining rights and 67, 98, 107–9, 176–9, 183–9, 191–4, 196, 252
  competing priorities within 16, 24–5, 27, 34, 37, 43–5, 63, 249–51, 264–5
  conservative activists' participation in 14, 24, 46–8, 52–4, 60, 62–3, 250, 264–5
  conservative foundations' funding for 33, 41–2, 244, 249
  consumer-facing companies and 86–7, 133–4, 138, 261
  corporate donors to xi–xii, 13–16, 23–6, 33–4, 36–7, 41–2, 45–9, 55, 57–63, 83–4, 86–7, 105, 114–28, 130, 132–9, 226, 250, 261, 264–5
  corporate sponsorships for legislators to attend meetings of 87–8, 123
  corporate tax policies and 23, 65, 253–4
  corporations' decision to leave 16, 58–9, 133–9, 261, 277
  corporations' desire to stymie competitors as reason for participating in 121–2, 135
  corporations' exposure to state regulation as factor predicting participation in 118–22, 125, 135–6
  corporations' exposure to unionization at industry level as factor predicting participation in 122–3, 125, 135
  corporations' other forms of political engagement as factor predicting participation in 124–5, 135–6, 138
  corporations' size as factor predicting participation in 123–5
  criminal sentencing policies and 37–8, 44, 49–51, 54, 69, 76, 300n114
  cross-state advocacy efforts by xiv, 82, 246–8, 263
  education policy and 69–71, 74–6, 98–9, 157, 253–4
  energy policy and xi–xii, 45, 69, 75–6, 99, 254
  English-language laws and 37
  extractive resource companies and 44, 46, 99, 103–4, 118–19, 261
  fast-food companies and 240
  financial services sector and 138
  food production companies and 118
  foreign policy issues and 69, 74–6
  gun legislation and 32, 37, 49, 58–9, 68–9, 76, 133, 138, 250, 261–2
  healthcare companies and 15–16, 115, 118–20, 126–30, 261
  healthcare policies and 4, 16, 69, 75–6, 99, 126–30, 199, 201–3, 205, 207–10, 253, 289–90
  Heritage Foundation and 34
  housing policies and 68–69
  immigration policy and 51–2, 55, 63
  increasingly conservative legislative membership of 48–9, 52–5, 63, 79, 97
  information technology companies and 15, 115, 118–20, 130–3
  Jeffersonian Project and 300n95
  Koch Brothers and 24, 42, 45
  lack of disclosure requirements regarding activities of 57, 257
  legislative spouse training offered by 83–4
  LGBT rights and 24, 32–3, 218
  Madison Group and 147–8
  membership dues for ix–x, 26, 266
  membership levels in x, 5–6, 26, 41, 48, 262
  minimum wage laws and 62
  model legislation drafted by x–xiii, 5, 10, 13, 15, 23, 32, 35, 41, 48, 51–2, 54, 57–9, 64–77, 79–83, 90–111, 114, 127–9, 156, 158, 176, 189, 199, 205, 209, 240, 246, 248, 258–64, 286–7
  National Education Association as a model for 30–1
  National Education Association opposed by 39, 58
  National Rifle Association and 49–51, 53, 58, 83
  networking and tourism opportunities in x, 80, 83–8, 109, 123, 264
  online retail companies and 130–3
  origins of 14, 25–34
  paid sick leave policies and 240, 254
  pharmaceutical companies and 137
  political action committee of 40, 246
  private sector business model for operations of 42–3
  progressive organizations' efforts to counter 16–18, 41, 58, 211–13, 218–19, 224–38, 242, 261–8
  public employee pension fund-held companies and 134–5, 137, 261
  public policy as a means of reshaping political landscape for 16, 35–6, 54, 210, 246, 251–2
  Public Safety and Elections Task Force and 50, 54–5, 59
  public sector unions and 31–2, 70–1, 74, 76, 101, 103, 107–9, 178–9, 181–92, 210, 219, 252–3
  railroad companies and 118
  Reagan and 40, 218, 263
  recruitment strategies at 107, 110
  representative democracy potentially harmed by 17, 253–7, 266
  right-to-work laws and 73, 144, 160, 247
  school busing and 37

INDEX

school prayer and 37
school vouchers and 70–1, 74, 253–4
secrecy prioritized by 26–7, 55, 57–60
senior legislative leaders and 107–10
state chairs of 46–8, 107, 265, 272–3
State Policy Network and 16, 147–50, 156–60, 173, 265–6
state pollution regulations drafted by 114
survey of state legislators regarding 92–96, 103–4, 278–80
task forces of 38, 41–6, 49–51, 54–5, 81, 114, 123, 127–8, 157, 173, 199, 240, 250, 265
tax-exempt status of 34
tobacco industry and 36, 118, 128, 137, 240
tort and liability reform and 34–6, 38, 74, 126–7, 251
tourism industry and 138
transportation sector and 69, 76, 118, 123
voter ID laws and 2–4, 18, 23, 50–2, 54–5, 59, 63, 68–9, 72, 76, 250, 252
welfare policy issues and 33, 69, 76
Weyrich and 29–31, 219
American Legislators' Association (ALA) 214–18
Americans for Prosperity (AFP):
  Affordable Care Act 4–5, 16, 166, 200–204, 207–10, 253
  American Legislative Exchange Council and 16, 171, 173
  anti-government stances of 172–3
  in Arizona 168–9, 180
  budget for, 164, 166–7
  Citizens for a Sound Economy as predecessor of 129, 163, 165–6
  climate change legislation and 170–1
  collective bargaining rights and 176–8, 180, 183, 187–9, 191–4, 196
  competing priorities within 16, 250, 265
  cross-state advocacy efforts and 246
  Defending the American Dream Summit and 169
  education policy and 166, 209, 253–4
  energy policy and 254
  in Florida 167
  grassroots volunteers organized by 166–70, 176, 263
  in Iowa 176–7
  Koch Brothers and 16, 129, 145, 160, 164–8, 200, 209–10, 245–6, 249
  libertarian viewpoints promoted by 166, 210, 245
  in Maine 169–71, 180
  membership levels in 5–6
  in Michigan 145–6, 166, 171, 180

primary elections and 9
progressive organizations' efforts to counter 17–18, 211–13, 219, 234, 262–8
public policy as a means of reshaping political landscape for 210, 251–2
public sector unions and 31, 166, 169, 179–80, 183, 210, 252–3
representative democracy potentially harmed by 17, 253–7, 266
Republican Party and 166, 173
right-to-work laws and 145–6
school vouchers and 253–4
scorecards developed by 168
state elections and 245–6
State Policy Network and 169–73
tax policy and 166–9, 253–4
Tea Party and 167
in Wisconsin 166, 171, 188, 208–9
American Society of Association Executives 34
American Tort Reform Association 34
Analysis and Research Association 28
Arizona:
  American Legislative Exchange Council and 72, 74, 87, 201
  Americans for Prosperity in 168–9, 180
  Federation of Taxpayers in 168
  Goldwater Institute and 70, 154–6, 158–9, 169, 181, 244
  Medicaid expansion in 199, 206–7
  part-time nature of state legislature in 89
  public funding for private schools in 155–6
  public sector unions and collective bargaining rights in 70–1, 155, 169, 181, 191, 222
  racial profiling in 52
  state legislature's halting of municipal initiatives in 61
  "Troika" index in 181–2
  voter ID law in 52
Arkansas 153, 206–7
Armey, Dick 163
Arpaio, Joe 52
Article V Constitutional Convention proposal xiii–xiv
Association of Community Organizations for Reform Now (ACORN) 54–5
Atkins, Joe 65
Atlantic Richfield (ARCO) 36
AT&T 45, 58, 86–8, 137

balanced budget amendment proposals xiv, 30, 75
Baldacci, John 157
Beacon Hill Institute 113
Becker, Bill 157

Bezos, Jeff 131
Blue Cross Blue Shield 261
Bond, Christopher 204
Bradley Foundation 41, 243–4, 249
Branstad, Terry 29, 108, 174–7, 194
Brat, Dave 258
Brewer, Jan 169
Brock, David 228
Broockman, David 255
Brownback, Sam 203
Brunelli, Sam:
  American Legislative Exchange Council state chairs and 47–8, 107, 265
  American Legislative Exchange Council task forces and 38, 41, 44
  biographical background of 39
  Clinton healthcare plan and 128
  Department of Education experience and 39
  Madison Group and 147–8, 159
  Reagan and 39
Burgin, Rachel 65
Bush, George W. 229
Business Roundtable 25–6, 45, 125, 135

California:
  American Legislative Exchange Council and 99, 201
  legislative professionalism index and 90–3, 97, 109
  pollution control standards passed in 114
  public sector unions in 222
  Reason Foundation in 169
  State Innovation Exchange in 227
  state legislators' salaries in 89
  state legislature staff in 90
  State Policy Network and 155
Carleson, Robert 29
Castle Doctrine 2, 50–1, 58
Cato Institute 162
Caudle, Reece A. 215
Caughey, Devin 247
Center for Media and Democracy 24, 59, 68, 249
Center for Policy Alternatives (CPA) 212, 224–6, 228–9, 242, 263
Center for Popular Democracy 212
Center for State Innovation (CSI) 212, 227
Center on Budget and Policy Priorities 230
Chemical Manufacturers Association 35
Chevron 86, 137
childcare subsidies 233
Citizens for a Sound Economy (CSE) 129, 162–6
Citizens United case (2010) 258
climate change:
  American Legislative Exchange Council's effort to stop laws addressing 43–4, 75, 113, 261

  Americans for Prosperity and 170–1
  carbon tax proposals and 103
  extractive industries' contribution to 103
  Kyoto Protocol and 46, 75
  net-metering policies and 112
  online retail companies and 130
  public opinion regarding 255
  renewable energy portfolio standards (RPS) and 112–13
  state legislatures' actions on 12, 61, 112
Clinton, Bill 127–8
Clinton, Hillary 128–9, 196
Clinton healthcare plan 126–9
Coca-Cola 58
Collective Bargaining and the Battle of Ohio (McNay) 18
collective bargaining rights:
  American Legislative Exchange Council's efforts to limit 67, 98, 107–9, 176–9, 183–9, 191–4, 196, 252
  individual legislators' partisan affiliation and ideology as factor predicting approach to 184–7
  in Iowa 107–8, 174–7, 183, 194
  National Education Association's efforts regarding 219
  national increase (1960s and 1970s) of 31
  public opinion regarding 176, 183–4, 254, 280–3
  right-to-work laws and 143
  state budget deficits as factor predicting cuts to 184
  State Policy Network and 31, 152, 155, 177–81, 183–9, 191–6, 210, 252–3
  states under full Republican control and 183
Colorado:
  Americans for Prosperity in 171
  "Four Horsemen" donors to liberal causes in 237
  lobbying disclosure laws in 57
  public sector unions and collective bargaining rights in 191, 194, 222
  State Innovation Exchange in 227
  State Policy Network in 171
Color of Change 58
Comcast 137
Commission on Uniform State Laws 214–15
Committee for the Survival of a Free Congress 28
Committee on the States 237
Common Cause 23, 58–9, 105
Conference on Alternative State and Local Policies (CASLP) 212, 223–4
Connecticut 72, 74
ConocoPhillips 137
Coors, Adolph 36

Coors, Joseph 28
Coors Foundation 33, 41–2, 249
Corrections Corporation of America (now CoreCivic) 55
Council of State Governments (CSG) 215–18, 224
Coverdell, Paul 130
Coyne, James 34
Crane, Phil 29
CSX 133
Culver, Chet 174
Cunningham, Jane 205

Dagan, David 54
Defenders of Wildlife 58, 83
Delaware 201, 231
DeLay, Tom 109
Democracy Alliance 227, 236–7, 266
Democratic Party:
 education policy and 99
 elections (2010) and 1
 federal government focus of 213, 229, 262
 medical liability reforms and 99
 public sector unions and 102, 130–3, 175, 179, 196
 tort reform and 35
 trial lawyers' support for 35, 251
 urban strength of 238
DentaQuest 87
Diageo 87
Dix, Bill 108, 174, 176
Dobson, James 27
Drutman, Lee 136
Ducey, Doug 156
Duke, Charlie 218
Duke Energy 137
Durbin, Dick 59

earned income tax credits 233
eBay 130, 132–3
Economic Analysis and Research Network (EARN):
 admission criteria for 230–1
 budget of 231–4
 childcare subsidies and 233
 earned income tax credits and 233
 establishment (1998) of 212, 230
 geographic reach of 232
 membership benefits and 231
 minimum wage laws and 233
Economic Policy Institute 225, 230
Edison Electric Institute 36, 45
electricity deregulation xi–xii, 23, 45
Electricity Freedom Act proposal (2012) 113

Eli Lilly 36, 137
Ellison, Keith 225
Encore Capital Group 87
Engler, John 29
Enron xi–xii, 23, 45–6
Enzi, Michael 109
Equal Rights Amendment 32
Exxon 87, 113, 133, 137

Facebook 44
Fallin, Mary 129
The Fall of Wisconsin (Kaufman) 18
Farnam, Henry W. 267
Federation of Taxpayers 168
FedEx 86
Feigenbaum, James 196–7
Feulner, Edwin J. 28–9
Fight for $15 campaign 239
Fitzgerald, Jeff 108–9, 188
Fitzgerald, Scott 108–9, 188
Flemming Leadership Institute 224–5
Florida:
 Americans for Prosperity and Tea Party in 167
 consumer packaging regulations in 114
 Madison Institute in 153
 Martin killing (2012) in 2, 58, 133–4, 138, 261–2
 Medicaid expansion and 201–2, 206
 public funding for private schools and 155
 stand-your-ground law and Castle Doctrine in 2, 51, 58
 State Chamber of Commerce in 206
 state legislature's halting of municipal initiatives in 61
 State Policy Network and 201, 244
 sugar industry in 163
 "Troika Index" and 202
 voter ID law in 55
FMC Corporation 116–17
Focus on the Family 32
Foundation for Government Accountability (FGA) 201, 244
Free Congress Foundation 147
Freedom Foundation xiii, 195
Freedom Partners Chamber of Commerce 162, 164–5
FreedomWorks 163
Friedman, Milton 29
Fulghum, Jim 78

Gates Foundation 59
Georgia:
 American Legislative Exchange Council in 114
 legislative professionalism index and 93

Georgia: (*cont.*)
  public sector unions and collective bargaining rights in 191, 194
  voter ID law in 52
Georgia Public Policy Foundation 151–2
Gerken, Heather 236
Giffords, Gabby 225
Gilens, Martin 253
Gingrich, Newt 27
Golden Rule Insurance Company 127–8
Goldstein, Amy 18
Goldwater, Barry 27
Goldwater Institute:
  Affordable Care Act and 156
  American Legislative Exchange Council and 156, 158–9
  Americans for Prosperity and 169
  Bradley Foundation and 244
  budget of 154–6
  Center for Constitutional Litigation at 155, 244
  Donors Capital Fund and 156
  Ducey and 156
  Koch Brothers and 156
  public funding for private schools and 70, 155–6
  public sector unions and 70, 155, 181
Goodman, John 128–9
Google 44
Gottwalt, Steve 65
Graham, Lindsey 109
Great Society legislation 28, 216–17
Grogan, Colleen 202
Grumbach, Jake 14
Guarantee Trust Life 87
Guardian Interlock Systems 49
gun legislation:
  American Legislative Exchange Council and 32, 37, 49, 58–9, 68–9, 76, 133, 138, 250, 261–2
  Castle Doctrine and 2, 50–1, 58
  concealed carry legislation and 50–1
  stand-your-ground laws and 2–3, 55, 58

Hacker, Jacob 245
Hammer, Marion 51
Hastert, Dennis 109
Hawaii 93, 99, 182, 231
healthcare companies:
  American Legislative Exchange Council and 15–16, 115, 118–20, 126–30, 261
  Clinton healthcare plan and 126–8
  Republican Party and 130
Health Security Act, *see* Clinton healthcare plan
Heartland Institute 113, 147

Heckman, Constance 147
Heritage Foundation 28, 34, 55, 147, 149
Herrera, Christie 159, 201
Home Depot 50
"Homosexuals: Just Another Minority Group?" (American Legislative Exchange Council report) 32–3
Hope, Patrick 80–1
Humana Insurance Company 127
Hyde, Henry 29

Idaho:
  American Legislative Exchange Council and 72
  legislative professionalism index and 91, 109–11
  part-time legislature in 110
  public sector unions and collective bargaining rights in 184–6, 191
  state legislature's halting of municipal initiatives in 61
  state legislature staff in 78
  State Policy Network in 201
Illinois:
  Americans for Prosperity in 171
  Clinton Healthcare Plan and 129
  legislative professionalism index and 90, 260
  public sector unions and collective bargaining rights in 180, 184–6, 194–5
  State Policy Network in 171, 195
Indiana:
  American Legislative Exchange Council and 74
  education reform bill in 74
  lobbying disclosure laws in 57
  Medicaid expansion in 199, 207
  public sector unions and collective bargaining rights in 179–80, 184–6
  state legislature's halting of municipal initiatives in 61
  voter ID law in 54–5
Institute for Policy Studies 223
Iowa:
  Americans for Prosperity and 176–7
  online sales taxes and 132
  Public Interest Institute in 177
  public sector unions and collective bargaining rights in 107–8, 174–7, 183, 194
  Republican takeover of legislature (2017) in 10, 174
  state legislature's halting of municipal initiatives in 61

Janesville (Goldstein) 18
Janus, Mark 195

Janus v. AFSCME 195–6, 222
Johnson Controls 133–4
Josiah Bartlett Center for Public Policy 159–60

Kansas:
  American Legislative Exchange Council and 74
  Americans for Prosperity in 171
  legislative professionalism index and 91, 111
  Medicaid expansion and 202–3
  state legislators' salaries in 89
  State Policy Network in 171
  "Troika" index in 181–2, 202
  voter ID law in 52
Kashin, Konstantin 67–70
Kasich, John 29
Kasten, Robert 29
Kaufman, Dan 18
Kentucky 91, 99, 222
Kiffmeyer, Mary 3
Kirkpatrick, Chad 168
Koch Brothers (Charles and David Koch):
  American Legislative Exchange Council and 24, 42, 45
  Americans for Prosperity and 16, 129, 145, 160, 164–8, 200, 209–10, 245–6, 249
  Cato Institute 162
  donor meetings convened by 164–5, 244
  election utilities supported by 162
  electricity deregulation and xi, 45
  Freedom Partners Chamber of Commerce and 162, 164–5
  Goldwater Institute and 156
  grassroots mobilization organizations supported by 162
  Koch Industries and xi, 24, 42, 45, 160–1
  libertarian principles advocated by 162, 164, 166, 210, 245
  lobbying organizations supported by 162–3
  National Rifle Association 165
  Republican candidates supported by 161, 165
  think tanks supported by 162–3
  US Chamber of Commerce and 165
Kraft 58
Krimmel, Katherine 7
Kyl, Jon 128–9
Kyoto Protocol 46, 75

Lafer, Gordon 23, 249–50
LaMarche, Gara 237
Lay, Kenneth xi, 45
LePage, Paul 157–8, 170–1
LGBT rights:

American Legislative Exchange Council and 24, 32–3, 218
Center for Policy Alternatives on 251
North Carolina "bathroom bill" and 241
urban politics and 241
Lorillard Tobacco 45
Louisiana 74, 90, 114, 130
Luminant 87
Lund, Pete 144, 146

MacIver Institute 188–9
Mackinac Center for Public Policy:
  American Legislative Exchange Council and 145
  Bradley Foundation and 243–4
  budget of 155
  education policy and 243–4
  public sector unions and 181, 195
  right-to-work laws and 144–6
  State Policy Network and 145–7
Madison Group 147–8, 159
Madison Institute 153
Maine, *see also* Maine Heritage Policy Center
  American Legislative Exchange Council and 74
  Americans for Prosperity in 169–71, 180
  Castle Doctrine law in 51
  collective bargaining laws in 1
  Medicaid expansion and 157–8, 198
  tax policy in 157, 170–1
Maine Heritage Policy Center:
  Affordable Care Act and 157
  Americans for Prosperity and 170
  budget of 156–7
  education policy and 157
  healthcare policy and 157
  LePage and 157–8
  Maine Wire and 158
  Medicaid expansion and 157–8
  right-to-work law and 157
  Searle Freedom Trust and 159
  tax policy and 157, 170
Malott, Robert 116–17
Manchin, Joe 109
Marathon Petroleum 46
Marcellais, Richard 102–3
Martin, Trayvon 2, 58–9, 133–4, 138, 261–2
Mary Kay Cosmetics 36
Maryland 114
Massachusetts:
  American Legislative Exchange Council and 74, 87
  Americans for Prosperity in 180
  legislative professionalism index and 91
  Medicaid expansion and 202

Massachusetts: (cont.)
  State Innovation Exchange in 227
  state legislature staff in 79
  "Troika" index in 181–2
McCarty, Nolan 7, 53
McMillin, Tom 144
McNay, John T. 18
Meany, George 221
Mechanical Contractors Association 34
Medicaid:
  Affordable Care Act's efforts to expand 4–5, 16, 152, 177–8, 197–210, 244, 246, 253, 267, 289–90
  eligibility requirements for 197, 203
  Foundation for Government Accountability and 201, 244
  Republican-controlled states and 199
  states' roles in administering 1, 5, 197–9
  Supreme Court ruling (2012) on 198
medical liability reform 74, 99
Meekhof, Arlan 144
Mercatus Center 162
Michigan:
  Americans for Prosperity in 145–6, 166, 171, 180
  election (2012) in 143
  election (2016) in 196
  full-time nature of state legislature in 89, 260
  industrial labor unions in 143
  legislative professionalism index and 91
  Medicaid expansion in 199, 207
  public sector unions and collective bargaining rights in 179, 181, 184–6
  right-to-work law and 143–7, 160, 196
  state legislature's halting of municipal initiatives in 61
  "Troika" index in 181–2
Microsoft 55, 130, 150–1
Miliken Family Foundation 41
minimum wage laws:
  Fight for $15 campaign and 239
  municipal governments' attempt to set 62, 238–41
  progressive organizations' efforts regarding 227, 233, 238, 242
  public opinion regarding 254–5
  right-to-work laws and 197
  state Chambers of Commerce efforts regarding 206
  state legislatures and 239–40
  State Policy Network and 152
Minnesota:
  American Legislative Exchange Council in 72, 74
  Americans for Prosperity in 171
  Clinton Healthcare Plan and 130
  State Innovation Exchange in 227
  State Policy Network in 171
  voter ID law in 3
Mississippi 110, 114, 155
Missouri:
  Affordable Care Act and Medicaid expansion in 64, 204–6
  American Legislative Exchange Council and 72, 74, 99, 205
  Americans for Prosperity in 204
  business community in 204–6
  Navigator Background Check Act (SB 508) in 64
  state legislature's halting of municipal initiatives in 61
  State Policy Network in 205
Mizruchi, Mark 25
Mobil Oil 46
Mock, Corey 102–3
Monaco, Charles 83
money in politics reform:
  Citizens United case (2010) and 258
  corporate donation limits and 111, 258
  independent expenditure limits and 258
  potential problems with 111
  public opinion regarding 258
  state legislatures' corporate contribution bans and 258–9
  support across political spectrum for 258
Montana 89, 91, 97, 110, 207
Mugwumps 215

National Association for the Advancement of Colored People (NAACP) 58
National Association of Independent Insurers 35
National Association of Manufacturers 125, 135
National Center for Policy Analysis 4
National Conference of State Legislative Leaders 216
National Conference of State Legislatures (NCSL):
  bipartisan aspirations of 216, 219, 223
  conservative opposition to the work of 217–18
  establishment (1950s) of 216
  media coverage of 56
  professionalization of state legislatures advocated by 217
  state legislators' automatic membership in ix
National Education Association (NEA):
  American Legislative Exchange Council's efforts to combat influence of 39, 58
  American Legislative Exchange Council's efforts to copy organizing techniques of 30–1
  declining power of state affiliates of 191–2, 195–6, 222
  model legislation and 30

political action committee of 219
political participation among members
  of 219–21
in Wisconsin 189–90
National Federation of Independent
  Business 34–5
National Legislative Conference 216
National Rifle Association (NRA):
  American Legislative Exchange Council
    and 49–51, 53, 58, 83
  Castle Doctrine and 51, 58
  concealed carry legislation and 50–1
  Koch Brothers and 165
  Madison Group and 147
  politically active profile of 7
  stand-your-ground laws and 55, 58
National Society of State Legislators 29, 216
Natural Resources Defense Council 58, 82
Nebraska 74, 182
Nelson, Marvin 102–3
Nevada 89, 152
Nevada Policy Research Institute 152
New Deal 216–17
New Federalism (Reagan) 218
New Hampshire:
  Josiah Bartlett Center for Public Policy
    in 159–60
  legislative professionalism index and 90–1
  public sector unions and collective bargaining
    rights in 183–6
  state legislators' salaries in 89
  state legislature staff in 90
New Jersey 194
New Mexico 93, 154
New York State:
  full-time nature of state legislature in 89
  legislative professionalism index and 90–1, 93,
    97, 109
  Medicaid expansion in 202
  online retail taxes and 131–2
  public sector unions in 222
  state legislature staff in 79
  State Policy Network and 155
  "Troika Index" in 202
Nichols, John 105
Nickles, Don 109, 129
Nixon, Jay 64, 204
Nonprescription Drug Manufacturers
  Association 127
Nordquist, Jeremy 80
North Carolina 78, 201, 222, 241
North Dakota:
  American Legislative Exchange Council
    and 72, 102–3
  Castle Doctrine law in 51
  legislative professionalism index and 90, 102

part-time nature of state legislature in 89
public sector unions and collective bargaining
  rights in 191
Quill v. North Dakota and 131–2
state legislature staff in 90
State Policy Network in 201, 231

Obama, Barack:
  Affordable Care Act and 4, 197, 199
  American Legislative Exchange Council's
    accusations of voter fraud regarding 54–5
  climate change legislation and 170
  election (2008) and 229, 262
  election (2010) and 1, 5
  election (2012) and 143
  Organizing for America organization and 59
  Taiwan Free Trade Agreement and 75
Ogles, Andrew 5
Ohio:
  American Legislative Exchange Council
    and 72, 87–8
  Americans for Prosperity in 166, 171
  public sector unions and collective bargaining
    rights in 184–6, 194
  renewable energy portfolio standards
    repealed in 114
  State Policy Network in 171
Oklahoma:
  American Legislative Exchange Council
    and 72, 74, 99
  Clinton Healthcare Plan and 129
  public funding for private schools and 155–6
  public sector unions and collective bargaining
    rights in 184–6, 222
Olin Foundation 41
online retail companies 130–3
Oregon:
  electricity regulations in xii
  legislative professionalism index and 109
  part-time legislature in ix
  public sector unions and collective bargaining
    rights in 194–5
  State Innovation Exchange in 227
  state legislature staff in 78–9
  State Policy Network in 195
  "Troika" index in 181–2
Overstock.com 131–3
"Overton Window" 247

Page, Benjamin 253
paid sick leave policies 239–41, 254
Park, Ethan 202
Parson, Mike 64
Passannante, William F. 218

Paycheck Protection Act proposal (ALEC) 66–7
Pearce, Russell 52–5
Pennsylvania:
   American Legislative Exchange Council
      and 72
   Americans for Prosperity in 166
   consumer packaging regulations in 114
   legislative professionalism index and 90–1, 93,
      97, 109
   public sector unions and collective bargaining
      rights in 180, 184–6, 194
   state legislators' salaries in 89
   state legislature staff in 78–9
People for the American Way 58–9
Pepsi 58
Pfizer 83, 137
Pharmaceutical Research and Manufacturers of
   America (PhRMA) 127, 150
Philip Morris 45, 87, 137, 163
Phillips, Tim 166, 179, 188–9, 200
Phillips Petroleum 46
Pierson, Paul 14, 245, 252
Pingree, Chellie 225
Planned Parenthood 7, 235
plastic bag regulations 61
Pocan, Mark 226
policy plagiarism of American Legislative
   Exchange Council model bills:
   bills to restrict Affordable Care Act and 64
   business-labor spending ratio and 106–7
   campaign contribution levels and 105–7,
      110–11, 258–9
   Democratic-controlled legislatures
      and 97–100, 248
   extractive industries' strength
      and 103–4
   legislative professionalism index and 89–94,
      97, 110–11, 260, 270–1
   public sector union strength and 101–3
   Republican-controlled legislatures
      and 97–100, 248
   state legislators' salaries and 89
   state legislators' tenure in office and 95–6, 104,
      107, 110
   state-level data on 72–4
   survey of state legislators regarding
      American Legislative Exchange Council
      and 92–6, 103–4
   text reuse detection techniques and 65
Poliquin, Bruce 158
Polletta, Francesca 265
Pollution Prevention Act (ALEC) 114
Pratt, Lawrence 81
Priorities USA 235
prison privatization 37, 49, 55
Procter & Gamble 36

Progressive Legislative Action Network
   (PLAN) 225–6, 229, 242, 263
Progressive Majority 212, 228–9, 242
Progressive States Network (PSN) 212, 226–9, 242
Public Citizen 58
Public Interest Institute 177
public sector unions:
   American Legislative Exchange Council
      and 31–2, 70–1, 74, 76, 101, 103, 107–9,
      178–9, 181–92, 210, 219, 252–3
   certification elections and 175, 194
   collective bargaining rights and 1, 16, 31,
      107–9, 221
   declining membership and budgets for 17,
      189–93, 196–7, 222
   Democratic Party and 102,
      130–3, 175, 179, 196
   in Iowa 107–8, 174–7, 183, 194
   Janus v. AFSCME and 195–6, 222
   low-income Americans' political representation
      improved through 257
   opt-out provisions and 195–6, 247
   Paycheck Protection Act proposal
      and 66–7
   pension funds of 134–5, 137
   political activity by members of 70–1, 155,
      193–4, 219–23, 247, 287–9
   public opinion regarding 176, 183, 253–4
   Republican Party 102
   strength during late twentieth century of 30
   teachers' unions and 31, 74, 98, 103, 178,
      189–90, 194, 219–23
   in Wisconsin 1, 107–9, 175–7, 179–80, 184–92,
      194, 196, 220–1

Quill v. North Dakota 131–2

Rathod, Nick 227
Reagan, Ronald 27, 38–40, 218, 263
Reason Foundation 149, 151, 169
renewable energy portfolio standards
   (RPS) 112–14
Republican Party:
   Americans for Prosperity and 166, 173
   conservative movement and 27, 52–4, 97
   elections (2010) and 1–2
   Koch Brothers and 161, 165
   Obamacare repeal efforts and 4, 144, 199
   public sector unions and 102
   tort reform and 35
Republican Study Committee 28
Rhoads, Mark 29
Rhode Island 74, 114, 182, 201–2
right-to-work laws:

INDEX 353

American Legislative Exchange Council
    and 73, 144, 160, 247
  collective bargaining rights and 143
  electoral outcomes impacted by 196–7
  expansion (2010-14) of 3
  labor unions targeted by 2
  Michigan and 143–7, 160, 196
  public sector unions' opposition to 30
  State Policy Network and 144–7, 152,
    157, 160
Right-Wing Troika, see American Legislative
    Exchange Council; Americans for Prosperity;
    State Policy Network
R.J. Reynolds Tobacco 42, 83, 86, 137
Rogers, Joel 226–7
Rothenberg, Lawrence 7
Rothschild, Rick 37

Safeway 133
Scaife, Richard 28
Scaife Foundation 28–9, 33, 41–2, 249
Schneider, Mac 102–3
school vouchers 70–1, 74, 253–4
Schuette, Bill 260
Seagram Liquors 86
Searle Freedom Trust 159
Senate Steering Committee 28
Service Employees International Union
    (SEIU) 220–1, 239
sharing economy 62
Sharp, Tracie 146–7, 159–60, 196
Shelby, Richard 109
Shell Oil 46, 113
Shor, Boris 53
Show-Me Institute 205
Sierra Club xii
Sirota, David 225
Skocpol, Theda 234–5
Skovron, Christopher 255
Snyder, Rick 143–5
Social Security 252
Solar Energy Industries Association 45
solar power 45, 61, 103, 112
South Carolina 57, 201–2, 231
South Dakota 114, 180–1
Speier, Jackie 225
stand-your-ground laws 2–3, 55, 58
State Action Collaborative 225–6, 229
State Fiscal Analysis Initiative (now State Priorities
    Partnership) 230, 232
State Innovation Exchange (SIX):
  budget of 227, 229
  establishment (2014) of 212, 227
  focus on states with strong progressive base
    and 265
  SIX Action and 228

state legislators:
  government experience levels among 9–10
  limited understanding of public opinion
    among 254–6
  policy platforms of 10
  salary levels for ix, 80, 84, 86, 89
  survey regarding views of American
    Legislative Exchange Council among 92–6,
    103–4, 278–80
The State Legislators Guide to Repealing Obamacare
    (ALEC report) 199
state legislatures:
  cities' policy initiatives halted by 11,
    61, 239–41
  climate change policies and 12, 61, 112
  Democratic Party dominance during 1960s and
    1970s of 31
  education policy as major focus of 75
  federalism and policy opportunities
    for 11–12, 14, 17, 115–17, 236–7,
    247–8, 262–3
  healthcare policy as major focus of 75
  legislative resources and staff at ix, 11, 15, 62,
    78–84, 89–93, 97, 105, 109–10, 137, 213–14,
    248, 252–3, 259–62
  national patterns of partisan
    control of 247–8
  partisan polarization and 10, 97–8
  part-time *versus* full-time sessions for 89,
    110, 260–1
  Progressive Movement and 213, 215
  tort reform and 35
State Policy Network (SPN):
  Affordable Care Act and 4, 16, 146, 152,
    156–7, 199–203, 205, 207–10, 253,
    289–90
  American Legislative Exchange Council
    and 16, 147–50, 156–60, 173, 265–6
  Americans for Prosperity and 169–73
  annual meeting of 146–7, 151
  budgets and revenues of 151, 154
  competing priorities in 250, 265–6
  corporate donors to 14, 113, 150–1
  cross-state policy initiatives by 11, 246, 263
  education policies and 152, 157, 243–4,
    253–4
  energy policy and 254
  extractive industry companies
    supporting 113
  growth of 148–9
  "IKEA" model for 146–7
  intended audiences of 152–3
  Janus v. AFSCME and 195–6
  lack of disclosure requirements regarding 257
  Mackinac Center and 145–7
  Madison Group and origins of 147–8
  Medicaid expansion and 4, 152, 160

State Policy Network (SPN): (cont.)
  minimum wage laws and 152
  policy forums held by 153
  progressive organizations' efforts to counter 17–18, 211–13, 219, 234, 242, 262–8
  public funding for private schools and 155–6
  public policy as a means of reshaping political landscape for 179, 210, 251–2
  public sector unions and collective bargaining rights targeted by 31, 152, 155, 177–81, 183–9, 191–6, 210, 252–3
  regional meetings of 149
  representative democracy potentially harmed by 17, 253–7, 266
  right-to-work laws and 144–7, 152, 157, 160
  school vouchers and 253–4
  scorecards developed by 153
  tax policy and 152, 253–4
  trainings offered by 150
  wealthy individual donors to 150–1, 156, 159, 209, 244, 249
State Priorities Partnership (SPP; previously State Fiscal Analysis Initiative):
  admission criteria for 230
  budget of 231–4
  childcare subsidies and 233
  earned income tax credits and 233
  establishment (1993) of 212, 230
  geographic reach of 232
  membership benefits and 231
State Voices organization 212
Steyer, Tom 7

Taiwan 75
Takeda 87
Task Force on Federalism 38
Taxpayer and Citizen Protection Act 51–2
Taylor, Chris 60
Teague, Kathy 82
Tea Party 167, 169
Teles, Steven 54
Tennessee:
  American Legislative Exchange Council and 114
  Castle Doctrine law in 51
  legislative professionalism index and 93
  Medicaid expansion in 4–5, 202
  public sector unions and collective bargaining rights in 191, 194
  State Policy Network in 231
  "Troika Index" and 202
Tester, Jon 225
Texas:
  Clinton Healthcare Plan and 130
  online sales taxes and 132

  part-time nature of state legislature in 89
  public sector unions in 155
  state legislators' salaries in 89
  State Policy Network and 154–5, 199–200
Thompson, Andy 57
Thompson, Tommy 29, 81
Thomson, Meldrim 29
Thwing, Alfred 215
Tillerson, Rex 113
Time Warner 86, 137
tobacco industry 36, 42, 45, 128, 137, 240
Toll, Henry W.:
  as advocate of increasing state legislatures' legislative resources 213–14, 218
  American Legislators' Association and 214–15, 218
  Council of State Governments and 216
  Ku Klux Klan opposed by 214
tort reform:
  American Legislative Exchange Council and 34–6, 38, 74, 126–7, 251
  increasing insurance costs during 1980s and 34
  medical liability reform and 74
  state legislatures' passing of laws regarding 35
  trial lawyers and 35, 251
Totten, Don 29
The Troika, see American Legislative Exchange Council; Americans for Prosperity; State Policy Network
Trump, Donald 4–5, 52, 196, 237, 263

Uber 261
United Auto Workers (UAW) 143
Upmeyer, Linda 108, 176
UPS 86–7
urban politics:
  American City County Exchange and 60–2
  Democratic Party strength in 238
  legislative resources and 62
  LGBT rights and 241
  minimum wage laws and 62, 238–41
  paid sick leave policies and 239–41
  plastic bag laws and 61
  progressive policy opportunities in 238–9
  sharing economy and 62
  state legislatures' halting of municipal government initiatives in 11, 61, 239–41
US Chamber of Commerce:
  business-friendly expansions of government and 172–3
  competing priorities within 45
  corporations' collective action through 25

Koch Brothers and 165
  participation in American Legislative Exchange
    Council among members of 124–5
  political spending by 13
  public employee pension fund-held companies
    and 134–5
  tort reform and 35
US West 163
Utah 72, 89–90, 191

Vermont 90–1, 201–2
Virginia:
  American Legislative Exchange Council
    and 80–2
  Americans for Prosperity in 171
  Medicaid expansion and 201–2
  online sales taxes and 132
  State Policy Network and 169, 171, 201
  "Troika Index" in 202
voter ID laws:
  American Legislative Exchange Council
    and 2–4, 18, 23, 50–2, 54–5, 59, 63, 68–9,
    72, 76, 250, 252
  in Arizona 52
  expansion (2010–2014) of 2–3, 55
  in Florida 55
  in Georgia 52
  in Indiana 54–5
  in Kansas 52
  Minnesota and 3
  partisan implications of 2
  populations of voters most affected by 2, 18
  Taxpayer and Citizen Protection Act as model
    for 51–2
Vukmir, Leah 189

Walgreens 58
Walker, Mark 104
Walker, Scott:
  American Legislative Exchange Council
    and 108, 188
  criminal sentencing laws and 108
  paid sick leave policies and 240
  public sector unions' collective bargaining
    rights eliminated by 108–9, 177, 180, 184,
    187–90, 194, 196
  recall campaign (2011) against 189–90
  on Wisconsin's budget deficit 184
Walmart xii, 50, 55, 58–9, 133
Warren, Elizabeth 258
Warshaw, Christopher 247
Washington Policy Center 150–1
Washington State 89, 114, 227
Wasserman Schultz, Debbie 225

Webb, Lee 224
Weihl, Bill 44
Weir, Margaret 221
Wendy's 58
Weston, Carol 170
West Virginia:
  American Legislative Exchange Council
    and 72, 74
  public sector unions in 179, 222
  renewable energy portfolio standards repealed
    in 113–14
Weyrich, Paul:
  American Legislative Exchange Council
    and 29–31, 219
  biographical background of 27–8
  on conservative movement's goals 35–6
  Free Congress Foundation and 147
  Heritage Foundation and 28
Whisnant, Gene:
  American Legislative Executive Council
    and ix–x, xi–xiii
  as Oregon state legislator ix, 78–9, 252–3
  on private sector checks on public sector xiv
Will, George 28
Williams, Bob xiii–xiv
Williamson, Vanessa 196–7
Willis, Kathleen 104
Winner-Take-All Politics (Hacker and Pierson) 245
Wisconsin:
  American Legislative Exchange Council
    and 74, 81, 176, 208
  Americans for Prosperity in 166, 171,
    188, 208–9
  Bradley Foundation and 243
  budget deficit in 184, 187
  election (2016) in 196
  Medicaid expansion and 208–10
  paid sick leave policies in 240
  private-sector unions in 220–1
  public sector unions and collective bargaining
    rights (Act 10) in 1, 107–9, 175–7, 179–80,
    184–92, 194, 196, 220–1
  right-to-work legislation in 196
  school voucher proposal in 70–1
  state Chamber of Commerce in 208–10,
    220–1
  state legislature's halting of municipal
    initiatives in 61
  State Policy Network in 171, 188–9, 208
  teachers' unions in 189–91, 220–1
  "Troika" index in 181–2
Wisconsin Education Association 190–1
Wisconsin Manufacturers and Commerce (trade
  organization) 208, 220–1
Wisconsin Policy Research Institute 189
Woodward, George 215

Wyoming:
  American Legislative Exchange Council and 74
  Americans for Prosperity in 180
  legislative professionalism index and 90–2, 97, 109, 111
  state legislators' salaries in 89

Yelp 261
Yiqing Xu 247
YUM! Brands 240

Zimmerman, George 2

www.ingramcontent.com/pod-product-compliance
Ingram Content Group UK Ltd.
Pitfield, Milton Keynes, MK11 3LW, UK
UKHW021307071025
8279UKWH00019B/110